Guide
to the
PRADO

© SILEX® : 1991
I.S.B.N.: 84-85041-46-1
Depósito Legal: M. 25.689 - 1991
Layout: J. M. Domínguez
Printed in Spain by: Gráficas Marte, S. A.
(Printed in Spain)
Translated by: Evelyne Colchero

Revised and corrected edition

CONSUELO LUCA DE TENA & MANUELA MENA

Guide to the PRADO

Sílex

CONTENTS

FOREWORD

If we cast a glimpse at the long list of bibliography published on the subject of the Prado since its inauguration in 1819 (that year its first Catalogue of Paintings of the Spanish School *was published), we will be struck by the large number of different angles from which this art museum has been studied. We will find histories of the building and of the collections, studies of definite pictures and sculptures, critical commentaries, both artistic and literary, analyses of the paintings from the point of view of* genres *or subject-matter, etc. If the tireless art scholar Juan Antonio Gaya Nuño had lived to publish his «Critical bibliography» of the Prado, the quantity and quality of publications quoted there would have caused surprise and admiration. But the basis of all these works are the* Catalogues *and* Guides. *The former, starting with the first summary catalogue written by Luis Eusebi in 1819, are drawn up in the Prado since this work of cataloguing requires a conscientious, day-to-day effort and constitutes one of the prime tasks of any institution that guards such a priceless treasure. Although it could also be considered part of the activities of a museum, the publishing of* Guides *can be assumed by other private organizations. The object of these guide-books is to bring the works of art closer to the spectator; they must show the way and provide a clear, concise orientation —the shorter the better— for the visitor to understand what he has before him.*

This should all be taken into account to judge the present Guide
to the Prado. *The authors and publishers set themselves a difficult task: to offer compact information about the works of art
kept in this Neo-Classical building (it is to be hoped that in future
editions the 19th and 20th-century works housed in the nearby
Casón del Buen Retiro will also be included), adjusting the length
of the text to the importance of each work, but with the object in
mind of making a comprehensive survey of all the paintings listed
in the Prado Catalogue. Thanks to the abundance of information
it contains (along with the text 217 black and white illustrations and
79 colour plates are included), this book combines the advantages
of a «catalogue» and a «guide» and is thus of great use as a
hand-book.*

*After reading the first few pages of this guide, intended to help
the visitor on his way around our Museum, he would be well
advised to read the introductory note on the history of the Prado
and its collections. The following sections refer to the different
schools of painting with commentaries on the artists and their
works. In this way the authors of this* Guide, *Manuela Mena and
Consuelo Luca de Tena, have succeeded in presenting a wealth
of information in its correct proportion and with the addition of
brief critical comments to help the visitor judge the artists and
their works.*

This Guide to the Prado *appears at a moment when important
re-modelling work is in progress in the Prado. Serious air pollu-
tion in this area of Madrid has made it necessary to achieve
complete air-conditioning and humidity control. The underground
machine room has fortunately been completed already under the
East façade and is unique in its kind. Other important innovations include new lighting and security systems against theft and
fire. At the same time the rooms are being re-arranged, a conference room with audiovisual equipment is being installed, other
rooms have been adapted for temporary exhibitions, the restoration workshop (in urgent need of being put to greater use) is
being modernized, as well as the laboratories and store-rooms
(thus making the latter more accessible to visitors wishing to see
definite paintings not on show in the exhibition rooms); the library is also being extended, a spacious cafeteria installed, etc.
All this requires time. In the meanwhile this* Guide *will continue
to be of great help to visitors due to the way in which it is
set up. It would be desirable if future editions could be extended to include the collection kept in the Casón del Buen Retiro, which is also being re-modelled. Apart from the 19th and
20th-century paintings exhibited there this building will also
house the Department of Drawings under the direction of one of
the authors of the present* Guide, *Manuela Mena, who has amply
proved her capacity in this branch of art so closely connected
with painting and which needs to be furthered in the Prado.*

We trust that this Guide *will prove to be a real help to Prado
visitors to appreciate the message of this great Museum. We
should like to stress this point because it is particularly important
when visiting an art gallery and admiring first-rate works of art
to be able also to understand how the artistic sensibility of the
great masters was formed through contact with the work of*

others. Here in the Prado the links between the Spanish masters and Italian and Flemish art are particularly revealing. The development of geniuses such as El Greco and Velázquez can be traced when we see their work in such close vicinity to magnificent canvases by Titian and Tintoretto. The paintings that decorated the royal palaces and were later hung in the Prado made a highly significant impression on our artists. It was a fortunate circumstance in the history of both the Habsburg and Bourbon dynasties in Spain that practically all the kings felt the inclination to collect works of art. How far did their personal preferences influence Spanish painting? The answer to this question can be found in the exhibition rooms of the Prado, not only by observing the works of artists who painted directly for the Spanish kings, but also in those of other painters who must have visited the old Alcázar in Madrid or other royal seats like El Escorial. The pictures in the Prado that originally belonged to the royal collections, as well as those that came from suppressed convents and monasteries all throw interesting light on this subject. In spite of a somewhat unequal distribution of its rich collection (it must be admitted that there are some notable shortcomings), the Prado thus bears witness to the way in which Spain opened up to the world in the field of painting, assimilating creative influences from abroad but producing such exceptional artists as El Greco, Velázquez, Goya and many others who gave their distinctive character to artistic centres in Andalusia, Castile and elsewhere.

José Manuel Pita Andrade
Director of the Prado Museum

HOW TO USE THIS GUIDE

This *Guide to the Prado* includes all the paintings listed in the Prado Catalogue with the exception of the 19th-century works exhibited in the nearby *Casón del Buen Retiro*. It therefore contains both the paintings on view in the exhibition rooms and those that are kept in storage and only exhibited periodically. The Guide is divided into schools of painting, following the arrangement of the works in the museum, although these are subdivided according to centuries in the exhibition rooms. Each section opens with a short introduction in which attention is drawn to the principal artists and their most important works, as well as to the origin of the collection. The artists are then listed in alphabetical order accompanied by their dates of birth and death when known. Biographical notes together with comments on their style and significance follow in the case of the most important and many of the lesser artists. The paintings are listed in the order of their catalogue numbers; their material and measurements are quoted in brackets and mention is made if they are signed and dated.

In order to locate paintings or artists in this Guide the reader must therefore first refer to the school to which they belong, where he will find the artist listed alphabetically and the paintings under the catalogue number quoted on the frames (1).

The Guide also contains brief chapters on other collections on show in the Prado: sculptures, silverware, coins and medals, drawings and furniture. Finally, an index is added to help the visitor locate a definite artist rapidly.

(1) If the visitor cannot identify the school to which they belong, the catalogue number and corresponding page number or the name of the artist can be found in the index.

9

ARRANGEMENT OF THE EXHIBITION ROOMS

SPANISH MASTERS

15th and 16th-century painting:
Ground floor: Rooms 48, 49, 55B, 56B, 57B.
16th-century painting:
Upper floor: Rooms 8B, 9B, 10B (Greco).
17th-century painting:
Ground floor: Room 51B (temporarily, Ribera).
Upper floor: Rooms 18, 18A; 16 A (Ribera); 16B (Murillo), 17A (Zurbarán); 12, 13, 14, 16, 17 (Velázquez).
18th-century painting: Goya
Ground floor: Rooms 66 (drawings) and 67 (Black Paintings).
Upper floor: Rooms 19, 20, 21, 22 and 23 (tapestry cartoons), 34, 35, 36, 37 and 38 (portraits), 32 and 39.

FLEMISH AND DUTCH MASTERS

Ground floor
15th and 16 th-century painting: Rooms 55A, 56A, 57A, 58A; 56 (Antonio Moro).
17 th-century Flemish painting: Rooms 60A, 61A, 62A, 63A; 61, 61B, 75 (Rubens); 62, 63 (Jordaens); 62B, 63B (Van Dyck).
17 th-century Dutch painting: Rooms 64 and 65.

ITALIAN MASTERS

Upper floor
15th-century painting: Rooms 4 (Fra Angelico) and 3 (Botticelli, Mantegna, Antonello).
16th-century painting: Rooms 2 (Raphael), 5 (Andrea del Sarto), 6 (Parmigiano, Pontormo, Barocci), 9 (Tintoretto, Veronese), 10, 10A (various Venetian painters) and 9 (Titian).

FRECH MASTERS. Upper floor: Rooms 11, 11B.

GERMAN MASTERS. Ground floor: Room 54.

THE DAUPHIN'S TREASURE: Ground floor: Room 72.

NOTE: It is a common practice in all Art Galleries to change the position of paintings within a room or from one room to another. This applies al the more in the case of the Prado where important renovation work is in progress, in addition to the fact that this Museum possesses more paintings than could ever be exhibited simultaneously.

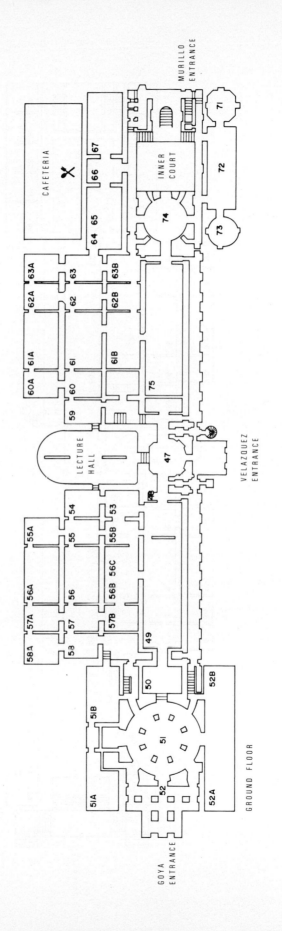

CAFETERIA

MURILLO ENTRANCE

INNER COURT

LECTURE HALL

VELAZQUEZ ENTRANCE

GOYA ENTRANCE

GROUND FLOOR

58A 57A 56A 55A 54
58 57 56 55 53
57B 56B 56C 55B
53
49
50
51B
51A
52
51
52A
52B

47
75
60A 61A 62A 63A
59 60 61 62 63
61B 62B 63B
64 65 66 67
71
72
73
74

11

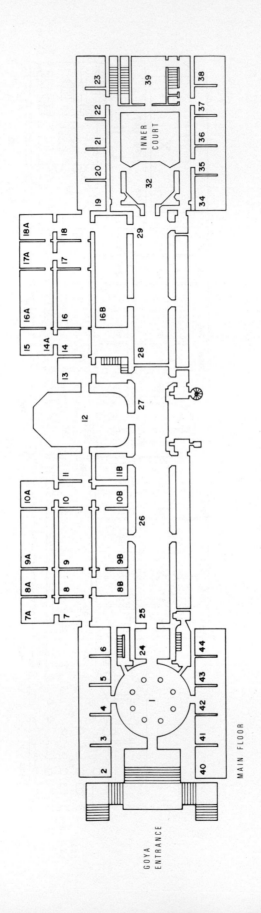

GOYA ENTRANCE

MAIN FLOOR

23 22 21 20 19 39 32 38 37 36 35 34

INNER COURT

18A 17A 16A 15 14A 13 18 17 16 14 16B 12 29 28 27

11 10A 9A 8A 7A 11B 10 9 8 7 10B 9B 8B 26 25 24

6 5 4 3 2 44 43 42 41 40

100 SELECTED WORKS

A guide-book, it seems elementary, should guide the visitor. However, in the case of the Prado a room-to-room guide following definite itineraries would probably only mislead the reader.

Important reconditioning work has been undertaken over the past few years, some of which is still in progress, making it necessary to close certain parts of the building to the public while others are being re-arranged and gradually re-opened. For this reason instead of suggesting an itinerary around the Prado we have preferred to offer a list of the museum's most interesting works which we recommend the visitor not to miss.

FLEMISH MASTERS

ITALIAN MASTERS

INTRODUCTION

One of the most important works undertaken by King Charles III to urbanize the capital of Spain was a new layout of the so-called *Prado de San Jerónimo* or «St. Jerome's Meadow» which stretched over an area comprising the gardens of the former monastery of the same name as well as those of the Buen Retiro Palace, a favourite promenading spot for the population of Madrid at the end of the 18th century. The great Neo-Classical architect Juan de Villanueva (1739-1811), the most interesting figure in 18th-century Spanish architecture, was commissioned to carry out this project; at the king's wish he designed the Botanical Gardens, the Astronomical Observatory and in 1785 began work on a magnificent building, the present-day Prado, which was originally intended to house the royal collection of natural science and thus become a Natural History Museum. The idea was to convert the site of the former «Meadow» into an area dedicated to Learning. Construction work advanced rapidly and the museum was finished early in the 19th century. However, due to the Napoleonic invasion the natural history collection could not be installed in the new building, which on the other hand suffered as a result of being used as headquarters by the French cavalry troops.

Velázquez Entrance of the Prado.

Villanueva had built one of the finest examples of Spanish Neo-Classical architecture, in keeping with its surroundings and at the same time enhancing them. The combination of stone and brick on the outside gives the building an attractive colouring, whereas the different architectonic elements with their salients and re-entrants produce an interesting *chiaroscuro* effect on the façades. The sober end pavilions are attached to the central part of the building by means of Ionic galleries, now covered in with windows, over a base consisting of arches and niches.

View of the Central Gallery. Main Floor.

Villanueva's design contained the three classic orders or styles. For the monumental main portico in the centre of the building, which he conceived as a classic temple, he used the austere Doric style. The more elegant and stylized Ionic order can be found in the galleries and the raised Northern entrance. Finally, if we walk round to the Southern façade we will recognize the Corynthian style in the exquisite moulding of the capitals when the sun plays around the great balcony overlooking the Botanical Gardens.

The interior of the building no longer reflects Villanueva's ideas since what he designed as a scientific museum was later turned into a picture-gallery. However, the general lines of the original layout can still be distinguished. Spacious vaulted galleries on two floors join the end pavilions to the central part of the building. The rotunda on the main floor with its elegant Ionic columns supporting a caissoned cùpola crowned by a large circular sky-light, imitating the famous Roman Pantheon, is probably the finest part of the museum. The architect planned the centre of the building as a «Temple of Science», but this original design can no longer be detected as it has been completely altered and divided up to form exhibition rooms, such as the Velázquez Room on the first floor.

This magnificent building had been ruined as a result of the French invasion, but when Ferdinand VII after his return to Spain decided, on his ministers' advice and with his wife Isabella of Braganza's support, to create an art museum to display the royal collections, the choice fell on the abandoned Prado building and restoration work commenced.

The idea of exhibiting the royal collection of paintings to the public was not a new one; since the 16th century artists and art connoisseurs had been permitted to visit the picture galleries in the royal palaces, but it was not until the late 18th century that the great Neo-Classical painter at the court of Charles III, Anton Raffael Mengs, suggested to the king the idea of creating a museum, possibly connected with the Natural History Museum, where the finest works from the royal collection could be displayed to the public in general. The death of Charles III brought the project to a halt and his successor Charles IV did little to further it, although privately he promoted the arts and enlarged the collection inherited from his predecessors. During the French invasion the new king Joseph Bonaparte (1808-1813) wanted to create a museum along the lines of the Napoleon Museum in Paris in order to exhibit works from public buildings and former convents and monasteries, together with the most interesting paintings from the royal collection. However, this project was thwarted by the fall of Napoleon and Joseph Bonaparte's departure from Spain. It was not until after Ferdinand VII returned that the plan finally materialized and on November 19, 1819 the «Royal Prado Museum» at last opened its doors to the public. The first paintings exhibited were all by Spanish artists, but the display was gradually extended to include works of other schools. The sculptured decoration on the exterior of the building dates from this period, for example the monumental *Allegory of the Arts* by Jerónimo Suñol on the Northern façade, the relief over the main portico representing *Minerva and the Fine Arts paying tribute to Ferdinand VII* by Ramón Barba, who also made the medallions with portraits of the principal Spanish artists, and the allegories of the Arts in the form of female figures that adorn the niches on the front façade, which are the work of the sculptor Valeriano Salvatierra.

This collection based on paintings from the royal palaces has been considerably enlarged during the 19th and 20th centuries by a series of important private donations and in 1870 the Prado merged with the Trinity Museum, created in 1836 to house works of art from the convents and monasteries that had been suppressed as a result of the Liberal minister Mendizábal's Disentailment Decree. In this way the Prado received the addition of a very large number of religious paintings.

Since it was primarily formed by paintings collected by the royal family, the Prado has certain characteristics that distinguish it from other European museums; it is of immense historical interest as it reflects the taste of the Spanish kings who controlled the fate of Europe in the 16th and 17th centuries and of their political allies. Apart from Spanish painting, for the most part works commissioned from artists in the service of the Spanish kings, foreign schools are also well represented here, although some more magnificently than others for political reasons. The finest section after the Spanish one is that devoted to Italian painting; the works of Venetian masters commissioned by Charles V and Philip II or purchased in the 17th century by the great patron of the arts Philip IV are world-famous. Due to family ties between the reigning houses of France and Spain a large number of French works reached this country during the 17th and 18th centuries, but without doubt the political ties with the Netherlands were the most beneficial for the field of art; from the early Flemish masters of the 16th century to the great figures of the 17th century, such as Rubens and Van Dyck, Flemish painting is admirably represented in the Prado and includes some of the most famous masterpieces of European art. Also for political reasons, the traditional hostility between Spain on the one hand and England, Germany and Holland on the other was responsible for a poor representation of these schools of painting in the royal collections, although this has partly been compensated by subsequent bequests and purchases.

General view of the Black Paintings Room.

The Prado collection is at present divided up between Villanueva's building, where painting from the Middle Ages to the 19th century is kept, as well as sculptures, drawings, furniture and decorative arts, and the *Casón del Buen Retiro* with its collection of 19th-century works, which is the result of the merger of the Modern Art Museum, created in the past century, with the works of modern art previously kept in the Prado. It is worthwhile remembering that the Prado houses nearly 3,000 paintings within its walls, but that these only represent part of its real treasure since a large number of works are on loan to provincial museums or other public institutions in order to enrich art galleries in provincial towns or adorn official buildings. The quantity and quality of its works make the Prado stand out as the most important art museum in the world.

1323. Bartolomé Bermejo. St. Dominic of Silos.

618. Pedro Berruguete. Auto-da-fe.

SPANISH MASTERS

The collection of works by Spanish masters on show in the Prado is the most complete and exceptional display of Spanish art to be found in any Museum in the world. The most important part of the paintings owned by the Kings of Spain were works by their Court painters, in particular two outstanding figures who break out of the context of Spanish painting and rank among the masters of universal art: Velazquez and Goya. Their works are amply represented in the Prado since they were present at Court from their youth practically until their death, so that a study of their masterpieces here is indispensable for anyone wishing to acquaint himself with their work.

In 1870 the Prado collection was enriched in number and quality by the addition of works from the Trinity Museum, where a large amount of paintings from convents and monasteries had been assembled after the secularization of the monasteries. This accounts for the excellent representation of Medieval art and religious painting, especially of the Schools of Madrid and Toledo.

Other famous sections of the Prado collection have been built up gradually in different ways. El Greco, for example, was only represented in the royal collection by a few portraits; the Trinity Museum added some religious paintings and the rest have been acquired through purchases and donations later. Ribera, who lived nearly all his artistic life in Naples, is present here thanks to the esteem of the Spanish viceroys in Naples who sent his works to Spain, where they were highly appreciated. Although the collection of works by Zurbarán is not extensive, it is nonetheless very varied and many of these paintings are the result of relatively recent purchases. Murillo is so well represented in the Prado thanks to Queen Elizabeth Farnese, who held him in high esteem and acquired as many of his works as possible.

Along with these great names the visitor to our Museum will find a long list of other artists whose works offer a fine panorama of the history of Spanish painting.

AGÜERO, Benito Manuel de Agüero (b. Burgos 1626; d. Madrid 1670). School of Madrid. Agüero was a pupil of Mazo and worked in his studio; his style resembles that of his master. His landscapes are generally rugged and agitated and sometimes almost Romantically dramatic; they often include small figures as a mythological pretext.

890 «A fortified port» (Canvas, 54 × 196 cm.).
893 «Landscape with a nymph and a shepherd» (Canvas, 56 × 199 cm.).
894 «Landscape» (Canvas, 56 × 199 cm.).
895 «Landscape with Dido and Aeneas» (Canvas, 246 × 202 cm.).
896 «Landscape: Aeneas' departure from Carthage» (Canvas, 293 × 205 cm.).
897 «Landscape with Leto and the peasants transformed into frogs» (Canvas, 244 × 219 cm.).
898 «Landscape with two figures» (Canvas, 246 × 325 cm.).
899 «Landscape with Mercury and Argus» (Canvas, 248 × 325 cm.).

ANDRES Y AGUIRRE, Ginés de Andrés y Aguirre (b. 1727; d. ?).
2893 «Dog and cats» (Canvas, 149 × 114 cm.). This was a tapestry cartoon.

ANTOLINEZ, Francisco Antolínez (b. Seville c. 1644; d. Madrid before 1700). Sevillian School. He was related to José Antolínez and painted religious scenes in landscape or architectural backgrounds, with numerous figures, very elongated and rather ghostlike due to their sketchy handling. The quality of his works is very unequal.

585 «The Presentation of the Virgin» (Canvas, 45 × 73 cm.). Together with the following three, this work comes from the convent of San Felipe el Real in Madrid.
587 «The Betrothal of the Virgin» (Canvas, 45 × 73 cm.). See No. 585.
588 «The Nativity» (Canvas, 45 × 73 cm.). See No. 585.
590 «The Flight into Egypt» (Canvas, 45 × 73 cm.). See No. 585.

ANTOLINEZ, José Antolínez (Madrid 1635-1675). School of Madrid. He was a pupil of Francisco Rizi, whose Baroque style he adopted along with Venetian and Rubensian influences, which all goes to make a dynamic, highly colourful style.

591 «Death of Mary Magdalene» (Canvas, 205 × 163 cm.). This is one of the most representative works of the Baroque style in Madrid.
2443 «The Immaculate Conception» (Canvas, 216 × 159 cm.). Antolínez is best known for his paintings of this subject, which he repeated frequently.

ARELLANO, Juan de Arellano (b. Santorcaz, Madrid 1614; d. Madrid 1676). School of Madrid. He specialized in flower paintings and was the best representative of his time and school in this branch. His large bouquets, silhouetted against dark backdrops, derive from Flemish and Italian models, which he had probably seen at Court (Van Kessel, Mario Nuzzi, Margarita Caffi), but he developed his own style with a masterly technique.

592 «**Flowers**» (Canvas, 83 × 63 cm.).
593 «**Flowers**» (Canvas, 83 × 63 cm.). Companion piece to the preceding No.
594 «**Flowers**» (Canvas, 103 × 77 cm.).
595 «**Flowers**» (Canvas, 103 × 77 cm.). Companion piece to the preceding No.
596 «**Flowers**» (Canvas, 60 × 45 cm.).
597 «**Flowers**» (Canvas, 60 × 45 cm.). Signed. Pendant to the preceding No.
2507 «**Flowers and a landscape**» (Canvas, 58 × 73 cm.). Signed.
2508 «**Flowers and a landscape** (Canvas, 58 × 73 cm.). Signed. Companion piece to the preceding No.
3030 «**Flowers**».
3138 «**Flowers**» (Canvas, 84 × 105 cm.). Signed.
3139 «**Flowers**» (Canvas, 84 × 105 cm.). Signed. Pendant to the preceding No.

3139. Arellano. Flowers.

ARGUIS, Master of (anonymous, active about 1450). Aragonese School.
1332 «**The Legend of St. Michael**» (Predella and six panels of an altar-piece, in order of size, 79 × 80, 78 × incomplete width, 65 × 46 and 57 × 80 cm). This altar-piece belongs to the pure International style which spread in Spain particularly in the regions of Catalonia and Valencia. Fondness for narrative and picturesque elements and the decorative aspect of costumes, landscapes and architectures are all typical of this style. The main figures are stylized and elegant, whereas the secondary ones appear caricature-like. In this work the most engaging scenes are those of the souls, with the devil standing watch to carry one off, and of St. Michael's victory over the Antichrist.

ARIAS, Antonio Arias Fernández (Madrid c. 1614-1684). School of Madrid. This artist's style is somewhat archaic with its simplified, full sense of mass and its closed contours.
598 «**Tribute money**» (Canvas, 191 × 230 cm.). Signed and dated 1646.
599 «**The Virgin and Child**» (Canvas, 91 × 129 cm.). Signed and dated 1650.
3079 «**St. Thomas the Apostle**» (Canvas, 193 × 105 cm.). This work might have belonged to a series on the Apostles now divided up.
3080 «**St. James the Younger**» (Canvas, 193 × 105 cm.). See No. 3079.

BARTOLOMEUS, Master. He was a 15th-century Hispano-Flemish artist, possibly related to Fernando Gallego.
1322 «**The Virgin of the milk**» (Wood, 52 × 35 cm.). Signed.

BAYEU, Francisco Bayeu y Subías (b. Saragossa 1734; d. Madrid 1795). Bayeu was an interesting personality on the artistic scene in Madrid prior to Goya. He started studying in Saragossa, but soon moved to Madrid with a scholarship to complete his studies at the Academy of San Fernando.

This period of his life was important since he trained with Antonio González Velázquez, from whom he learnt Rococo refinement, and worked as an
assistant to Mengs, whose Neo-Classical influence can be observed in the
frescoes he painted in the Royal Palace, the palace of El Pardo, the convent of the Encarnación, etc. His fame was such that in 1788 he was
appointed Director of the Academy of San Fernando, at the height of his
career, and received a large number of royal commissions; he prepared
cartoons for the Royal Tapestry Factory with the everyday street scenes en
vogue in the 18th century. Some of these charming, delicately coloured
sketches bring him close to the best European masters of the Rococo.

600   «The Assumption of the Virgin» (Canvas, 137 × 81 cm.). This sketch
      was for a segment of the cupola of the Santa Engracia church in Saragossa.
601   «The Triumph of the Lamb» (Canvas, 48 × 58 cm.). This was a sketch
      for one of the lunettes of the chapel on the ground floor of the palace at
      Aranjuez; it dates from 1788 and shows the artist's Neoclassical trend.
603   «St. Francis of Sales» (Canvas, 56 × 34 cm.). This was probably a sketch
      for an altar painting and is presumed to be the work of Ramón Bayeu.
604   «Olympus: the fight with the giants» (Canvas, 68 × 123 cm). This was
      a sketch for a ceiling decoration in the Royal Palace, Madrid, and repre-
      sents a scene from Greek mythology: the giants being driven out of
      Olympus by Jupiter with the aid of Hercules and Pallas Athena.
605   «The bridge over the canal in Madrid» (Canvas, 36 × 95 cm). This
      fine sketch for a tapestry was attributed to Goya in the past.
606   «The Paseo de las Delicias in Madrid» (Canvas, 37 × 55 cm). This was
      a sketch for a tapestry now kept in El Escorial. It is one of the most
      interesting due to its realistic rendering and beautiful landscape.
607   «Picnic in the country» (Canvas, 37 × 55 cm). Signed. This is another of
      the sketches for the tapestries for El Escorial.
740h «Feliciana Bayeu, the painter's daughter» (Canvas, 38 × 30 cm). In
      the artist's handwriting below: rto. de Feliciana niña de 13 años (portrait of
      Feliciana as a child of 13). It was painted in 1788 and is a very intense
      portrait, similar in style to ·works by Goya.
2480 «The creation of Adam» (Canvas, 59 × 33 cm). Together with Nos.
      601, 2482, 2485-8, 2491-3, this work belonged to a series of prepara-
      tory sketches for the fresco decoration of the cupola in the collegiate
      church at La Granja, carried out in 1772; his Neo-Classical approach is
      evident in the clear positioning of the figures, the sense of balance and
      harmony of the compositions and the pale tones of the colouring.
2481 «The Spanish monarchy» (Canvas, 63 × 59 cm). This is a grisaille sketch
      for the decoration of a salon.
2482 «Abraham praying» (Canvas, 59 × 33 cm). This sketch was for the decor-
      ation of the cupola in the collegiate church at La Granja. It represents the
      angel announcing to Abraham that the Messiah will be born among his
      descendents.
2483 «The surrender of Granada» (Canvas, 54 × 57 cm). This sketch for the
      ceiling decoration of the state dining hall in the Royal Palace represents
      the Catholic Kings receiving the keys from the Moorish king.
2485 «St. Luke» (Canvas, 58 × 58 cm). See No. 2480.
2486 «St. John the Evangelist» (Canvas, 58 × 58 cm). See No. 2480.
2487 «St. Matthew» (Canvas, 58 × 58 cm). See No. 2480.
2488 «St. Mark» (Canvas, 58 × 58 cm). See No. 2480. These four sketches of
      the Evangelists were for the fresco decoration of the pendentives in the
      collegiate church at La Granja.
2489 «The prophecy of Isaiah» (Canvas, 47 × 57 cm). This sketch for a lu-
      nette represents the prophet announcing the coming of the Messiah.
2491 «Adam and Eve reproached for their sin» (Canvas, 59 × 32 cm). See
      No. 2480.
2493 «The sacrifice of the Law of Moses» (Canvas, 59 × 32 cm). See No. 2480.
2520 «The picnic» (Canvas, 278 × 173 cm). This was a tapestry design.
2531 «St. Theresa in Glory» (Canvas, 43 × 100 cm). This was a preparatory
      sketch for a fresco no longer preserved.
2634 «The Flight into Egypt» (Canvas, 14 × 21 cm). This is an unfinished
      sketch.
      BAYEU, Ramón Bayeu y Subías (b. Saragossa 1746; d. Aranjuez 1793).
      He received a similar artistic training to that of his brother, with whom
      he collaborated all his life; he studied together with Goya in the family
      workshop and also worked with him on the frescoes for the Cathedral of
      Saragossa, St. Anne's church in Valladolid and the church of Valdemoro.

629. Alonso Cano. Dead Christ supported by an angel. (detail)

In 1775 he also began to paint tapestry cartoons full of gay, vivid street scenes that reflect the lively atmosphere of Madrid, painted with clear colouring and close observation of reality.

2451 «**The sausage-vendor**» (Canvas, 222 × 106 cm). This tapestry design shows an ambulant tradesman.

2452 «**Fans and pastries**» (Canvas, 147 × 187 cm). This tapestry design shows a similar scene enlivened by the presence of young women.

2453 «**Country scene**» (Canvas, 183 × 146). This was also a tapestry cartoon.

2521 «**Youth with a guitar**» (Canvas, 184 × 137 cm). In its simplicity this tapestry design is one of the most attractive of Bayeu's works in the Prado.

2522 «**The blind musician**» (Canvas, 93 × 145 cm). This must have been a very frequent street scene in Madrid.

2523 «**The boy with a fruit basket**» (Canvas, 93 × 141 cm). This was also a tapestry design.

2599 «**Thirteen sketches for tapestry cartoons**» (Canvas, 45 × 100 cm). Some of these small sketches were for cartoons kept in the Prado.

BECERRIL, Master of.

2682 «**St. Barbara**» (Wood, 145 × 65 cm). Early 16th century.

BERMEJO, Bartolomé de Cárdenas Bermejo or «Rubeus» (b. Córdoba?). Hispano-Flemish School. This artist worked in Valencia, Aragon and Catalonia between 1474 and 1495; he painted in a vigorous, realistic style, with sound draughtsmanship and a sculptural sense of form. His work is the chief Gothic painting in the Prado.

1323 «**St. Dominic enthroned as Abbot of Silos**» (Wood, 242 × 130 cm). This work was painted for the altar-piece of St. Dominic's church at Daroca before 1477.

BERRUGUETE, Pedro Berruguete (b. Paredes de Nava ?, Palencia c. 1450; d. before 1504). He was the artist from Castile known as «Pietro spagnuolo» when he was working in Urbino in 1477 for Federigo da Montefeltro, who had also commissioned the Flemish artist Just of Ghent and the Italians Melozzo da Forlì and Piero della Francesca. After 1483 he is known to have worked in Spain, particularly in Toledo, in the provinces of Burgos, Palencia and Avila, where he began an altar-piece for the Cathedral which he left unfinished when he died. His style combines elements of Flemish realism with a sense for space and lighting effects learnt in Italy, together with a fondness for rich decorativeness that led him to make abundant use of gilded backgrounds. Although his quality is at times somewhat unequal, in his best works he reached a degree of technical quality and maturity in the use of perspective and light that distinguishes him among his contemporaries in Spain.

123 «**St. Peter**» (Gouache on canvas, 350 × 206 cm). This work forms a series with the three following ones. They come from Avila and were probably wings of an organ or an altar-piece. Like in its companion piece *St. Paul*, the figure of the saint is framed in a semi-circular Renaissance arch. There is an Italian flavour about the monumental figure, his poise and the way he is situated in the architectonic framework; with this manner of placing the figure on the edge and making him slightly exceed the framework Berruguete uses a *trompe l'oeil* effect which appears in various of his works.

124 «**St. Paul**» (Gouache on canvas, 350 × 206 cm). See No. 123.

125 «**The Adoration of the Kings**» (Gouache on canvas, 350 × 206 cm). This work and its companion piece (No. 126) make a single scene.

126 «**Two of the Magi**» (Gouache on canvas, 350 × 206 cm). Like the three preceding works this one also has an Italian flavour, an impression that is heightened by the technique which makes it resemble fresco.

609 «**St. Dominic and the Albigenses**» (Wood, 122 × 83 cm). This work was part of the St. Dominic altar-piece in the convent of Santo Tomás in Avila, together with Nos. 610, 615 and 616. The composition is partially repeated in No. 1305.

610 «**St. Dominic restoring a young man to life**» (Wood, 122 × 83 cm). It is interesting to observe how the artist connects the different parts of the picture space by means of light.

611 «**St. Peter the Martyr preaching**», (Wood, 132 × 86 cm). This work comes from the St. Peter the Martyr altar-piece in the convent of Santo Tomás in Avila, together with Nos. 612, 613, 614 (?) and 617.

612 «**St. Peter the Martyr praying**» (Wood, 133 × 86 cm). The portrayal of saints in ecstasy is a highly important pictorial form in religious art; Berruguete uses it here with extreme simplicity and concentration.

613 «**Death of St. Peter the Martyr**» (Wood, 128 × 85 cm).

614 «The sepulchre of St. Peter the Martyr» (Wood, 131 × 85 cm). The light entering the high windows is rendered in a masterly fashion.

615 «The Virgin appearing to a community» (Wood, 130 × 86 cm).

616 «St. Dominic de Guzmán» (Wood, 177 × 90 cm).

617 «St. Peter the Martyr» (Wood, 170 × 90 cm).

618 «Auto-da-fe presided over by St. Dominic de Guzmán» (Wood, 154 × 92 cm). This work represents the story of the heretic Raimond, who was pardoned by the saint. The scene is divided into two parts; the upper part in particular recalls Italian painting of the *quattrocento*.

1305 «Trial by fire» (Wood, 113 × 75 cm). Heretical books are being burnt, while the orthodox ones are saved.

2709 «The Virgin and Child» (Wood, 58 × 53 cm).

BERRUGUETE, Follower.

2574 «St. Anthony of Padua» (Wood, 105 × 53 cm).

BOCANEGRA, Pedro Atanasio Bocanegra (Granada 1638-1689). School of Granada. He was a follower of Alonso Cano, whose style and models he imitated, although in a softer and more popular vein.

619 «The Virgin and Child with St. Elizabeth and the infant St. John» (Canvas, 127 × 166 cm).

626 See Cano.

2797 «The Virgin Mary» (Canvas, 67 × 48 cm).

BORGOÑA, Juan de Borgoña (b. ?; d. Toledo 1534). He was an important figure in the School of Toledo in the 16th century. Possibly of Northern origin, he was trained in Italy. His work reveals a Tuscan influence in his fondness for clear, spacious composition, frequently framed in 15th-century architectural elements, as well as for idealized, enhanced figures.

3110 «Mary Magdalene and three Dominican saints» (Wood, 156 × 107 cm).

BORRASA, Luis Borrasá, Follower. 14th-15th century. Catalan School.

2675 «The Crucifixion» (Wood, 48 × 35 cm). The background has been repainted.

2677 «Miracle of St. Cosme» (?) (Wood, 69 × 62 cm).

CABEZALERO, Juan Martín Cabezalero (b. Almadén, Ciudad Real 1633; d. Madrid 1673). School of Madrid. He was a pupil of Carreño.

621 «Scene from the life of St. Francis» (Canvas, 232 × 195 cm).

CAJES. See Caxés.

CALLEJA, Andrés de la Calleja (b. Rioja 1705; d. Madrid 1785). He was a restorer.

3126 «Portrait of a Knight of the Order of Santiago» (Canvas, 87 × 78 cm).

CAMARON, José Camarón (b. Segorbe, Castellón 1730; d. Valencia 1803).

622 «Mater Dolorosa» (Canvas, 160 × 118 cm). This is probably the work of his son, José Camarón y Mediá (1761-1819), whose style is often mistaken for that of his father.

2786 «Bull-fighter» (Canvas, 42 × 28 cm). See No. 2787.

2787 «Dashing young lady» (Canvas, 42 × 28 cm). These two works were previously attributed to Carnicero.

CAMILO, Francisco Camilo (Madrid c. 1615-1673). School of Madrid. He painted a large number of pious, sentimental works which evolved towards Baroque dynamism; he worked at Court.

623 «The Martyrdom of St. Bartholomew» (Canvas, 205 × 249 cm).

2966 «St. Jerome scourged by angels» (Canvas, 206 × 249 cm).

3201 «Cardinal Albergati» (Canvas, 112 × 84 cm).

CANO, Alonso Cano (Granada 1601-1667). School of Granada. Alonso Cano is one of the most striking figures in Spanish art in the 17th century. His life reads like a novel, including a duel, a trial for the murder of his wife (in which he was acquitted) and a continuous series of disputes with the ecclesiastical tribunal of Granada; he was an attractive personality and a cultured and talented man, an architect, sculptor, painter and a prolific draughtsman, an unusual quality among Spanish artists, an enthusiastic collector of drawings and engravings and owner of a library that bore witness to his extensive culture. His father was a joiner of altar-pieces in Granada. At the age of 13 Alonso Cano went to Seville, where he was apprenticed in the workshop of Pacheco along with Velázquez. He probably also studied under the sculptor Martínez Montañés. In 1638 he went to Madrid, where he was protected by the Conde-Duque de Olivares and worked for the Court. On the death of his wife he lived for a short time in Valencia before returning to Madrid. He applied for a post as prebendary at the Cathedral in Granada, which he obtained in 1652. Apart from a few

723. Francisco de Goya. Self-portrait. (detail)

726. Francisco de Goya. The Family of Charles IV. (detail)

visits to Madrid he spent the rest of his life in his native city. At the outset of his artistic career he followed the Tenebrist naturalistic trend common to all the artists of his generation; however he soon gave it up and developed his own mature style, on the advice of Velázquez and other painters at Court, especially Van Dyck. His palette turned paler and silvery and he applied his colours with delicate velaturas. In his figures he aimed at dignity, beauty and harmonious proportions; his debt to Van Dyck is undeniable. His compositions are simple and well-balanced and in general his painting marks a moment of calm on the Spanish artistic scene.

625 «St. Benedict in the vision of the three angels» (Canvas, 166 × 123 cm). This work dates from about 1657-60.

626 «Penitent St. Jerome» (Canvas, 177 × 107 cm). This work is now attributed to Bocanegra.

627 «The Virgin and Child» (Canvas, 162 × 107 cm). This work dates from about 1646-50. The model resembles that of the Virgin called «del Lucero», now on loan to the Museum of Granada. The face of the Virgin is characteristic of all of Cano's Virgins with delicate features and large eyes.

629 «Dead Christ supported by an angel» (Canvas, 178 × 121 cm). This work dates from about 1646-52. This kind of representation is rather unusual; there are precedents in 15th-century Flemish and Italian art. Cano shows a deeply dramatic, but restrained interpretation of the scene.

632 «A Spanish king» (Canvas, 165 × 125 cm). This work was painted for the Golden Salon of the Alcázar together with no. 633. Although documentary evidence seems to indicate that Jusepe Leonardo was commissioned to carry out this one, art critics consider both works to be by Cano.

633 «Two Spanish kings» (Canvas, 165 × 227 cm). See No. 632.

2529 «Christ on the Cross» (Wood, 34 × 24 cm).

2637 «Dead Christ supported by an angel» (Canvas, 137 × 100 cm). Signed. This work dates from about 1646-52. See No. 629.

2806 «The miracle of the well» (Canvas, 216 × 149 cm). This work dates from about 1646-48. It refers to the miracle in which an angel saved the son of St. Isidore, who had fallen into a well. It is an important work painted by Cano during the time he lived in Madrid and very characteristic of his taste: he has portrayed the scene after the miracle has occurred, when calm has returned to the saint's family, the angel has disappeared and St. Isidore is giving thanks for the child's rescue, while the women are discussing the event and the children and dog add an anecdotic note. The composition is calm and balanced and the figures are quietly realistic. Cano's fluid brushwork, pleasing impasto and especially his colouring, which here begins to show the luminous quality of his later works painted in Granada, all bear witness to his study of the Venetian masters in the royal collection and the influence of Velázquez.

3041 «St. Anthony of Padua» (Canvas, 28 × 19 cm). This was a preparatory sketch for a painting now kept in the *Pinakothek* in Munich.

3134 «St. Bernard and the Virgin» (Canvas, 276 × 185 cm).

3185 «Christ at the column» (Canvas, 203 × 103 cm). This work is ascribed to Cano without documentary evidence due to the great similarity in style between this and other paintings by Cano, in particular one kept in a convent in Avila. It reveals obvious interest in the Classical anatomy and nude. Its sentimental tone, with its restrained pathos and emphasis on the impression of solitude surrounding the figure, is similar to the mood of the two *Dead Christ supported by an angel* kept in the Prado.

CARDENAS. See Bermejo.

CARDUCHO, Bartolomé. See Carduccio, Bartolomeo in Italian Masters.

CARDUCHO, Vicente Carducho or Vicencio Carduccio (b. Florence 1576/8; d. Madrid 1638). He was brought to Spain as a child by his brother Bartolomeo in 1585 and received his artistic training from him and the other painters working at El Escorial. In 1609 he was appointed Court Painter to succeed his brother; from then on he carried out a large number of royal commissions until his place was taken by Velázquez, who rapidly became the King's favourite painter. However Carducho continued to receive commissions from religious orders for important works, for example for the decoration of the Carthusian monastery of El Paular near Segovia. In keeping with his Italian background, Carducho attached special importance to the theoretical aspects of painting and his intellectual approach was higher than that of most of his Spanish colleagues; although he was acquainted with Caravaggesque naturalism, he only used it to the extent he considered necessary to give his subjects a life-like touch. His works reveal extremely correct draughtsmanship and a composition that is always easy and clear, with a well-balanced distribution of mass and figures arranged parallel to the picture-plane.

67 See Leonardo.

635 «The victory of Fleurus» (Canvas, 297 × 365 cm). Signed; it dates from 1634. Together with Nos. 636 and 637, this work was painted for the Hall of Realms in the Buen Retiro Palace. The three pictures have a rather archaic composition, with the main figures in a corner, in somewhat grandiloquent poses, and the battle scene in the background depicted with a high horizon line and topographical feeling. The battle of Fleurus (Belgium) was won by the Spanish troops commanded by Gonzalo de Córdoba in 1622, during the Thirty Years' War.

636 «The relief of Constance» (Canvas, 297 × 374 cm). Signed; it dates from 1634. The Duke of Feria, the commander of the Spanish troops, is seen freeing the city of Constance. See No. 635.

637 «The storming of Rheinfelden» (Canvas, 297 × 357 cm). Signed; it dates from 1634. The Duke of Feria is seen taking the town by storm. See No. 635.

638 «Large head of a man» (Canvas, 246 × 205 cm).

639 «The death of the venerable Odo of Novara» (Canvas, 342 × 302 cm). Signed; it dates from 1632. Together with Nos. 639a, 2227, 2501, 2956, 3061 and 3062, this work belonged to the cloister decoration of the monastery of El Paular, for which 54 large-scale canvases were commissioned. This series is the most important of Carducho's production and shows the extent of his creative ability since he had to portray a large number of complex scenes including numerous figures for which no iconographic precedents were available. In this work he painted his self-portrait in the first kneeling figure on the left and the figure seen in profile next to him is his friend, the Spanish dramatist Lope de Vega.

639. Carducho. The death of the venerable Odo of Novara.

650. Carreño. The Duke of Pastrana.

639a «The miracle of the water» (Canvas, 345 × 315 cm). This work dates from between 1626 and 1632. See No. 639.

643 «The Holy Family» (Canvas, 150 × 114 cm). Signed and dated 1631.

2227 «The superior of the Order, Don Bosson, restores a dead mason to life» (Canvas, 345 × 315 cm). Signed and dated 1626-32. See No. 639.

2501 «Father Basil of Burgundy appearing to his disciple St. Hugh of Lincoln» (Canvas, 345 × 315 cm). Signed and dated 1632. See No. 639.

2502 «St. Bruno renounces the mitre of Reggio» (Canvas, 345 × 315 cm). Signed. This work dates from about 1626-32. The grand but simple architectural elements in the background lend the composition a solemn air.

2956 «The martyrdom of the Ven. Fathers Herk and Leodiense of the monastery of Roermond» (Canvas, 345 × 315 cm). Signed; about 1626-32.

3061 «St. Bruno and six disciples attempting to retire to live in solitude» (Canvas, 345 × 315). This work dates from about 1626-32. See No. 639.

3062 «St. Bernard of Clairvaux visits the Rev. Father Guido, Prior of the monastery of Grenoble» (Canvas, 345 × 315 cm). Signed and dated 1632. See No. 639.

3265 «St. Jean de Matha renounces his doctorate and accepts it later by divine inspiration» (Canvas, 240 × 243 cm). This work belonged to a series of twelve paintings that Carducho was commissioned to paint for the church of the Trinitarian Order in Madrid in 1634, after completing the series for El Paular, on the life of St. Felix de Valois and St. Jean de Matha.

CARNICERO, Antonio Carnicero (b. Salamanca 1748; d. Madrid 1814). He chiefly painted portraits in a style directly influenced by Goya. He was Court painter after 1796.

640 «View of the Albufera, Valencia» (Canvas, 64 × 85 cm).

641 «Ascent of a Montgolfier balloon in Madrid» (Canvas, 170 × 284 cm). The event portrayed is apparently the ascent of the Frenchman Bouché in Aranjuez.

2649 «Doña Tomasa de Aliaga, widow of Salcedo» (Canvas, 93 × 69 cm). This portrait was attributed in the past to Goya.

2786 See Camarón.

2787 See Camarón.

CARREÑO, Juan Carreño de Miranda (b. Avilés 1614; d. Madrid 1685). School of Madrid. Carreño came to Madrid early in life from his native Asturias and studied under Pedro de las Cuevas and Bartolomé Román. At Velázquez's suggestion he was invited to participate in the decoration of the Hall of Mirrors in the Alcázar, thus entering in contact with the Court. In 1671 he was appointed Court painter and, like Velázquez, he also carried out administrative duties at Court. His known works all belong to his mature period; they reveal the characteristic features of the School of Madrid, that is, excellent impasto, fluid brushwork that blends the contours in space, and Venetian-style colouring. Carreño executed portraits, altar paintings and fresco decorations in churches in Madrid. In his portraits he enhanced his sitters with an elegant and sensitive air in the manner of Velázquez and Van Dyck. His other paintings and frescoes reveal true Baroque inspiration with stage-like positioning of the figures and settings and masterly use of light effects.

642 «Charles II» (Canvas, 201 × 141 cm). Charles II, known as «el Hechizado» («the Bewitched»), was the last offspring of the Spanish Habsburgs, the son of Philip IV and his second wife Mariana of Austria. He was weakly and retarded and after a chaotic reign died childless, appointing as his heir Philip of Anjou, who reigned as Philip V. Although he does not attempt to enhance his degenerate features, Carreño portrays the adolescent king with a certain air of Velazquenian elegance with which he tries to compensate his expressionless, fragile appearance, overwhelmed by the showy decorations of the Hall of Mirrors in the Alcázar.

644 «Queen Mariana» (Canvas, 211 × 125 cm). This work dates from about 1669 and shows Queen Mariana in widow's weeds, portrayed against the same background as her son, the young Charles II, in the preceding picture, conveying a rather gloomy image of the Court of Madrid as Carreño saw it.

645 «Piotr Ivanowitz Potemkin, the Russian ambassador» (Canvas, 204 × 120 cm). This portrait dates from 1681. The Russian ambassador was in Madrid twice, in 1668 and again in 1681. The work reveals Carreño's response to colour when his subject-matter permitted.

646 «Eugenia Martínez Vallejo, the freak» (Canvas, 165 × 107 cm). The child was portrayed by Carreño at the age of five. This kind of portrait of freakish figures is comparatively frequent in Spanish Baroque painting, the most famous examples being Velázquez's dwarfs and Ribera's Bearded Woman.

647 «The Court jester Francisco Bazán» (Canvas, 200 × 101 cm).

648 «Charles II» (Canvas, 75 × 60 cm). Dated 1680.

649 «St. Sebastian» (Canvas, 171 × 113 cm). Signed and dated 1656.

650 «The Duke of Pastrana» (Canvas, 217 × 155 cm). The Duke is portrayed outdoors, standing next to his horse and accompanied by two servants as a reference to his high rank; like Van Dyck in his famous portrait of Charles I of England, Carreño has combined elements of Baroque portraiture, which could not omit such allusions to the sitter's position, with a search for reality to give the painting a more spontaneous, true-to-life appearance.

651 «St. Anne teaching the Virgin» (Canvas, 196 × 168 cm). Signed.

2533 «The Immaculate Conception» (Canvas, 208 × 145 cm). Doubtful.

2800 «Naked freak» (Canvas, 165 × 108 cm). The figure is portrayed with attributes of Bacchus. The work is the companion piece to No. 646.

3088 «Herod's feast» (Canvas, 80 × 59 cm). This is a preparatory sketch.

749. Francisco de Goya. The executions of the third of May 1808 on the Principe
Pio hill in Madrid. (detail)

CASCESE. See Caxés.

CASTELO, Felix Castelo or Castello (Madrid 1595-1651). School of Madrid. He was a pupil of Vicente Carducho, whose style he followed. He worked for the Court and convents.

653 See Caxés.

654 «**The Reconquest of St. Kitts**» (Canvas, 279 × 311 cm). Signed and dated 1634, this work was previously attributed to Caxés. It was painted for the Hall of Realms in the Buen Retiro Palace and represents Don Fadrique de Toledo recapturing the island.

CASTILLO, Antonio del Castillo Saavedra (Córdoba 1616-1668). School of Córdoba. He worked in Córdoba and also for a while in Seville. He was a good draughtsman and his compositional schemes were skilful, but the colouring of his paintings is rather poor.

951 «**Joseph and his brethren**» (Canvas, 109 × 145 cm). This series on the life of Joseph (Nos. 951, 952, 953, 954, 955 and 956) is the best of Castillo's artistic production. The scenes have spacious Flemish-style settings and some of them architectural backgrounds. The paintings illustrate the episodes related in Genesis, xxxvii *et seq.*

952 «**Joseph sold by his brethren**» (Canvas, 109 × 145 cm). See No. 951.

953 «**Joseph's chastity**» (Canvas, 109 × 145 cm). See No. 951.

954 «**Joseph interpreting the Pharaoh's dream**» (Canvas, 109 × 145 cm). See No. 951.

955 «**Joseph's advancement in Egypt**» (Canvas, 109 × 145 cm). See No. 951.

956 «**Joseph orders Simeon to be imprisoned**» (Canvas, 109 × 143 cm). See No. 951.

2503 «**Penitent St. Jerome**» (Canvas, 141 × 105 cm). Signed.

2940 «**St. Francis**» (Canvas, 164 × 108 cm).

CASTILLO, José del Castillo (Madrid 1737-1792). After studying in Rome under Corrado Giaquinto, he painted designs for the Tapestry Factory.

2894 «**Still life with game**» (Canvas, 134 × 134 cm). This was a tapestry design.

CAXES, Eugenio da Cascese, Caxés or Cajés (Madrid 1574-1634). School of Madrid. He learnt the rudiments of his art from his father, one of the Italian artists who came to work at El Escorial, and completed his training in Rome before 1598. From this date on he worked in Madrid, for the Court (he was appointed Court painter in 1612), churches and convents, and frequently collaborated with Vicente Carducho. The unattractive human types he painted do not make his style very appealing, but it is certainly very personal: he combined Mannerist-style composition and elongated figures with a realistic touch in the details and strangely soft modelling. His best quality is possibly his bright, contrasted colouring.

119-20 See Correggio, copies.

653 «**The Reconquest of San Juan de Puerto Rico**» (Canvas, 290 × 344 cm). This work was painted for the Hall of Realms in the Buen Retiro Palace in 1634. In the foreground Don Juan de Haro converses with an *aide-de-camp* while the Dutch flee towards their ships. This event ocurred in 1625. The work was previously attributed to Castelo and has now been ascribed to Caxés on the basis of not conclusive documentary evidence.

654 See Felix Castelo.

657 «**Bestowal of the chasuble on St. Ildefons**» (Wood, 40 × 51 cm). Signed.

3051 «**Cardinal Cisneros**» (Canvas, 209 × 145 cm). Signed and dated 1604.

3064 «**The incredulity of St. Thomas**» (Canvas, 131 × 98 cm).

3120 «**Virgin with the sleeping Child**» (Canvas, 160 × 135 cm). This work is very characteristic of his style with the sharp contrast between the very slim, stereotyped figure of the Virgin and the highly precise details of the cradle in the foreground and the carpenter's workshop in the background.

3180 «**The Adoration of the Kings**» (Canvas, 123 × 103 cm). This is a workshop painting.

3228 «**The miracle of St. Leocadia**».

CEREZO, Mateo Cerezo (b. Burgos c. 1626; d. Madrid 1666). School of Madrid. He was one of Carreño's pupils and possibly his assistant. He specialized in religious painting with beautiful colouring and a very fluid technique, although without neglecting the draughtsmanship, which is always correct. His restrained Baroque style retains the composure and elegant bearing of his figures. Cerezo must have known the paintings of the royal collection since his works reveal the influence of Titian and Van Dyck.

620 «**The judgement of a soul**» (Canvas, 145 × 104 cm). This work was previously attributed to Cabezalero. It is very much in line with the Counter-Reformation, with the soul accompanied by interceding saints.

658 «**The Assumption**» (Canvas, 237 × 169 cm).
659 «**The mystic betrothal of St. Catherine**» (Canvas, 207 × 163 cm). Signed and dated 1660. This composition with its setting of columns and hangings is more scenographic than usual in Cerezo's works.
2244 «**St. Augustine**» (Canvas, 208 × 126 cm). Signed and dated 1663.
3159 «**Still life**» (Canvas, 100 × 227 cm). This work has been attributed to Cerezo recently; it had been listed as anonymous, close to the style of Pereda. Only two signed still lifes by Cerezo are known.
3256 «**The stigmata of St. Francis**» (Canvas, 170 × 110 cm). Dated 1660.

CIEZA (?), Vicente Cieza (active in Madrid between 1677 and 1701).
571 «**The Judgement of Solomon**» (Canvas, 110 × 140 cm).

COELLO, Claudio Coello (Madrid 1642-1693). School of Madrid. Coello is the best representative of the School of Madrid in the late 17th century. The son of a Portuguese bronze worker, he began his training under Francisco Rizi, whose Baroque style he adopted, but subordinated it to a high degree of extremely correct draughtsmanship. Other influences are those of Carreño and of the Venetian and Flemish masters, particularly Rubens, whose works he studied in the royal collection. Coello's frescoes and altar paintings mark the height of Spanish decorative Baroque art; he was a master in spatial illusionism and created ambitious compositions in stage-like settings full of columns, staircases, balustrades and hangings. In the human types he painted he portrayed beauty and dignified bearing unruffled by the bustling movement around them. From 1685 on he was Court painter, which allowed him to demonstrate his abilities as a portraitist.
660 «**The Virgin and Child among the Theological Virtues and Saints**» (Canvas, 232 × 273 cm). Signed and dated 1669. As in the following work, the scene is depicted like an Italian-style «Holy Conversation», unusual in Spanish art, which Coello situated in an opulent courtly setting.
661 «**The Virgin and Child adored by St. Louis of France**» (Canvas, 229 × 249 cm). See No. 660.
662 «**St. Dominic de Guzmán**» (Canvas, 240 × 160 cm). This is the companion piece to No. 663. An unusual modification of the traditional representation of the saint in a niche, which derives from Medieval altar-pieces, has been made by opening the niche to a landscape background; in this way Coello gives free rein to his Baroque taste which would have been constricted by the classic iconography of the saint in a cramped space and against a neutral background.
663 «**St. Rose of Lima**» (Canvas, 240 × 160 cm). See No. 662.
664 «**The Triumph of St. Augustine**» (Canvas, 271 × 203 cm). The traditional manner of representing the saint in ecstasy surrounded by angels bearing his emblems is enriched here with magnificent Classical architectonic elements.
665 «**Doña Mariana, Queen of Spain**» (Canvas, 97 × 79 cm). The attribution of this work to Coello is doubtful.
992 «**Father Cabanillas**» (Canvas, 76 × 62 cm). This is a portrait of a Franciscan monk.
2504 «**Charles II**» (Canvas, 66 × 56 cm).
2583 «**Jesus as a Child at the Temple door**» (Canvas, 168 × 122 cm). This work was attributed in the past to Carlo Dolci, it bears what is believed to be a false signature of Coello.

COELLO, Copy.
1316 «**Death of the Virgin**» (Canvas, 190 × 120 cm).

COLLANTES, Francisco Collantes (Madrid 1599-1656). School of Madrid. He was the most important figure of his time in Spanish landscape painting; his style shows the influence of both Italian and Flemish landscapes with figures and architectural elements.
666 «**The vision of Ezekiel**» (Canvas, 177 × 205 cm). Signed and dated 1630.
2849 «**Landscape**» (Canvas, 75 × 92 cm). Signed.
3027 «**St. Onofrius**» (Canvas, 168 × 108 cm). In his figure painting Collantes was clearly influenced by Ribera's realistic style, with vigorous modelling and thick impasto, but with clear light effects.
3086 «**The burning of Troy**» (Canvas, 144 × 197 cm).

CORREA, Juan Correa de Vivar (b. ?; d. Toledo 1566). He worked in Toledo, painting in the manner of Juan de Borgoña. His style is Italianate and contains a variety of Mannerist elements combined with architectural or still-life details that denote interest in observation of reality.
671 «**The Death of the Virgin**» (Wood, 254 × 147 cm). The donor, Don Francisco de Rojas, plays a prominent part in the composition. The fruit

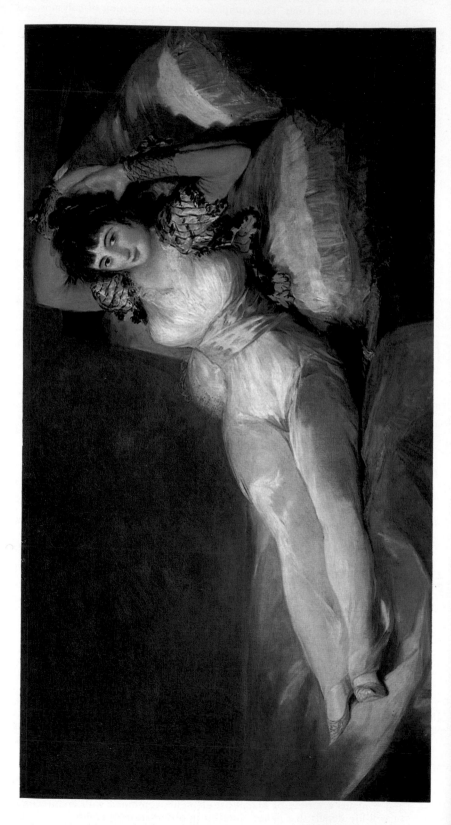

741. Francisco de Goya. The clothed maja.

742. Francisco de Goya. The nude maja.

bowl on the Virgin's table seems to anticipate the Toledan still lifes and illustrates the characteristic contradiction in Spanish painting of the time between the realistic, Flemish-style essence and the Italian forms.

672 «The Virgin and Child with St. Anne» (Wood, 94 × 90 cm). This work comes from the altar-piece of the church at San Martín de Valdeiglesias, together with Nos. 673 and 2832. The Italian influence can be observed in the sweetened, idealized figures, but the way in which the interior is combined with the landscape through a triple arch is typically Flemish.

673 «St. Benedict blessing St. Maur» (Wood, 94 × 87 cm). See No. 672.

680 «St. Bernard» (Wood, 91 × 35 cm).

687 «The Presentation of Jesus in the Temple» (Wood, 219 × 87 cm). Together with No. 689, this work comes from the monastery of Guisando.

689 «The Visitation» Reverse: «Penitent St. Jerome» (Wood, 212 × 77 cm).

690 «The Nativity» (Wood, 228 × 183 cm).

2828 «The Annunciation» (Wood, 225 × 146 cm).

2832 «The Virgin appearing to St. Bernard» (Wood, 170 × 130 cm).

CORTE, Juan de la Corte (b. ? 1597; d. Madrid 1660). He was of Flemish extraction and worked for the Spanish Court. He painted landscapes and battle scenes in a highly-detailed, elaborate style.

3102 «The Rape of Helen of Troy» (Canvas, 150 × 222 cm).

3103 «The burning of Troy» (Canvas, 140 × 238 cm).

DELEITO, Andrés Deleito or Deleyto. His biography is unknown; he worked around 1680, painting chiefly still lifes in a very personal style.

3125 «Christ driving the traders out of the Temple» (Canvas, 60 × 80 cm). This is the only known work with figures by Deleito.

DONOSO. See Jiménez Donoso.

ESCALANTE, Juan Antonio de Frías y Escalante (b. Córdoba 1633; d. Madrid 1670). School of Madrid. He was probably trained in the circle around Rizi and in his brief career left works that reveal excellent technical ability and refinement. With his pale pearl-like colouring, fine, elegant figures and somewhat doll-like female models with long limbs and tapering fingers, and his preference for grace and delicacy, he anticipates aspects of Rococo art.

696 «The Infant Jesus and St. John» (Canvas, 46 × 122 cm).

697 «Dead Christ» (Canvas, 133 × 152 cm).

698 «The prudent Abigail» (Canvas, 113 × 152 cm). Signed and dated 1667. Abigail is seen offering David provisions for the troops. Together with Nos. 699 and 2957 this work formed part of a series of 18 paintings on biblical subjects painted by Escalante for the Merced convent in Madrid between 1666 and 1668, the most important of his artistic production.

699 «The triumph of Faith over the senses» (Canvas, 113 × 152 cm). Signed and dated 1667. See No. 698.

2957 «The water from the rock» (Canvas, 104 × 143 cm). See No. 698.

3046 «The Communion of St. Rose of Viterbo» (Canvas, 215 × 190 cm). Signed.

3114 «Ecce Homo» (Canvas, 105 × 82 cm). Signed.

3135 «Elijah and the angel» (Canvas, 114 × 103 cm).

3220 «Jesus and the Samaritan woman» (Canvas, 104 × 123 cm).

ESPINOSA, Jerónimo Jacinto Espinosa (b. Cocentaina, Valencia 1600; d. Valencia 1667). School of Valencia. He received his training under his father, an artist who settled in Valencia about 1612; his style reveals the influence of the Ribaltas and Orrente, as well as Zurbarán, whose work he must have seen in Seville between 1640 and 1647, although there is no documentary evidence of his visit. He painted harshly realistic religious scenes with the use of *chiaroscuro* that modelled the forms vigorously. The colours are extremely deteriorated due to defective preparation.

700 «Mary Magdalene» (Canvas, 112 × 91 cm). This is the companion piece to the following No.

701 «St. John the Baptist» (Canvas, 112 × 91 cm). Pendant to No. 700.

3087 «St. Raymond Nonnatus» (Canvas, 245 × 180 cm).

ESPINOSA, Juan de Espinosa. This artist worked in the first half of the 17th century; his identity is difficult to ascertain as it is confused with that of other figures with the same name whose biographies are practically unknown. This one was a masterly painter of fruit pieces.

702 «Apples, plums, grapes and pears» (Canvas, 76 × 59 cm).

703 «Grapes and apples» (Canvas, 50 × 39 cm).

ESTEVE, Agustín (b. Valencia 1753; d. Madrid after 1820). He was a follower of Goya's style and is primarily known as a portraitist.

2581 «Joaquina Téllez-Girón, daughter of the Duke of Osuna» (Canvas, 190 × 116 cm). Signed. On the lower part of the canvas her age can be read: 13 years 4 months (*Su edad: 13 años y 4 meses*). The portrait reveals the same sober approach and delicate colouring, combined with intense psychological study, as Goya in his portraits.

2876 «Don Mariano San Juan y Pinedo, Conde Consorte de la Cimera» (Canvas, 128 × 89 cm).
ESTIMARIU, Master of Estimaríu. 14th-century anonymous master of the Catalan School. He might have been schooled in the workshop of Destorrents; his style is simple, candid and predominantly narrative.

2535 | «The Legend of St. Lucy» (Wood, 161 × 97 cm each panel). The panels
2536 | relate episodes of the saint's martyrdom in horizontal bands, avoiding monotony by means of simple architectural elements that change the background tones, thus making a clearer distinction between the scenes. The importance attached to the silhouettes and fondness for pure, bright colouring are characteristic of the Catalan School, which is influenced by Sienese painting.
EZQUERRA, Jerónimo Antonio de Ezquerra. He is known to have lived around 1725, but his biography is unknown.

704 «Water» (Canvas, 248 × 160 cm). This work completes a series of three «elements» by Palomino.
FERNANDEZ, Alejo Fernández (b. Córdoba c. 1475; d. Granada 1545/6). He was the pioneer of the Sevillian Renaissance School, which was still closely related to the Flemish style.

1925 «The flagellation» (Wood, 42 × 35 cm).
FERNANDEZ NAVARRETE. See Navarrete «the Deaf».
FERRO, Gregorio Ferro (b. Sta. María de Lamas, Corunna 1742; d. Madrid 1812).

2780 «The Count of Floridablanca (?), the protector of trade» (Canvas, 35 × 27 cm). This was a preparatory sketch and bears a false signature of Goya, who was Ferro's rival on several occasions.
FLANDES, Juan de Flandes (b. ?; d. Palencia before 1519). Hispano-Flemish School. The real name and origin of this artist, called «John of Flanders», are unknown; there is evidence of his presence in Spain from 1496 on, the year he entered the service of Queen Isabella. His style reveals Flemish origin, but already influenced by the Italian Renaissance. He was an excellent painter, his draughtsmanship was sound and his modelling delicate and sensitive; his sense of space was Renaissance. He used unified colouring, with cold tones and predominance of blues and whites.

2935 «The resurrection of Lazarus» (Wood, 110 × 84 cm).
2936 «Agony in the Garden» (Wood, 110 × 84 cm).
2937 «The Ascension» (Wood, 110 × 84 cm).
2938 «The descent of the Holy Ghost» (Wood, 110 × 84 cm).
FLANDES, Follower of Juan de Flandes.

2541 «The Visitation of the Virgin to St. Elizabeth» (Wood, 52 × 36 cm).
GALLEGO, Fernando Gallego (active 1466/67-1507). Hispano-Flemish School. He was a capital figure in painting in Castile and left numerous works, some of them signed, as well as exercising an important influence on the large number of artists who passed through his workshop. His style derives from Flemish painting and also reveals similarities with German art, although it is a very personal style and tends towards dramatic touches.

2647 «Christ giving His blessing» (Wood, 169 × 132 cm). The work shows Christ enthroned between the Church and the Synagogue and surrounded by the Tetramorph.

2997 «Calvary» (Wood, 92 × 83 cm). The deep pathos of the scene inclines one to overlook the incorrect details of the draughtsmanship. The massive, rugged landscape is very typical of Gallego.

2998 «Pietà or The Fifth Sorrow» (Wood, 118 × 102 cm). This work is characteristic of the artist's expressionist taste and dry, angular form of modelling. The Flemish landscape reflects the roughness of the Castilian countryside.

3039 «The Martyrdom of St. Catherine» (Wood, 125 × 109 cm). This work is probably by Francisco Gallego, a pupil and possibly a relative of Fernando.
GARCIA DE BENABARRE, Pedro García de Benabarre (active in Barcelona in 1455 and 1456). Catalan School. He was a pupil of Martorell and took over his workshop on his master's death.

1324 «St. Sebastian and St. Polycarp destroying idols» (Wood, 160 × 68 cm).
1325 «The Martyrdom of St. Sebastian and St. Polycarp» (Wood, 160 × 68 cm).
GILARTE, Mateo Gilarte (Valencia c. 1620-1690). Valencian School.

763. Francisco de Goya. Saturn devouring one of his sons. (detail)

761. Francisco de Goya. The witches' Sabbath. (detail)

2998. Gallego. Pietà.

He was a somewhat archaic artist; his compositions are Mannerist-style, compact and static.

714 **«The Birth of the Virgin»** (Canvas, 228 × 147 cm). Signed.

GOMEZ, Jacinto Gómez Pastor (San Ildefonso 1746-1812). He was a pupil of Bayeu and painted fresco decorations.

715 **«Angels adoring the Holy Ghost»** (Canvas, 46 × 45 cm). This was a preparatory sketch for the ceiling of the Oratory in the Palace at La Granja.

GONZALEZ, Bartolomé González (b. Valladolid 1564; d. Madrid 1627). He was a Court portraitist who painted in the manner of Coello and Pantoja, portraying his sitters in stiff poses and with great attention to detail in the draperies and jewelry.

716 **«Queen Margarita»** (Canvas, 116 × 100 cm). Signed and dated 1609.

1141 Copy after Anthonis Mor.

2918 **«Philip III»** (Canvas, 160 × 109 cm).

GONZALEZ VELAZQUEZ, Zacarías González Velázquez (Madrid 1763-1834). He received his training in the Fine Arts Academy and worked for the Royal Tapestry Factory.

2495 **«Don Antonio González Velázquez»** (Canvas, 80 × 58 cm). The sitter was the painter's father, an artist who specialized in fresco decorations.

2897 **«Angler»** (Canvas, 110 × 196 cm).

GOYA, Francisco de Goya y Lucientes (b. Fuendetodos, Saragossa 1746; d. Bordeaux 1828). Goya was one of those titanic figures who stand out in history not only for their achievements but also because their many-sided and independent genius defies all attempts at classifying them within the restricting limits of one or another artistic trend. His long life coincided with a critical period of Spanish history: the beginnings of the age of Enlightenment under Charles III, the upheavals of the reign of Charles IV, the Peninsular War and finally the reactionary government of Ferdinand VII. In spite of his strong constitution, Goya fell very seriously ill several times and as a result of one of these illnesses lost his hearing in the prime of life. But on each occasion his indomitable temperament and universal curiosity enabled him to surmount his personal misfortune and face life with renewed vigour and still greater mastery of his brush. The process by which his character matured was a slow and at times painful one; his whole artistic career is marked by an inner tension produced by his extremely lucid mind that led him to question the meaning of everything his eyes perceived and to seek means to express it, always experimenting to convey the ideas with which his inner world was overflowing.

After studying in Saragossa under José Luzán, Goya tried to make his way in Madrid, but after two unsuccessful attempts at obtaining a scholarship to the Academy of San Fernando, he decided to go to Italy (1770). On his return the following year he received his first important commission, moved to Madrid and married the sister of Francisco Bayeu, Josefa. Partly through his brother-in-law he was introduced at the Royal Tapestry Factory and subsequently prepared tapestry cartoons for many years. This was the opportunity to make contact with courtly circles, visit the royal art collections and receive commissions to portray noble sitters; he gradually became the favourite portraitist of aristocratic circles. At this stage he was still the gay, bright artist of the tapestries, who combined Rococo delicacy and hedonism with wise academic principles in a style of painting that, although not yet brilliant, was extremely pleasing, refined in colour and enlivened by keen observation of reality.

The influence of his enlightened liberal environment was important in converting him into a mature and cultured man. His outlook on life and the world around him became more critical as he began to reflect on the problems of the society in which he lived. This criticism found expression in his canvases, where he denounced the vices of the Court, religious obscurantism, vanity, stupidity and ignorance, not with the cold moralizing tone of a passive onlooker, but with the impassioned interest of someone directly involved in the problems of his time.

Goya was highly regarded at Court and in 1799 his appointment as first Court painter marked the height of his artistic career. However, in 1792 he had undergone the terrible illness that had deprived him of his hearing. This crisis was one of the important thresholds of his life and contributed to the birth of a new Goya, a bitter, sarcastic Goya isolated by his lack of communication, who began to reveal the depth of his amazing personality. By this time he was already a magnificent artist. His art was essentially pictorial and he drew on Baroque sources for his inspiration («Velázquez, Rembrandt and nature», as he declared). Light and colour were his prime interests. If his draughtsmanship was not entirely correct, it did however denote a freedom that gave him ample means of expressing himself and conveying reality rapidly and directly. The strict Classical trend prevailing in Europa at the time did not correspond to his concept of art and he concentrated on his own study of light effects that relate his work directly to the Impressionists.

The Peninsular War was another landmark in his life; this terrible conflict brought to the fore one of Goya's chief preoccupations, latent in all his work: his concern for the irrational side of human behaviour, the animal instincts in human nature waiting for the slightest opportunity to break loose. The sinister, diabolical elements present in his work almost from the start and which to a certain extent foreshadow aspects of Romanticism and even Surrealism, coincided with the state of deep pessimism the war had caused in his spirit. The result was a new turn of his painting. With his astonishing ability to find the most adecuate artistic language to communicate his innermost anxieties, Goya turned to a distorted form of expressionism.

The reign of Ferdinand VII proved to be the final disenchantment. Aged and ailing, Goya left Spain for France and settled in Bordeaux. Here he found himself again and lived these last few years in comparative calm. The great artist who had executed oil paintings, fresco decorations, innumerable drawings, who revolutionized the art of engraving and touched on all possible themes in his artistic life, spent his last years preparing lithographies and miniatures. Like the old man in one of his famous drawings who says «I am still learning», Goya maintained his creative force and intellectual curiosity intact till the very end in spite of all his bitterness and frustrations.

719. Goya. Charles IV on horseback.   720. Goya. Queen María Luisa.

2899. Francisco de Goya. The milk-maid from Bordeaux. (detail)

809. El Greco. Nobleman with his hand on his chest. (detail)

719 «**Charles IV on horseback**» (Canvas, 305 × 279 cm). Goya's admiration for Velázquez is exemplified in the series of engravings he made after works by the great 17th-century artist. In the case of this portrait the influence is completely evident: not only the general idea of the equestrian portrait and the way the figure is placed in a landscape setting, but also the horse is copied from that of Margaret of Austria in the Prado portrait by Velázquez. It is not a heroic portrait and for this reason Goya has chosen a promenading horse, although possibly he took into consideration that the clumsy figure of Charles IV would not have been seen at its best on one of the elegantly prancing horses of Velázquez's masculine equestrian portraits. The predominant colours in this work are grey tones, not the silvery greys used by Velázquez, but rather leaden grey shades that give the landscape a somewhat stormy air.

720 «**Queen Maria Luisa on horseback**» (Canvas, 335 × 279 cm). This work dates from 1799 and is the companion piece to the preceding portrait. Goya portrayed the Queen on her horse «Marcial», a gift from Godoy. In this case the horse's silhouette copies that of Queen Elizabeth, the wife of Philip IV, in Velázquez's portrait. The light effect of its figure against the landscape is interesting and avoids the monotony of the dark shades. As in all the portraits Goya painted of Queen Maria Luisa, she has the same pert, self-assured expression; her figure lacks dignity, but she has the defiant air of a person who knows herself mistress of the situation.

727. Goya. Charles IV.   **724. Goya. Ferdinand VII.**

721 «**The painter Francisco Bayeu**» (Canvas, 112 × 84 cm). It dates from 1791; it is a posthumous portrait, for which Goya used the painter's own self-portrait. From the point of view of its colouring, this is one of Goya's finest works, where he used the range of grey shades with extreme delicacy. He learnt much from Bayeu who introduced him at the Tapestry Factory.

722 «**Josefa Bayeu de Goya**» (?) (Canvas, 81 × 56 cm). The sitter has traditionally been identified as Goya's wife, although without certainty. The portrait has an intimate, familiar air that could support this belief. It dates from about 1790.

723 «**Self-portrait**» (Canvas, 46 × 35 cm). Signed and dated 1815. In this portrait Goya is 69 years old, has been deaf for many years and a widower; the war is over. His face here reflects bitterness and disappointment. The handling is very free and as in all his mature works he makes generous use of blacks. His unkempt appearance and the way he seems to «look out of» the picture give it an intimate, almost self-revealing air.

724 «**Ferdinand VII in an encampment**» (Canvas, 207 × 140 cm). Signed (with the letters upside-down). The work dates from about 1814. Ferdinand VII tried to avoid Goya (and he was right in doing so). The portraits that exist were not commissioned by the King himself and Goya used the same head to paint them, proof that the King was not willing to sit to him. In these portraits Goya gives free rein to his animosity and does not make the slightest effort to enhance the ugly face, indolent expression and gracelessness of the heavy figure. Strangely enough, Goya's portraits of Ferdinand VII are his most pompous ones; they contain a certain Baroque

flamboyance which the portraits of Charles IV totally lack and which only accentuate the ridiculous appearance of the monarch.

725 **«General Don José de Palafox on horseback»** (Canvas, 248 × 224 cm). Signed and dated 1814. Palafox played an important part in the defence of Saragossa against the Napoleonic troops in 1808. Goya knew him personally. This portrait is clearly inspired in Velázquez's *Conde Duque de Olivares*.

726 **«Charles IV and his family»** (Canvas, 280 × 336 cm). Dating from 1800, this is one of Goya's most famous works and is all the more surprising if one bears in mind that it was painted the same year as his contemporary David's famous *Mme. Recamier*. Although the general arrangement of the figures, like in a frieze parallel to the picture plane, and the sober setting could be considered Neo-Classical touches, the picture contains nothing of the cool aloofness, reverent attitude towards delineation and severely sculptural forms that are characteristic of the Neo-Classical style. Goya's work is essentially pictorial; light plays a foremost role, invading the scene from the left, making jewelry and medals sparkle and silk sashes and gold-embroidered organdy dresses shine, bringing out all the splendour of the predominant yellow tones. Goya employs all his skill as a painter to capture forms with fluid, vibrating brushstrokes, unencumbered by the limits of the design. As on other occasions he pays tribute to Velázquez when he paints his own self-portrait in the background, as the great master does in his *Meninas;* but what interests Goya here is not the subtle depiction of space in the manner of Velázquez, but rather the use of his self-portrait as a witness to the scene. His face seems to send a conniving look from the back of the picture over the heads of the figures thus making us witnesses of his not very favourable impression of that family. King Charles IV, well meaning and good-natured but completely dominated by the Queen, is shown with an absent, foolish expression; Maria Luisa, on the contrary, is portrayed with her usual typically defiant look and regally stretched neck (of which she was so proud). The female figure who turns her face away from the spectator is surprising and probably represents the future, still unknown, wife of Ferdinand VII. Among all these plain, unattractive faces, the figures of the children are treated by Goya, as usual, with sympathy and delicacy.

727 **«Charles IV»** (Canvas, 202 × 126 cm). This work dates from 1798/9. It is a replica of one kept in the Royal Palace. Like its companion piece (No. 728), it belonged to Godoy, the all-powerful favourite and chief minister who ruled Spain during the reign of Charles IV with the unlimited support of Queen Maria Luisa.

728 **«Queen Maria Luisa with a mantilla»** (Canvas, 209 × 125 cm). This work dates from 1798/9. The Queen is dressed as a *maja,* with the popular costume that was used on occasions by members of the aristocracy. It is known that the Queen found herself «very much herself» in this portrait, as she wrote in one of her letters to her *protégé* Godoy.

729 **«The Infanta Maria Josefa»** (Canvas, 74 × 60 cm). She was the sister of Charles IV. Like Nos. 730 to 733, this is a preparatory life study for the group portrait *Charles IV and his family;* all of them are extremely vivacious. The red priming that Goya generally used shines through.

730 **«The Infante Don Francisco de Paula Antonio»** (Canvas, 74 × 60 cm). He was one of the sons of Charles IV.

731 **«The Infante Don Carlos Maria Isidro»** (Canvas, 74 × 60 cm). He was

725. Goya. General Palafox.   **2785. Goya. The Colossus or Panic.**

810. El Greco. A nobleman. (detail)

another of Charles IV's sons, brother of Ferdinand VII, and a pretendent to the Spanish throne on the death of the latter, which gave rise to the Carlist Wars between his absolutist followers and the liberal followers of Ferdinand VII's daughter Isabella.

732 **«Don Luis de Borbón, Prince of Parma and King of Etruria»** (Canvas, 74 × 60 cm). He was Charles IV's son-in-law.

733 **«The Infante Don Antonio Pascual»** (Canvas, 74 × 60 cm). He was Charles IV's brother.

734 **«Isidoro Máiquez»** (Canvas, 77 × 58 cm). Signed and dated 1807. The sitter was a famous actor; Goya portrayed him with all the flourish and naturalness he used when his sitter was a person of his confidence, barely outlining the background and concentrating his attention on the face with its sparkling eyes, described with vivid, expressive strokes.

735 **«Ferdinand VII in his robes of State»** (Canvas, 212 × 146 cm). It dates from 1814. This is without doubt the most grotesque of all the portraits of Ferdinand VII. The clumsy figure, the graceless way in which he holds the sceptre and his total lack of majesty make a striking contrast to the pompous regal robes that Goya depicts in a simple, masterly manner, with fluid, forceful brushstrokes full of impasto.

736 **«General Urrutia»** (Canvas, 200 × 135 cm). Signed. This interesting portrait dates from 1798 and reveals a sober elegance that gives some of Goya's portraits a vaguely English flavour.

737 **«Charles III in hunting costume»** (Canvas, 210 × 127 cm). This portrait dates from 1786/8 and is known in several almost identical versions; it is clearly inspired by Velázquez's style.

738 **«Cardinal Don Luis María de Borbón y Vallabriga»** (Canvas, 214 × 136 cm). This portrait dates from about 1800. There is another earlier version in São Paulo with the sitter facing the other direction.

739 **«The Duke and Duchess of Osuna with their children»** (Canvas, 225 × 174 cm). Dated 1788. The family portrait is a branch of painting with little tradition in Spain. It has its origin in 17th-century Dutch art and was very popular in England in the 18th century. Here Goya has painted a simplified version, omitting the domestic interior which is usually part of the scene. The pyramid-shaped composition gives the group unity, as well as the clear, harmonious colouring with its delicate tints. The Osunas protected Goya and were important figures in Madrid society at the time; the Duchess was a refined and very cultured woman, to a certain extent a rival or counterpart to the Duchess of Alba. In the children the Aragonese painter has once again shown his sentimental angle; their fragile figures and the childish curiosity expressed in their transparent gaze make them unforgettable.

740 **«Doña Tadea Arias Enríquez»** (Canvas, 190 × 106 cm). Signed. This work dates from about 1793/4. Always receptive to feminine appeal, Goya has painted in this case a very Rococo portrait, with pale, porcelain-like tones against an ethereal garden background very much in keeping with the sitter's aloof air and upright bearing characteristic of Goya's models.

740a **«Charles IV»** (Canvas, 126 × 94 cm). This is probably a workshop copy.

740b **«Charles IV»** (Canvas, 152 × 110 cm). See No. 740a.

740c **«Queen María Luisa»** (Canvas, 114 × 81 cm). Pendant to No. 740 b.

740i **«The beheading»** (Tin, 29 × 41 cm). This is a repetition of an original on wood with the same subject-matter. It is a disturbing work, especially if it was painted, as some art critics allege, before the Peninsular War. The theme of blind fury, of senseless violence, was later treated in detail by Goya in the *Disasters of War*.

740j **«The bonfire»** (Tin, 32 × 46 cm). See the preceding No.

741 **«The clothed maja»** (Canvas, 95 × 190 cm). See No. 742.

742 **«The nude maja»** (Canvas, 97 × 190 cm). These are two of the most mythical paintings in the history of art and have always been surrounded by an air of mystery and scandal, primarily due to their supposed connection with the Duchess of Alba. Quite apart from the fact of the probable intimacy between Goya and the Duchess, renowned for her beauty and wit, these *majas* bear little or no likeness to existing portraits painted by Goya of the Duchess, so that it is very unlikely that she sat to him for these two pictures. The nude resembles the feminine prototype found in many of Goya's paintings and drawings. The smooth, polished handling gives the impression of an academic, ideal type of nude rather than of a definite woman. In the clothed figure Goya seems to take pleasure in depicting the play of sheens and tints in the fine, transparent textiles. The

handling is much freer than in the other picture and in particular the bolero reveals bold strokes characteristic of Goya's mature period. These two works are mentioned in the inventory of Godoy's estate confiscated in 1808, so that it is possible that they were painted for him. It has also been suggested that the clothed portrait was originally intended to hide the nude one by means of a double frame, which is maybe not too far-fetched a supposition considering that these works came into conflict with the Inquisition. They were probably painted around 1800.

728. Goya. Queen María Luisa with a mantilla.

743 «The majo with a guitar» (Canvas, 135 × 110 cm). It dates from 1779/ 1780. Goya worked for the Royal Tapestry Factory from 1775 on, to begin with simply as an assistant to his brother-in-law Francisco Bayeu. For a long time the Factory's output had consisted of a constant repetition of Flemish designs, until Mengs conceived the idea of commissioning young artists to prepare new cartoons with gay, popular themes to renew the designs. Goya supplied the Factory with cartoons until 1790. This work was an interesting form of apprenticeship and Goya's gradual maturing process can be followed in these designs, which he regarded as independent paintings, without giving too much thought to the ultimate object so that he sometimes ran into difficulties due to the problems his designs caused the weavers. The pyramid-shaped composition of this cartoon complies with the Neo-Classical style which Goya often used in his early period.

744 «A goader on horseback» (Canvas, 56 × 47 cm). The world of bull fighting was a constant source of inspiration to Goya and he illustrated it perfectly in the *Tauromaquia* etchings.

745 «Christ crucified» (Canvas, 255 × 153 cm). Dating from 1780, this was Goya's admission piece when he was accepted as a member of the Academy of San Fernando. It is very Classical, with a polished, enamel-like technique; the way in which the subject is treated once again recalls Velázquez.

746 «The Holy Family» (Canvas, 200 × 148 cm). Like the preceding, this work, dating from 1780 (?), is Neo-Classical and reveals the influence of Mengs in the closed composition and smooth handling.

747 «The exorcized man» (Canvas, 48 × 60 cm). This work dates from 1813-18. Goya often treated the subject of religious obscurantism and sometimes in an extremely violent manner. The positioning of the figures, light effects, the relation between the different figures and the ample surrounding space reveal the influence of Rembrandt, whose engravings Goya probably studied with particular interest.

748 «The 2nd of May 1808 in Madrid: the charge of the Mamelukes» (Canvas, 266 × 345 cm). This work dates from 1814. Without being a man of great culture, Goya belonged to the liberal circles, whose ideas he

shared and who were generally *afrancesados* or Francophile. The fact that the invaders who brought war to Spain should have been the French caused a deep conflict in Goya's spirit, which combined with the terrible experience of the war itself, together with his deafness and feeling of isolation, to cause an indelible impression in his mind. The artistic production of his last period reflects all the bitterness and disappointment that this produced. This painting represents the encounter between Napoleon's Egyptian troops (Mamelukes) and the anonymous people of Madrid; it is not a heroic scene, but one of blind, atavistic fury that distorts the faces in convulsed expressions and poses, filling the whole picture with unaccustomed violence. It is the companion piece to the following No.

749 «The 3rd of May 1808 in Madrid: the executions on Príncipe Pío hill» (Canvas, 266 × 345 cm). This work dates from 1814. Both these pictures were painted «to perpetuate... the memorable and heroic feats... of our glorious rebellion against the tyrant of Europe». However, they contain few heroic elements and a great deal of anguish. Goya emphasizes the irrational effect of the war on human beings rather than its heroic or gallant aspects. The destructive power of war is regarded as something stronger than human nature, dominating both the executioners and the executed. The way in which the scene is presented pictorially is as violent as the scene itself and this brings Goya very close to the Expressionists, exaggerating contrasts, distorting features and doing away with any kind of refinement in order to convey the whole drama of the terrible events.

750 «St. Isidore's Meadow» (Canvas, 44 × 94 cm). This tapestry design dates from 1788. A view of Madrid can be seen in the background.

751 «A dead turkey» (Canvas, 45 × 63 cm). Signed. This is the companion piece to No. 752.

752 «Dead fowl» (Canvas, 46 × 64 cm). This is the pendant to No. 751.

753 «Dogs on the leash» (Canvas, 112 × 170 cm). This work dates from 1775 and was a tapestry design.

The Black paintings from the «Quinta del Sordo». *Nos. 754 to 768.* These works were painted between 1819 and 1823 and covered the walls of the salon and dining room of the house Goya had bought on the banks of the Manzanares river. He painted them in oil paints on the wall; in

748. Goya. The Charge of the Mamelukes (2nd of May 1808).

1873 they were removed, transferred to canvas and restored by Martínez Cubells. Their name comes from the predominant black colour blended with ochres and earthen tones. The paintings are disconcerting to say the least, not only because their ultimate meaning is not clear, in spite of various possible interpretations, but also due to the strange, hallucinating, almost visionary scenes. Goya was already old and had just overcome one of the most serious crisis of his illness when he chose to fill his house with these monstruous images; since he was painting them for himself, he did so without any outward restraint, giving free rein to his fantastic visions and rendering them with an unprecedented bold technique which even today, after Expressionist and abstract art, produces astonishment. Even at the height of his pessimism Goya remained an artist full of creative force, capable of discovering new ways of artistic expression and producing at the end of his life some of the most personal and surprising works of modern painting.

754 «Doña Leocadia Zorrilla» (Canvas, 147 × 132 cm). Doña Leocadia shared the last few years of Goya's life and accompanied him into exile.

755 «Pilgrimage to St. Isidore's well (The Holy Service)» (Canvas, 123 × 266 cm). The names quoted in brackets are those that appeared in the inventory of the *Quinta* and are therefore probably the original names that Goya gave them.

756 «Fantastic vision (Asmodeus)» (Canvas, 120 × 265 cm). Two beings can be seen flying towards a mountain, while two soldiers are preparing to fire at them from the right-hand angle.

757 «Fate (Atropos)» (123 × 266 cm). The figure on the right seems to represent Death waiting to sever the thread of life.

758 «Duel with cudgels» (123 × 266 cm). Two men with mud up to their knees struggle unable to separate.

759 «Two monks» (144 × 66 cm).

750. Goya. St. Isidore's Meadow.

760 «St. Isidore's Day» (140 × 438). This theme was painted by Goya in a tapestry design (No. 750) full of light and merry-making; here it has turned into a terrible nightmare.

761 «Witches' Sabbath (Aquellare)» (140 × 438 cm). The witches gather around a he-goat dressed in monk's attire.

762 «Two old men eating» (53 × 85 cm).

763 «Saturn devouring one of his sons» (146 × 83 cm). The classical theme is represented with exceptional cruelty and probably alludes to the destructive force of Time. Although it is sometimes difficult to interpret each work individually, as a whole these paintings seem to contain bitter reflexions on the futility of life, the inevitableness of destiny and the foolishness and lack of communication between men.

764 «Judith and Holofernes» (146 × 84 cm).

765 «Two women and a man» (125 × 66 cm).

766 «Reading» (126 × 66 cm).

767 «Dog half-submerged» (134 × 80 cm).

768 «Picnic on the banks of the Manzanares» (Canvas, 272 × 295 cm). This tapestry design dates from 1775 and like the others (see explanation to No. 743) reflects the gay, carefree world of Goya's youthful period. These scenes of ordinary people enjoying themselves are the Spanish counterpart to the *fêtes champêtres* of the French Rococo with the gallant ladies and noblemen substituted by popular figures like the *majas* and *majos*, *manolas* and *manolos*. They offer a vital, easy-going view of life in Madrid, full of colour and picturesque aspects that in part anticipate Romanticism.

Cartoons for tapestries to decorate the dining-room at the Pardo Palace (1777-8):

769 «A dance at San Antonio de la Florida» (Canvas, 272 × 295 cm). Goya

756. Goya. Fantastic Vision (Asmodeus).

is known to have been satisfied with the result of this skilful design.

770 «The quarrel in the New Tavern» (Canvas, 275 × 414 cm). This subject recalls the usual *genre* scenes of Flemish tapestry cartoons.

771 «The maja and the cloaked men» (Canvas, 275 × 190 cm). The cloaked men wear the fashionable wide capes which had been prohibited under Charles III by the minister Esquilache, causing a famous popular uprising.

772 «The drinker» (Canvas, 107 × 151 cm).

773 «The parasol» (Canvas, 104 × 152 cm). This is one of the finest paintings of this series; the filtered light on the lady's face is particularly subtle.

774 «The kite» (Canvas, 269 × 285 cm).

775 «The card-players» (Canvas, 270 × 167 cm). This is the usual compositional scheme for tapestry cartoons at the time: the figures are arranged in a pyramid while some branches enliven the scene on the left.

776 «Boys blowing up a balloon» (Canvas, 116 × 124 cm). Goya often recorded children's pastimes in his tapestry designs.

777 «Boys picking fruit» (Canvas, 119 × 122 cm).

Cartoons for tapestries to decorate the Prince's bedroom at the Pardo Palace (1778-80):

778 «The blind man with a guitar» (Canvas, 260 × 311 cm). The scene takes place in the *Plaza de la Cebada* in Madrid.

779 «The Madrid fair» (Canvas, 258 × 218 cm). The scene is set in the same square as No. 778.

780 «The pottery vendor» (Canvas, 259 × 220 cm). Here we can see how the compositions gradually become more complicated.

781 «The soldier and the lady» (Canvas, 259 × 100 cm).

782 «The hawthorn-seller» (Canvas, 259 × 100 cm).

783 «Boys playing at soldiers» (Canvas, 146 × 94 cm).

784 «Basque ball game» (Canvas, 261 × 470 cm).

785 «The swing» (Canvas, 260 × 165 cm).

786 «The washerwomen» (Canvas, 218 × 166 cm)

754. Goya. Doña Leocadia Zorrilla.   764. Goya. Judith and Holofernes.

787 «**The young bulls**» (Canvas, 259 × 136 cm). Apparently the bull-fighter dressed in red who turns towards the spectator is a self-portrait of Goya.

788 «**The tobacco guards**» (Canvas, 262 × 137 cm).

789 «**Boy and a tree**» (Canvas, 262 × 40 cm). Goya has made a rather skilful composition to fit the extremely high, narrow canvas.

790 «**The boy with a bird**» (Canvas, 262 × 40 cm). Like in the preceding work, the narrow canvas is filled with a tree.

791 «**The woodcutters**» (Canvas, 141 × 114 cm). In these early series scenes of work are treated in exactly the same way as scenes of pastimes.

792 «**The appointment**» (Canvas, 100 × 151 cm).

Cartoons for tapestries to decorate the King's dining-room at the Pardo Palace (1786-88):

793 «**The flower girls (Spring)**» (Canvas, 277 × 192 cm). In these cartoons Goya's style is already more mature, the compositions are more skilful, the figures have better movement and the colouring is extremely delicate. The graceful silhouette of the kneeling flower girl is admirable.

794 «**The threshing-floor (Summer)**» (Canvas, 276 × 641 cm). The composition overflows Goya's usual favourite pyramid shape in a pleasing manner; the yellow tones give it special warmth.

795 «**The wine harvest (Autumn)**» (Canvas, 275 × 190 cm). This is one of the finest of Goya's works of this period; the accustomed pyramid-shaped composition is enlivened by the interweaving figures with their gay, graceful poses which Goya was so expert at portraying.

796 «**The injured mason**» (Canvas, 268 × 110 cm). Now and again a touch of social criticism begins to appear in Goya's paintings; among the carefree, merry, pleasing scenes he depicted to decorate the Palace rooms and entertain the royal family Goya suddenly added a dissonant note like this, no doubt not very «appropiate» for the King's dining-room.

797 «**Poor children at the well**» (Canvas, 277 × 115 cm). Here again Goya's changing sensibility comes to the fore, possibly as a result of his contacts with liberal circles; he gradually begins to reflect other aspects of the life of the common people whom he had until now portrayed in picturesque pursuits and pastimes.

798 «**The snowstorm (Winter)**» (Canvas, 275 × 293 cm). This work reflects the same vein; the tones are very fine, but the figures, labouring against the icy wind, show life at its hardest.

Cartoons for tapestries to decorate the King's study at El Escorial (1790-92):

799 «**The wedding**» (Canvas, 267 × 293 cm). Possibly due to the experience of the dining-room decorations, when the King commissioned these cartoons he specified that the subject-matter should be rural and gay. By this time Goya was already famous and painting tapestry cartoons did not offer him much scope; he carried out the commission unwillingly and delayed submitting the designs. Goya used this subject of a marriage between a young girl and an old man in various drawings and etchings, insisting on the injustice of these marriages of convenience.

800 «**Young girls with pitchers**» (Canvas, 262 × 160 cm). This is a very simple composition; in order to arrange the picture space Goya has used large, simple architectonic elements.

800a «**Children playing**» (Canvas, 137 × 104 cm).

801 «**The stilts**» (Canvas, 268 × 320 cm).

802 «**The straw manikin**» (Canvas, 267 × 160 cm).

803 «**Boy climbing a tree**» (Canvas, 141 × 111 cm).

804 «**Blind-man's buff**» (Canvas, 269 × 350 cm). This is one of Goya's best-known cartoons and dates from 1787; the style is almost Rococo, the slender, fragile, doll-like figures are painted in a range of pale colours.

805 «**The huntsman with his dogs**» (Canvas, 262 × 71 cm). Dating from 1775, this was one of a series of cartoons of hunting scenes.

2446 «**Cornelio van der Gotten**» (Canvas, 62 × 47 cm). This work bears a signature and a date (1782), possibly false, although the picture is definitely by Goya. The sitter was the son of the director of the Royal Tapestry Factory and kept the inventory of cartoons supplied by Goya between 1775-86.

2447 «**Doña María Antonia Gonzaga, Marchioness of Villafranca**» (Canvas, 87 × 72 cm). The face reveals refinement and sensitivity; the portrait is extremely elegant and painted in a range of sober colours applied in very subtle velaturas.

2448 «**The Marchioness of Villafranca**» (Canvas, 195 × 126 cm). Signed and dated 1804. The sitter is portrayed painting a portrait of her husband.

2449 «**The Duke of Alba**» (Canvas, 195 × 126 cm). This portrait dates from 1795 and represents one of Goya's patrons, the music and art-loving Duke of Alba, leaning against a piano with a score in his hand. The patch of light behind the figure is a device Goya used very often to set off his figures against the background. He found it difficult to be impartial in his portraits and these always reflect his personal feelings towards his sitters; this portrait of the duke as a cultured, elegant man devoted to his favourite pastime reveals Goya's friendly attitude towards him.

798. Goya. The Snowstorm (Winter).

2450 «**Don Manuel Silvela**» (Canvas, 95 × 68 cm). It dates from 1809-12.

2524 «**Two children with a mastiff**» (Canvas, 112 × 145 cm). This was a tapestry design.

2546 «**Trade**» (Canvas, 227 cm in diameter). This work dates from about 1797-1800 and was painted, like the following two, for Godoy's palace.

2547 «**Agriculture**» (Canvas, 227 cm in diameter). See No. 2546.

2548 «**Industry**» (Canvas, 227 cm in diameter). See No. 2546.

2650 «**St. Justa and St. Rufina**» (Wood, 47 × 29 cm). This was the preparatory sketch for the painting in the Seville Cathedral done in 1817.

2781 «**Blind-man's buff**» (Canvas, 41 × 44 cm). This is a reduced version, with variations, of the cartoon No. 804. It was painted for the Alameda de Osuna palace, together with Nos. 2782 and 2783.

2782 «**The drunken mason**» (Canvas, 35 × 15 cm). This is a reduced version of cartoon No. 796, in which the subject-matter has also been altered.

2783 «**St. Isidore's Day at the saint's hermitage**» (Canvas, 42 × 44 cm). 1799.

2784 «**General Don Antonio Ricardos**» (Canvas, 112 × 84 cm). About 1793-94.

2785 «**The Colossus or Panic**» (Canvas, 116 × 105 cm). This work dates from before 1812 and was given the name *Colossus* because it resembles a drawing with this name; however, in an inventory in 1812 Goya called it *A giant*. The enormous figure seems to terrify a long trail of people and animals who flee in all directions, although it does not threaten them directly. The strange theme seems to foreshadow the Black Paintings and has been interpreted in various different ways.

2856 «**Hunting with decoys**» (Canvas, 111 × 176 cm). This was a tapestry design and dates from 1775.

2857 «**A hunting match**» (Canvas, 290 × 226 cm). Tapestry design from 1775.

773. Goya. The Parasol.

2862 «Queen María Luisa with a bustle» (Canvas, 222 × 140 cm). This work dates from 1789. The queen wears a strange dress in part inspired in 17th-century fashion; it was probably an attempt to introduce a «national» way of dressing and depart from French fashions.

2895 «Shepherd playing the flageolet» (Canvas, 131 × 130 cm). This was a tapestry cartoon and dates from 1786-87.

2896 «Huntsman by a spring» (Canvas, 131 × 130 cm). This was another tapestry design from 1786-87.

2898 «Don Juan Bautista de Muguiro» (Canvas, 103 × 84 cm). Signed with a dedicatory inscription and dated 1827 in Bordeaux. Towards the end of his life Goya painted several portraits which surprise us with his vitality and ability to continue renewing his style. Black tones predominate here and are characteristic of this period; face and hands are rendered with fine, broken brushstrokes that enliven the picture surface and make it vibrate.

2899 «The milkmaid of Bordeaux» (Canvas, 74 × 68 cm). At a time when he still had the will and energy to learn new techniques (miniatures, lithographies, etc.), in 1827, Goya painted this famous work, generally considered one of the clearest forerunners of Impressionist art; its pure colouring and luminous quality seem the result of Goya's last reconciliation with life and a fresh attempt to try out new means of artistic expression.

2995 «Don Joaquín Company, Archbishop of Saragossa and Valencia» (Canvas, 44 × 31 cm). This portrait dates from about 1800 (?).

3045 «Strolling players» (Tin, 43 × 32 cm). This was probably painted in 1793 while Goya was convalescing from his serious illness, like other

788. Goya. The Tobacco Guards.   795. Goya. The Wine Harvest.

804. Goya. Blind-man's Buff.

works painted on tin. It bears the inscription *Aleg, Men.*, which has been interpreted as *Alegoria Menandrea*.

3047 «Bull-fight» (Canvas, 38 × 46 cm). It dates from 1824.

3113 «The Taking of Christ» (Canvas, 40 × 23 cm). This was the preparatory sketch for the painting Goya did in 1788 for the Sacristy of the Toledo Cathedral.

3224 «Charles IV» (Canvas, 220 × 140 cm).

3236 «Gaspar Melchor de Jovellanos» (Canvas, 205 × 123 cm). Signed. This splendid portrait of Jovellanos dates from 1798 and is one of the most important among the Prado's recent purchases. Jovellanos was an eminent lawyer and writer who became Minister of Justice for a brief period (until his liberal ideas were the cause of his imprisonment and exile). He was an art-lover and a friend of Goya, whose way of thinking he influenced to a large degree. Goya has drawn on his ability of psychological characterization and the deep sympathy he displayed when painting personalities whom he appreciated in order to portray Jovellanos here as an intellectual with signs of preoccupation and disappointment in his features.

3254 «Cardinal Luis María de Borbón» (Canvas, 200 × 114 cm). This is a replica of an original kept in the Museum of São Paulo.

3255 «The Count of Floridablanca» (Canvas, 175 × 112 cm). This work dates from about 1783.

GRECO, Domenicos Theotocopoulos or Theotocopuli, called «El Greco» (b. Candia, Crete 1540/1; d. Toledo 1614). The earliest documentary evidence of El Greco dates from 1566 in Candia on the Venetian-ruled island of Crete; he was then 25 years old and it is surmised that he had already spent some years in Venice, where he returned the following year and possibly worked with Titian. In 1570 he left for Rome where the miniaturist Giulio Clovio recommended him to Cardinal Alexander Farnese describing him as «an excellent painter». He remained in Rome until 1573 or 1575 and possibly visited Venice again before travelling to Spain in 1576 or 1577. It is not known what prompted him to come to Spain, maybe the wave of plague that devastated Venice in 1576 or the hope of working on the decoration of El Escorial; in Italy in those days competition was hard: Tintoretto, Veronese, Bassano and Zuccaro were all at the height of their artistic careers and El Greco is not known to have received important commissions. After a short stay in Madrid he went to Toledo, where he was painting altar-pieces for Santo Domingo el Antiguo and the *Expolio* or Disrobing of Christ on Calvary in 1577. He rapidly achieved fame. His relations with Doña Jerónima de las Cuevas must have begun soon also because in 1578 his son Jorge Manuel was born. All these factors, combined with Philip II's lack of appreciation of his work, which closed the doors of Court to him, made him decide to settle in Toledo, where he remained, painting portraits and religious works for monasteries, convents and country parish churches, until his death in 1614.

Art scholars agree that El Greco's very particular style -so particular that it has given rise to the most absurd conjectures about a possible eye defect-did not fully develop until after his arrival in Spain, although its roots can be traced back to his Italian training; his ambiguous rendering of space, preference for vertical composition with the figures arranged on one plane, the elongated bodies, affected elegance, precarious poses and strong foreshortenings are all features that recall the international Mannerist style. But while in the rest of Europe Mannerism was on the wane, El Greco drove it to its ultimate extremes, discovering its unsuspected possibilities of dynamic, expressive power. The importance he attached to colour rather than draughtsmanship derived from Venetian artists, however in his palette the luscious Venetian colouring loses its sensitivity and the colours turn cold, absorbed by a powerful abstract light that dissolves contours, makes bodies appear insubstantial and gives his pictures their characteristic vibrating quality.

El Greco specialized in two kinds of painting: portraiture and religious subjects; outside courtly circles there was no scope for profane or mythological pictures in Spain. His portraits reveal the most realistic aspect of his painting; in the bust-length portraits he centres all the attention on the head, setting it off against the dark, neutral background without any further attributes than the features of the sitter's face. The full-length portraits reflect Greco's gift of close observation and realistic representation of textures and objects. In spite of their vigorous characterization, in both kinds of portraits the typical Mannerist-style dignified, distant qualities may be observed. The religious paintings exemplify his independence of traditional iconographic models, to the extent that he was on occasions accused of unfitting portrayals; however, the large number of copies and imitations that were made of his art bear witness to his popularity. What is known of El Greco's biography does not permit us to regard him as a man of deep devotional feeling; he appears rather as a refined humanist, who took pride in his culture and enjoyed life. However, he is generally regarded as a mystic painter. It was indeed in the field of religious painting that Greco excelled and showed the most original side of his work; the above-mentioned features of Greco's art (insubstantial bodies, unreal colouring and unearthly light effects) reflect the mysterious and prodigious nature of religion at a time when the Counter-Reformation was trying to present religious feeling in its homely, emotional, every-day aspect.

806 «Aged nobleman» (Canvas, 46 × 43 cm). Signed. This portrait dates from the period 1585-95. The very fluid technique consists of short parallel brushstrokes that leave the contours indistinct, giving the face vibrating expressiveness.

807 «The doctor (Dr. Rodrigo de la Fuente?)» (Canvas, 93 × 82 cm). Signed. This work was painted before 1598.

808 «Don Rodrigo Vázquez, President of the Councils of Castile and of Finance» (Canvas, 62 × 40 cm). This portrait dates from 1594-1604.

809 «The nobleman with his hand on his chest» (Canvas, 81 × 66. cm). Signed. It dates from the period 1577-84; it is one of the first portraits, and probably the most popular, painted by Greco in Spain. The sitter has been generally identified as Don Juan de Silva, probably when knighthood was conferred on him to judge by the position of the hand and the presence of the sword. The smooth and somewhat tight handling shows that it belongs to his early Spanish period.

810 «A nobleman» (Canvas, 64 × 51 cm). Signed. This portrait dates from Greco's last period, between 1600-14.

811 «Young nobleman» (Canvas, 55 × 49 cm). It dates from 1597-1614.

812 «The Licentiate Jerónimo de Cevallos» (Canvas, 64 × 54 cm). Dating from 1604-14, this portrait is a splendid example of Greco's mature style, with extremely broken contours rendered with long, loose brushstrokes.

813 «A nobleman» (Canvas, 65 × 55 cm). This work dates from 1584-94.

814 «St. Paul (or St. Bartholomew)» (Canvas, 70 × 56 cm). This work dates from the period 1594-1601.

815 «St. Anthony of Padua» (Canvas, 104 × 79 cm). Signed. Dating from the period between 1577-1604, this work, although it is signed, lacks El Greco's usual quality; it is extremely darkened.

817 «St. Benedict» (Canvas, 116 × 81 cm). Signed. This work was painted for Santo Domingo el Antiguo (in Toledo) between 1577-79.

819 «St. Francis of Assisi» (Canvas, 152 × 113 cm). Signed. This work dates from 1585-95 and according to some art critics a large part of it was

painted by Greco's assistants. The subject was very popular and various different versions are known.

820   See Greco, Copies.

821   «**The Baptism of Christ**» (Canvas, 350 × 154 cm). Signed. This work was commissioned in 1596 for the convent popularly known as *Colegio de Doña María de Aragón* in Madrid and delivered in 1600. It is very characteristic of El Greco's religious compositions; in the vertical format the figures are distributed on two levels, heaven and earth, separated by Greco's typical, almost solid clouds. The relationship of space is confused and ambiguous and this impression is heightened by the combination of differently proportioned figures, a device often used by El Greco.

822   «**Christ clasping the Cross**» (Canvas, 108 × 78 cm). Signed. This work dates from the period 1591-1605. The subject became very popular and there are various different versions. The technique is brisk, with very long brushstrokes. The greyish tones of the flesh accentuate the pathos of Christ's expression and contrast with the intense colour of the cloaks.

823   «**The Crucifixion**» (Canvas, 312 × 169 cm). Signed. Dating from 1600-1610, this is one of Greco's finest mature works and illustrates his use of light as a dramatic element; light falls forcefully on the figures, making them shine and giving them a ghostly appearance; the light concentrates attention on these figures while the rest of the scene remains in the shadows, thus producing the impression of pathos and desolation that emanates from the picture.

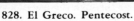

| 828. El Greco. Pentecost. | 823. El Greco. The Crucifixion. |

824   «**The Trinity**» (Canvas, 300 × 179 cm). This was the first work that El Greco painted in Toledo for the convent church of Santo Domingo el Antiguo between 1577-79. It reveals his still recent Italian training in the fondness for vigorously modelled bodies in the manner of Michelangelo and the pale colouring which appealed to Mannerist taste.

825   «**The Resurrection**» (Canvas, 275 × 127 cm). Signed. This work was painted between 1584 and 1610. It has been surmised that this work could have been the companion piece to *Pentecost* (No. 828), but they belong to different periods. The vision of the risen Christ suspended in space dazzles

the sentries who throw themselves to the ground; Greco has rendered their convulsed bodies in violent foreshortenings. His insistence on the nude bodies is unusual in Spanish art and reveals his Italian training.

826 **«The Holy Family with St. Anne and the infant St. John»** (Canvas, 187 × 69 cm). Signed. This work dates from 1594-1605.

824. El Greco. The Trinity.   **826. El Greco. The Holy Family.**

827 **«The Annunciation»** (Wood, 26 × 18 cm). This work dates from 1570-73 and stylistically speaking belongs to Greco's Venetian period. The influence of Tintoretto is evident in the architectural elements that form a deep recession. The style is very different from that of his mature period in its rendering of space, clear, bright colouring and smooth enamel-like finish.

828 **«Pentecost»** (Canvas, 275 × 127 cm). Signed. Dating from 1604-14, this is the only version of this subject by El Greco. It is executed with the characteristic technique of his mature works, with straight, parallel brush-strokes that give the figures a flame-like appearance. Towards the end of his life the Mannerist elements, far from becoming tempered, reached new heights. Greco's son Jorge Manuel collaborated on this work.

829 **«The Virgin Mary»** (Canvas, 52 × 77 cm). Signed. It dates from 1594-1604.

2444 **«St. John the Evangelist»** (Canvas, 90 × 77 cm). This work was painted between 1597 and 1607. Although it resembles in style the *St. John* of the series of the Apostles in the Toledo Cathedral, this is an individual work and does not belong to any series.

2445 **«Julián Romero and his patron saint»** (Canvas, 207 × 127 cm). The inscription was added at a later date; the work belongs to the period 1594-1604.

2644 **«A Trinitarian or Dominican friar»** (Canvas, 35 × 26 cm). 1600-10.

2645 **«The Coronation of the Virgin»** (Canvas, 90 × 100 cm). Signed. Dating from 1590-1604, this seems to be the first version of a subject that Greco repeated later.

2819 **«St. Andrew and St. Francis»** (Canvas, 167 × 113 cm). Signed. This work dates from the period 1590-1600. The two saints are represented conversing and gesticulating in a manner that is very characteristic of Greco. The long figures seem still taller through the use of a very low view-point, which makes them appear silhouetted against the sky.

2874 **«The Holy Face»** (Canvas, 71 × 54 cm). This work has been very much restored and reveals the hands of Greco's assistants.

2889 **«The Saviour»** (Canvas, 72 × 55 cm). Together with Nos. 2890, 2891 and 2892, this work belonged to a series of Apostles for the parish church of Almadrones, near Guadalajara. Due to their poor quality, they are considered to have been painted almost completely by Greco's workshop.

2890 **«St. James the Elder»** (Canvas, 72 × 55 cm). See No. 2889.

2891 **«St. Philip or St. Thomas»** (Canvas, 72 × 55 cm). See No. 2889.

2892 **«St. Paul»** (Canvas, 72 × 55 cm). See No. 2889.

2988 «The Adoration of the Shepherds» (Canvas, 319 × 180 cm). This important canvas dates from Greco's last period (between 1603-14) and was intended for his own burial chapel. He uses the figure of the Child as a light focus, a device often found in important Italian paintings. The general colouring is warmer than usual in Greco's works and the glow produced by the light reflections gives life to the scene.

3002 «St. Sebastian» (Canvas, 115 × 85 cm). It dates from about 1600-05.

3262 «Penitent St. Jerome» (Canvas, 91 × 90 cm). This is another version of an original kept in Edinburgh; some art critics consider it a workshop painting. It dates from about 1595-1600.

GRECO, Copies by his son Jorge Manuel.

830 «The Burial of the Lord of Orgaz» (lower part) (Canvas, 189 × 250 cm). This is a copy after the famous work in Santo Tomé in Toledo.

832 «The Disrobing of Christ on Calvary» (Canvas, 120 × 65 cm). This is a copy after Greco's *Expolio* in the Toledo Cathedral.

GRECO, anonymous copies.

820 «St. John the Evangelist and St. Francis of Assisi» (Canvas, 64 × 50 cm).

831 «St. Eugene» (?) (Canvas, 241 × 162 cm).

HAMEN, Juan van der Hamen (Madrid 1596-1631). School of Madrid. He specialized in still lifes with a balanced composition and carefully depicted objects silhouetted against a dark background.

1164 «Still life» (Canvas, 52 × 88 cm). Signed and dated 1622.

1165 «Fruit» (Canvas, 56 × 110 cm). Signed and dated 1623.

2877 «Offering to Flora» (Canvas, 216 × 140 cm). Signed and dated 1627. This is one of the few known works by Hamen with a figure.

HERRERA «the Younger», Francisco de Herrera (b. Seville 1622; d. Madrid 1685). He was the son of Herrera «the Elder» and received his training in Italy, where he developed a theatrical, sensational style that exercised an influence on Spanish painting on his return by showing the way towards a more dynamic Baroque style.

832a See Herrera «the Elder».

833 «The Triumph of St. Hermengild» (Canvas, 328 × 229 cm). This is one of his best-known works, characteristic of his spirited style; the saint is represented in apotheosis with Leovigild and an Arian bishop at his feet.

HERRERA «the Elder», Francisco de Herrera (b. Sevilla (?) c. 1590; d. Madrid 1656). Sevillian School. He was the father of Herrera «the Younger» and lived and worked in Seville. He played an important part in the transition from Mannerism to naturalism; his style was bold and free, he modelled his forms energetically with fluid, vigorous brushwork. About 1650 he moved to Madrid, where he died.

832a «Pope St. Leo the Great» (Oval canvas, 164 × 105 cm). The handling of this work seems closer to that of Herrera «the Younger», to whom it probably belongs.

2441a «St. Bonaventura receiving St. Francis' habit (Canvas, 231 × 215 cm). This work from about 1628 belonged to a series on St. Bonaventura that was completed by Zurbarán. It is regarded as one of his finest paintings.

3058 «Head of decapitated saint» (Canvas, 61 × 65 cm). Signed

2773 ⎫ HERRERA «the Elder» (?)
2774 ⎬ «Apostle's head» (Canvas, 39 × 32 cm each). These two works do not
     ⎭ appear to have been painted by Herrera.

HUGUET, Jaume (b. Valls, Tarragona 1414/15; d. Barcelona 1498). Catalan School.

2683 «A prophet» (Wood, 30 × 26 cm). This work shows the melancholy expression characteristic of Hughet's figures, as well as his delicate style and excellent draughtsmanship.

HUGHET, Follower.

2680 «The Crucifixion» (Wood, 88 × 63 cm).

INGLES, Jorge Inglés. Hispano-Flemish School. This artist introduced Flemish influences into Castilian art; in 1458 he was working on the altarpiece for the Hospital of Buitrago for the Marquis of Santillana.

2666 «The Trinity surrounded by angels» (Wood, 97 × 86 cm).

INZA, Joaquín Inza (Madrid, works between 1763 and 1808).

2514 «Don Tomás Iriarte (Canvas, 82 × 59 cm).

IRIARTE, Ignacio Iriarte (b. Santa María de Azcoitia, Guipúzcoa 1621; d. Seville 1685). Sevillian School. Iriarte moved to Seville in his youth and entered the Art Academy there. He specialized in spacious landscapes with rugged backgrounds in orange tones and small figures; his handling is very ethereal. They resemble those of Murillo.

836   «**Landscape with a torrent**» (Canvas, 112 × 198 cm). This work is probably the companion piece to No. 2970.

837   «**Landscape with ruins**» (Canvas, 97 × 101 cm).

2970   «**Landscape with shepherds**» (Canvas, 106 × 109 cm). Signed and dated 1665.
       JIMENEZ, Miguel. See Ximenez.
       JIMENEZ DONOSO, José Jiménez Donoso (b. Consuegra 1628; d. Madrid 1690). School of Madrid. He received his training in Rome.

694   «**The Vision of St. Francis of Paola**» (Canvas, 172 × 163 cm).
       JUANES, Vicente Juan Masip, called «Juan de Juanes» (b. Valencia [?] c. 1510; b. Bocairente, Valencia 1579). School of Valencia. He was the son of Vicente Masip and continued his father's Raphaelesque style, although in a clearly Mannerist way, at times somewhat affected and soft and with an overpolished execution. His religious works with their sweet, sentimental character were very popular, particularly some of his iconographic types, like the *Saviour*. He founded an important workshop whose influence can be traced down to Ribalta.

838   «**St. Stephen in the Synagogue**» (Wood, 160 × 123 cm). Together with Nos. 839-842 this work was part of the main altar-piece of the church of San Esteban in Valencia and is considered one of his finest paintings. Like in the following work, this scene takes place inside a profusely decorated Renaissance interior and Juanes modells the sculptured forms in the same soft manner as the bodies of the figures; the room looks out over one of Juanes' typical landscapes, full of Flemish-style ruins. The rhetorically gesticulating figures give the work a narrative character.

839   «**St. Stephen accused of Blasphemy**» (Wood, 160 × 123 cm). See No. 838.

840   «**St. Stephen led to Martyrdom**» (Wood, 160 × 123 cm). See No. 838.

841   «**The Martyrdom of St. Stephen**» (Wood, 160 × 123 cm). See No. 838.

842   «**The Burial of St. Stephen**» (Wood, 160 × 123 cm). This work is very directly inspired in Raphael's *Entombment of Christ*. The figure dressed in black who does not participate in the scene is presumed to be a self-portrait of Juanes. See No. 838.

844   «**The Saviour**» (Wood, 73 × 40 cm). This iconographic type by Juanes became very popular and he repeated it on numerous occasions, usually holding the chalice preserved in the Cathedral at Valencia which is traditionally identified as the one used by Christ at the Last Supper. Juanes' use of a gilded background was an archaic note at his time.

846   «**The Last Supper**» (Wood, 116 × 191 cm). This is one of Juanes' most famous works; it is inspired in Leonardo's *Last Supper*, but representing it as the institution of the Eucharist.

848   «**Ecce Homo**» (Wood, 83 × 62 cm).

853-4 «**Melchizedek, king of Salem**» and «**The high priest Aaron**» (Wood, 80 × 135 cm). These two works were the wings of a Sagrario. Both figures were forerunners of Christ in the Old Testament.

855   «**Don Luis de Castelvi**» (Wood, 105 × 80 cm). Both sitter and artist are identified by a label apparently stuck to the back of the picture in the 18th century. Recently it has been suggested that the work could have been painted by Vicente Masip. At all events it is an exceptionally fine portrait and strongly influenced by Titian.

844. Juanes. The Saviour.   **3018. Maino. Pentecost.**

JUANES. Follower of Juan de Juanes.

1262 «**St. Stephen ordained a deacon**» (Wood, 160 × 123 cm).

JUANES, father of. See Masip, Vicente.

JULIA, Ascensio Juliá (b. Valencia c. 1771; d. Madrid 1816). He was one of Goya's pupils.

2573 «**Scene from a comedy**» (Canvas, 42 × 56 cm).

JUNCOSA, Fray Joaquín Juncosa (b. Cornudella 1631; d. Rome 1708).

2652 «**St. Helena and her daughter**» (Canvas, 170 × 124 cm). This work is tradicionaly attributed to Juncosa although it is of finer quality than is usual in this artist.

LEONARDO, Jusepe Leonardo (b. Calatayud, Saragossa 1601; d. Saragossa before 1653). School of Madrid. He studied in Madrid under Pedro de las Cuevas and Cajés. His work reflects the influence of Carducho and particularly of Velázquez, whose atmospheric effects interested him and whose light handling he imitated, as well as some of his types. He was a very able draughtsman and used pale, refined colouring.

3017. Machuca. The Descent from the Cross.

67 «**St. Sebastian**» (Canvas, 192 × 58 cm). Previously ascribed to Carducho, this work is now unanimously attributed to Leonardo.

858 «**The Surrender of Jülich**» (Canvas, 307 × 381 cm). This work dates from 1635 and was painted like No. 859 for the Hall of Realms of the Buen Retiro Palace. The principal figure is Ambrosio Spinola, as in Velázquez's *Las Lanzas,* who is seen receiving the keys of the city from the Dutch ambassador, an event that occurred in 1622.

859 «**The Capture of Breisach**» (Canvas, 304 × 360 cm). The Duke of Feria is the principal figure in this episode from the Thirty Years' War that occurred in 1633. Compared with the other pictures of this series for the Hall of Realms, these two works reveal a natural positioning of the figures, together with atmospheric effects and a way of setting the scene in a landscape background that bear witness to Velázquez's influence.

860 «**Birth of the Virgin**» (Canvas, 180 × 122 cm). This work dates from 1640.

2229 «**The beheading of John the Baptist**» (Canvas, 104 × 143 cm). 1635-39.

LLORENTE, Bernardo Germán Llorente (Seville 1680-1759).

871 «**The Divine Shepherdess**» (Canvas, 167 × 127 cm). This was a subject he repeated constantly in a manner directly imitating the style of Murillo.

LUNA CHAPEL, Master of the. Hispano-Flemish School. The name is taken from an altar-piece in the chapel of Don Alvaro de Luna in the Cathedral of Toledo, documented in 1483 and 1485. The artist could have been Juan de Segovia, one of the artists commissioned to paint the altar-piece, some of whose subjects are repeated in the following works.

1289 «**The Virgin of the Milk**» (Wood, 112 × 71 cm).

2425 «**The Seventh Sorrow of the Virgin Mary**» (Wood, 105 × 71 cm).

MACHUCA, Pedro Machuca (b. Toledo in the late 15th century; d. Granada 1550). He studied in Italy, where he was still in 1517; after 1520 he worked in Granada, mainly as an architect. Together with Berruguete he is one of the most important representatives of Spanish Mannerism.

2579 «**The Virgin of the Milk**» (Wood, 167 × 135 cm). Signed and dated 1517. The theme of the Virgin succouring the souls in Purgatory with her milk is an Italian one. The influence of Michelangelo (contemporary sources consider Machuca to have been his pupil) is tempered by the use of diffused light and unified colouring.

3017 «The Descent from the Cross» (Wood, 141 × 128 cm). This work, dated 1547, reflects an ambiguous, mysterious mood is completely Mannerist and reflects an ambiguous, mysterious mood that is heightened by the night lighting. It retains its original frame.

MAELLA, Mariano Salvador Maella (b. Valencia 1739; d. Madrid1819). Maella came to Madrid in his youth to study at the Academy of San Fernando, where he showed great talent and won a scholarship to study in Rome in 1758. On his return to Spain in 1765 he was appointed a member of the San Fernando Academy. From then on his works reflect Mengs' Neo-Classical influence, which partly attenuated the Roman Baroque and Rococo styles he had learnt in Italy. In 1774 he was appointed Court painter and his fame in courtly circles even eclipsed that of Goya. In 1795 he became Director of the Academy of San Fernando and in 1799 First Court Painter. However, due to his collaboration with the French invaders, he was removed from Court by Ferdinand VII after the Napoleonic War.

873 «Seascape» (Canvas, 55 × 28 cm). This is an example of a branch of painting seldom cultivated by Maella and related in this case to Italianate landscape painting.

874 «Seascape» (Canvas, 56 × 74 cm). The scene is realistically portrayed.

875 «Fishermen» (Canvas, 56 × 75 cm). It is related to the preceding ones.

2440 «Carlota Joaquina, Spanish Infanta and Queen of Portugal» (Canvas, 177 × 116 cm). She was a daughter of Charles IV, born in 1775, and married the Portuguese king John VI.

2484 «The vision of St. Sebastian de Aparicio» (Canvas, 171 × 121 cm). This saint was of Galician origin and saw two angels making music in a vision while he was praying. The composition is related to numerous similar scenes in Italian Baroque painting.

2497 «The Seasons: Spring» (Canvas, 144 × 77 cm). See No. 2500.

2498 «The Seasons: Summer» (Canvas, 144 × 77 cm). See No. 2500.

2499 «The Seasons: Autumn» (Canvas, 142 × 77 cm). See No. 2500.

2500 «The Seasons: Winter» (Canvas, 144 × 77 cm). The subject of the four seasons has been repeated time and again; Maella gives the scenes a rural flavour, some of them with idealized mythological figures.

3140 «St. Joseph's dream» (Paper on cardboard, 27 × 19 cm). This was a sketch.

3141 «The freeing of St. Peter» (Paper on cardboard, 27 × 19 cm). This was also a sketch.

MAINO, Fray Juan Bautista Maino or Mayno (b. Pastrana, Guadalajara 1581; d. Madrid 1649). He studied in Italy as a young man. In 1611 he was back in Spain and in 1613 became a Dominican friar at the convent of St. Peter the Martyr in Toledo. About 1620 he was appointed drawing master to the young prince Philip (later Philip IV) and from then on he frequently worked for Court. His style reveals his direct acquaintance with the Italian Classicist movement (Annibale Carracci, Guido Reni) and Caravaggio's early naturalism. His realism is tempered, his draughtsmanship sound and his compositions are easy; he used focussed lighting, but without Tenebrist shadows, and clear colouring with smooth brushwork.

885 «The Recovery of Bahia in 1625» (Canvas, 309 × 381 cm). This work dates from 1634/5 and shows Don Fadrique de Toledo after recapturing Bahia (Brasil) from the Dutch. It was painted for the Hall of Realms in the Buen Retiro Palace. The scene has a less heroic and more realistic character due to the fact that the foreground is occupied by secondary figures, while the main actors are to be found in the middle distance.

886 «The Adoration of the Magi» (Canvas, 315 × 174 cm). Signed. This work was commissioned in 1612 for an altar-piece at St. Peter the Martyr's convent, together with Nos. 3018, 3128, 3212 and 3227. The textures of the Kings' draperies are admirably depicted. The composition does not show the ceremonious air frequently found in portrayals of this scene; it is realistic, pleasing and sentimental.

1276 «Portrait of a gentleman». This work was attributed to Maino in an inventory in 1794. See Tristán.

2595 «Gentleman with a gloved hand» (Canvas, 96 × 73 cm). Signed. This work dates from about 1600-05. It is the only definitely known portrait by this artist, renowned in his time as a portraitist.

3018 «Pentecost» (Canvas, 285 × 163 cm). See No. 886.

3128 «St. John the Evangelist in a landscape» (Canvas, 74 × 163 cm). The figure is set easily in a calm, spacious landscape, which is not frequent in

2988. El Greco. The Adoration of the Shepherds. (detail)

Spanish painting and reveals the influence of Annibale Carracci. See No. 886.

3129 «**St. Catherine of Siena**» (Wood, 118 × 92 cm). This was the upper part of an altar-piece.

3130 «**St. Dominic**» (Wood, 118 × 92 cm). This is the pendant to No. 3129; some art critics have raised the question of whether it is a self-portrait.

3212 «**St. John the Baptist in a landscape**» (Canvas, 74 × 163 cm). See Nos. 886 and 3128.

3225 «**Repentant Mary Magdalene**» (Wood, 58 × 155 cm). This work was painted in the same period as Nos. 3128 and 3212.

3226 «**St. Anthony Abbot**» (Wood, 61 × 155 cm). This is the companion piece to No. 3225.

3227 «**Adoration of the Shepherds**» (Canvas, 315 × 174 cm). This realistic work shows Caravaggesque influence and still-life details. See No. 886.

MARCH, Esteban March (Valencia 1610-1668). Valencian School. He was influenced by Orrente, who was probably his master.

883 «**The Crossing of the Red Sea**» (Canvas, 129 × 176 cm).

MARCH (?)

878 «**Old man drinking**» (Canvas, 73 × 62 cm).

879 «**Old woman drinking**» (Canvas, 73 × 62 cm).

880 «**Old woman with a tambourine**» (Canvas, 80 × 62 cm).

874. Maella. Seascape.

MASIP, Vicente Masip (b. about 1475; d. Valencia 1545). Valencian School. He introduced the Raphaelesque influence into Valencian painting. He frequently worked with his son, Juan de Juanes, whose style is so directly related to his father's that the attribution of their works is sometimes difficult. However, the father's style is more serene and classical with preciser draughtsmanship and tighter modelling.

843 «**The Martyrdom of St. Inés**» (Wood, 58 cm in diameter). This is the companion piece to No. 851; both were painted for the convent of Santo Tomás de Villanueva in Valencia. The influence of Raphael's tapestry cartoons is evident, especially in the arrangement of the scene and the poses of the figures.

849 «**Christ bearing the Cross**» (Wood, 93 × 80 cm).

851 «**The Visitation**» (Wood, 60 cm in diameter). See No. 843.

852 «**The Coronation of the Virgin**» (Wood, 23 × 19 cm). Oval panel.

855 See Juanes.

MASIP, Vicente Juan Masip (b. Valencia c. 1565; d. after 1606). He was the son of Juan de Juanes and a faithful follower of his father's style.

850 «**Deposition**» (Wood, 108 × 98 cm).

MAZO, Juan Bautista Martínez del Mazo (b. ? c. 1615; d. Madrid 1667). School of Madrid. Mazo was the son-in-law of Velázquez, who introduced him at Court, where he was appointed Court painter on Velázquez's death. In 1657 he visited Naples. He painted in the manner of his father-in-law and master and his works reveal a high level of accomplishment, which together with the excellent quality of his copies often makes it extremely difficult to ascertain the correct attribution. He specialized in portraits and landscapes with small figures and buildings.

888 «**The Empress Margaret of Austria**» (Canvas, 209 × 147 cm). This is the same Infanta Margarita whom Velázquez portrayed in *Las Meninas;* the inscription that erroneously identifies her as Dona María Teresa was added at a later date. The scene glimpsed through the door in the background bears witness to Mazo's interest in Velázquez's spatial effects.

889 See Velázquez and Mazo.

899a «**The death of Adonis**» (Canvas, 246 × 217 cm).

1212 See Velázquez, workshop.

1213 See Velázquez.

1214 «**The Queen's Street in Aranjuez**» (Canvas, 245 × 202 cm). This work, which is definitely known to be by Mazo, shows how difficult it is to ascertain the correct attribution of many works to Velázquez or Mazo due to their fluid, rapid execution and finely depicted light effects.

1215 «**The lake in the Buen Retiro Park**» (Canvas, 147 × 114 cm).

1216 «**Palace garden**» (Canvas, 148 × 111 cm).

1217 «**Landscape with a temple**» (Canvas, 148 × 111 cm). Previously attribu-

2571. Mazo. Hunt at Aranjuez.

ted to Velázquez, this work is now considered to be by Mazo.

1218 «**Classical building with a landscape**» (Canvas, 148 × 111 cm). See No. 1217.

1221 «**Prince Balthasar Carlos**» (Canvas, 209 × 144 cm). This work dates from 1645 and was previously attributed to Velázquez.

1706 See Rubens, copies. In flemish school.

1708 See Rubens, copies. In flemish school.

1711 See Rubens, copies, In flemish school.

1712 See Jordaens, copies. In flemish school.

2571 «**Hunt at Aranjuez**» (Canvas, 249 × 187 cm).

MELENDEZ, Luis Eugenio Meléndez or Menéndez (b. Naples 1716; d. Madrid 1780). He was born in Naples of Spanish parents and brought to Spain as a child; he studied in the artistic environment of 18th-century Madrid, specializing in still lifes, although not exclusively. His sober, realistic approach, clear arrangement of his objects and strongly contrasted light and shade effects recall works by Zurbarán or Sánchez Cotán. The Prado possesses a splendid series of his still lifes painted for a room at the Palace in Aranjuez intended to illustrate the variety of food produced in Spain.

902 «**Piece of salmon, a lemon and three vessels**» (Canvas, 42 × 62 cm). The highly-detailed depiction and technical mastery make this one of the most interesting works of this series.

2683. Jaume Huguet. A prophet. (detail)

886. Fray Juan Bautista Maino. Adoration of the Magi. (detail)

903   «Sea-bream and oranges» (Canvas, 42 × 62 cm). Signed and dated 1771.
906   «Box of sweetmeats» (Canvas, 49 × 37 cm). Signed and dated 1770.
907   «Fish, spring onions and bread» (Canvas, 50 × 36 cm).
909   «Plate of cherries and cheese» (Canvas, 40 × 62 cm). Signed and dated 1771. The colouring of the fruit and the perfect depiction of the popular ceramic plate are outstanding.
910   «Oranges, water-melons, a jar and a box of sweetmeats» (Canvas, 47 × 34 cm). Signed.
911   «Cherries, plums, cheese and a jar» (Canvas, 47 × 34 cm). Signed.
912   «Pears, bread, a jar, a flask and a pan» (Canvas, 47 × 34 cm). Signed and dated 1760.
915   «Water-melon, bread and biscuits» (Canvas, 34 × 47 cm). Signed.
919   «Pears, melon and a barrel» (Canvas, 48 × 35 cm). Signed and dated 1764.
924   «Plums, figs and bread» (Canvas, 35 × 48 cm). Signed.
927   «Pomegranates, apples, jars and a box of sweetmeats» (Canvas, 37 × 49 cm).Signed.
929   «Chocolate set» (Canvas, 48 × 36 cm). Signed and dated 1770. The skilful placing of the objects and their varied colouring make this one of Meléndez's most refined and sober compositions.
930   «Cucumbers and tomatoes» (Canvas, 41 × 62 cm). Signed and dated 1772.
931   «Quinces, peaches, grapes and pumpkins» (Canvas, 36 × 62 cm). Signed.
932   «Jug and bread» (Canvas, 48 × 34 cm). Signed.
933   «Pigeons and a basket» (Canvas, 49 × 36 cm). Signed.
934   «Ham, eggs and bread with earthenware vessels» (Canvas, 49 × 37 cm).
935   «Basket of grapes, plums and an apple» (Canvas, 48 × 35 cm). Signed and dated 1762.
936   «Apples, walnuts, a jar and boxes of sweetmeats» (Canvas, 36 × 49 cm). Signed and dated 1769.
937   «Plate of figs and pomegranates and a bottle of white wine» (Canvas, 36 × 49 cm). Signed.
938   «Piece of meat, ham and earthenware and copper vessels» (Canvas, 41 × 63 cm). This is one of Meléndez's most complicated works and bears relation to 17th-century Neapolitan still lifes.
MELENDEZ, Miguel Jacinto Meléndez (Oviedo 1679-c. 1731).
958   «St. Augustine warding off a plague of locusts» (Canvas on wood, 85 × 147 cm). Like the following work, this was a preparatory sketch for a painting intended for the convent of San Felipe el Real. After Meléndez's death they were painted by Andrés de la Calleja.
959   «The burial of the Lord of Orgaz» (Canvas on wood, 85 × 147 cm). See No. 958.
901   «The Holy Family» (Canvas, 19 cm in diameter). The attribution of this work to Meléndez is doubtful.
MENENDEZ. See Meléndez.
MOHEDANO, Antonio Mohedano (Lucena, Córdoba 1563-1625).
2911a «St. John the Evangelist» (233 × 130 cm). This is a wall canvas from a chapel at Lucena. Its attribution is doubtful.
MORALES, Luis de Morales, called «the Divine» (Badajoz c. 1500-1586). A painter of religious works, Morales became particularly famous for his small devotional pictures with their emphasis on sentimental aspects. His style recalls Flemish art, his brushwork is blending and smooth, his works lack colour and have a vaguely Leonardesque shading; his figures are elongated and stereotype, softly modelled and usually seem to emerge from a dark background.
943   «The Presentation» (Wood, 146 × 114 cm).
944   «The Virgin and Child» (Wood, 57 × 40 cm). Morales repeated this subject many times (cf. Nos. 946 and 2656); these works are very representative of his style, reflecting deep devotional feeling in an intimate, emotional manner. He has portrayed the Virgin and Child silhouetted against a dark background and lost in mutual contemplation.
946   «The Virgin and Child» (Wood, 43 × 32 cm). See No. 944.
947   «St. John of Ribera» (Wood, 40 × 28 cm).
948a «St. Stephen» (Wood, 67 × 50 cm). The saint is portrayed in a Flemish-style landscape with a stone alluding to his martyrdom to identify him.
2512 «The Annunciation» (Wood, 109 × 83 cm).
2656 «The Virgin and Child» (Wood, 84 × 64 cm). This is the finest example of Morales' paintings of this subject (cf. Nos. 944 and 946).
2770 «Ecce Homo» (Wood, 40 × 28 cm). This subject was also frequently portrayed by Morales, always in the same poignant mood.

3147 «The Holy Family» (Wood, 40 × 57 cm). By one of Morales' followers.

MORENO, José Moreno (Burgos c. 1642?-1674). School of Madrid.
He studied under Francisco de Solís and painted with a fluid touch and
pleasing colouring.

2872 «The Flight into Egypt» (Canvas, 209 × 250 cm). Signed; about 1668.

2994 «The Visitation» (Canvas, 185 × 132 cm). Signed and dated 1662.

MUÑOZ, Sebastián Muñoz (b. Segovia c. 1654; d. Madrid 1690).
School of Madrid. He studied under Claudio Coello and travelled to Italy.

957 «Self-portrait» (Canvas, 35 × 33 cm).

MUR, Master of the Archbishop Dalmau of Mur (15th century).

1334 «St. Vincent, deacon and martyr» (Wood, 185 × 117 cm).

961. Murillo. The Adoration of the Shepherds.

MURILLO, Bartolomé Esteban Murillo (Seville 1618-1682). Sevillian
School. Murillo was born in a large Sevillian family and also had many
children himself; of cheerful disposition, he led an uneventful life in Seville, where he was highly renowned as an artist. He trained in Juan del
Castillo's workshop, where he possibly came into contact with Alonso
Cano, as his works bear more resemblance to the latter's sensitive and
elegant style than to his master's. Although it is not known how long he
stayed, he was in Madrid in 1658, at a time when Velázquez was at the
height of his career and this master's works must have impressed Murillo,
as well as the Flemish and Italian paintings in the royal collection. When
the Arts Academy was founded in Seville in 1660, Murillo served as its
first president together with Herrera the Younger, who had recently returned from Italy; other famous Sevillian artists were among its founding
members, for example Valdés Leal. Murillo represents a turn in Spanish
art. With him painting abandoned the grandiloquent style followed by the
chief 17th-century artists and began to search for grace and delicacy, anticipating the style of the following century. With this aim in view Murillo
used an extremely light technique, a technique that art critics have called
«vaporous» in his mature works and that dissolves the forms, making them
insubstantial and intangible and transforming them into purely pictorial
visions of light and colour. Although they may appear too sweet for
present-day taste, Murillo's religious pictures complied with the principles
of the Counter-Reformation, which required religious feeling to be
brought close to the people and their every-day life using plain, pleasing
language to move and appeal to them; these figures of the Holy Family,
the beautiful Virgin playing with her Child or the candid Immaculate
Conception are all more moving and appealing than the great hermits and
heroic martyrs painted by earlier masters. In his *genre* pintures Murillo

71

2656. Luis de Morales. The Virgin and Child. (detail)

902. Luis Eugenio Meléndez. A slice of salmon, a lemon and three vessels. (detail)

portrayed children with a freshness and spontaneity that made these original works very popular.

960 **«The Holy Family with a little bird»** (Canvas, 144 × 188 cm). This popular work is a fine example of Murillo's simple, homely religious feeling. It is an appealing scene of the Holy Family during a pause in their everyday life to play with the Child. It still reveals a very Zurbaranesque influence in its sensibility and technique, with somewhat Tenebrist lighting effects and special attention to still-life details.

961 **«The Adoration of the Shepherds»** (Canvas, 187 × 228 cm). This work dates from about 1650; the scene is imagined as a night piece with the Child as the only source of light, a symbolic device used constantly since Mannerism. The figures of the shepherds with their offerings, like the lamb, add a naturalistic touch.

962 **«The Good Shepherd»** (Canvas, 123 × 101 cm). Dating from about 1665, this picture was always very popular. The Boy Shepherd reflects a somewhat grave mood and the ruins and flock give the painting a classical, bucolic air.

963 **«The infant St. John the Baptist»** (Canvas, 121 × 99 cm). This work dates from about 1665 and was painted for the inauguration of the church of Santa María la Blanca in Seville. Like the preceding and the following pictures, it reflects Murillo's constant interest in children and their world.

964 **«The Holy Children with the shell»** (Canvas, 104 × 124 cm). The pyramid-shaped composition reveals Classicist influence; it follows an engraving after Guido Reni. The soft handling and warm, golden colouring are characteristic of Murillo's mature period.

965 **«Ecce Homo»** (Canvas, 52 × 41 cm). This is the companion piece to No. 977 and dates from about 1668-70.

966 **«Christ on the Cross»** (Canvas, 183 × 107 cm). Dating from about 1675-80, this work shows an unusual subject-matter in Murillo's artistic production, interpreted in a conventional manner. It seems to be inspired in a work by Van Dyck.

967 **«Christ on the Cross»** (Canvas, 71 × 54 cm). This work also dates from about 1675-80.

968 **«St. Anne and the Virgin»** (Canvas, 219 × 165 cm). Dating from about 1665, this work shows the Virgin listening attentively to St. Anne, who has put aside her sewing basket. As in other paintings, Murillo imagines the holy figures in their everyday life, in this case in a very candidly clean and orderly setting.

969 **«The Annunciation»** (Canvas, 183 × 225 cm). It dates from about 1655.

970 **«The Annunciation»** (Canvas, 125 × 103 cm). This is a replica of a work kept in the Hermitage in Leningrad. It was painted later than No. 969 and shows a more developed technique, with lighter and more energetic brushwork. Although similar, the positioning of the figures is more successful in this work. The radiance of the *Gloria* bathes the whole of the picture in golden light and closes it harmoniously in the upper part.

972 **«The Immaculate Conception of El Escorial»** (Canvas, 206 × 144 cm). This work dates from about 1656-60. All of Murillo's *Immaculate Conceptions* are typical of the High Baroque prototype which started with Ri-

963. Murillo. The infant John the Baptist. 968. Murillo. St. Anne and the Virgin.

bera's version for the Augustinian convent in Salamanca, in which the subject-matter closely resembles in form that of an *Assumption,* thus giving rise to a very dynamic representation with billowing draperies and angels in flight, but without the traditional attributes of the litany. Murillo's skill lies not only in the beauty of his models, but more particularly in his technique. His subtle brushwork seems to suggest the forms without touching them and is therefore a perfect medium for conveying the idea of the mystery of the Immaculate Conception. This work is one of the most famous versions.

973 «**The Immaculate Conception**» (Canvas, 91 × 70 cm). About 1665.

974 «**The Immaculate Conception of Aranjuez**» (Canvas, 222 × 118 cm). This is an earlier and more Baroque work than No. 972, dating from about 1656-60. The windblown mantle and the diagonals crossing the picture add to the dynamic effect and the angels continue the Virgin's silhouette downwards, making it slimmer and airier.

964. Murillo. The Holy Children with the shell.

975 «**The Virgin with the Rosary**» (Canvas, 164 × 110 cm). This work from about 1650 shows a theme painted many times by Murillo, very much in keeping with his artistic sensibility for feminine beauty and child-like grace. The Classical pyramid-shaped composition is reminiscent of Raphael.

976 «**The Virgin and Child**» (Canvas, 151 × 103 cm). It dates from about 1660.

977 «**Mater Dolorosa**» (Canvas, 52 × 41 cm). This is the companion piece to No. 965 and dates from about 1668-70.

978 «**The Virgin appearing to St. Bernard**» (Canvas, 311 × 249 cm). In this work, dating from about 1660, the saint is rewarded for his eloquence in defending and praising the Virgin with her milk; the usual iconographic scheme is slightly altered, setting the Virgin closer to the saint's level, so that the composition is more compact.

979 «**The Virgin descending to reward St. Ildefons**» (Canvas, 309 × 251 cm). This work dates from about 1660 and the similar subject-matter and measurements could indicate that it was the companion piece to the preceding painting. Instead of portraying the more awkward act of the bestowal of the chasuble, Murillo has preferred to paint the Virgin simply offering it to the saint while the angels seem to be admiring her beauty, one of Murillo's typically candid touches. The great diagonal ray of light from the clouds enlivens the composition and makes the colours shine.

980 «**St. Augustine between Christ and the Virgin**» (Canvas, 274 × 195 cm). This work from about 1665 represents St. Augustine meditating and is taken from an engraving after Van Dyck.

981 «**Vision of St. Francis during the Porciuncula**» (Canvas, 206 × 162 cm). This work dates from about 1667. When Murillo painted supernatu-

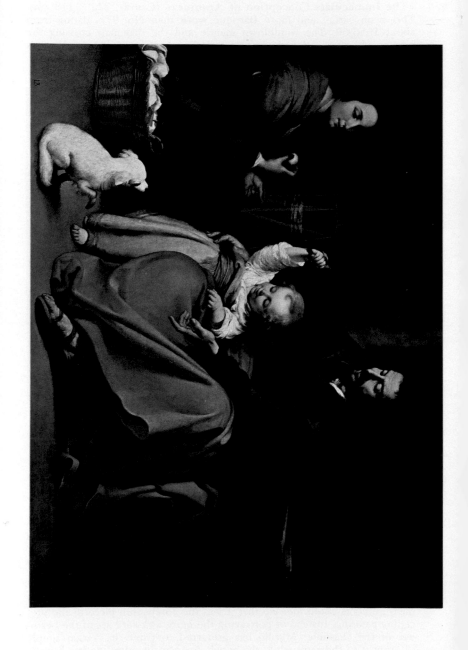

960. Bartolomé Esteban Murillo. Holy Family with a little bird.

972. Bartolomé Esteban Murillo. The El Escorial Immaculate Concepcion.

ral visions he attempted as far as possible to blend them into the earthly part of the picture, pervading it with brilliant light effects.

982 «**The Martyrdom of St. Andrew**» (Canvas, 123 × 162 cm). In this work, painted between 1675 and 1680, Murillo's lack of interest in dramatic effects led him to surround the main subject with anecdotic details and bustling activity. The repoussoir figure on the left is clearly reminiscent of Velázquez's tapestry-weaver, although facing the other direction.

984 «**The Conversion of St. Paul**» (Canvas, 125 × 169 cm). This work is the companion piece to the preceding one and dates from the same period. It is a very Baroque composition with splendid light effects.

987 «**St. Jerome**» (Canvas, 187 × 133 cm). This is a work from Murillo's early period (about 1652) revealing a naturalistic approach. It is still very Tenebrist and the subject is unusual in his artistic production.

989 «**St. James the Apostle**» (Canvas, 134 × 107 cm). This work, dating from about 1656-60, resembles Ribera's *St. Simon* (in the Prado), although with the saint facing the opposite direction.

994. Murillo. The patrician's dream.

994 «**The foundation of Santa Maria Maggiore in Rome: the patrician's dream**» (Canvas, 232 × 522 cm [the arch has been cut down]). This work, painted about 1665, is the first of a series of four canvases that Murillo was commissioned to paint for the church of Santa María la Blanca in Seville when it was remodelled in 1665. It represents the Virgin appearing to the patrician in a dream to order him to build a church on Mount Esquilino. The composition describes a soft curve contrary to that of the arch. The sleeping figures with the book left on the table, the small dog curled up and the sewing basket all make a homely scene that remains undisturbed by the appearance of the Virgin, so lightly portrayed with Murillo's delicate touch. This series (the two canvases in the Prado, a third in the Louvre and a fourth in a private collection in England) mark Murillo's mature period, when he had reached the height of his pictorial mastery. The four canvases were taken to France by the French marshal Soult during the Napoleonic War; the spandrels were added in Paris, giving them their present rectangular shape. These two returned to Spain in 1816.

995 «**The foundation of Santa Maria Maggiore: the patrician reveals his dream to the Pope**» (Canvas, 232 × 522 cm). This is the companion piece to the preceding work and represents the patrician relating his dream to Pope Liberius. The subsequent episode is seen on the right: when the group goes to visit the Mount Esquilino they find it covered with snow in high summer. Murillo's mastery with the brush is seen here at its best, giving the forms grace and freshness. The pale, harmonious colouring, applied in fine velaturas, reveals an almost 18th-century sensibility.

996 «**Rebekah and Eliezer**» (Canvas, 107 × 171 cm). Dating from about 1665, this is a very Classicist composition, although the subject is treated like a *genre* painting.

996a «**Jesus and the Samaritan woman**» (Canvas, 30 × 37 cm). This was a preparatory sketch.

997 «**The Prodigal Son taking his due**» (Canvas, 27 × 34 cm). Dating from about 1675, this work and Nos. 998, 999 and 1000 were preparatory sketches for a series of six pictures now kept in the Beit Collection (Blessington, Russborough); they are taken from engravings after Callot.

998 «**The Prodigal Son taking leave**» (Canvas, 27 × 34 cm). See No. 997.

965. Murillo. Ecce Homo.   **977. Murillo. Mater Dolorosa.**

999 «The dissipation of the Prodigal Son» (Canvas, 27 × 34 cm). See No. 997.

1000 «The Prodigal Son abandoned» (Canvas, 27 × 34 cm). See No. 997.

1001 «Old woman weaving» (Canvas, 61 × 51 cm). This is a youthful work, painted with a naturalistic approach, and reveals Murillo's fondness for *genre* scenes.

1002 «Galician woman with a coin» (Canvas, 63 × 43 cm).

1005 «Landscape» (Canvas, 95 × 123 cm). Its attribution to Murillo is doubtful.

1006 «Landscape» (Canvas, 95 × 123 cm). Pendant to the preceding No.

2657 «Portrait of an unknown man» (Canvas, 49 × 41 cm).

2809 «The Immaculate Conception of Soult» (Canvas, 274 × 190 cm). This work was commissioned for the Priests' Hospital in Seville about 1678 by Don Justino de Neve, who also commissioned the series for Santa Maria la Blanca. It takes its name from the French marshal Soult, who took the work to France in 1813; it was returned to Spain in 1940. Its compositional scheme is more static than other *Immaculate Conceptions,* while Murillo has taken particular pleasure in developing the glory of the angels, thus creating a splendid golden aureole around the Virgin with a diffused, sensuous handling worthy of the Venetian masters.

2845 «Gentleman with a ruff collar» (Canvas, 198 × 127 cm). This work, painted about 1670, is an interesting example of Murillo's style as a portraitist and follows the sober pattern of Velázquez's portraits.

3008 «Mountain landscape» (Canvas, 194 × 130 cm). This is an imaginary landscape painted with a fluid, soft kind of handling. It bears a very close resemblance to landscapes by his pupil Iriarte.

3060 «Nicolás Omazur» (Canvas, 83 × 73 cm). Dated 1672. The sitter was a Flemish merchant, hobby poet and a friend of Murillo. The portrait shows him with a skull in his hand, thus creating a *vanitas* portrait, rare in

**1002. Murillo. Galician woman with   3060. Murillo. Nicolas Omazur.
a coin.**

2422. Luis Paret y Alcázar. Charles III lunching in front of his courtiers. (detail)

Spanish painting but relatively frequent in Flemish art. This interpretation was confirmed by an inscription now cut off, but known by a transcription by Ceán Bermúdez.

MURILLO (?).

971 «Immaculate Conception» (Canvas, 96 × 64 cm).
983 «St. Ferdinand» (Canvas, 56 × 38 cm).
985 «Head of St. Paul» (Canvas, 50 × 77 cm).
986 «Head of St. John the Baptist» (Canvas, 50 × 77 cm).
990 «St. Francis of Paola» (Canvas, 104 × 100 cm).
991 «St. Francis of Paola» (Canvas, 111 × 83 cm).
2777 «Two angels» (Canvas, 44 × 68 cm).
2912 «Self-portrait» (Canvas, 103 × 77 cm).

NAVARRETE, Juan Fernández de Navarrete, called «the Deaf» (b. Logroño c. 1526; d. Toledo 1579). He was trained in various Italian cities and in Titian's workshop. From 1568 on he worked at El Escorial. His style combines reformed Mannerist grandeur and decorum with a fondness for vivacious anecdotic details and contrasted light effects that already anticipate the naturalistic style.

1012 «The Baptism of Christ» (Wood, 49 × 37 cm). Signed. This is his earliest known work.

NICOLAS FRANCES, Master Nicolás Francés (active in Leon before 1434; d. 1468). He introduced the International Gothic style in Leon.

2545 «Retable of the Life of the Virgin and St. Francis» (Wood, 557 × 558 cm). Predella: *bust-length portraits of saints.* Central panel: *The Virgin and Child among angelic musicians, the Assumption and Calvary.* Right: *The Annunciation, Nativity and Purification.* Left: *St. Francis before the Sultan, the dream of Honorius III and the founding of the Franciscan Order* and *the Stigmata.* This altar-piece is characteristic of Nicolás Francés' style with its sound, delicate draughtsmanship and fresh, lively colouring. Its spaciousness reveals Italian influence; the figures are varied and expressive and elegantly portrayed.

NUÑEZ DE VILLAVICENCIO. See Villavicencio.

ONCE MIL VIRGENES, Master of the Eleven Thousand Virgins. (Active in Segovia about 1475-1500). Hispano-Flemish School. This artist shows an independent style within the circle of painters working in Segovia, with a tendency to stylize his figures and abundant use of *mudéjar* details.

1290 «The Coronation of the Virgin» (Wood, 129 × 92 cm).
1293 «St. Ursula with the Eleven Thousand Virgins» (Wood, 112 × 79 cm). This is the panel that gave the anonymous master his name. It represents the saint on the way to Rome with her surprising entourage, according to the account of Jacobo de Vorágine in the *Golden Legend.*
1294 «The Bestowal of the Chasuble upon St. Ildefons» (Wood, 165 × 91 cm).

ORRENTE, Pedro de Orrente (b. Murcia 1588; d. Valencia 1645). Toledan School. He worked in Valencia, Toledo and Madrid and probably travelled to Venice (before 1612) and painted in the workshop of Leandro Bassano, whose influence on his style is evident. His compositions contain numerous figures in spacious Venetian-style landscapes where the artist takes pleasure in introducing animal figures and still-life details.

1015 «The Adoration of the Shepherds» (Canvas, 111 × 162 cm).
1016 «The Crucifixion» (Canvas, 153 × 128 cm).
1017 «Laban overtaking Jacob» (Canvas, 116 × 209 cm). This is an excellent work and like No. 1016 entirely by Orrente.
1018 «Exodus» (Canvas, 113 × 180 cm). This is probably a workshop copy.
1020 «Return to the fold» (Canvas, 74 × 89 cm). Its attribution is doubtful.
2421 «The parable of the sower» (Canvas, 100 × 140 cm).
2771 «A donkey and a sheep» (Canvas, 34 × 51 cm).
2772 «A horse with vessels» (Canvas, 34 × 51 cm). This is the companion piece to No. 2771.
3052 «St. Peter receiving the keys» (Canvas, 103 × 102 cm).
3229 «The journey of Tobias and Sarah» (Canvas, 100 × 139 cm).
3242 «Self-portrait» (Canvas, 45 × 36 cm).

PACULLY COLLECTION, Master of the Pacully Collection. Anonymous 15th-century Castilian master.

2971 «The Apostles Philip, Bartholomew, Matthias, Simon, Judas and
2972 Thomas» (Wood, 25 × 40 cm each panel). These panels belong to an altar-piece previously attributed to the Master of St. Ildefons.

PACHECO, Francisco Pacheco (b. Sanlúcar de Barrameda 1564; d. Seville 1654). Sevillian School. Pacheco was the master and later father-in law of Velázquez and his contribution to Spanish art as a theoretician (*The Art of Painting,* 1649) is more important than as an artist. He travelled to Flanders and also visited Toledo (before 1612) and Madrid (1623). His personal style is retardataire and somewhat dry. His pencil-drawn portraits *(Book of Portraits)* are the most interesting part of his work.

2545. Nicolás Francés. Retable of the Life of the Virgin.

1022 «St. Inés» (Wood, 103 × 144 cm). Signed and dated 1608. This and the following three works are companion pieces.
1023 «St. Catherine» (Wood, 102 × 43 cm).
1024 «St. John the Evangelist» (Wood, 99 × 45 cm).
1025 «St. John the Evangelist» (Wood, 99 × 45 cm).
PALOMINO, Acislo Antonio de Palomino (b. Bujalance 1655; d. Madrid 1726). School of Madrid. Palomino was primarily a fresco painter and decorated various churches in Madrid, sometimes in collaboration with Coello. His dynamic, spirited style shows the influence of Luca Giordano. He was an art scholar and his book *Pictorial Museum and Optical Scale,* published in two volumes in 1715 and 1724, earned him the title «the Spanish Vasari».
1026 «The Immaculate Conception» (Canvas, 193 × 137 cm). Signed.
3161 «St. Inés» (Canvas, 250 × 168 cm).
3186 «St. Inés» (Canvas, 250 × 160 cm).
3187 «Air» (Canvas, 246 × 156 cm). Signed.
PANTOJA DE LA CRUZ, Juan Pantoja de la Cruz (b. Valladolid 1553; d. Madrid 1608). He was Court painter to Philip III and a pupil of Sanchez Coello, whose style he continued without reaching his teacher's standard. He also painted religious works.
1030 See Sánchez Coello, Copies.
1031 See Sánchez Coello, Copies.
1032 «Margaret of Austria, wife of Philip III» (Canvas, 112 × 97 cm). Signed and dated 1607.
1034 «A Knight of the Order of Santiago» (Canvas, 51 × 47 cm). Signed and dated 1601.
1035 «Portrait of an unknown lady» (Canvas, 56 × 42 cm).
1038 «The Birth of the Virgin» (Canvas, 260 × 172 cm). Signed and dated 1603.
1040a «St. Augustine» (Canvas, 264 × 115 cm). Signed and dated 1601. See No. 1040 b.
1040b «St. Nicholas of Tolentino» (Canvas, 264 × 135 cm). Signed and dated 1601. Like the preceding work, this one was painted for the convent popularly known as *Colegio de Doña María de Aragón.*
2562 «Philip III» (Canvas, 204 × 122 cm). Signed. This is the companion piece to No. 2563.
2563 «Queen Margaret» (Canvas, 204 × 122 cm). Signed and dated 1606.
PAREJA, Juan de Pareja (b. Seville c. 1610; d. Madrid 1670). He was Velázquez's servant and began painting in secret since his condition did not permit him to do so openly, until Philip IV saw his works and granted him freedom to paint; Velázquez made a famous portrait of him.

1041 «The Vocation of St. Matthew» (Canvas, 225 × 325 cm). Signed and
dated 1661. The figure on the left is a self-portrait.
PARET, Luis Paret y Alcázar (Madrid 1746-1798/9). Paret is a rather
unusual figure on the artistic scene of his time; his work reflects the
influence of 18th-century Venetian art which he had studied during his
stay in Italy (1763-66), and French Rococo painting which his master La
Traverse, a pupil of Boucher, had passed on to him.

1042 «Flowers» (Canvas, 39 × 37 cm). Signed.

1043 «Flowers» (Canvas, 39 × 37 cm). Signed.

1044 «The Royal couples» (Canvas, 232 × 365 cm). Signed. This work represents a riding show attended by Charles III and María Luisa of Parma and
the royal family.

1045 «Ferdinand VII taking the oath as Prince of Asturias» (Canvas,
237 × 159 cm). Signed and dated 1791.

2422 «Charles III lunching before his Court» (Wood, 50 × 64 cm). Signed
in Greek: «Luis Paret, son of his father and mother, did it».

2875 «Masked ball» (Wood, 40 × 51 cm). This work dates from about 1767
and shows the Prince's Theatre in Madrid.

2991 «A rehearsal» (Canvas, 38 × 51 cm).
PEREAS, Master of the Pereas. Valencian School. He was an anonymous
master who worked towards the end of the 15th century and included some
Renaissance novelties in his style.

2678 «The Visitation» (Wood, 176 × 155 cm).
PEREDA, Antonio de Pereda y Salgado (b. Valladolid 1611; d. Madrid 1678). School of Madrid. This artist painted works of very unequal
quality; his depictions of material things (highly-detailed objects, draperies
in luscious Venetian colouring and striking shot fabrics) are excellent,
whereas he failed to adapt his style to the dynamic requirements of contemporary decorative Baroque. He also painted famous *vanitas* still lifes.

1032. Pantoja. Margaret of Austria, wife of Philip III.

1046 «St. Jerome» (Canvas, 105 × 84 cm). Signed and dated 1634.

1047 «Christ, Man of Sorrows» (Canvas, 97 × 78 cm). Signed and dated 1641.

1317a «The Relief of Genoa» (Canvas, 290 × 370 cm). Signed. Dating from
about 1634/5, this work shows the 2nd Marquis of Santa Cruz relieving
the city of Genoa, besieged by the French troops in 1625. It was painted
in his best period, when he was in the service of the Court, for the Hall of
Realms in the Buen Retiro Palace.

1317b «The Virgin appearing to St. Felix of Cantalicio». See Van de Pere.

1340 «St. Peter freed by an angel» (Canvas, 145 × 110 cm). Signed and dated
1643.

2555 «The Annunciation» (Canvas, 134 × 77 cm). Signed and dated 1637.

PEREZ, Bartolomé Pérez (Madrid 1634-1693). School of Madrid. He was the son-in-law and principal assistant of Juan de Arellano. He painted intensely coloured flower bouquets against dark backgrounds in the manner of his father-in-law with an excellent fluid, succulent technique. He also painted figures for Arellano's garlands and theatrical decorations.

1048 «**Flowers**» (Canvas, 86 × 76 cm).

1049 «**Flowers**» (Canvas, 86 × 76 cm).

1050 «**Flowers**» (Canvas, 107 × 72 cm).

1051 «**Flowers**» (Canvas, 112 × 71 cm).

1052 «**Flowers**» (Canvas, 75 × 56 cm). Together with the following five Nos., this work comes from the convent of St. Diego in Alcalá de Henares.

1053 «**Flowers**» (Canvas, 75 × 56 cm).

1054 «**Flowers**» (Canvas, 62 × 84 cm).

1055 «**Flowers**» (Canvas, 62 × 84 cm).

1056 «**St. Francis Xavier in a garland**» (Canvas, 95 × 73 cm). This is the companion piece to No. 1057.

1057 «**St. Theresa of Jesus in a garland**» (Canvas, 95 × 73 cm). This is the pendant to the preceding work.

PEREZ SIERRA, Francisco Pérez Sierra (b. Naples 1627; d. Madrid 1700). School of Madrid. He collaborated with Carreño and Rizzi.

3181 «**St. Joachim**» (Canvas, 214 × 122 cm).

PICARDO, León Picardo (resident in Burgos between 1514 and 1530; d. 1547). He was painter to the Constable of Castile, in whose chapel in the Cathedral of Burgos he worked. Possibly a native of Picardy, he was probably trained in Flanders and only made the acquaintance of Italian art through Flemish Romanists.

2171 «**The Annunciation**» (Wood, 171 × 139 cm). Like the two following works, this comes from the Monastery of Tamara.

2172 «**The Purification**» (Wood, 170 × 139 cm).

2173 «**Landscape near Jerusalem**» (Wood, 170 × 139 cm).

POLO, Diego Polo (b. Burgos c. 1610; d. Madrid 1665). School of Madrid. He was influenced by Titian in his colouring and diffused technique.

3105 «**St. Roch**» (Canvas, 193 × 142 cm).

PRADO, Blas de Prado (b. Camarena (?), Toledo c. 1546/7; d. between 1593-1600). He worked in Toledo and at the Moroccan Court.

1059 «**The Holy Family, St. Ildefons, St. John the Evangelist and the Master Alonso de Villegas**» (Canvas, 209 × 165 cm). Signed and dated 1598.

PUGA, Antonio Puga (b. Orense 1602; d. Madrid 1648). School of Madrid. He studied with Caxés and painted some popular *genre* scenes.

3004 «**The painter's mother**» (Canvas, 147 × 109 cm).

RAMIREZ, Cristóbal Ramírez (first half of the 17th century). The biography of this artist is unknown.

1060 «**The Saviour giving His blessing**» (Canvas, 207 × 129 cm). Signed and dated 1628.

RAMIREZ, Felipe Ramírez (first third of the 17th century). Toledan School (?).

2802 «**Still life**» (Canvas, 71 × 92 cm). Signed and dated 1628. This canvas is the only known work by this artist, who was connected with Sánchez Cotán. For this reason the rare perfection of this still life with its rigorously mathematical composition and masterly rendering of the objects is all the more surprising. The lilies in the gold goblet add an extremely refined note between the sober thistle and grapes; this sober character is typical of Castilian still lifes and has given rise to the expression «Lenten still lifes» to describe them.

RIBALTA, Francisco Ribalta (b. Solsona, Lerida 1565; d. Valencia 1628). Valencian School. A native of Catalonia, Ribalta studied in Madrid and settled in Valencia before 1599, where he was highly renowned and received important commissions to paint altar-pieces; he was also the master of many artists who passed through his large workshop where he was assisted by his son Juan. His early style is related to that of the artists who worked at El Escorial and shows naturalistic tendencies and an interest in contrasted light effects. But after 1620 this trend becomes more pronounced, his realism directer and harsher and his lighting more Tenebrist; his knowledge of Caravaggism seems to indicate a visit to Italy, although this has not been sufficiently documented. At all events his contribution to introducing naturalism in Spain is important and his severe, monumental and intensely expressive style exerted a considerable influence.

1061 «**Christ with two angels**» (Canvas, 113 × 90 cm).

1062 «**St. Francis comforted by an angel**» (Canvas, 204 × 158 cm). There are several versions of this work, which is a fine example of his style; he concentrates on light effects and realistic depiction of figures and objects, rendering the textures with excellent technique.

1063 «**Blessed soul**» (Canvas, 58 × 46 cm). See No. 1064.

1064 «**Soul in Purgatory**» (Canvas, 58 × 46 cm). The attribution to Ribalta is not generally accepted.

1065 «**St. Matthew and St. John the Evangelist**» (Canvas, 66 × 102 ·cm). This is the companion piece to No. 2965; they probably belonged to an altarpiece and have been considered the work of Orrente or Juan Ribalta.

2804 «**Christ embracing St. Bernard**» (Canvas, 158 × 113 cm). This is one of Ribalta's most popular works; the dramatic use of light and the vigorous plasticity of the two figures are admirable.

2965 «**St. Mark and St. Matthew**» (Canvas, 166 × 102 cm). See No. 1065.

RIBALTA, Juan Ribalta (b. Madrid 1596/7; d. Valencia 1628). Son and assistant of Francisco Ribalta, he only survived him by a few months.

3044 «**St. John the Evangelist**» (Canvas, 182 × 113 cm). Signed.

1121. Ribera. Archimedes.

2804. Ribalta. Christ embracing St. Bernard.

RIBERA, Jusepe de Ribera, called «Lo Spagnoletto» (b. Játiva, Valencia 1591; d. Naples 1652). Nothing is known about Ribera's youth and training; he must have gone to Italy at an early age as his presence there is documented already in 1615. He stayed in Rome and probably also in Parma before settling in Naples in 1616, where he spent the rest of his life in a comfortable economic position and protected by the Spanish viceroys. His artistic career is therefore Italian, but he always signed his works as a Spaniard; these were sent to Spain by the viceroys and exerted a considerable influence in his native country, so that Spanish art scholars always include him among Spanish masters. His biographies are full of tales about his bloodthirsty character, which probably have no other foundation than the fact that he lived at a time and place of constant upheaval and popular revolts against Spanish domination, heightened in the public imagination by Ribera's violent temperament. On the other hand, the portrayal of violent scenes in art, that made such an impression on the Romanticists, was completely normal at the time in religious painting, which abounded in scenes of martyrdoms.

His contemporaries regarded Ribera as a follower of Caravaggio and indeed of Caravaggesque origin are his extremely naturalistic approach and Tenebrist lighting that gives his forms a vigorously sculptural modelling, highlighting the essential parts of the picture and thus producing an effect of concentration that Ribera cultivates very consciously by reducing the elements and arrangement of his composition to simple schemes. The way he uses impasto is very personal, with thick brushwork underlining the tensions of the forms, the movements of tendons and muscles under the skin, and rendering textures in a masterly manner. His work as an etcher was fundamental in forming his style since it was probably the basis of the unfaltering accuracy of his draughtsmanship. Ribera is primarily known as one of the foremost painters of ascetic saints and hermits, heroic martyrs, old men with wrinkled faces consumed by penitence and suffering, that is, of the most dramatic aspect of art at the time of the Counter-Reformation; however, it is often forgotten that a large amount of his works deal with mythological subjects and that he shows a first-hand knowledge of Classical art. This knowledge is exemplified in his compositional precision, in the sober, dignified bearing of his figures that maintain an intimate and profound poise in spite of all their tortures, solitude and penitence. Contact with Venetian art enriched his painting with a fondness for colour that led him to place his figures in outdoor settings and study atmospheric effects with a palette of brighter, richer colours. Originally Tenebrist, then splendidly colourist towards the end of his artistic career, Ribera was always inspired by an interest in the human being as an individual. Doing away with rhetoric approaches and superfluous anecdotic details, he gave his figures a dignified, monumental character, so that his works include some of the most sober, intense examples of Baroque religious painting.

1067 «The Saviour» (Canvas, 77 × 65 cm). This is the first of a series of the twelve Apostles and Christ formed by Nos. 1071, 1074, 1077, 1082, 1084, 1087, 1088, 1089, 1090, 1092 and 1099. Although Ribera is known to have painted several *Apostolados,* this is the only almost extant one. *The Saviour* is the most classical in style of this series; the rest are excellent, expressive portraits. They were probably painted about 1630/32.

1069 «The Trinity» (Canvas, 226 × 181 cm). Dating from about 1635/36, this is one of Ribera's most famous and outstanding creations. The composition is developed in curved diagonals, an accustomed scheme in Ribera's works. In spite of the intense shadows, the colouring, especially in the upper part, achieves Venetian splendour. The theme of the Trinity with the dead Christ, which is the most human version of the dogma, was treated by several distinguished artists in the 16th century (Dürer, Michelangelo, El Greco); Ribera takes this humanizing aspect a step further, for example in God the Father's expression as He rests His hands on the crown of thorns lost in grief and also in the waxen grey body of Christ whose rigid arms recall His death on the Cross.

1070 «The Immaculate Conception» (Canvas, 220 × 160 cm). This work, which dates from about 1637/40, is a lesser version of Ribera's important *Immaculate Conception* in the Augustinian convent in Salamanca.

1071 «St. Peter» (Canvas, 75 × 64 cm). See No. 1067.

1072 «St. Peter» (Canvas, 128 × 100 cm). Dating from about 1632 (?), this work possibly belonged to a series of Apostles now divided up, of which No. 1110 could have been another. The aged saint, of noble bearing, almost fills the picture with his yellow cloak. The triangular composition gives the work a monumental aspect.

1073 «St. Peter freed by an angel» (Canvas, 177 × 232 cm). Signed and dated 1639. The lighting is clearly Caravaggesque and sets off the beautiful figure of the angel. The composition resembles that of *Jacob's dream* (No. 1117).

1074 «St. Paul» (Canvas, 75 × 63 cm). See No. 1067.

1075 «St. Paul the hermit» (Canvas, 143 × 143 cm). Signed and dated 1640. Ribera painted many hermit saints, a particularly cherished theme at the time of the Counter-Reformation since it exalted the virtue of penitence; he seems to take pleasure in describing the half-naked bodies wasted by fasting and their intent expressions deep in meditation. The way the figures are placed on a slant to the picture plane and the diagonal compositional scheme are characteristic of Ribera.

1076 «St. Andrew» (Canvas, 76 × 64 cm). This is a workshop painting.

1077 «St. Andrew» (Canvas, 76 × 63 cm). Signed. The date (1641) is false. See No. 1067.

1078 «St. Andrew» (Canvas, 123 × 95 cm). Dating from about 1630/32, this is a fine example of Ribera's ability in representing all kinds of hair and skin textures realistically; the saint's curly hair, wrinkled skin, hairy chest and coarse fisherman's hands all go to make an unforgettable image, dignified and melancholic in spite of his haggard appearance.

1079 «St. Andrew» (Canvas, 127 × 100 cm). This is a replica of an original kept in the Museum of Brussels.

1082 «St. James the Elder» (Canvas, 78 × 64 cm). See No. 1067.

1083 «St. James the Elder» (Canvas, 202 × 146 cm). Signed and dated 1631 or 1651. This is considered a companion piece to *St. Roch* (No. 1109) which poses the same problems with regard to the interpretation of its date; both are monumental full-length figures of saints with the serious aspect of classical philosophers.

1084 «St. Thomas» (Canvas, 75 × 62 cm). See No. 1067.

1087 «St. Matthew» (Canvas, 77 × 65 cm). See No. 1067.

1088 «St. Philip» (Canvas, 76 × 64 cm). See No. 1067.

1089 «St. James the Younger» (Canvas, 75 × 63 cm). See No. 1067.

1090 «St. Simon» (Canvas, 74 × 62 cm). See No. 1067.

1091 «St. Simon» (Canvas, 107 × 91 cm). As usual in his pictures of saints, Ribera portrays a definite man, known and observed; these are generally aged, wrinkled men whose gaze seems to convey the depth of their resignation.

1092 «St. Judas Thaddeus» (Canvas, 76 × 64 cm). See No. 1067.

1094 «St. Augustine praying» (Canvas, 203 × 150 cm).

1095 «St. Sebastian» (Canvas, 127 × 100 cm). This work dates from about 1635/40. Here Ribera has completely departed from Tenebrism; the figure is depicted in full light and reveals the artist's relation with the Bolognese Classicists in his search for harmonious, full forms as an expression of inner poise, which was the ultimate aim of the Classical spirit and the characteristic feature of this saint's traditional iconographic representation.

1096 «St. Jerome» (Canvas, 109 × 90 cm). Signed and dated 1644. This work is unfinished, particularly the cloak and the background, which the artist began to brighten behind the saint's head.

1098 «Penitent St. Jerome» (Canvas, 77 × 71 cm). Signed and dated 1652. This work from the last year of his life is one of Ribera's finest paintings of this hermit saint, not only due to his strangely wild aspect with his long hair and beard, but also due to his intense expression and Ribera's masterly technique in rendering light with loose brushstrokes loaded with paint.

1099 «St. Bartholomew» (Canvas, 77 × 64 cm). See No. 1067.

1100 «St. Bartholomew» (Canvas, 183 × 197 cm). Dating from about 1640, this work is part of a remarkable series that includes Nos. 1103, 1106 and

1103. Ribera. Mary Magdalene or St. Thais.

1108 and combines simple, imposing forms with growing refinement in the use of light and splendid Venetian-style colouring. The four canvases have been enlarged on some unknown occasion so that the original composition has been somewhat altered.

1069. Ribera. The Trinity.

1101 «**The Martyrdom of St. Philip**» (Canvas, 234 × 234 cm). Signed and dated 1630 or 1639 (the latter is more probable). This work, which was traditionally considered to represent the scene prior to the martyrdom of St. Bartholomew, has recently been newly interpreted as the martyrdom of St. Philip. It bears a certain resemblance to Caravaggio's painting of the same subject, especially in the figure of the executioner pulling the ropes and the addition of spectators. The compositional scheme consists of a long diagonal that crosses the foreground, counterbalanced by another in the opposite direction in the middle distance, a frequent scheme in Ribera's works, that is reinforced in its balance here by the vertical and horizontal lines of the mast and the Classical column. The dramatic effect of the scene is heightened by the contrast between the saint's strong body and his helplessness, between his anguished expression and the impassive attitude of the onlookers; however it is not a gruesome scene of martyrdom that we find here, but a much more profound expression of pain and a dignified attitude in the face of suffering.

1102 «**St. Joseph and the Christ Child**» (Canvas, 126 × 100 cm).

1103 «**Mary Magdalene or St. Thais**» (Canvas, 181 × 195 cm). This work belongs to the above-mentioned series (see No. 1100) and is without doubt the most attractive of the four canvases. The beautiful model can be found in several of Ribera's works and is generally considered to represent the features of the artist's daughter, who is said to have been seduced by Don Juan José de Austria, illegitimate son of Philip IV, and later obliged to spend the rest of her life in a convent. Her rich red mantle, the subtle balance of the composition and the masterful use of light contribute to set off the repentant saint's beauty.

1104 «**Repentant Mary Magdalene**» (Canvas, 97 × 66 cm).

1105 «**Repentant Mary Magdalene**» (Canvas, 153 × 124 cm). Recently some art scholars have attributed this work to Luca Giordano.

1106 «**St. Mary of Egypt**» (Canvas, 183 × 197 cm). See No. 1100.

1107 «**The Vision of St. Francis of Assisi**» (Canvas, 120 × 98 cm). This work dates from about 1630/38. In his vision an angel appears to the saint with a flask of water, a symbol of purity.

1108 «**St. John the Baptist in the Wilderness**» (Canvas, 184 × 198 cm). See No. 1100.

1109 «**St. Roch**» (Canvas, 212 × 144 cm). Signed and dated 1631. See No. 1083.

1110 «**St. Roch**» (Canvas, 126 × 93 cm). This work possibly belongs to an untraceable series, like No. 1072.

1111 «**St. Christopher**» (Canvas, 127 × 100 cm). Signed and dated 1637. In this work, with its very Venetian colouring, the huge figure of St. Christopher contrasts with that of the delicate child.

1112 «The blind sculptor Gambazo» (Canvas, 125 × 98 cm). Signed and dated 1632. The sitter's identity is incorrect; the work is probably a representation of the sense of touch and possibly one of a series on the five senses, a subject Ribera is known to have painted.

1113 «Tityus» (Canvas, 227 × 301 cm). Signed and dated 1632. Like the following work, this was previously considered one of a series of four pictures of giants that Ribera painted for Lucas van Uffel, who returned them to him because they terrified his wife to such a degree that she gave birth to a deformed child. They are indeed not agreeable subjects and probably contributed to Ribera's bloodthirsty reputation, which the Romanticists further exaggerated. The giant Tityus was condemned by Jupiter to have his entrails constantly devoured by a vulture for having attempted to rape Latona. The paint is so darkened, like in other works by Ribera, that it is difficult to distinguish the vulture. The subject is a rare one in painting, but there is a notable example by Titian (in the Prado).

1114 «Ixion» (Canvas, 220 × 301 cm). Signed and dated 1632. The giant is shown tied to the burning wheel to which he was condemned by Jupiter. See No. 1113.

1115 «St. Paul the hermit» (Canvas, 118 × 98 cm).

1116 «An anchorite» (Canvas, 128 × 93 cm). Apparently a workshop painting.

1117 «Jacob's dream» (Canvas, 179 × 233 cm). Signed and dated 1639. Ribera has avoided the traditional representation of the ladder with the ascending and descending angels and has converted the dream into a golden haze around Jacob's head where subtly drawn angels can be distinguished, while attention is centred on the recumbent figure of the patriarch completely absorbed in his dream. The horizontal composition, scarcely broken by the line of the tree-trunk, the warm light that bathes the scene and the sleeping Jacob's state of complete oblivion all make an intensely lyrical picture.

1118 «Isaac and Jacob» (Canvas, 129 × 289 cm). Signed and dated 1637. Colour plays an important part in this work, one of Ribera's most Venetian-style paintings. Light, tinted by the shades of the red curtains, is captured in a masterly fashion as it falls on the two main figures and colour is the element that structures the different parts of the picture.

1120 «Aesop» (Canvas, 118 × 94 cm). Art critics generally consider this a workshop painting.

1121 «Archimedes» (Canvas, 125 × 81 cm). Signed and dated 1630. This is a particularly expressive work and resembles in tone some of Velázquez's paintings, both in the type of model and in his spontaneous gesture.

1122 «The Triumph of Bacchus: Head of a woman» (Canvas, 67 × 53 cm). This and the following No. are two of four surviving fragments of a painting known thanks to a copy and which was inspired by a Classical relief still extant in the National Museum at Naples. These two fragments

1117. Ribera. Jacob's dream.

in the Prado bear witness to the vital sensuousness that must have characterized the work with its dense golden light and vibrating colouring.

1123 «The Triumph of Bacchus: Silenus» (Canvas, 55 × 46 cm). See No. 1122.

1124 «Women fighting» (Canvas, 235 × 212 cm). Signed and dated 1636. This work was apparently inspired by an actual event that occurred in Naples when two women fought for the love of a man. Dating from Ribera's mature period, the colours are homogeneous and warm.

2506 «Old money-lender» (Canvas, 76 × 62 cm). Signed and dated 1638. This restored work probably comes from Ribera's workshop.

3053 «St. Francis receiving the stigmata» (Canvas, 277 × 175 cm). Signed with a repainted signature and dated 1644, this work is a replica of an original kept at El Escorial.

2549. Rincón. The Miracle of SS. Cosme and Damian.

RICI, RICCI. See Rizi.

RINCON, Fernando del Rincón de Figueroa (active in Guadalajara in the late 15th century; d. after 1517).

2518 «Don Francisco Fernández de Córdoba y Mendoza» (Wood, 51 × 40 cm with frame). This portrait reveals an undeniable Italian influence.

2549 «The miracle of St. Cosme and St. Damian» (Canvas, 188 × 155 cm).

RIZI, Francisco Rizi (or Rizzi) de Guevara (b. Madrid 1614; d. El Escorial 1685). School of Madrid. He was the son of one of the Italian artists who came to Spain to work at El Escorial; he trained under Vicente Carducho at Court and worked as a Court painter from 1656 on. He painted fresco decorations, theatrical scenery and large-scale altar-pieces in a dynamic flamboyant Baroque style with a bold technique in which the forms dissolve in airy masses of vibrating colour. The Venetian colourist tradition is combined in his work with the influence of Rubens, all-important in his human types and way of composing. Although he was criticized in his time for inaccuracy in his draughtsmanship, Rizi nevertheless represents an advance in technique that influenced the school of Madrid. In his important workshop Antolínez, Escalante and Claudio Coello learnt their craft.

1126 «Auto-da-fe on the Plaza Mayor in Madrid» (Wood, 277 × 438 cm). Signed and dated 1683. This work was painted to commemorate an event held on June 30, 1683 in the presence of King Charles II, his wife and mother, who can be seen on the royal stand in the centre.

1127 «An artillery general» (Canvas, 202 × 135 cm). The sitter is represented with a dignified bearing that recalls Van Dyck.

1128 «The Annunciation» (Canvas, 112 × 96 cm). This work is characteristic of his style with its energetic brushwork and brilliant colouring enlivened by luminous touches. It is similar in style to the two following works and possibly belonged to the same altar-piece.

1129 «The Adoration of the Kings» (Canvas, 54 × 57 cm). This is the companion piece to No. 1130, possibly from an altar-piece.

1130 «The Purification» (Canvas, 54 × 57 cm). Pendant to No. 1129.

1130a «The Immaculate Conception» (Canvas, 289 × 174 cm). Signed.

2870 «St. Agueda» (Canvas, 184 × 108 cm).

2962 «The Purification» (Canvas, 206 × 291 cm). Like No. 3136, this is one of a series painted about 1663.

3136 «The Visitation» (Canvas, 206 × 291 cm). See No. 2962.

RIZI, Fray Juan Andrés Rizi (or Rizzi or Ricci) de Guevara (b. Madrid 1600; d. Montecassino, Italy 1681). School of Madrid. He was the son of the Italian painter Antonio Ricci and elder brother of Francisco. In 1627 he became a Benedictine monk at Montserrat, moving to Madrid in 1640, where he worked for almost twenty years before going to Italy. His style is realistic and monumental with fondness for chiaroscuro and sober colouring.

887 «Don Tiburcio de Redin y Cruzat» (Canvas, 203 × 124 cm). The sitter's identity was added at a later date. The work was attributed to Mazo.

2510 «St. Benedict blessing a loaf of bread» (Canvas, 168 × 148 cm).

2600 «St. Benedict's supper» (Canvas, 185 × 216 cm).

3108 «St. Benedict blessing St. Maur» (Canvas, 188 × 166 cm).

3214 «St. Benedict destroying the idols» (Canvas, 193 × 219 cm).

ROBREDO, Master of. Anonymous 15th-century artist from Burgos.

2596 «The dinner at the Pharisee's house» (Wood, 39 × 51 cm).

ROMAN, Bartolomé Román (or Romano) (b. Montoro, Córdoba c. 1590; d. Madrid 1647). School of Madrid. He studied under Carducho.

3077 «The Venerable Bede» (Canvas, 205 × 110 cm).

ROMANA, Pedro Romana (Córdoba 1488-1536). He was a Cordoban artist who painted in the manner of Alejo Fernández.

3233 «St. Catherine of Siena» (Wood, 95 × 72 cm).

RUIZ GONZALEZ, Pedro Ruiz González (b. Arandilla, Cuenca 1640; d. Madrid 1706).

2807 «Christ in the night of His Passion» (Canvas, 123 × 83 cm). Signed and dated 1673.

RUIZ DE LA IGLESIA, Francisco Ignacio Ruiz de la Iglesia (Madrid 1648-1704). School of Madrid. He studied with Camilo and Carreño.

3029 «The Duchess of Aveiro» (Canvas, 81 × 60 cm). Oval-shaped portrait.

SALMERON, Francisco Salmerón (b. ? 1608; d. Cuenca 1632).

1135 «Gideon's troops» (Canvas, 114 × 210 cm). Attribution is doubtful.

SAN NICOLAS, Master of. Anonymous 15th-century Hispano-Flemish artist.

2684 «St. Augustine as a Bishop» (Wood, 127 × 53 cm).

SANCHEZ, Mariano Sánchez (Valencia 1740-1822). He painted a large number of views of ports for Charles III, for which he was appointed Court painter.

2919 «Bridge at Badajoz» (Canvas, 57 × 111 cm).

2922 «Bridge at Martorell» (Canvas, 67 × 102 cm).

1138. Sánchez Coello. Infantas Isabella Clara Eugenia and Catalina Micaela.

SANCHEZ COELLO, Alonso Sánchez Coello (b. Alqueria Blanca, Benifayó, Valencia 1531/2; d. Madrid 1588). As a child he moved to Portugal with his parents and was later protected by the Portuguese King John III, who sent him to Flanders, where he lived with Cardinal Granvelle and studied under the great portrait-painter Anthonis Mor from 1550-54. From 1555 on he worked for the Spanish Court in Valladolid, Toledo and Madrid painting portraits and altar pictures. In his portraits he followed the style of Mor's courtly portraits with three-quarter length figures against a neutral background, resting one hand on an armchair or table while the other holds a handkerchief or gloves. Sánchez Coello sweetens Mor's Flemish influence (his detailed description of surfaces, draperies and jewelry, the realistically portrayed faces of his sitters and their aloof, distant pose) by making them appear more human by means of golden tones and a more sensuous impasto that reveals the influence of Titian, whose works he knew and copied. In his religious paintings he followed the general style used at El Escorial where the Italian influence was predominant.

1036   «**Philip II**» (Canvas, 88 × 72 cm). Although it resembles his style, this is not conclusively a work by Sánchez Coello; it was attributed to Pantoja and has also been regarded as an Italian work. It was painted before 1582.

1136   «**Don Carlos**» (Canvas, 109 × 95 cm).

1137   «**Infanta Isabella Clara Eugenia**» (Canvas, 116 × 102 cm). Signed and dated 1579. This is a touching portrait and reflects the grace and gentleness of Philip II's favourite daughter.

1138   «**The Infantas Isabella Clara Eugenia and Catalina Micaela**» (Canvas, 135 × 149 cm).

1139   «**Catalina Micaela of Austria, Duchess of Savoy**» (Canvas, 111 × 91 cm).

1140   «**Portrait of an unknown young lady**» (Wood, 26 × 28 cm).

1142   «**Lady with ermine**» (Wood, 67 × 56 cm).

1143   «**Knight of the Order of Santiago**» (Wood, 41 × 30 cm). This portrait was previously attributed to Anthonis Mor.

1144   «**The mystic betrothal of St. Catherine**» (Cork, 164 × 80 cm). Signed and dated 1578.

2511   «**Self-portrait**» (?) (Wood, 38 × 32 cm).

2861   «**St. Sebastian between St. Bernard and St. Francis**» (Wood, 295 × 196 cm). Signed and dated 1582.

SANCHEZ COELLO, Copies by Pantoja.

1030   «**Elizabeth of Valois, third wife of Philip II**» (Canvas, 119 × 84 cm).

1031   «**Elizabeth of Valois, third wife of Philip II**» (Canvas, 205 × 123 cm).

SANCHEZ COELLO, followers.

861   «**Isabella Clara Eugenia and Magdalena Ruiz**» (Canvas, 207 × 129 cm).

1284   «**Anne of Austria, fourth wife of Philip II**» (Canvas, 84 × 67 cm).

SANCHEZ COTAN, Juan Sánchez Cotán (b. Orgaz, Toledo 1560; d. Granada 1627). Toledan School. He was renowned as a still-life painter.

3222   «**The bearded woman of Peñaranda**» (Canvas, 102 × 61 cm).

SERRA, Workshop. Jaime and Pedro Serra worked in Catalonia in the last third of the 14th century.

3106   «**Scenes from the life of Mary Magdalene**» (Wood 280 × 29 cm). See No. 3107.

3107   «**Scenes from the life of John the Baptist**» (Wood, 280 × 92 cm). These two panels are companion pieces and related to the Virgin of the Milk of the Tobed altar-piece, to which they could have belonged as side panels.

SEVILLA, Juan de Sevilla Romero (Granada 1643-1695). Granadine School.

1160   See Valdés Leal.

2509   «**The rich man and the beggar Lazarus**» (Canvas, 110 × 160 cm). Signed.

SIGUENZA, Master of. His name is taken from the altar paintings in the Cathedral at Siguenza, but he has now been identified as Juan de Peralta (also known as Juan from Seville or «Juan Hispalense»), who worked in the mid-15th century in the International Gothic style.

1327   «**St. Luke**» (Wood, 95 × 55 cm).

1336   «**Retable of St. John the Baptist and St. Catherine**» (Five panels: central panel, 161 × 127 cm; side panels, 135 × 64 cm).

SISLA, Master of La Sisla. Hispano-Flemish School. He was an anonymous master to whom the following six panels from the Monastery of La Sisla, near Toledo, have been attributed; their style bears a certain relation to that of the Master of St. Ildefons (active 1483-85). Although the six panels are listed here under the same name, two different styles can be distinguished: Nos. 1254, 1255 and 1259 reveal a more Northern influence, whereas in Nos. 1256, 1257 and 1258 Italian Renaissance elements have been introduced. They are of extraordinarily high quality; the draughtsmanship is firm and sure, the modelling conveys sense of bulk and the tactile values are precisely depicted. The artist takes pleasure in ennobling his figures, which on the other hand he has made very human.

1254   «The Annunciation» (Wood transferred to canvas, 200 × 100 cm).
1255   «The Visitation» (Wood transferred to canvas, 200 × 114 cm).
1256   «The Adoration of the Magi» (Wood transferred to canvas, 214 × 109 cm).
1257   «The Presentation of the Child in the Temple» (Wood transferred to canvas, 203 × 100 cm).
1258   «The Circumcision» (Wood transferred to canvas, 213 × 102 cm).
1259   «The Death of the Virgin» (Wood transferred to canvas, 212 × 113 cm).

SOPETRAN, Master of. Anonymous 15th-century Hispano-Flemish artist. He takes his name from the following panels from the Benedictine monastery of Sopetrán (Guadalajara). His style derives from that of Jorge Inglés, although it is more advanced and with a greater sense of spaciousness; it also reveals the influence of Van der Weyden.

2575   «The Annunciation» (Wood, 103 × 60 cm).
2576   «Young man praying» (Wood, 105 × 60 cm). Some art historians identify the sitter as the son of the Marquis of Santillana, 1st Duke of Infantado.
2577   «The Nativity» (Wood, 103 × 60 cm).
2578   «The Death of the Virgin» (Wood, 103 × 60 cm).

TOBAR, Alonso Miguel de Tobar (b. Higuera, Huelva 1678; d. Madrid 1758).

1153   «Bartolomé Esteban Murillo» (Canvas, 101 × 76 cm). This is a copy of Murillo's self-portrait.

TOLEDO, Captain Juan de Toledo (b. Lorca, Murcia 1611; d. Madrid 1665). As a soldier he went to Italy, where he trained under Cerquozzi. He painted battle scenes, frequently naval battles, with small, bustling figures.

1154   «Naval combat between Spaniards and Turks» (Canvas, 62 × 110 cm). This is the companion piece to Nos. 1155, 1156 and 1157.
1155   «Shipwreck» (Canvas, 62 × 110 cm). See No. 1154.
1156   «Landing and combat» (Canvas, 62 × 110 cm). See No. 1154.
1157   «Attack at sea» (Canvas, 48 × 84 cm). See No. 1154.
2775   «Battle» (Canvas, 62 × 146 cm). Pendant to the following No.
2776   «Battle» (Canvas, 63 × 146 cm). See No. 2775.

TRISTAN, Luis Tristán (b. ? in the last third of the 16th century; d. Toledo 1624). Toledan School. He studied under El Greco, visited Italy and was acquainted with Ribera. His style reveals the influences of El Greco and the Mannerists working at El Escorial, as well as early traces of naturalism.

1158   «Portrait of an old man» (Canvas, 47 × 34 cm).
1159   «St. Anthony Abbot» (Canvas, 167 × 110 cm).
1276   «El Calabrés» (Canvas, 108 × 95 cm). According to Angulo and Pérez Sánchez, this work cannot be ascribed to Tristán due to the date indicated by the man's clothing.
2836   «St. Monica» (Canvas, 42 × 40 cm). Signed and dated 1616. This work comes from an altar-piece at Yepes.
2837   «Lamenting saint» (Canvas, 42 × 40 cm). See No. 2836.
2975   «Pietà» (Canvas, 61 × 48 cm). Its attribution is doubtful; it could have been painted by a non-Spanish artist.
3078   «St. Peter of Alcántara» (Canvas, 169 × 111 cm).

VALDES LEAL, Juan de Valdés Leal (Sevilla 1622-1690). Sevillian School. He studied in Cordoba in his youth under Antonio del Castillo, whose influence is evident in some of his works. In 1656 he returned to Seville where he participated in the foundation of the Art Academy in 1660. His most famous works are those on the *vanitas* theme and the triumph of death commissioned by Don Miguel de Mañara in 1672. In Spanish Baroque art Valdés Leal represents the counterpole to his contemporary Murillo; he was an energetic, violent artist who worked rapidly, which did not benefit his draughtsmanship, and whose best qualities were his brilliant colouring and spirited technique.

1160   «The Presentation of the Virgin in the Temple» (Canvas, 153 × 138 cm). Its attribution is listed as doubtful in the Prado Catalogue; recently art critics have suggested Juan de Sevilla as its possible author.
1161   «Jesus with the doctors» (Canvas, 200 × 215 cm). Signed and dated 1686. This is a very scenographic composition with decorative details.

2582   «A Jeronymite martyr» (Canvas, 249 × 130 cm). See No. 2593.

2593   «St. Jerome» (Canvas, 211 × 131 cm). Signed. This is the first of a series of Jeronymite saints painted for the church of Santa Isabel in Seville (see No. 2582). These two works are more reserved and monumental than usual in Valdés Leal.

3149   «St. Michael» (Canvas, 205 × 109 cm). This is taken from an engraving after Raphael.

VALERO, Cristóbal Valero (b. Alboraya, Valencia ?; d. 1789).

1162   «Don Quixote in the tavern» (Canvas, 56 × 79 cm).

1163   «Don Quixote knighted» (Canvas, 56 × 79 cm).

VAN DE PERE, Antonio van de Pere (b. Madrid ? c. 1618/20; d. c. 1688). School of Madrid.

1317b «The Virgin appearing to St. Felix of Cantalicio» (Canvas, 77 × 75 cm). Signed and dated 1665. This work was previously attributed to Antonio de Pereda due to mistaken reading of the signature.

1167. Velázquez. Christ crucified.

VELAZQUEZ, Diego Velázquez de Silva (b. Seville 1599; d. Madrid 1660). After a brief period in the studio of Herrera «the Elder», he was apprenticed in 1610 to Francisco Pacheco, whose daughter he married in 1617, a year after finishing his apprenticeship. Probably already conscious of his exceptional talent, Velázquez aimed at becoming Court painter, the ultimate ambition of all artists at the time. On his first visit to Madrid in 1622 he tried in vain to get a commission to paint royal portraits, but a year later Philip IV's all-powerful minister Count-Duke of Olivares summoned him to Court to portray the king. The work caused such a favourable impression that Velázquez was immediately appointed painter to the King, moving to Madrid with his family. From then on his career as an artist ran parallel to his other duties at Court, at first royal valet and usher to the King's privy chamber, later assistant superintendent of royal building projects and Grand Chamberlain of the Palace in charge of the decoration of the royal palaces, public festivities and royal journeys. At the end of his life he achieved his ambition of a knighthood when he was finally accepted in the Order of Santiago in 1658, usually reserved for the highest nobility. Velázquez's position at Court and especially his friendship with the King placed him in a privileged situation to pursue his art and also his studies in the two principal sources for an artist of his time: the paintings of the royal collections and Italy, which he visited on two occasions (1629-31 and 1649-51) with the purpose of acquiring works of art for the King.

Thus favoured by fortune, that gave him both his talent and the best means of developing it, Velázquez was to carry out an artistic revolution in the history of European painting which was to open up new paths for future generations of artists and consisted chiefly in stressing the predominant role of painting as a visual art that interprets reality in terms of light and colour as perceived by our sense of sight, freeing it of characteristics perceived by other senses (bulk, tactile qualities) or intellectual preconceptions (draughtsmanship, linear perspective). With this purpose in view Velázquez observed reality with new, unprejudiced eyes, which enabled him to discern the subtlest gradations of light and the finest shades of colouring, as well as to discover unexplored effects like the fact that our eyes are only able to perceive distinctly the object they are focussing on at a given moment, whereas all the surrounding objects appear blurred. Velázquez used different techniques, precise or sketchy as the case may be, to represent these effects. In this way he conveys the impression of space without resorting to geometric aids, thus producing the effect known as «aerial perspective» and also the often cited instantaneous photograph effect. Does that mean that we should only regard Velázquez as an artist endowed with a perfect eye and the mastery to capture immediate reality with his brush? Surely not. Velázquez painted his early works in the Tenebrist naturalistic style which implied the use of violent, contrasted light effects that modelled the forms with sculptural harshness; from these beginnings until the culmination of his mature style Velázquez underwent a long intellectual process, consciously assimilating influences, in particular that of Venetian painting, and making use of new motifs. He composed his pictures with great precision, carefully balancing the masses, choosing the most natural poses for his sitters, correcting the position of an arm or a leg at a later date in overpaintings that now come to light in X-ray examinations; he distributed the light in alternative planes to heighten the impression of depth and emphasize the object or detail he wanted to highlight. The final result, which seems like a piece of reality chosen at random, is the outcome of a mental process by which Velázquez linked all the elements of the work, blending masses and space by means of light until he had obtained the perfect optical synthesis.

1166 «The Adoration of the Magi» (Canvas, 203 × 125 cm). This work dates from 1619 and therefore belongs to his Sevillian period, when Velázquez still used contrasted light effects and precise modelling. The various figures have sometimes been considered portraits of members of his family: his wife Juana Pacheco as the Virgin, his father-in law Francisco Pacheco as one of the Magi and Velázquez himself as the youngest king. At all events, they are very concrete and individual models. Like in his other (not very frequent) religious works, the artist aims at an appearance of authenticity, showing emotional restraint and avoiding an exalting tone.

1171. Velázquez. Vulcan's Forge.

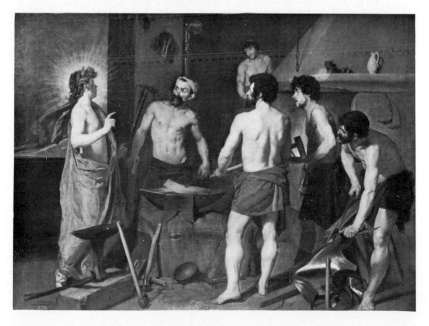

1167   «Christ crucified» (Canvas, 248 × 169 cm). This work was painted about 1630 at the wish of Philip IV for the convent of San Plácido. It is a serene picture in which Velázquez has avoided pathetic features; the classically beautiful body of Christ reveals no tension or stiffness and the face is discreetly covered by hair.

1168   «The Coronation of the Virgin» (Canvas, 176 × 124 cm). This work was painted for the Queen's Oratory about 1641-42. Its rigorous, heart-shaped compositional scheme has been interpreted symbolically (J. Gallego), considering that the crimson shades of the colouring and the Virgin's gesture heighten this symbolism.

1169   «St. Anthony the Abbot and St. Paul the first hermit» (Canvas, 257 × 188 cm). Traditionally considered a late work, it was probably painted about 1642; an important element is the landscape, where the various episodes of the saints' lives are related along a winding path leading into the background.

1170   «The Topers» or «The Triumph of Bacchus» (Canvas, 165 × 225 cm). Also known as The Drinkers, this work, dating from 1628, is the earliest known mythological subject painted by Velázquez. Such subjects are rare in Spanish painting since there was neither a humanistic tradition that justified them nor clients to purchase them, apart from the Kings and high nobility, who preferred to acquire such works from Italian or Flemish artists. When Velázquez treated mythological subjects he did so by associating them with reality in a manner not wholly lacking in ironic touches. In this respect the popular title of The Drinkers given to this work is very expressive. Although the scene takes place outdoors, Velázquez's fondness for contrasted light effects can still be observed, but here he is a complete master of his art. There is a notable difference in the way he treats the figure of Bacchus, more carefully portrayed and luminous, and those of the remaining figures depicted with Velázquez's characteristic long, fluid brushstrokes; these are extremely vivavious and expressive, some of them seeking the spectator's complicity with their frank, open gaze.

1171   «Vulcan's Forge» (Canvas, 223 × 290 cm). Painted in 1630, during Velázquez's first stay in Italy, this work relates the episode in which Apollo notifies Vulcan, the divine blacksmith, of his wife Venus' infidelity. It is considered by art critics his most Italian-style work and the one in which he shows the greatest interest in the portrayal of the nude. As usual, Velázquez does not want to convey the intemporal aspect of the mythological scene, but to bring it closer to contemporary reality. The centre of attention is the figure of Apollo, especially his head, silhouetted against the light background and stressed by its greater luminosity, brighter colouring and more finished handling; the other figures turn towards him, surprised and incredulous, in one of Velázquez's characteristic momentary «snapshot» portrayals. These figures half in the shade show a magnificent play of light, one of Velázquez's chief preoccupations in this picture.

1172   «The Surrender of Breda» (Las Lanzas) (Canvas, 307 × 367 cm). This work was painted before 1635 for the Hall of Realms of the Buen Retiro Palace to commemorate the Spanish military victory over the Dutch at Breda in June 1625. Justin of Nassau is seen giving the key of the city to the commander of the Spanish troops, Ambrosio Spinola, who receives it courteously, stretching out his arm to prevent the defeated general kneeling down in an attitude which has become famous as a model of courtliness and fair dealing. But there are also other important figures: the soldiers on both sides are a fine display of portraits, revealing concrete persons, individuals. Some address the spectator directly with their gaze as if wanting to make him a witness to the historic scene. The composition is simple: the two counterbalanced masses of figures are divided in the centre by a space through which our eyes are led into the background; the picture space is thus divided up into parallel planes like the flies on a stage, an effect that is stressed by the famous lances. Velázquez is known to have consulted abundant documentary evidence to prepare this picture, as well as eye-witness accounts and engravings, which all goes to prove Velázquez's ability to integrate given elements into a unified, coherent whole. It has been thought that the figure looking at the spectator on the extreme right might be a self-portrait of the artist.

1101. Jusepe de Ribera. The Martyrdom of St. Philip.

1172. Velázquez. The Surrender of Breda.

1173   «The Tapestry-weavers» or «The Fable of ·Arachne» (Canvas, 220 × 289 cm). Dating from 1657, this work was traditionally considered to represent the interior of the tapestry workshop of Santa Isabel, but it is now generally regarded (according to Angulo's theory, confirmed by documents brought to light by Mrs Caturla) as a representation of the story of Arachne as related in Ovid's *Metamorphoses*. The goddess of the Arts, Minerva, disguised as an old woman, is seen competing with Arachne, famous for her skill in spinning, in weaving a tapestry. In the background Minerva is represented without disguise rebuking Arachne for her daring in portraying the sins of the gods in her tapestry (the tapestry behind them depicts the rape of Europa by Zeus in the shape of a bull). The women watching the scene are the nymphs who, according to Ovid, used to come to contemplate Arachne at work and the bass viol symbolizes music, considered the best antidote against poisonous spider bites (Arachne was transformed into a spider by way of punishment for daring to challenge the goddess). In a different interpretation, De Tolnay considers the spinners and weavers in the foreground to symbolize the handicrafts, while the figures on the stage illuminated by the light of the intellect represent, apart from Minerva, Painting (Arachne), Music (the lady next to the bass viol), Architecture and Sculpture (the other two ladies), thus converting the scene into the triumph of the Fine Arts over the handicrafts. Whatever the meaning may be, Velázquez seems to intentionally avoid being too explicit in order to make a coherent picture in which the legend is no more than a plausible explanation. The spinners, whoever they may be, are working fast, their figures reveal movement and the spinning wheel turns so rapidly that the spokes cannot be distinguished. In spite of the simplicity of the rigorously right-angled composition, the artist avoids monotony by alternating the poses and leading our eyes from the spinner on the right, moulded by the light, to the more blurred figure on the left and from her over the head of the assistant in the shade to the brightly lit scene in the background. As usual Velázquez involves the spectator in the picture, although less directly than usual in Baroque painting; instead of addressing the spectator by means of rhetoric gestures or movements, here it seems to be the spectator who has attracted the attention of the picture, making one of the figures in the background turn to look.

1174 «**The Maids of Honour**» *(Las Meninas)* or «**The Family of Philip IV**» (Canvas, 318 × 276 cm). This work, painted in 1656, includes several different branches of painting (self-portrait of the artist, courtly portrait, interior group scene) in an unusual combination; it is unanimously considered by art critics to be Velázquez's finest work, the sum of his pictorial achievement in portraying space in terms of light, and one of the masterpieces of universal art. The exceptionally bold technique, fascinating effect of depth, the «impressionistic» aspect of a scene that appears to be captured «on the spur of the moment» have all been commented on at length many times. The work shows Velázquez painting an unseen picture and the Infanta Margarita accompanied by two maids of honour, a duenna, a male escort and two dwarfs, while through the doorway in the background we catch a glimpse of José Nieto, head of the Queen's tapestry workshops. The most complete interpretation of the scene has been ventured recently by J. Brown: the Infanta has come to watch Velázquez at work. While one of her maids of honour offers her a glass of water, the King and Queen enter the room and are reflected in the mirror on the opposite wall. Several of the figures look towards them and out of the picture. Velázquez is painting neither the Infanta nor the King and Queen, but the greatest picture he ever made: *The Maids of Honour.* Apart from demonstrating his familiarity with the royal family, Velázquez is making them witnesses of his most important creation. Their presence in his studio confirms the nobility of his art, denied him by the strict rules of his time which regarded painting as a purely manual craft, thus excluding him for a long time from the knighthood he aspired to. In this picture Velázquez not only involves the King in his assertion; the look that the figures direct at the King and Queen in practice reaches the spectator, drawing him into the picture space, which the composition prolongs towards us. In this intelligent and

1174. Velázquez. The Maids of Honour.

1036. Sánchez Coello. Philip II.

1173. Diego Velázquez. The tapestry-weavers. (detail)

discreet, subtle and apparently natural way Velázquez achieves the object of Baroque illusionism, doing away with the limits of the picture and confusing fiction and reality in the mind of the beholder.

1175 **«Mercury and Argus»** (Canvas, 127 × 248 cm). This work was painted in 1659 for the Hall of Mirrors in the Alcázar; it is extremely rich and reveals very fluid brushwork.

1176 **«Philip III on horseback»** (Canvas, 300 × 314 cm). See No. 1179.

1177 **«Queen Margaret of Austria, wife of Philip III»** (Canvas, 279 × 309 cm). See No. 1179.

1178 **«Equestrian portrait of Philip IV»** (Canvas, 301 × 314 cm). See No. 1179.

1179 **«Queen Isabella of Bourbon, wife of Philip IV»** (Canvas, 301 × 314 cm). These four equestrian portraits were painted for the Hall of Realms in the Buen Retiro Palace. With the exception of No. 1176, which seems to be entirely by Velázquez, the rest are supposed to have been started by the great master before his first journey to Italy, continued by another artist and repainted by Velázquez on his return. The whole conception of the portraits, with the elegant, solemn figures set in a spacious landscape bathed in silvery light, is characteristic of Velázquez.

1180 **«Prince Balthasar Carlos on horseback»** (Canvas, 209 × 173 cm). Dating from about 1635/6, this work was painted, like the preceding ones, for the Hall of Realms, where the young prince should be represented as heir to the throne. He was the great hope of his father, King Philip IV, and the whole of the Spanish Court and his birth in 1629, after Queen Isabella's repeated miscarriages, had been one of the happiest events of Philip's reign. Unfortunately the prince died at the age of seventeen. This equestrian portrait is one of Velázquez's most touching works; mounted gracefully on his horse, the child adopts a serious air as if trying to assume the heroic role expected of him for the portrait, obviously unfitting for his tender age. His fragile little figure, dressed in pink and gold, makes a delicate image and the whole picture with its fine colouring, light handling and silvery atmosphere is one of Velázquez's most successful works.

1181 **«Conde-Duque de Olivares»** (Canvas, 313 × 239 cm). With this heroic pose the Count-Duke is commemorating the battle of Fuenterrabía. The foreshortening of the horse stresses the impression of depth, with the figure set into the landscape.

1182 **«Philip IV»** (Canvas, 201 × 102 cm). With this work, painted before 1628, Velázquez set up a new model for courtly portraits, centring the spectator's whole attention on the figure and reducing to a minimum the attributes of his rank or social position, then deemed essential in courtly portraits. In this picture the King's rank is merely indicated by his impassive expression which reflects the attitude of absolute composure expected of a monarch, as well as by the tautness and luminosity of his face, where Velázquez never uses light touches or sketchiness.

1183 **«Philip IV»** (Canvas, 57 × 44 cm). Dating from 1628 (?), this is apparently a fragment of an equestrian portrait. (See No. 1182).

1184 **«Philip IV»** (Canvas, 191 × 126 cm). This work was painted about 1634-36 for the *Torre de la Parada,* the King's hunting lodge in El Pardo,

1175. Velázquez. Mercury and Argus.

like Nos. 1186 and 1189. These portraits provided Velázquez with an excellent pretext for outdoor effects in the countryside around El Pardo.

1185 «Philip IV» (Canvas, 69 × 56 cm). This portrait dates from 1655-60.

1186 «Cardinal-Infante Don Fernando» (Canvas, 191 × 107 cm). Dating from about 1632-36, this work portrays one of Philip IV's brothers. See No. 1184.

1187 «Queen María of Hungary» (Canvas, 55 × 44 cm). This portrait was painted in 1630 in Naples, where Velázquez coincided with Doña María, Philip IV's sister, on her way to meet her husband, Ferdinand of Hungary, later Emperor Ferdinand III.

1188 «Infante Don Carlos» (Canvas, 209 × 125 cm). This portrait dates from 1626-27. Don Carlos was one of Philip IV's brothers and, like the King, an art-lover; he died young. It is an exceptionally sober and elegant portrait; the Infante is dressed entirely in black, as was the custom at the Spanish Court, and holds a glove carelessly between his fingertips in a very different attitude from that of Titian's famous *Man with a glove*. There is an air of restraint and melancholy about him that is also frequent in Velázquez's portraits of the King. The figure is sharply silhouetted in space, moulded exclusively by the effect of the light.

1189 «Infante Balthasar Carlos in hunting dress» (Canvas, 191 × 103 cm). Painted in 1635-36, this is a portrait of the heir to the throne at the age of six. See No. 1184.

1191 «Queen Mariana» (Canvas, 231 × 131 cm). Mariana of Austria was the second wife of Philip IV, the daughter of his sister Maria and the Emperor Ferdinand III; the marriage took place in 1649, Philip's first Queen, Isabella of Bourbon, having died in 1644. This portrait dates from 1652-53; it can be observed that in his portraits of the Queen and the Infantas Velázquez's style is more conventional and showy. They are fine examples of his colouristic ability, reproducing the play of light on magnificent draperies, embroideries and jewelry with light brushwork and extremely delicate painting.

1192 «Infanta Margarita in pink» (Canvas, 212 × 147 cm). Velázquez left this portrait unfinished when he died in 1660; the face was probably painted by Mazo, but the dress reveals Velázquez's masterly technique.

1193 «Don Juan Francisco Pimentel, 10th Count of Benavente» (Canvas, 109 × 88 cm). This portrait, painted in 1648 (?), is influenced by Titian.

1194 «The Sculptor Martínez Montañés» (Canvas, 109 × 107 cm). Martínez Montañés (1568-1649) was the most distinguished sculptor of his time. In 1635-36 he was summoned to Court to make a bust of the King to be sent to Italy together with drawings by Velázquez as model for the bronze equestrian statue of Philip IV commissioned from Pietro Tacca, with the technical assistance of Galileo Galilei, that now stands in the Plaza de Oriente in Madrid. Velázquez portrayed the sculptor at work, although this part of the picture has been left unfinished; indeed, some parts of the figure were also left half-finished and were apparently completed by the artist many years later. It is the portrait of a mature, but still energetic man with a noble head crowning a sturdy, upright figure.

1195 «Don Diego de Corral y Arellano» (Canvas, 215 × 110 cm). This portrait was painted in 1631 and is the companion piece to the following one; the sitter was a judge of the Supreme Court of Castile.

1196 «Doña Antonia de Ipeñarrieta and her son» (Canvas, 215 × 110 cm). This work is not unanimously accepted as an original by Velázquez.

1197 «A Sibyl (the artist's wife?)» (Canvas, 62 × 50 cm). It dates from 1632.

1198 «Pablo de Valladolid» (Canvas, 209 × 123 cm). Dating from about 1632, the effect of this portrait is surprisingly modern due to its completely bare background. Velázquez's portraits of Court jesters, buffoons and dwarfs are extraordinarily interesting in his artistic output, not only due to the human and personal way in which he portrays them, but also because he gives free rein to experiment, unencumbered by the constraints of official portraiture. These works (cf. Nos. 1198 to 1205) are characterized by bold execution as well as economy of means in moulding the figures in dense, enveloping space and rich nuances that give their faces an expressiveness that makes them unforgettable.

1199 «The jester "Barbarossa", Don Cristóbal de Castañeda» (Canvas, 198 × 121 cm). The jester is dressed up as the famous Turkish pirate Khair-el-Din, who held sway over the Mediterranean and was defeated at the battle of Lepanto. The picture was left unfinished, but the parody of the fierce pirate can be seen in the jester's facial expression and movement of the hands clutching the swords.

103

1174. Diego Velázquez. *Las Meninas* or maids of honour (detail).

1180. Diego Velázquez. Prince Baltasar Carlos on horseback. (detail)

1181. Velázquez. Conde-
Duque de Olivares.

1182. Velázquez. Philip IV.

1200   «The jester known as "Don Juan de Austria"» (Canvas, 210 × 123 cm).
The counterpart of «Barbarossa», the victorious «Don Juan de Austria», is
personified by this jester with a languid air and surrounded by his accoutrements while a fictitious battle scene is being fought in the background. The buffoon's real name is unknown. The work dates from about 1632.

1201   «The dwarf Don Diego de Acedo, known as "El Primo"» (Canvas,
107 × 82 cm). In this work, dating from 1644, the size of the Court
dwarf, who was made Secretary of the Council of the Signet, contrasts
with the enormous book; his absent-minded expression and pretentiously
grave costume give him a deeply melancholic air.

1202   «The Court dwarf Don Sebastián de Morra» (Canvas, 106 × 81 cm).
This work dates from about 1643-44 and the penetrating gaze with which
the dwarf addresses the spectator makes it one of the most touching.

1203   «The Court jester Don Antonio, wrongly called "El Inglés"» (Canvas,
142 × 107 cm).

1204   «The Court dwarf Don Francisco Lezcano, called "The Child of Va-
llecas"» (Canvas, 107 × 83 cm). This work dates from 1637.

1205   «Don Juan de Calabazas, called "Calabacillas" or "The Idiot of Co-
ria"» (Canvas, 106 × 83 cm). With his cross-eyed look and strange grin,
this is probably the most disconcerting of these buffoons.

1206   «Aesop» (Canvas, 179 × 94 cm). Dating from 1640, this work was painted,
like the following two, for the *Torre de la Parada*. They reveal Velázquez's
sceptical tone, totally lacking in heroism, when he treats Classical subjects.

1207   «Menippus» (Canvas, 179 × 94 cm). About 1639-40. See No. 1206.

1208   «Mars» (Canvas, 179 × 95 cm). See No. 1206.

1209   «Francisco Pacheco (?)» (Canvas, 40 × 36 cm). Dating from 1619, this is
believed to be a portrait of Velázquez's father-in-law, painted in Seville;
the handling is still very tight.

1186. Velázquez. Cardinal-
Infante Don Fernando.

1189. Velázquez. Infante
Balthasar Carlos.

1191. Velázquez. Queen Mariana.   1192. Velázquez. Infanta Margarita.

1210 «The Medici Gardens in Rome» (Canvas, 48 × 42 cm). This work and the one that follows mark a turning point in the history of landscape painting. There is no sign here of the Flemish influence observed in the landscape backgrounds of his portraits; here Velázquez broaches the subject directly, conveying light effects with a rapid, sketchy technique and justifying the title of forerunner of Impressionism sometimes attributed to him. On the other hand, they have also been considered to reflect a melancholy mood that relates them to the Classicist landscape *en vogue* in Rome at the time. They date from Velázquez's second visit to Italy (1650-51).

1211 «The Medici Gardens in Rome» (Canvas, 44 × 38 cm). See No. 1210.

1213 «The Fountain of the Tritons in Aranjuez» (Canvas, 248 × 223 cm). The attribution of this work is uncertain (Velázquez or Mazo).

1219 «Philip IV in armour» (Canvas, 231 × 131 cm). This work is apparently not totally by Velázquez.

1224 «Self-portrait» (?) (Canvas, 56 × 39 cm). This work dates from about 1623.

2873 «Sor Jerónima de la Fuente» (Canvas, 160 × 110 cm). Signed and dated 1620.

2903 «Christ on the Cross» (Canvas, 100 × 57 cm). Signed and dated 1631.

3265 «Stag's head» (Canvas, 66 × 52 cm). 1634 (?).

VELAZQUEZ and MAZO.

889 «View of Saragossa» (Canvas, 181 × 331 cm). Although this work was commissioned from Mazo and bears an inscription stating that it was done by him, its exceptional quality leads art critics to recognize Velázquez's hand in several parts, although they disagree as to how much is due to each artist.

VELAZQUEZ, Workshop.

1212 «The Arch of Titus in Rome» (Canvas, 146 × 111 cm). This work is now attributed to Mazo, who visited Rome towards the end of his life.

1220 «Philip IV praying» (Canvas, 209 × 147 cm). Pendant to the following.

1222 «Queen Mariana praying» (Canvas, 209 × 147 cm). Pendant to No. 1220.

1194. Velázquez. The sculptor   1195. Velázquez. Don Diego
      Martínez Montañés.   de Corral y Arellano.

1202. Diego Velázquez. The Court dwarf Don Sebastián de Morra. (detail)

1239. Francisco de Zurbarán. St. Casilda.

1205. Velázquez. The jester «Calabacillas». 1201. Velázquez. Diego de Acedo.

2961 «An Italian palace» (Canvas, 56 × 36 cm).
2996 «Prince Balthasar Carlos» (Canvas, 121 × 96 cm).
VELAZQUEZ, Copies.
1223 «The poet Don Luis de Góngora y Argote» (Canvas, 59 × 46 cm). Copy of an original painted in 1622, now kept in the Museum in Boston.
1230 «Boar hunt in El Hoyo» (Canvas, 188 × 303 cm). This is a copy of the *Boar hunt in El Pardo (La tela real)*, painted about 1638 and now kept in the National Gallery in London.
2553 «Aesop» (Canvas, 180 × 93 cm). This is a copy of No. 1206.
2554 «Menippus» (Canvas, 179 × 93 cm). This is a copy of No. 1207.
VELAZQUEZ, Followers.
1225 «Portrait of Alonso Martínez de Espinar» (Canvas, 74 × 44 cm).
1233 «Prince Balthasar Carlos» (Canvas, 158 × 113 cm).
VIDAL, Pedro Antonio Vidal (active in Madrid in 1617).
1950 «Philip III» (Canvas, 200 × 135 cm). This is the only known work by this artist, who painted it in 1617.
VILADOMAT, Antonio Viladomat (Barcelona 1678-1755).
2662 «St. Augustine and the Holy Family» (Canvas, 107 × 72 cm).
VILLAFRANCA, Pedro de Villafranca (b. Alcolea, La Mancha; active between 1632 and 1678). This artist was primarily an engraver.
1232 «Philip IV» (Canvas, 203 × 125 cm).
VILLANDRANDO, Rodrigo de Villandrando (?-1621). This artist was a Court portraitist in the manner of Pantoja and Coello, who painted with particular care details of dress and royal attributes.
1234 «Philip IV and the dwarf Soplillo» (Canvas, 204 × 110 cm). Signed.
1234a «Isabella of Bourbon, wife of Philip IV» (Canvas, 201 × 115 cm). Signed.
VILLAVICENCIO, Pedro Núñez de Villavicencio (Seville 1644-1700). Sevillian School. He painted popular scenes influenced by Murillo.

1200. Velázquez. The jester   1206. Velázquez.   1208. Velázquez.
«Don Juan de Austria».   Aesop.   Mars.

1210. Velázquez. The Medici Gardens. 1213. Velázquez. The Fountain of the Tritons.

1235 «Boys playing dice» (Canvas, 238 × 207 cm).
XIMENEZ, Miguel Ximénez or Jiménez (documented between 1466 and 1503). Aragonese School.

2519 «The Resurrection between episodes from the Life of St. Michael and the Martyrdom of St. Catherine» (Wood, 70 × 40 cm each of the five panels). Signed. These panels come from an altar-piece in Ejea de los Caballeros and their quality is unequal, possibly due to the collaboration of another artist.
YAÑEZ, Fernando Yáñez de la Almedina (active between 1501 and 1531 in Valencia, Barcelona and Cuenca). He was a Castilian artist who trained in Florence, possibly in the workshop of Leonardo da Vinci. It is often difficult to distinguish his artistic personality from that of his permanent assistant Fernando de los Llanos. His works have a spacious composition with unadorned Renaissance architecture and Italian landscapes. His very Leonardesque figures are delicately modelled and light acts as a unifying element, fusing forms and contours with the characteristic *sfumato*.

1339 «St. Damian» (Octogonal panel, 95 × 73 cm).

2805 «St. Anne, the Virgin, St. Elizabeth and the infants St. John and Jesus» (Wood, 140 × 119 cm). This work possibly comes from the altarpiece of La Almedina and is one of the clearest examples of Leonardo's influence on the work of this artist.

2902 «St. Catherine» (Wood, 212 × 112 cm). This is considered one of the finest examples of Spanish Renaissance painting.

3081 «Madonna and Child» (Wood, 58 × 46 cm). Its attribution is doubtful.
YEPES, Tomás Yepes (or Hiepes) (Valencia c. 1600-1674). Valencian School. He was the chief Valencian still-life and flower painter.

3203 «Still life» (Canvas, 102 × 175 cm).

889. Velázquez and Mazo. View of Saragossa.

2803. Francisco de Zurbarán. Still life.

ZURBARAN, Francisco de Zurbarán (b. Fuente de Cantos, Extremadura 1598; d. Madrid 1664). Sevillian School. Zurbarán started his artistic training in Seville in 1614 and on completing his apprenticeship in 1617 moved back to his native region and settled in Llerena, where he married twice and where his son Juan, later also a painter, was born. From 1628 he was in Seville again working on important commissions at the head of his large workshop; Velázquez had left the city and Zurbarán and Cano were the foremost painters there until the latter left for Madrid in 1638 and Zurbarán remained the unrivalled master. In 1634 he spent several months in Madrid, probably invited by his friend Velázquez, and painted for the Hall of Realms in the Buen Retiro Palace. He was appointed Court painter, a purely honorary title because he returned to Seville at the end of the year. There he painted some of his greatest works, including series for the Carthusian monastery in Jerez and the Jeronymite convent in Guadalupe. However, a few years later his artistic career began its decline; the death of his wife affected him profoundly and commissions became scarcer. Financial difficulties obliged him to paint without respite for export to Spanish America, especially after the rapid success of Murillo in Seville. He had remarried in 1644 and moved to Madrid in 1658, where he died six years later.

Like his contemporaries Velázquez and Cano, Zurbarán received his artistic schooling at a time when the naturalistic style was at its height, combining objective representation of reality with the use of dramatic contrasted light effects that modelled the figures vigorously. He always remained faithful to this style, ignoring the changes in trend of the art of his time and concerning himself with the palpable nature of things in which he revealed a sort of hidden sculptural vocation. He simplified his compositions, discarded complicated narrative elements and showed no interest in atmospheric effects or the play of colours. Each object or figure in his paintings stands by itself, disconnected from its surroundings; this lack of a unified vision, which could be considered a defect, is what makes his works so attractive because Zurbarán seems to feel each piece of reality as something exceptional and unrepeatable and conveys this sense of uniqueness to his canvases. In this way, Zurbarán's figures and objects are extraordinarily plastic, his forms, although simple, acquire sober solemnity and his full colours shine with unusual splendour; the compelling physical presence of figures and objects in his pictures is heightened by their stillness and silence, thus making them strangely mysterious.

656 «The Defence of Cádiz against the English» (Canvas, 302 × 323 cm). This work was painted in 1634 for the Hall of Realms to commemorate an event occurred in 1625. The very static composition is rigorously divided into two planes: in the foreground we see Don Fernando Girón, seated, giving orders to his generals (without looking at them, a typical detail of Zurbarán's narrative inconsequence), who are arranged opposite him, all very upright and more or less in the same posture. Behind them the battle scene, with a very high horizon line, has the appearance of a backdrop and this impression is confirmed by the dark architectural element on the left imitating stage flies. This is one of Zurbarán's few non-religious works and was commissioned on his first visit to Madrid, probably at Velázquez's suggestion.

1236 «The Vision of St. Peter Nolasco» (Canvas, 179 × 223 cm). Signed and dated 1629. An angel is seen appearing to the saint and showing him the Heavenly Jerusalem. Like the following No., this work was painted for the convent of the Merced Calzada in Seville, for which he did a large number of commissioned works. The Tenebrist-style scene has a very simple triangular composition and is illuminated by the light of the vision with hardly any reference to space. Very characteristic of his style is the way in which he concentrates the scene in a reduced number of elements, which he represents realistically, giving the miraculous event a homely, normal air. Observe the rather rustic appearance of the angel, who seems a young boy dressed up, hard to imagine in flight.

1237 «The Apostle St. Peter appearing to St. Peter Nolasco» (Canvas, 179 × 223 cm). Signed and dated 1629. See No. 1236. This work follows the same compositional scheme. The saint's splendid cloak is a fine example of Zurbarán's skill.

1239 «St. Casilda» (Canvas, 184 × 90 cm). This work dates from 1640. This representation of a saint (only identified by the roses she carries) is one of many done by Zurbarán which composed one of the most attractive parts of his production; dressed in fashionable contemporary costumes these saints parade their splendid draperies with a surprising mixture of sophistication and bashfulness. St. Casilda's dress with its bold colours against the dark background and the masterly tactile quality of the crisp folds give the saint a majestic air.

1241 «Hercules separating the mountains of Calpe and Abyla» (Canvas, 136 × 167 cm). Together with the following Nos. (1242-50), this work was part of a series painted in 1634 on the labours of Hercules for the Hall of Realms, like No. 656. They do not belong to Zurbarán's best works, although it should be taken into account that they were painted for a very high spot where only their general effect would be appreciated.

1242 «Hercules killing Geryon» (Canvas, 136 × 167 cm). See No. 1241.

1243 «Hercules fighting with the Nemean lion» (Canvas, 151 × 166 cm). See No. 1241.

1244 «Hercules capturing the boar of Erymanthus» (Canvas, 132 × 153 cm). See No. 1241.

1245 «Hercules and the Cretan bull» (Canvas, 133 × 152 cm). See No. 1241.

1246 «Hercules fighting with Antaeus» (Canvas, 136 × 153 cm). See No. 1241.

1247 «Hercules and Cerberus» (Canvas, 132 × 151 cm). See No. 1241.

1248 «Hercules changing the course of the River Alpheus» (Canvas, 133 × 153 cm). See No. 1241.

1249 «Hercules fighting with the Lernean hydra» (Canvas, 133 × 167 cm). See No. 1241.

1250 «Hercules scorched by the shirt of the centaur Nessus» (Canvas, 136 × 167 cm). See No. 1241.

2442 «St. Diego of Alcalá» (Canvas, 93 × 99 cm). Dating from 1640, this work shows the saint with the bread transformed in roses.

2472 «St. Jacob de la Marca» (Canvas, 291 × 165 cm). Signed. This work was painted towards the end of his life, in 1658, for the convent of St. Diego of Alcalá in Madrid; it reveals Zurbarán's attempt to match Velázquez's achievements.

2594 «St. Luke before Christ on the Cross» (Canvas, 105 × 84 cm). This work was painted about 1635 and it has been suggested that the painter could be Zurbarán himself; it is rather unusual as a representation of St. Luke since the saint is traditionally portrayed painting the Virgin. It is a very Tenebrist work with an intense, but restrained dramatic effect.

656. Zurbarán. The Defence of Cádiz against the English.

1236. Zurbarán. Vision of St. Peter Nolasco.

2803 **«Still life»** (Canvas, 46 × 84 cm). Not many still lifes by Zurbarán are known, which is somewhat surprising since all his painting is to a certain extent still life, that is pleasure in materials, surface textures, bulk and consistencies. For this reason when he paints «just» a still life, Zurbarán produces such a prodigiously true and fascinating image. The four simple vessels lined up on the table suggest a serene, orderly domestic world where everything has its place and its individuality.

2888 **«Flowers»** (Canvas, 44 × 34 cm). Its attribution is doubtful, but it is an exceptional work.

2992 **«The Immaculate Conception»** (Canvas, 139 × 104 cm). Dating from 1630-35, this work shows an Immaculate Conception in the form of a modest, reserved girl who reflects the tenderness and purity that so many of Zurbarán's paintings transmit. It represents the traditional kind of static Immaculate Conception firmly standing on the waning moon and surrounded by the attributes of the litany, far removed from the upward movement of the High Baroque Immaculate Conceptions.

3009 **«Fray Diego de Deza, Archbishop of Seville»** (Canvas, 211 × 161 cm). Dating from 1631, this portrait was not painted from life as the sitter had died in 1623.

3010 **«St. Anthony of Padua»** (Canvas, 148 × 108 cm). In spite of the late date of this work (1640), Zurbarán still uses harsh light effects. The saint is portrayed contemplating the Christ Child he is holding in his arms. The compositional scheme is derived from the traditional representation of hermit saints: kneeling in front of a cave with a triangular opening where a landscape background can be observed.

3148 **«St. Euphemia»** (Canvas, 83 × 73 cm). This saint, who bears a saw as a symbol of her martyrdom, is another excellent example of this series of saints (see No. 1239), which should probably be regarded as «saintly portraits» or portraits of ladies in the guise of their patron saints.
ZURBARAN (?).

2572 **«A deceased ecclesiastic»** (?) (Canvas, 50 × 68 cm).

3006 **«St. Clare»** (Canvas, 152 × 79 cm). This is probably a work done by Zurbarán's studio.
ANONYMOUS SPANISH MASTERS.

s. n. **«Mural paintings from the church of San Baudelio in Casillas de Berlanga»** These six fragments, transferred to canvas, come from the Mozarabic church (11th century) of San Baudelio in Casillas de Berlanga in the province of Soria. They represent hunting scenes and reveal a strong Oriental character; they recall ivory and ceramic designs from the

115

time of the Caliphate. These paintings were removed and exported in 1926 to the United States, where they are now divided up among various museums. The ones on display here in the Prado are an unlimited loan from the Metropolitan Museum of New York.

s. n.   **«Mural paintings from the Santa Cruz hermitage in Maderuelo»** (Transferred to canvas). This interesting group of wall paintings reproduces the original state of the decoration of the hermitage in Maderuelo, in the province of Segovia, which was completely covered with murals by an anonymous artist whose style is closely related to that of the Master of Tahull, who worked in 1123.

295   **«Don Diego Hurtado de Mendoza»** (?) (Wood, 45 × 33 cm). 16th century.

528   **«Portrait of a 54-year-old man»** (Walnut wood, 57 × 44 cm). 16th century.

584   **«Christ bearing the Cross»** (Wood, 65 × 51 cm). Dated 1543.

652   **«Maria Louisa of Orleans, Queen of Spain»** (Canvas, 96 × 68 cm). School of Madrid: about 1680.

705 ⎫
to ⎬   **«Scenes from the life of John the Baptist»** These six panels, of different sizes, come from the Carthusian Monastery of Miraflores. They are by a 15th-century Hispano-Flemish artist.
710 ⎭

1249. Zurbarán. Hercules fighting with the Lernean hydra.

1037   **«Queen Isabella of Bourbon, first wife of Philip IV»** (Canvas, 126 × 91 cm). 17th century.

1066   **«A singer»** (Canvas, 68 × 56 cm). 17th century. Attributed to Ribalta.

1227   **«A girl»** (Canvas, 58 × 46 cm). School of Madrid; about 1660. Angulo attributes it to Antolínez, together with the following No.

1228   **«A girl»** (Canvas, 58 × 46 cm). This is the companion piece to No. 1227.

1260   **«The Virgin of the Catholic Kings»** (Wood, 123 × 112 cm). This Hispano-Flemish work from about 1490 represents the Virgin enthroned with the Child between St. Thomas and St. Dominic, adored by King Ferdinand and Queen Isabella, Prince Don Juan and Princess Doña Isabella, Fray Tomás de Torquemada and the chronicler Pedro de Anglería. It is an excellent work and reveals typically Flemish fondness for meticulous, realistic representation combined with a tendency to enhance the figures. It has been ascribed to Master Bartolomeus, who painted No. 1322.

1298   **«The Deposition»** (Wood, 128 × 78 cm). 15th-century Hispano-Flemish work based on a composition by D. Bouts.

1299   **«A conquistador»** (?) Wood, 33 × 24 cm). 16th century.

1311   «St. Gregory the Great» (Canvas, 138 × 99 cm). See No. 1314.

1312   «St. Jerome» (Canvas, 133 × 99 cm). See No. 1314.

1313   «St. Ambrose» (Canvas, 138 × 99 cm). See No. 1314.

1314   «St. Augustine» (Canvas, 133 × 99 cm). These four works are all by the same artist and date from the mid-17th century.

1317a «Juan José de Austria» (Canvas, 83 × 60 cm). School of Madrid; 17th c.

1321   «Retable of the Archbishop Don Sancho de Rojas». This splendid Gothic altar-piece comes from the church of San Benito in Valladolid, where it was substituted by another by Berruguete. It represents the life of Christ with episodes of His childhood and Passion. The central panel shows the Virgin and Child surrounded by angelic musicians, with St. Benedict, St. Bernard, the Archbishop Don Sancho de Rojas (identified by his coat-of-arms) being crowned by the Virgin, while the Child is crowning King Ferdinand of Aragón, the conqueror of Antequera. Italian influence can be observed in the general style. The colouring is fresh and bright, as can be appreciated in the panels that have been cleaned. 15th century.

1326   «The Archangel St. Michael» (Wood transferred to canvas, 242 × 153 cm). This work was painted by a Hispano-Flemish master about 1475. Post considers it the work of Juan Sánchez de Castro or one of his immediate followers. It is an excellent work with particularly fine draughtsmanship.

1329   «St. Gregory» (Wood, 76 × 60 cm). 16th c. Pendant to the following.

1331   «St. James the Elder» (Wood, 76 × 60 cm). Pendant to No. 1329.

1335   «The Virgin with a Knight of Montesa» (Wood, 102 × 96 cm). This is an exceptionally fine panel. It represents the Virgin and Child enthroned in a church between St. Benedict and St. Bernard with a knight of the Order of Montesa at her feet. The iconographic scheme is Flemish, but in the formal aspect the Italian influence predominates, not only in the Renaissance architectural elements, but also in the fullness of the forms and the use of light. The execution reveals great refinement and the figure of the Virgin is very beautiful, sweet and idealized. The work is closely related in style to those of Paolo di Sancto Leocadio, an Italian artist who worked in Valencia after 1472 summoned there by Alexander Borgia, later Pope Alexander VI.

1338   «The Virgin of the Rosary between St. Dominic and St. Peter the Martyr» (Wood, 134 × 150 cm). Valencian School; 16th century.

1955   «Knight of the Order of Santiago» (Canvas, 109 × 80 cm). 16th century.

2505   «A son of Francisco Ramos del Manzano» (Canvas, 168 × 85 cm). 17th c.

2516   «St. John the Baptist» (Wood, 96 × 60 cm). Late 15th-c. Castilian work.

2517   «The Martyrdom of St. Ursula» (Wood, 97 × 122 cm). 15th century.

2530   «Mater Dolorosa» (Canvas, 103 × 84 cm). 17th century.

2532   «Our Lady of Grace and the Masters of the Order of Montesa» (Wood, 128 × 105 cm). 15th century, repainted in the 18th century.

2534   «Charles II» (Canvas, 118 × 99 cm). 17th century.

2537   «Christ triumphant» (Wood, 151 × 173 cm). 15th-century Castilian work.

2538   «Scenes from the Life of Christ» (Triptych; central panel, 78 × 67 cm; side wings, 78 × 33 cm). This is possibly a work by the artist from Bruges Luis Alimbrot, who settled in Valencia. 15th century.

2665   «Two huntsmen» (Wood, 94 × 30 cm). 15th-century Castilian work.

2668   «Transfer of the body of St. James the Elder: embarkation in Jaffa» (Wood, 79 × 73 cm). This is the companion piece to the following No.

2669   «Transfer of the body of St. James the Elder: arrival in Galicia» (Wood, 79 × 73 cm). Pendant to No. 2668, 15th-c. Aragonese work.

2670   «The Martyrdom of St. Vincent» (Wood, 250 × 84 cm). See No. 2671.

2671   «The Martyrdom of St. Vincent» (Wood, 250 × 84 cm). These two panels were probably painted by a Valencian artist towards the end of the 15th century; they show a delightfully ingenuous representation of the martyrdom of the Levantine saint. They reveal a curious mixture of styles, in which the attempt to achieve linear perspective in some scenes contrasts with the treatment of the figures, painted like flat silhouettes, although with charming doll-like faces and tiny proportions.

2673   «The Martyrdom of St. Sebastian» (Wood, 86 × 80 cm). 15th-century Aragonese work.

2674   «St. Irene removing the arrows from St. Sebastian». This is the companion piece to the preceding work.

2676   «The Virgin of the Milk» (Wood, 58 × 32 cm). 16th-c. Aragonese work.

2681   «Beheaded saint and two donors» (Wood, 72 × 47 cm). 16th century.

2686   «Angelic musicians» (Wood, 130 × 33 cm). 16th century.

2687   «Still life» (Canvas, 30 × 44 cm). 17th century.

1260. Anonymous. The Virgin of the Catholic Kings.

2693a «The Saviour» (Wood, 34 × 25 cm). This work is by a 15th-century
Valencian artist, together with its companion piece. They are fine works,
related to the style of Rodrigo de Osona and Paolo di Sancto Leocadio.

2693b «Mater Dolorosa» (Wood, 34 × 25 cm). Pendant to the preceding No.

2707 «The Virgin and Child» (Wood, 161 × 92 cm). 15th century.

2717 «Pentecost» (Wood, 52 × 39 cm). 16th century Castilian work.

2720-1 «The Annunciation» (2 panels, 34 × 23 cm each). These two small panels
were painted by an unknown 15th-century Valencian artist and in spite of
their poor state of preservation the richness of the gilded or graffito-
decorated backgrounds can still be appreciated. The figures kneeling on the
tiled floor reveal elegant, refined draughtsmanship.

2778-9 «Pair of flower pieces» (Canvas, 104 × 65 cm). 17th century.

2829 «SS. Peter and Andrew» (Wood, 106 × 64 cm). 15th-cent. Aragonese work.

2830 «Alonso Cano» (Canvas, 47 × 40 cm). 17th century.

2833 «Brother Lucas Texero before the dead Venerable Father Bernadino of
Obregon» (Canvas, 108 × 163 cm). Dated 1627.

2834 «The Nativity» (Wood, 78 × 44 cm). This is the companion piece to the
following work. Angulo attributes it to Rodrigo de Osona the Younger, who
worked in Valencia between 1505 and 1513.

2835 «The Adoration of the Magi» (Wood, 78 × 44 cm). See No. 2834.

3015 «St. Nicholas» (Wood, 84 × 22 cm). 15th-century Aragonese work.

3016 «St. Thecla» (Wood, 83 × 23 cm). 15th-century Aragonese work.

3028 «Christ on the Way to Calvary» (Canvas, 181 × 283 cm). This work is by a
17th-century artist of the School of Madrid.

3055 «Altar frontal from Guills» (Wood, 92 × 175 cm). This frontal comes
from the church of San Esteban in Guills, Gerona. It represents the Pantocra-
tor surrounded by symbols of the Evangelists. Late 13th century.

3111 «St. Dominic». This work is by a 15th-century Valencian artist.

3112 «St. Gregory, St. Sebastian and St. Tirso» (Wood, 147 × 124 cm). This
work is by a 16th-century artist from Toledo.

3150 «Retable of St. Christopher». This 14th-century altar-piece with its emphasis on contours and a purely decorative use of colour is a good example of
Gothic linear style. The large figure of St. Christopher fills the centre; the
way water is represented around the saint's legs, full of fishes, is original.
The side wings show scenes from the lives of SS. Peter and Millan.

3159 «Still life» (Canvas, 100 × 227 cm). See Cerezo.

3196 «The earth» (Canvas, 245 × 160 cm). 17th-century Madrid work.

3197 «Water». This is a pendant to the preceding work.

FLEMISH MASTERS

The Prado houses a truly exceptional collection of paintings by Flemish masters. Spain's close commercial relations with the Netherlands from the 15th century onwards brought about a constant flow of artistic works, which influenced the style of Spanish painting until well into the 16th century. In this Museum we can admire really outstanding examples of the exquisite work of Rogier van der Weyden, Dieric Bouts, Hans Memling and many others and obtain a considerably complete vision of the splendour of Flemish art.

When the Netherlands became part of the Spanish dominions, under the Emperor Charles V, these artistic ties were further intensified. Philip II was both a fervent admirer of Titian and an enthusiastic collector of Flemish works, tracking them down where he could and having copies made of the works he could not purchase; he was responsible for bringing to Spain the excellent collection of pictures by Hieronymus Bosch, which is one of the Prado's chief attractions. It was in the 16th century that the differences began to become evident between the artists from the Northern part of the Netherlands, the part that was to become Holland in the 17th century, and those from Flanders in the South, where the Reformation had begun, already in the early 17th century, to divide the country between Catholics and Protestants, thus accentuating the existing national differences. 16th-century painting is represented here by several interesting panels of the Antwerp Mannerists, but mainly by the Romanists, the painters who studied in Italy and brought Renaissance ideas and styles to Flanders, for example Gossaert, called Mabuse, Van Orley, Pieter Coecke, Van Hemessen and other lesser-known but interesting artists. Together with these we find some of the best works by Patenier, the first great landscape painter, by Marinus van Reymerswaele, the precursor of *genre* painting, and above all Bruegel the Elder's famous *Triumph of Death*. The Prado also possesses a large number of portraits by Philip II's Court Painter, Anthonis Mor.

The Netherlands were definitively divided in the 17th century. Holland, independent and Protestant, created its own school of painting, which will be studied separately. Flanders remained within the Spanish orbit and Catholic. The greatest figure in 17th-century Flemish art was without doubt Peter Paul Rubens. He worked as Court Painter for the Duke of Mantua and later for the Governor-General of the Netherlands, Archduke Albert and his wife, the Infanta Isabella Clara Eugenia. He also visited Spain on two occasions and was highly admired by the King and his ministers, who tried to persuade him to stay in Spain as Court Painter. Rubens did not stay, but an astonishingly large number of his works ended up in the royal collection and can now be admired in the Prado. They are magnificent examples of his work, some of them having been kept by the artist in his own collection and acquired by Philip IV after Rubens' death at the auction of the artist's estate. The Prado also possesses a considerable number of works by Van Dyck, both religious and mythological scenes as well as portraits, the branch in which he excelled. Apart from these two exceptional representatives of 17th-century Flemish art, the Museum exhibits works by a host of painters who specialized in still lifes, flowers, landscapes and *genre* pictures that all reveal the high level of this school of painting, which constitutes one of the Prado's most complete sections.

ADRIAENSSEN, Alexander van Adriaenssen (Antwerp 1587-1661). A still life painter, he specialized in game and fish. He searched for compositional unity and balance, with homogeneous colouring and diffused light.

1341 **«Still life»** (Wood, 60 × 91 cm). Signed. The objects are arranged on a table parallel to the picture plane making them stand out against the dark background. The presence of a cat is a device resorted to frequently by some still-life painters to give a touch of life and «argument» to their pictures.

1342 **«Still life»** (Wood, 60 × 91 cm). Signed.

1343 **«Still life»** (Wood, 60 × 91 cm). Signed. In this work the handling is somewhat drier; as in the other still lifes, the objects slightly overlap the edges of the table.

1344 **«Still life»** (Wood, 59 × 91 cm). Signed.

AEKEN, Hieronymus van Aeken. See Bosch.

AELST. See Coecke.

ALSLOOT, Denis van Alsloot (b. Mechlin 1570; d. Brussels 1628). He worked at the Court of the Archduke Albert and Infanta Isabella Clara Eugenia and painted pictures commemorating solemn events and festivities, of great historical interest.

1346 «**Masked figures skating**» (Wood, 57 × 100 cm).

1347 «**Festival of the Ommeganck, the guildsmen's procession**» (Canvas 130 × 380 cm). Signed and dated 1616. This is the first of a series of paintings commemorating the Festival of the Ommeganck or Parrot, which the Infanta Isabella Clara Eugenia had restored in Brussels. The processions were held in the *Grande-Place*.

1348 «**Festival of the Ommeganck, the procession of Our Lady of the Sand**» (Canvas, 130 × 382 cm). Signed and dated 1616. See No. 1347.

2570 «**Festivity of Our Lady of the Woods**» (Canvas, 156 × 238 cm). Signed and dated 1616.

ARTHOIS, Jacques d'Arthois (Brussels 1613-1686). Landscape painter; his works usually contain woodlands arranged on either side of the picture with a path or stream leading the eye into the background.

1351 «**Landscape**» (Wood, 115 × 144 cm). Signed.

1352 «**Landscape with a river**» (Canvas, 140 × 200 cm). This work is typical of his style, with trees and water suggesting pleasant, shady spots in a wood.

1353 «**Landscape with a lake**» (Canvas, 36 × 42 cm). Signed.

1354 «**Landscape**» (Wood, 41 × 66 cm).

1355 «**Landscape**» (Wood, 40 × 66 cm).

1359 «**Walk along a river-bank**» (Canvas, 245 × 242 cm). As in other paintings Arthois makes the landscape come to life with the addition of small figures enjoying the pleasing, calm countryside.

ARTHOIS, School.

2746 «**Landscape with huntsmen**» (Wood, 39 × 66 cm).

2747 «**Landscape with huntsmen**» (Wood, 39 × 65 cm).

BALEN, Hendrick van Balen. See Bruegel and van Balen.

BEERT. See Beet.

BEET, Osias Beet or Beert (Antwerp c. 1580-1624). He was the main Flemish still-life painter at the beginning of the 17th century.

1606 «**Still life**» (Wood, 43 × 54 cm). Signed. This work is characteristic of his style, descriptive and masterly. He used a raised viewpoint and homogeneous colouring.

BEKE, Joos van der Beke. See Cleve.

BENEDETTI, Andries Benedetti (active in Antwerp between 1636-1641). A follower of Jan de Heem (see Dutch Masters).

2091 «**Table with sweetmeats**» (Canvas, 121 × 145 cm). This work was previously attributed to an anonymous follower of Heem. It is a very scenographic still life, which seeks to convey spaciousness and a rich decorative effect.

2093 «**Cupboard**» (Canvas, 121 × 147 cm). See the preceding No.

BENSON, Ambrosius (b. ?; d. Bruges 1550). A native of Lombardy, Ambrosius Benson worked all his life in Bruges. His painting derives from the 15th-century Flemish masters, especially Gerard David, and catches the sense of calm and patterning of the latter's compositions, but interprets them with greater taste for plasticity and bulk of the figures. The Prado has seven panels by this artist brought from a chapel of the Holy Cross Church (Santa Cruz) in Segovia.

1303 «**Santo Domingo de Guzmán**» (Wood, 104 × 57 cm). A small scene from the life of the saint, praying in the desert, appears in the background.

1304 «**St. Thomas (?) and a donor**» (Wood, 104 × 57 cm). The donor could have been the Bachiller Juan Pérez de Toledo, who is buried in the chapel from which this altar-piece proceeds.

1927 «**Pietà**» (Wood, 124 × 60 cm). The draughtsmanship is particularly fine.

1928 «**Entombment of Christ**» (Wood, 125 × 60 cm). The artist avoids a dramatic treatment of the scene.

1929 «**The Nativity of the Virgin**» (Wood, 115 × 60 cm). This panel reveals the same clear, calm arrangement as the rest of the series.

1933 «**St. Anne, the Child Jesus and the Virgin**» (Wood, 125 × 90 cm). The different measurements of this panel presumably indicate that it comes from another altar-piece. In the fantastic architecture of the canopy elements of Gothic tradition are combined with some new Renaissance forms. It is interesting to observe the artist's precise, descriptive taste in portraying nature. An echo of Leonardo can be found in the technique and the landscape.

1935 «**The embrace before the Golden Gate**» (Wood, 115 × 60 cm).

BESCHEY, Jacob Andries Beschey (Antwerp 1710-1786).

2364 «**The raising of the Cross**» (Wood, 46 × 35 cm). This work is inspired in an original by Rubens in the Cathedral at Antwerp.

BLOEMEN, Jan Frans van Bloemen, «Orizzonte» (b. Antwerp 1662; d. Rome 1749). Resident in Rome from 1680, he painted landscapes in the Classicist style created by the French artists who worked in the Eternal City.

1607 **«Landscape near Rome»** (Canvas, 47 × 56 cm). Signed and dated 1704.
1608 **«Landscape»** (Canvas, 35 × 47 cm).

BLOEMEN, Peeter van Bloemen (Antwerp 1657-1720). A brother of Jan Frans van Bloemen, he also lived in Rome, painting landscapes in Classicist style, but full of figures, animals and ruins.

1362 **«Caravan»** (Canvas, 46 × 49 cm). Signed and dated 1704.
2155 **«Travellers' rest»** (Canvas, 61 × 80 cm).

BOEL, Peter Boel (b. Antwerp 1622; d. Paris 1674). A painter of landscapes and hunting scenes, he used a technique similar to that of Fyt. His still lifes follow the somewhat extravagant style common to Flemish painting of the time, tending to group his objects vertically. His compositions are less skilful than those of Snyders or Fyt, but his pictorial quality is equally excellent.

1363 **«Game and dogs»** (Canvas, 117 × 313 cm). Signed. The composition is dominated by the figure of the swan, a frequent motif in his still lifes, which traces a long diagonal.
1364 **«Provisions»** (Canvas, 172 × 251 cm). This is a motley composition in which game, fruit and other objects literally fill the whole scene.
1365 **«Provisions»** (Canvas, 172 × 251 cm).
1366 **«Still life»** (Canvas, 168 × 237 cm). This is a symmetrical composition, open to a seascape background; as usual, live animals give it a touch of life.
1367 **«Arms and accoutrements»** (Canvas, 169 × 313 cm). Signed.
1879 **«Otters attacked by dogs»** (Canvas, 64 × 177 cm). This work was previously ascribed to Paul de Vos, although with doubts.

BORKENS, Jan Baptiste Borkens (Antwerp 1611-1675). He was influenced by Rubens.

1368 **«The apotheosis of Hercules»** (Canvas, 189 × 212 cm). Signed. It follows a composition by Rubens.
1369 **«The apotheosis of Hercules»** (Canvas, 98 × 98 cm). This is a copy by Juan Bautista del Mazo.

2052. Bosch. The Path of Life (exterior of The Hay-Cart).

BOSCH, Hieronymous van Aeken Bosch, called «El Bosco» in Spain (b. 's-Hertogenbosch c. 1450-1516). Bosch was born in a small village in the North of the Netherlands, in the province that was to become Holland at the political division of the country, and far from the cultural and artistic centres of the time, such as Bruges, Ghent and Antwerp in the South or Haarlem and Utrecht in the North. Son and grandson of painters, he learnt the rudiments of his art in the modest family workshop, copying popular illustrations and engravings and familiarizing himself, although at a distance, with the stylistic development of the important 15th century Flemish masters. He possibly travelled in his youth because his work reveals first-hand acquaintance with Dieric Bouts, Massys and particularly with Northern artists like Geertgen Tot Sint Jans or the Master of the Virgo inter Virgines. However, Bosch must have spent the rest of his lifetime in his native village; very few biographical notes on Bosch exist, but thanks to archive documents we know that he was married and from 1486 on belonged to the Brotherhood of Our Lady, which maintained close ties with the more important Brethren of the Common Life, a deeply spiritual, reforming and ascetic movement, whose ideas are reflected in Bosch's enigmatic art. The Brothers considered that the pleasures and temptations of this world, cruelty and ambition were the sure way to Hell and could only be opposed with virtues, humility, charity and meditation; they censured the corrupt medieval clergy, a criticism that also appears in Bosch's pictures. This atmosphere of moralizing mysticism is without doubt reflected in his art. On the other hand, Bosch must have been a cultured man, well-acquainted with the religious and profane literature of his time, as is proved in his painting by constant quotations and allusions to definite works. He cannot deny, however, a certain popular vein, which comes out in his use of proverbs and sayings, sometimes almost acquiring the form of religious allegories with a deep symbolic and moralizing significance. On the other hand we find in his painting the esoteric world of alchemy, the medieval pseudo-science that represented a constant source of inspiration to Bosch and remains for us today in many cases wrapped in mystery. Some interpreters of Bosch's art have tried to identify the fantastic garments and headdresses that appear in his paintings with the costumes worn by the actors in the *Misterios* or religious miracle-plays so popular in the Middle Ages, or in the processions and other festivities organized by the Brotherhood of Our Lady. Other Bosch critics consider the artist a precursor of 20th-century surrealism and his paintings the work of a neurotic on the verge of insanity, whose pictures should be interpreted in the light of Freudian psychology. A great deal of this is no doubt true, particularly with regard to Bosch's constant repetition of erotic symbols, his obsessions and phantasies bordering on perversion, but on the other hand Bosch is also the portrayer of his fellow human beings and not only of his own intimate sentiments. Nobody has depicted as critically as he the passions and vices, anxieties and misery of mankind, the moral depravity and man's lack of sensibility with regard to his destiny. Bosch is more concerned with the contents of his paintings than with the form; his style is archaistic, his compositions are symmetrical and at times rigid, his figures delicate and almost transparent; in spite of his painstakingly scrupulous attention to detail, the artist does not dwell on these details with the exquisite care of the Flemish masters. On the contrary, a desire for abstractness can be felt in his long brushstrokes which sometimes contract his forms. In his spacious compositions with their high horizon-lines the landscape seems to be viewed from a tower, with the world stretching out at the feet of the artist, who gives free rein to his imagination; groups and scenes pass by in quick succession, nature is interwoven with the creatures of the artist's mind; the dividing-line between the human and the animal world is blurred so that the monstruous, deformed beings appear real. Bosch's works were highly admired by his contemporaries and Philip II of Spain was a particularly enthusiastic collector of his paintings. His fame spread abroad and although he had no followers, many artists tried to imitate him. Bruegel was probably the painter who caught Bosch's satirical and fantastic spirit best, without limiting himself to purely formal imitation as other artists.

2048 **«The Adoration of the Magi»** (Signed triptych. Central panel: 138 × 72 cm; wings: 138 × 34 cm). The closed triptych represents St. Gregory's Mass. Inside, the Adoration of the Magi and on the side wings St. Peter and St. Inés accompanying the donors. Dating probably from about 1510, it is one of Bosch's later masterpieces. It reveals an advanced technique in colouring and *chiaroscuro;* the figures have acquired a more monumental character and individuality; the landscape stretches into the distance more naturally and convincingly than in his earlier works, whereas the monochrome and abstract view of the city of Jerusalem in the background comes close to our modern sensibility. It is one of Bosch's clearest paintings, although some figures and elements are difficult to interpret. On the left-hand panel, which portrays St. Peter, St. Joseph can be seen in the background drying the Child's swaddling-clothes over a fire and still further back, in the landscape, a group of peasants dance to the music of a bagpipe, an instrument that symbolized carnal sins. On the right-hand panel the artist depicts violence and crime. Bosch's imagination appears at its freest in the central panel. The richly dressed Magi, whose clothes are decorated with biblical scenes, offer their gifts to the Child. In the shack, the most controversial point in the composition, there are disturbing figures, like the shepherds on the roof, where we see the bagpipe again, and the half-naked man in the doorway, who has been interpreted by some as representing the Antichrist, whose army is preparing in the background to attack the heavenly Jerusalem.

2052. Bosch. The Hay-Cart.   2049. Bosch. The Temptation of St. Anthony.

2049   **«The Temptation of St. Anthony»** (Wood, 70 × 51 cm). Like the preceding work, this is one of the artist's late panels, in which he expressed admirably his imagination and symbolism. The saint seems to have attained a state of spiritual serenity through meditation after his temptations. He is surrounded by monstrous, demon-like creatures. In the foreground an iridescent reptile with horns represents woman as temptation; at the saint's feet lies a pig, the symbol of St. Anthony, with a bell in its ear, which was a means of identifying animals in villages and towns as belonging to the convent.

2052   **«The Hay-Cart»** (Triptych. Central panel: 135 × 100 cm; side wings: 135 × 45 cm). Signed. The closed triptych shows the *Path of Life,* lined with dangers and temptations. Inside, the left-hand wing represents the creation of Adam and Eve, the Temptation and their expulsion from Paradise, the cause of all the ills of mankind. In the centre, we see the hay-cart, which is probably one of the easiest scenes to interpret of all Bosch's works as it is inspired by the old Flemish proverb: «The world is a hay-cart from which every man takes what he can». Watched by Christ, men are busy trying to grab what they can from an enormous cart laden with hay and drawn by demons, which symbolizes the misleading comforts and pleasures of life. On the left, the mighty, the Emperor and the Pope, followed by noblemen, arrive in ostentatious cavalcade; lower down, poor people and beggars also want their share; in the foreground we see members of the clergy who have already taken their stock in large sacks to the convent, where monks and nuns are enjoying it in private. The picture is full of violence and bloodshed, but here and there we can discover a peaceful scene; a group of women and children make up one of the most placid settings, although one of the women is a gypsy deceiving a lady by telling her fortune from her hand; another such haven of peace is formed by a couple of lovers making music on top of the hay-cart, oblivious to what is going on around them, although the owl and the jug, symbolizing malice and lust, and the strange demon playing a trumpet, imply that they are doomed to damnation. On the right-hand wing, Hell is depicted with all its punishments for Man's sins. *The Hay-cart* is one of the most important of Bosch's satirical and moralistic allegories that has fortunately been handed down to us intact.

2056 **«The Cure for Folly»** (Wood, 48 × 35 cm). This is one of Bosch's earliest and most controversial works. The inscription that surrounds the picture says: «Master, extract this stone from me, my name is castrated badger» (that is, a fool or simpleton). The painting has been interpreted by some art critics as a satire on medieval charlatans and quack doctors who took advantage of people's ignorance and claimed to cure insanity by extracting from a person's forehead the stone that was supposed to cause it. Other experts have ventured a more complicated interpretation. According to this, the surgeon is extracting not a stone, but a flower, a medieval symbol of castration. The jug and the funnel are frequent sexual representations and could therefore be associated with the main theme: castration of a man in order to be accepted in one of the numerous religious, heretical sects that flourished in the Middle Ages, which considered that castration eliminated the source of human passions. Possibly the most beautiful aspect of the picture is the landscape with its lyrical simplicity and serenity.

2695 **«A crossbowman»** (Wood, 28 × 20 cm). This painting is a repetition, with some variations, of the head of a soldier from a lost *Crown of Thorns,* known thanks to a copy preserved in the Museum of Antwerp.

2822. Bosch. The Table of the Seven Deadly Sins.

2822 **«The Table of the Seven Deadly Sins»** (Wood, 120 × 150 cm). Signed. This work belonged to Philip II, who kept it in his rooms at El Escorial. It is one of the artist's earliest known works, and in it he anticipated the particular style and subject-matter of his later production. Forming a circle around the central figure of Christ, we see seven scenes depicting the seven deadly sins, portrayed with all of Bosch's characteristic vitality and imagination. Each scene bears an inscription to identify it. Anger is a scene of violence and jealousy; Pride is represented by a demon holding up a mirror to a woman; Lust is portrayed by two couples of lovers inside a tent being entertained by a jester, while musical instruments lie abandoned on the ground, including a harp, a theme which will later be repeated in *The Garden of Delights;* Sloth is represented by a woman dressed for church trying to wake up a sleeping man; Gluttony is depicted by a table full of foodstuffs and two men devouring greedily; Avarice is a judge accepting a bribe and Envy illustrates the Flemish saying: «Two dogs seldom come to an agreement over the same bone».

2823 **«The Garden of Delights»** (Triptych. Central panel: 220 × 195 cm; side wings: 220 × 97 cm). This work probably dates from the last decade of the artist's life and is one of his most famous and enigmatic pictures. The closed triptych represents the *Creation of the World* in grisaille, seen inside a glass bowl symbolizing the fragility of the Universe. What we find inside is without doubt the height of the artist's creative imagination and its interpretation remains controversial. One art historian believes it to illus-

2822. Bosch. The Table of the Seven Deadly Sins (detail).

trate the doctrines of the Adamites or Brethren of the Free Spirit, a heretical religious sect that was widely spread in Northern Europe in the Middle Ages. They sought a return to a state of purity prior to the Fall which they hoped to attain by means of sexual liberty and rites involving nude men and women who tried to free their souls through their bodies. Bosch was maybe familiar with the doctrines of this sect and made use of its rites in his work, but it is unlikely that he actually belonged to it himself. For this reason, the traditional interpretation which considers *The Garden of Delights* a moralistic satire, similar to *The Hay-Cart,* is probably closer to the truth. As in the latter work, we see Paradise on the left, in the centre Mankind in pursuit of worldly pleasures, symbolized in this case by the strawberries and *madroño* berries which all are so keen to pick, and on the right, Hell with its punishments. Paradise abounds with plants, birds and animals; in the middle an owl looks out of a curiously-shaped fountain, which represents Knowledge for some critics and Evil for others. In the foreground Adam is seen sitting under an exotic dragon-tree, symbol of Life, whereas Eve, on the right, is shown introducing lust and vice into the world symbolized by rabbits, toads, serpents and fantastic monsters. The central panel contains groups of people and animals, plants and fabulous constructions, which has all been interpreted as an allegory on the pursuit of carnal pleasures, symbolized by the strawberries that everyone is eating and offering to others. Some groups are easy to explain, for example the lovers in a glass bubble, illustrating the popular saying: «Pleasure is as fragile as glass». The outsize clam or mussel shell, which represented the female sex in the Middle Ages, represents mankind as a prisoner of pleasure. A bit higher up there is a cavalcade of figures riding on the backs

2823. Bosch. The Garden of Delights (detail).

of animals and monsters; some critics have interpreted them as men carried by their vices. In the centre there is a pond, which apparently continues in the upper part of the picture and represents the Fountain of Youth. Bosch's vision of Hell in this work is probably the best and most dramatic he painted. A strange monster with an egg-shaped body and legs that resemble dried-up tree trunks balances on its head a round platform with a pink bagpipe, once again an allusion to the male and female sex. Some art historians are of the opinion that the face is a self-portrait of the artist, who appears in a hell of ice, no doubt an allusion to Dante's *Divine Comedy;* this figure has been considered by some critics to represent the alchemist in different stages of boiling mercury, while others believe it to represent the corrupt Universal Man. Lower down, the abandoned musical instruments symbolize punishments for carnal sins. In the foreground, gamblers are suffering punishment. On the right we see the dissolute clergy, personified by a pig dressed as an abbess trying to beguile a man into signing a will, representing those who get rich by means of false bequests, although some critics believe this scene to refer to the sale of Papal bulls, which was one of the reasons of the corruption of the Church in the Middle Ages and gave rise to the Reformation. The most beautiful part of this scene of Hell is without doubt the background of a city on fire.

2913 **«The Temptation of St. Anthony Abbot»** (Wood, 70 × 115 cm). This is another version of the saint's temptation. It is considered by some art historians to be an imitation by another artist copying Bosch's style.

3085 **«The Temptation of St. Anthony»** (Wood, 88 × 72 cm). This is possibly one of the three «Temptation» scenes that Philip II is known to have sent to El Escorial in 1574.
BOSCH, Copies.

2050 **«The Temptation of St. Anthony»** (Wood, 90 × 37 cm). This is a smaller-scale copy of one of the wings of a triptych on the same subject kept in the Museum of Lisbon.

2051 **«The Temptation of St. Anthony»** (Wood, 97 × 37 cm). This is a copy after an untraceable work by Bosch.
BOSCH, Imitations.

2054 **«Moral fantasy»** (Wood, 29 × 24 cm). This work is inspired by the scenes of Hell from Bosch's *Garden of Delights.*

2055 **«An angel leading a soul through Hell»** (Wood, 135 × 78 cm).

2096 **«Landscape in Hell»** (Wood, 49 × 64 cm). This painting has been ascribed to Bosch, in which case it would be a late work.
BOSMANS, Andries Bosmans (b. Antwerp 1621; d. Rome 1681). Painter specialized in flowers, in the manner of Seghers.

1370 **«Garland with St. Anne, the Virgin and Child»** (Wood, 85 × 55 cm). Signed. The figures are considered to be the work of Cornelius Schut.
BOUDEWYNS, Adriaan Frans Boudewyns (b. Brussels 1644; d. after 1700). His landscapes are well-balanced and serene, with sparse masses of trees bordering on placid open spaces containing figures and animals. He was a pupil of Van der Stock and worked in Paris at the Court of Louis XIV.

1371 **«Landscape with shepherds»** (Wood, 26 × 38 cm).

1372 **«Landscape with houses»** (Wood, 31 × 43 cm).

1373 **«Landscape»** (Wood, 31 × 43 cm). The influence of Arthois' landscapes on Boudewyns' style is evident. Nature is depicted as a harmonious setting for human activities (tending the flocks, hunting or just strolling) against a pleasing background of woods, streams and peaceful skies.

1374 **«Path on a river-bank»** (Wood, 31 × 43 cm).

1375 **«Landscape with shepherds»** (Wood, 25 × 35 cm).

1376 **«Flock»** (Wood, 32 × 43 cm).

1377 **«A harbour»** (Wood, 32 × 43 cm). Observe the beautiful effect of the sunset which bathes the scene in golden light blurring the contours.

1378 **«Landscape with shepherds»** (Wood, 25 × 35 cm).

1379 **«A harbour»** (Canvas, 35 × 57 cm).

1382 **«View of a village»** (Canvas, 35 × 44 cm). Previously attributed to Peter Bout.

2082 **«Landscape with shepherds and their flock»** (Canvas, 42 × 61 cm). This and the following paintings have been attributed to Jan Glauber, but the Museum's present Catalogue of Flemish Paintings ascribes them to Boudewyns.

2083 **«A rest on the way»** (Canvas, 43 × 63 cm). See No. 2082.

2084 **«Landscape with ruins»** (Canvas, 43 × 69 cm). See No. 2082.

2085 **«A halt on the way»** (Canvas, 43 × 62 cm). See No. 2082.

BOUT, Peter Bout (Brussels 1658-1719). A landscape and *genre* painter, he lived in Paris for many years.

1380 «Skaters» (Wood, 27 × 43 cm).

1381 «The village square» (Wood, 27 × 43 cm). Signed and dated 1678. It belongs to the typically Flemish type of anecdotic landscape painting.

1382 See Boudewyns.

BOUTS, Aelbrecht Bouts (Louvain c. 1460-1549). Son of Dieric Bouts, his painting is inferior to his father's and shows the influence of Hugo van der Goes.

2698 «Head of Christ» (Wood, 30 cm in diameter). This subject is frequently repeated by Bouts, often in conjunction with the Sorrowing Virgin. His inspiration was probably derived from his father's compositions.

BOUTS, Follower.

2672 «Portrait» (Wood, 33 × 32 cm). There is a similar one in Dijon.

BOUTS, Dieric Bouts (b. Haarlem c. 1420; d. Louvain 1475). He spent most of his life in Louvain. His work shows the influence of Van Eyck and particularly Rogier van der Weyden.

1461 «Annunciation - Visitation - Adoration of the Angels - Adoration of the Magi» (Triptych. Central panel, 80 × 105 cm; side wings, 80 × 56 cm). This is considered Bouts' earliest known work. Each scene is set in an arch with scenes on the archivolt, a style invented by Van der Weyden. However, the figures are reminiscent of Van Eyck in their fullness and have a completely personal lighting effect.

BRILL, Paul Brill (b. Antwerp 1554; d. Rome 1626). Landscape painter who worked in France and Italy. He was inspired by the Italian landscape and had contacts with Elsheimer; his work influenced Poussin and Claude Lorrain.

1385 See Coninxloo.

1386 See Anonymous Flemish Masters.

1388 See Gysels.

1849 «Landscape with Psyche and Jupiter» (Canvas, 93 × 128 cm). This work does not attempt to offer a panoramic effect, but a close vision of nature. A vaguely romantic mood underlies its solid, well-balanced composition.

BROECK (?), Crispin van der Broeck (Mechlin 1524-1591).

1389 «The Holy Family» (Wood, 88 × 104 cm). The Virgin with St. Joseph and the Child, accompanied by St. Elizabeth, Zacharias and the infant St. John. The artist insists on the linear values of the composition. Its attribution is doubtful.

BROUWER, Adriaen (b. Oudenarde 1605/6; d. Antwerp 1638).

1391-2 See Teniers, David.

2731 «The combing» (Wood, 17 × 14 cm). Brouwer was one of the first to paint rural *genre* scenes. His light style with its fluid technique was followed by David Teniers.

1461. Bouts. Triptych.

BRUEGEL, Jan Bruegel «de Velours» (Antwerp 1568-1625). Son of Pieter Bruegel «the Elder», he cultivated many different types of painting in a very original manner and with an extremely precise, meticulous technique, resembling that of the miniaturists. The heritage of the great Primitives comes to life and gives his works their luxurious appearance which earned him his nickname. Nature and life are represented in his paintings as a grand show, pleasing to the senses, which he observed with the utmost attention and a typically Flemish spirit of intellectual curiosity. This induced him to load his compositions with all kinds of objects without, however, losing sight of the work's unity. He spent some time in Italy, where Cardinal Borromeo protected him, and in Brussels he worked at the Court of the Archduke Albert and Infanta Isabella Clara Eugenia. He frequently collaborated with other artists (Franken II, Momper, Van Balen, Brill, Rubens) and was held in high esteem by his contemporaries. The Prado possesses an outstanding collection of his works.

1394 **«Allegory on Sight»** (Wood, 65 × 109 cm). Signed and dated 1617. This work is the first of a series of allegories on the five senses. Bruegel takes pleasure in the detailed description of objects with his characteristic, meticulous brush-strokes. *Sight* is illustrated by means of a «collector's cabinet» crowded with paintings, sculptures (almost all of them identifiable) and all kinds of valuable objects. These allegories are typical of Bruegel and he owed a great deal of his popularity to them. The human figures that appear in this series are now generally considered to be by Rubens.

1395 **«Allegory on Hearing»** (Wood, 65 × 107 cm). Venus (or possibly Euterpe) sings to the accompaniment of Cupid, surrounded by deer (symbol of hearing), birds and all kinds of musical instruments and clocks. The pictures on the wall refer to music. See No. 1394.

1396 **«Allegory on Smell»** (Wood, 64 × 109 cm). Signed. A nymph (or Flora) is portrayed in the midst of a variety of flowers in a garden. We should bear in mind that flowers were a favourite subject for Bruegel. See No. 1394.

1397 **«Allegory on Taste»** (Wood, 64 × 110 cm). A nymph and a satyr are dining at a splendid table; the opulent still life in the foreground is typical of Flemish art. See No. 1394.

1398 **«Allegory on Touch»** (Wood, 65 × 110 cm). The nymph who is kissing a little Cupid is surrounded by objects whose smoothness or roughness allude to the sense of touch. See No. 1394.

1399 See Bruegel and Van Balen.

1400 See Jan Bruegel II.

1403 See Bruegel, Van Balen and others.

1404 See Bruegel, Van Balen and others.

1406 See Bruegel, Workshop and copies.

1407 See Bruegel, Workshop and copies.

1408 See Jan Bruegel II.

1410 **«Heaven on Earth»** (Copper, 59 × 41 cm).

1411 See Bruegel and Rubens.

1412 **«St. John preaching»** (Copper, 44 × 57 cm). The subject is handled like a *genre* painting and at the same time importance is attached to the landscape.

1414 See Bruegel and Van Balen.

1416 **«Garland of fruit and flowers with the Virgin and Child»** (Wood, 48 × 41). This type of picture was invented by Bruegel and due to its great success was imitated by many artists.

1417 See Bruegel and Procaccini.

1418 See Rubens and Jan Bruegel.

1419 See Veerendael.

1421 **«Flowers»** (Copper, 48 × 35 cm). Flowers were one of Bruegel's favourite subjects. He painted them from life, waiting to observe them blossom each year. The colouring is particularly fresh.

1422 **«Flowers»** (Wood, 44 × 66 cm).

1423 **«Flowers»** (Wood, 49 × 39 cm).

1424 **«Flowers»** (Wood, 47 × 35 cm).

1425 **«Flowers on a plate»** (Canvas, 43 × 33 cm).

1426 **«Flowers»** (Canvas, 41 × 33 cm).

1427 **«Path in a wood»** (Wood, 40 × 62 cm). In his landscapes Bruegel gradually departed from the three conventional colour-schemes (browns, greens and blues) traditionally used by 16th-century Flemish artists to achieve a more homogeneous colouring.

1430 **«Landscape with windmill»** (Wood, 34 × 50 cm).

1431 **«Landscape»** (Wood, 40 × 62 cm).

1432 **«Gypsy gathering in a wood»** (Wood, 36 × 43 cm).

1433 **«Landscape with wagons»** (Wood, 33 × 43 cm). Signed and dated 1603.

1434 **«The Archduke and Infanta hunting»** (Canvas, 135 × 246 cm). Originally attributed to his son, this work reveals a sense of balance between the diagonals and horizontals, as well as a delicate handling of the foliage, that is characteristic of Bruegel de Velours.

1435 **«Windmills»** (Canvas, 16 × 27 cm).

2052. Hieronymus Bosch. The Hay-cart.

1395. Bruegel de Velours. Allegory on Hearing.

1436 «Mountain path» (Canvas, 16 × 27 cm).
1438 «Wedding banquet» (Canvas, 130 × 265 cm). Signed and dated 1623. Landscapes with figures illustrating popular customs were a very frequent subject in Flemish art, which liked to combine curious scenes with enjoyable surroundings. Bruegel is an excellent exponent of this kind of painting and the precision of his technique enables him to dwell on details without losing sight of the whole.
1439 «Peasant dance before the Archduke and Infanta» (Canvas, 130 × 226 cm). Signed and dated 1623.
1440 See Momper, Joost de.
1441 «Country wedding» (Canvas, 184 × 126 cm).
1442 «Wedding banquet presided over by the Archduke and Infanta» (Canvas, 84 × 126 cm). The Archduke and Infanta attending country fêtes and weddings seem to have lived a very different life from the strict rules of the Spanish Court. Bruegel has succeeded in reproducing in this scene the lively atmosphere of merry-making and high spirits.
1443 See Momper, Joost de.
1444 «Country life» (Canvas, 130 × 293 cm).
1445 See Anonymous Flemish Masters.
1447-50 See Bruegel, Workshop and copies.
1451 See Anonymous Flemish Masters.
1452 See Bruegel, Workshop and copies.
1453 «The Palace of the Infanta Isabella Clara Eugenia in Brussels» (Canvas, 126 × 153 cm). Previously listed as anonymous.
1455 See Bruegel, Workshop and copies.
1588-91 See Momper, Joost de.
1885 «Forest» (Wood, 47 × 80 cm).
2096 «Hell» (Wood, 54 × 78 cm). This painting repeats subjects from works by Bosch. It was previously listed as anonymous.

1439. Bruegel de Velours. Peasant Dance before the Archduke and Infanta.

BRUEGEL and Van Balen. Hendrick van Balen (Antwerp 1575-1632) frequently collaborated with landscape artists by painting the figures in their works.

1399 «The four elements» (Wood, 62 × 105 cm).

1414 «Garland with the offering to the goddess Cybele» (Wood, 106 × 73 cm).

BRUEGEL, Van Balen and others.

1403 «Sight and smell» (Canvas, 176 × 264 cm). Both senses are personified and portrayed in the spacious setting of a picture gallery. In the present catalogue of the Museum, M. Díaz Padrón identifies the style of various different artists, including Frans Franken II. This way of producing a work of art collectively was a normal practice among Flemish painters at the time and far from reducing its value, enhanced the picture's merits.

1404 «Hearing, touch and taste» (Canvas, 176 × 264 cm). This is the companion piece to the preceding work.

BRUEGEL and Procaccini.

1417 «Garland with the Virgin and Child and two angels» (Copper, 48 × 36 cm).

BRUEGEL and Rubens.

1411 «The vision of St. Hubert» (Wood, 63 × 100 cm). The figure of the saint, patron of huntsmen, is by Rubens.

1411. Bruegel and Rubens. The Vision of St. Hubert.

BRUEGEL, Workshop and copies.

1406 «Heaven on earth» (Copper, 57 × 88 cm).

1407 «The animals entering Noah's Ark» (Copper, 56 × 88 cm).

1447 «Flowers» (Wood, 37 × 27 cm).

1448 «Flowers» (Wood, 37 × 27 cm). Companion piece to No. 1447.

1449 «Flowers» (Canvas, 181 × 70 cm).

1450 «Flowers» (Canvas, 181 × 70 cm). Companion piece to No. 1449.

1452 «Heaven on earth» (Copper, 36 × 50 cm).

1455 «A forest and houses» (Wood, 57 × 86 cm).

1732 «Landscape» (Copper, 47 × 73 cm). Previously attributed to Schoevardts.

BRUEGEL II, Jan Bruegel «the Younger» (Antwerp 1601-1678). He inherited the workshop from his father, Bruegel «de Velours», and imitated his style.

1400 «The four elements» (Wood, 65 × 111 cm). This is a copy after a work (No. 1399) by Bruegel and Van Balen.

1402 «Abundance» (Copper, 40 × 58 cm). This work was previously attributed to his father; the son's precision in imitating his father's style leads to frequent confusion.

1408 «Adam and Eve in Paradise» (Copper, 40 × 50 cm).

1409 See Clerck and Van Alsloot.

1428 See Momper and Bruegel de Velours.

1429 See Momper and Bruegel de Velours.

1434 See Bruegel de Velours.

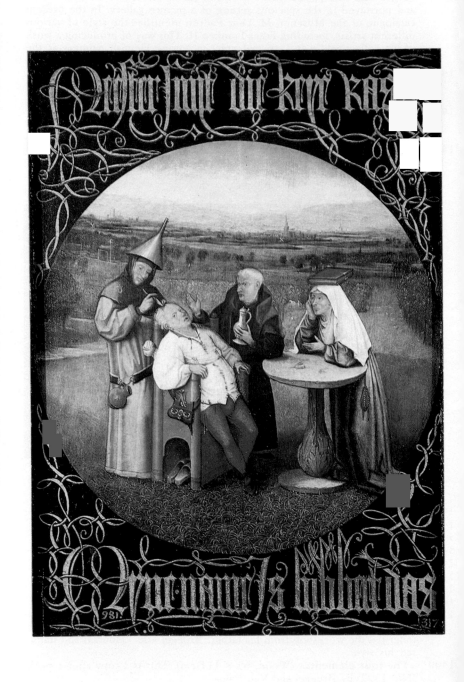

2056. Hieronymus Bosch. The Cure for Folly.

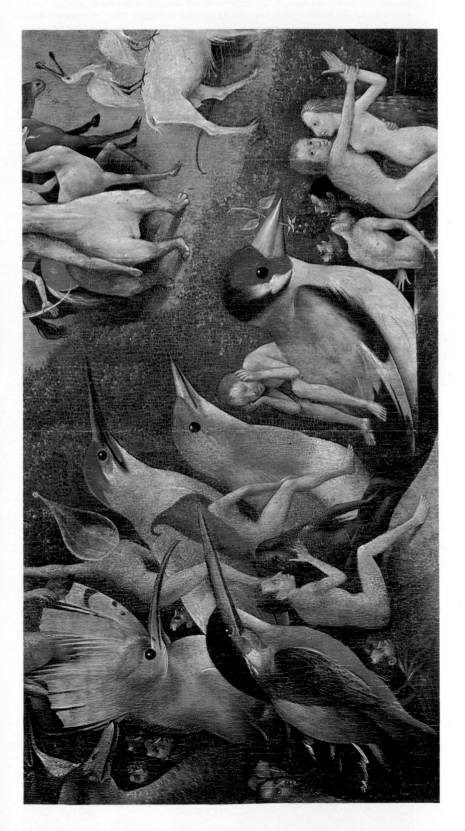

2823. Hieronymus Bosch. The Garden of Delights.

BRUEGEL, Pieter Bruegel «the Elder» (b. Breda (?) c. 1525/30; d. Brussels 1569). Although he received his artistic education in the tradition of the Romanist painters and travelled through Italy (Calabria, Messina, Naples and Rome), Bruegel's style does not in the least testify to his familiarity with Italian Renaissance art and its subject-matter. On the contrary, his painting is in the best tradition of the Flemish masters who, like Bosch, used their art to illustrate the popular, satirical and moralistic spirit of the Netherlands. He was interested in Patenier and his followers' discoveries in the field of landscape-painting, although Bruegel himself was an innovator and a unique and brilliant artist. He found inspiration in life with its many different aspects, in the tragic and comical side of everyday events and in country scenes of peasants at work or enjoying themselves. Nothing escaped Bruegel's attention and he painted reality with perfect objectivity. With him ugliness is introduced in art. Sober technique and colouring with fundamental tones emphasize the clear structure of his compositions, which are arranged in an orderly pattern in spite of the great variety of events he portrayed. Bruegel is also important as the founder of a family of painters that marked Flemish art until well into the 17th century.

1393 **«The Triumph of Death»** (Wood, 117 × 162 cm). This is one of the most famous of Bruegel's works, dated about 1562. It is inspired by the medieval literary theme of the Dance of Death and offers us a devastating vision of Death triumphing over all worldly things. The artist avoids any reference to religion as a means of consolation or to a belief in immortality and shows us an end full of grief and despair. The scenes of killing and destruction, battles, fires and shipwrecks reach into the background of the picture, which recalls the bay of Naples. In the centre, Death in the shape of one of the four horsemen of the Apocalypse rides into a crowd brandishing a huge scythe. Wherever the eye turns there are dramatic scenes portraying all kinds of encounters with Death. All fall under his merciless onslaught: the Emperor and dignitaries of the Church as well as the poor and humble. On the right, an army of skeletons hold up coffins to block the way and only a couple of lovers in the foreground seem oblivious to what is going on around them.

2470 **«The Adoration of the Magi»** (Canvas, 119 × 165 cm). This is a copy by Pieter Bruegel «the Younger» after one of his father's works now preserved in the Museum of Brussels.

BRUEGEL, Pieter Bruegel «the Younger» (b. Brussels 1564; d. Antwerp 1638). Son of Pieter Bruegel «the Elder». He copied his father's works and imitated his style.

1415 **«Garland with the Adoration of the Kings»** (Copper, 39 × 29 cm). Signed.

1454 **«The Rape of Proserpine»** (Wood, 43 × 64 cm).

1455 See Bruegel, Workshop and copies.

3232. Coecke. The Temptation of St. Anthony.

2045. Bruegel the Younger. Snowy Landscape with bird-trap.

1456 **«Landscape with wayfarers»** (Wood, 30 × 47 cm).
1457 **«Construction of the Tower of Babel»** (Originally round panel converted into a square 44 × 44 cm). Its attribution is doubtful, but it is inspired by compositions of Bruegel «the Elder».
1458 See Heil.
1459 See Heil.
1782 See Stalbent.
2045 **«Snowy landscape with bird-trap»** (Wood, 40 × 57 cm). Signed. This is a copy after a famous original by Bruegel «the Elder» of which there are several versions.
2816 **«Snowy landscape»** (Wood, 45 × 76 cm). This is a copy after an untraceable original by Bruegel «the Elder».
2817 See Momper, Joost de.
CHRISTUS, Petrus Christus (b. Baerle c. 1410; d. Bruges 1472/73). He carried on Van Eyck's style, assimilating his sense of space and bulk, but his execution is less precise.
1921 **«The Virgin and Child»** (Wood, 49 × 34 cm).
CLERCK, Hendrick de Clerck (Brussels c. 1570-1630). In 1578 he appeared in Italy. He painted religious and mythological themes in the manner of the Flemish Romanist artists. He collaborated frequently with other painters.
CLERCK and Van Alsloot.
1356 **«Landscape with Diana discovered by Actaeon»** (Wood, 70 × 150 cm).
1409 **«Paradise with the four elements»** (Copper, 58 × 74 cm). Signed. It dates from about 1607. The spindle-shaped figures recall Michelangelo and are typical of Clerck.
CLERCK and Bruegel «de Velours».
1401 **«Abundance and the four elements»** (Copper, 51 × 64 cm).
CLEVE (?), **Joos van der Beke or van Cleve** (b. Cleves c. 1485; d. Antwerp, c. 1540/41).
2182 See Holbein in German Masters.
2654 **«The Saviour»** (Wood, 60 × 47 cm). This panel possibly comes from Cleve's workshop without being his own work. It is difficult to define his style as he was an eclectic artist who painted in the manner of the most important masters of his time.
2213 **«The Emperor Maximilian I»** (Wood, 50 × 35 cm). This is a replica of an untraceable original.
COCK, Jan de Cock (active in Antwerp in 1506; d. before 1527).
2700 **«St. Anne, the Virgin and Child»** (Wood, 35 × 26 cm). Although Cock was a follower of Bosch, there is little in this picture to remind us of that artist. Soft, delicate forms in the figures and special attention to the landscape are the salient features of this composition.
COECKE, Pieter Coecke van Aelst (b. Aelst 1502; d. Brussels 1550). He lived in Italy and visited Constantinople in 1533, an interesting cir-

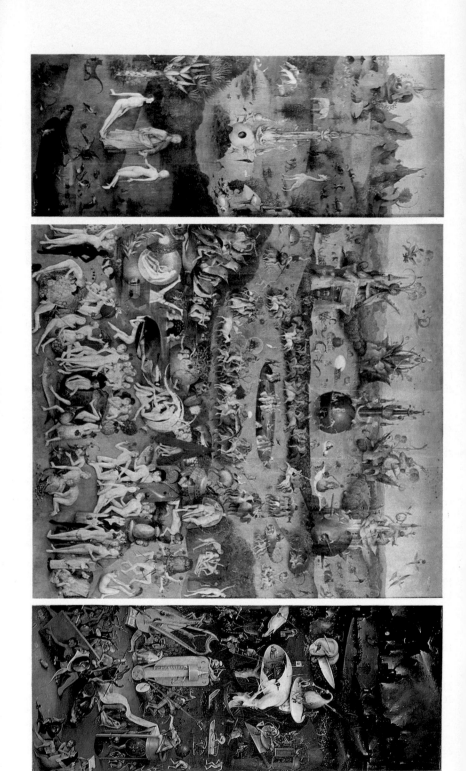

2823. Hieronymus Bosch. The Garden of Delights

1514. Master of Flémalle. St. Barbara.

cumstance since reminiscences of the Oriental world can be found in his works. His elegant, refined style, beautiful models and the bright, enamel-like surface of his panels all contribute towards making him one of the most stimulating painters of the Mannerist generation in the Netherlands. From 1534 on he worked at the Court of Charles V.

1609 «St. James and eleven figures praying» (Wood, 112 × 44 cm). See No. 1610.

1610 «St. John the Evangelist with two ladies and two girls in prayer» (Wood, 112 × 44 cm). Like the preceding panel, this is a wing of a triptych whose central panel has been lost. Its outstanding features are the extreme realism of the faces and the gracefulness and delicacy of the child models. The vision of Hell in the background of the second panel is interesting in that it recalls Bosch's compositions on the same subject.

2223 «Triptych of the Adoration of the Magi» (Central panel: 87 × 55 cm; side wings: 87 × 23 cm). The elongated figures derive from the Mannerist school of Antwerp.

2703 «The Annunciation, the Adoration of the Magi and the Adoration of the Shepherds» (Wood, 81 × 67 cm). This work abounds in features that make us appreciate Coecke's characteristic wealth and variety of detail.

3210 «The Holy Trinity» (Wood, 98 × 84 cm). Like the preceding panel, this work has been acquired recently and is an excellent example of the artist's later period. The symmetry of the upper half of the composition draws our attention, with the perfect anatomy of Christ, and the lovely landscape in the lower half.

3232 «The Temptation of St. Anthony» (Wood, 41 × 53 cm). The main figures of the Saint and the women who tempt him appear in a landscape full of small, monstrous figures that once again remind us of Bosch.

COFFERMANS, Marcellus Coffermans (active 1549-1575 in Antwerp).

2719 «Entombment of Christ» (Wood, 17 × 13 cm). This work is based on an engraving by the German master Schongauer.

2723 «Altar-piece with the Scourging of Christ, the Deposition, the Annunciation, St. Jerome and Rest on the Flight into Egypt» (Each panel 33 × 23 cm, except the last one: 21 × 14 cm). Nearly all the compositions are based on previous models.

CONINXLOO, Gilles van Coninxloo (Antwerp 1544-1607). He is the first fully Baroque Flemish landscape painter.

1385 «Landscape» (Copper, 24 × 19 cm). The forest landscape is dense and the trees acquire a splendid fullness. The work was attributed to Brill.

COOSEMANS, Alexander Coosemans (Antwerp 1627-1689). Still life painter and follower of Davidsz de Heem.

1462 «Still life» (Wood, 33 × 77 cm). Signed. This still life is more elaborate than those of his master.

2072 «Fruit» (Wood, 49 × 40 cm). Signed.

CORNELISZ VAN HAARLEM, Cornelis (Haarlem 1562-1638).

2088 «The Judgement of Apollo or the Tribunal of the gods» (Wood, 44 × 98 cm). Signed and dated 1594. Trained in the Mannerist tradition of the School of Fontainebleau, Cornelisz van Haarlem is one of the artists who tried to create in the late 16th century a new, more natural style, giving up the elongated and distorted bodies prized by the Mannerists, and introducing more classic figures with well-proportioned, harmonious forms. This work bears witness to the artist's transition and indicates acquaintance with Italian models.

COSSIERS, Jan Cossiers (Antwerp 1600-1671). He painted mythologies, biblical scenes, genre pictures and portraits. His figures recall Rubens, his colouring and light are closer to Jordaens. He collaborated with Rubens.

1463 «Jupiter and Lycaon» (Canvas, 120 × 115 cm). This work is based on a sketch by Rubens.

1464 «Prometheus» (Canvas, 182 × 113 cm).

1465 «Narcissus» (Canvas, 97 × 93 cm).

COSTER, Adam de Coster (Mechlin 1586-1643). Genre painter; he usually painted scenes illuminated by candle-light.

1466 «Judith» (Canvas, 144 × 155). Its attribution is very doubtful. The Prado's present Catalogue of Flemish Masters lists it as anonymous.

COXCIE, Michel van Coxcie (Mechlin 1499-1592). He was one of the most outstanding Flemish Romanists, being the one who spent the longest period in Italy (1530-1540), where he assimilated the style of Raphael and his followers. His success in Rome led to his being appointed a member of the Academy of San Luca. On his return to Flanders he worked in Mechlin and Brussels and was also Court Painter to Philip II. The Prado possesses several of his works that reveal his monumental and imposing style, which is however at times somewhat affected and cold.

1467 **«St. Cecilia»** (Wood, 136 × 104 cm). Signed. This work was commissioned by Philip II and kept in the old church at El Escorial. It dates from about 1569. It reveals the influence of Italian models, especially those of Raphael's Roman followers.

1468
1469 } **«Triptych of the Life of the Virgin»** (Central panel: 208 × 181 cm; side wings: 208 × 67 cm). The closed triptych shows on the left-hand
1470 wing the *Annunciation* and the *Adoration of the Shepherds*, and on the right-hand wing the *Visitation* and the *Adoration of the Magi*, painted in grisaille. On the inside, the left-hand wing shows us the *Birth of the Virgin* and the right-hand wing the *Presentation in the Temple*. On the central panel the *Death and Assumption of the Virgin* are depicted. The triptych was made for St. Gudule's Cathedral in Brussels and purchased by Philip II for El Escorial. All of the panels reveal the perfect combination of Italian models and the traditional Flemish taste for realism and highly finished detail. The sense of space is rendered in a masterly manner, as well as the way in which the figures blend with the Renaissance-style architecture.

2641 **«Jesus carrying the Cross»** (Wood, 81 × 50 cm). The theme is clearly taken from models by Sebastiano del Piombo (see Italian Masters).

CRAESBEEK, Joos van Craesbeek (b. Neerlinter c. 1605; d. Brussels 1654/61). *Genre* painter in the manner of Brouwer.

1390 **«The burlesque trio»** (Wood, 30 × 24 cm).

1471 **«The marriage contract»** (Wood, 71 × 54 cm). This work is typical of his style with its expressive, free and easy handling.

CRAYER, Gaspard de Crayer (b. Antwerp 1584; d. Ghent 1669). Painter of religious subjects (there is an excellent series of his works in the Church of San Francisco el Grande in Madrid), as well as mythologies and portraits. His style is delicate and sentimental.

1472 **«The Cardinal-Infante»** (Canvas, 219 × 125 cm).

1553 **«Philip IV on horseback»** (Wood, 28 × 22 cm). This preparatory sketch was previously attributed to Van Kessel.

CRONENBURCH, Adriaen van Cronenburch (Pietersbierun, Friesland, active in the second half of the 16th century). Little is known about this Dutch portrait painter, whose name was mistakenly read in the past as Anna Cronenburch due to the strange monogram he used to sign his pictures, which has only recently been deciphered. His clear-cut forms, precisely drawn outlines and the distant, aloof air of his figures in the splendid series of paintings on display in the Prado reveal him as an artist of the best Mannerist style. On the other hand, he is a representative of the Puritan world of the Reformation in the Northern Netherlands with his austere settings and constant allusions to Death in symbols and inscriptions.

2073 **«Lady with a yellow flower»** (Wood, 107 × 79 cm). Signed.

2074 **«Lady and girl»** (Wood, 104 × 78 cm).

2075 **«Lady and girl»** (Wood, 105 × 78 cm). Signed and dated 1537. This work is possibly the best of the series, which probably portrays ladies of the same family to judge by the architectural background. In all of them the models are stiff and distant; the ladies wear admirably described dark clothes and the scenes are enlivened by a colourful note in the form of flowers and other accessories. The strikingly realistic skull and the inscription on the wall allude to Death and the vanity of worldly things.

2076 **«Dutch lady»** (Wood, 100 × 79 cm). Signed.

DALEM, Cornelis van Dalem (active in Antwerp in 1545; d. 1573/76).

1856 **«Landscape with shepherds»** (Wood, 47 × 68 cm). This painting was previously attributed to Valckenborgh. In the panoramic vision of nature realistic elements are coupled with fantastic forms.

DAVID, Gerard David (b. Oudewater c. 1450/60; d. Bruges 1523). He lived in Bruges and became the town's chief artist after Memling's death. His work has its roots deep in the Pre-Renaissance tradition, but he adds a new sense of more homogeneous colour and soft, indistinctly traced lines *(sfumato)*. In many of his pictures considerable importance is attached to the landscapes.

1512 **«The Virgin and Child and two angels crowning her»** (Wood, 34 × 27 cm).

1537 **«The Virgin and Child»** (Wood, 45 × 34 cm). Its attribution is doubtful,

1394. Jan Bruegel «de Velours». Sight. (detail)

1393. Pieter Bruegel «the Elder». The Triumph of Death. (detail)

although it is a valuable work. The manner of framing the figures in a window is original and the flowers and book resting on a window-sill constitute the starting-point for a still life.

2643 «**Rest on the Flight into Egypt**» (Wood, 60 × 39 cm). This theme was very successful and he painted several versions. The artist's taste for solid composition is apparent in the mass of tree-trunks in the background and the almost square-cut rocks the Virgin is sitting on. The serious, vertical figure of the Virgin is imbued with a gentleness that accounts for the picture's success.

DAVID, Follower.

2542 «**The Crucifixion**» (Wood, 45 × 33 cm).

1921. Christus. Virgin and Child.   1537. David. Virgin and Child.

DYCK, Anthony van Dyck (b. Antwerp, 1599; d. London, 1641), also known in England as Sir Anthony Vandyke. Van Dyck is the second greatest figure in 17th-century Flemish painting. He studied under Van Balen; an early talent, when he entered Rubens' workshop his style was already sufficiently developed to avoid being unduly influenced by Rubens, so that in fact his relationship with the master was closer to that of a colleague than to that of a pupil. In 1621 he went to Italy and worked particularly in Genoa, where he began to specialize in portraiture. In this field his style is sober and somewhat pompous, similar to that of Rubens, but enriched by his own particular touch. After another period in Antwerp, he returned to England (where he had already been in 1620) and was appointed Court Painter by Charles I. After the Reformation, the crisis of art in the Protestant countries considerably reduced the scope of painting and, like many other artists, Van Dyck dedicated his efforts to portraiture (like his contemporary Velazquez at the Court in Madrid, although for entirely different reasons). It was in this field that he obtained his great popularity in aristocratic circles. He was a man of extraordinary sensibility, capable of identifying himself with his sitter's personality and catching his innermost mood. Van Dyck's masterly technique and psychological sharp-sightedness made it unnecesary for him to resort to scenic effects to enhance his models; expression and gesture are sufficient for the artist to create an image in which the apparent lack of pose emphasizes all the haughtiness of these courtiers.

1473 «**St. Jerome**» (Canvas, 100 × 71 cm). This work is now attributed to Van Dyck. His great influence on the Madrid school of painting is the main reason why this picture has sometimes been considered a Spanish work.

1474 «**The Crown of Thorns**» (Canvas, 223 × 196 cm). This painting dates from about 1618/20. Although he was better known as a portrait painter, Van Dyck also executed a considerable number of religious and mythological works. This one is inspired by a famous painting by Titian and reveals, as is to be expected in such an early work, the influence of Rubens; but his personal sensibility, more introspective than that of his master and much more aware of the psychological aspect of what he is portraying, comes out in the tense, although restrained dramatic effect of the scene with its contrast between the classic nobleness of the body of Christ and His serene expression and the figures of His persecutors.

1475 See Van Dyck, Workshop and copies.

1477 «Seizure of Christ» (Canvas, 344 × 249 cm). This work dates from about 1618/20. It is typical of Van Dyck's manner of handling religious themes, stressing their spiritual contents; here the movement of the soldiers about to seize Christ appears to come to a stop in front of Him as if halted by His dignified serious figure which contrasts with the threatening attitude of the soldiers. The painter's artistic maturity, at such an early stage, is revealed here in the perfect compositional scheme, together with firm, sound execution and clever illumination.

1478 «St. Francis of Assisi» (Canvas, 148 × 113 cm). It dates from 1627/32.

1479 «Martin Ryckaert» (Canvas, 148 × 113 cm). The sitter was a painter who had lost his left arm. Here the languid air we are accustomed to from other Van Dyck portraits is missing; the image is energetic, the profound look and half-opened mouth are full of life and the hand grasps the arm-rest forcefully. The sitter's somewhat dandyish costume stands out against the compact background. The portrait was painted in Antwerp about 1627/32.

1480 «The Cardinal-Infante» (Canvas, 107 × 106 cm). The Cardinal-Infante was a brother of Philip IV and Governor-General of the Netherlands. He is portrayed here with the sword used by Charles V at the Battle of Mühlberg.

1481 «Diana Cecil, Countess of Oxford» (Canvas, 107 × 86 cm). The proud pose of the sitter, with her stretched neck and ambiguous expression, half reserved, half conversing, gives the portrait a special charm which was without doubt highly appreciated by her contemporaries.

1482 «Frederick Henry of Nassau» (Canvas, 110 × 95 cm). The son of William the Silent, he was elected *Stadholder* in 1625. The portrait was painted in 1628.

1483 «Amalia of Solms-Nassau» (Wood, 105 × 95 cm). Dated 1628. She was the wife of Frederick Henry of Nassau, portrayed in the preceding picture. The sitter's pose is similar to that of Anne of Austria in Rubens' portrait (in the Prado); the pale complexion of her hands and face stand out against the dark dress.

1484 See Van Dyck, Workshop and copies.

1485 «Portrait of a lady» (Canvas, 106 × 75 cm). This portrait was painted about 1628. Its severe, vertical lines have much in common with the pictures Van Dyck painted during his Genoese period.

1486 «Count Henry of Bergh» (Canvas, 114 × 100 cm). Signed; it dates from about 1627/32. The rhetoric gesture of the hand which seems to address the observer as if to stress a point is a very Baroque invention already used by Rubens; the vigorous face reveals a strong, energetic personality.

1477. Van Dyck. Seizure of Christ.   1481. Van Dyck. Diana Cecil.

1487 «Jacob Gaultier» (?) (Canvas, 128 × 100 cm). Although Van Dyck normally painted portraits of the aristocracy, he left some portraits of intellectuals and artists that are very interesting because they are painted with greater freedom; his *«Jacob Gaultier»* is an example of sober, ingenious composition with the parallel diagonals he used frequently.

1488 «The engraver Paul de Pont» (?) (Canvas, 112 × 100 cm). The sitter has been identified as the engraver Paulus Pontius due to the portrait's likeness with one of his own engravings; however, his strange attitude and the sword hardly seem appropiate to his profession.

1930. Jan Gossaert «Mabuse». The Virgin and Child. (detail)

1489 «**Sir Endymion Porter and Van Dyck**» (Canvas, 110 × 114 cm, oval). This portrait dates from about 1623. Sir Endymion Porter was secretary to the Duke of Buckingham and a cultured man and art connoisseur; he was Van Dyck's protector and friend. The artist portrayed himself next to Sir Endymion Porter in a deferential, but none the less elegant pose. The delicately balanced face, combining both forehead and profile, the masterly reproduction of draperies, especially Porter's elegant white suit, together with the psychological depth of the men's expressions make this double portrait one of the masterpieces of Baroque portrait painting.

1489. Van Dyck. Sir Endymion Porter and Van Dyck.

1490 «**The musician Liberti**» (Canvas, 107 × 97 cm). Liberti was the organist of the Antwerp Cathedral. The portrait reveals Van Dyck's typical mixture of nonchalance and arrogance.

1491 «**Head of an old man**» (Canvas, 47 × 36 cm).

1492 «**Diana and Endymion discovered by a satyr**» (Canvas, 144 × 163 cm). Dating from Van Dyck's Italian period, it recalls Venetian works.

1493 «**Policena Spinola**» (Canvas, 204 × 130 cm). This portrait dates from 1622/27. It is of the sober, majestic type painted by Van Dyck in Genoa, with the sitter's Spanish ceremoniousness marking the distance.

1494 «**St. Rosalia crowned**» (Canvas, 106 × 81 cm). It dates from 1621/22.

1495 «**Maria Ruthwen**» (Canvas, 104 × 81 cm). The model was a widow when she married Van Dyck in 1639. Her identity has been in dispute and the portrait has sometimes been considered a copy.

1544 «**The mystic betrothal of St. Catherine**» (Canvas, 121 × 173 cm). The work dates from 1618/20. It has been attributed to Rubens and to Jordaens, but now it is unanimously accepted as a Van Dyck.

1545 «**The Child Jesus and St. John**» (Canvas, 130 × 74 cm). This work was previously attributed to Jordaens.

1637 «**The brazen serpent**» (Canvas, 205 × 235 cm). This work dates from 1618/20. It was painted in his youth, when he worked with Rubens, but its dramatic expression is different, less ostentatious and deeper-felt than in his master's works. The human types portrayed here, although they are full-blooded as in Rubens, are somehow more energetic and the expressiveness of the hands is characteristic of Van Dyck.

1642 «**Pietà**» (Canvas, 201 × 171 cm). This work dates from 1618/20. It maintains the scheme of the medieval *Pietà* sculptures, which Van Dyck imbues with deep religious feeling. Light falls on the emaciated body of Christ; the Virgin's apathetic figure reflects complete obliviousness.

1694 «**Head of an old man**» (Paper on cloth, 45 × 24 cm).

2526 See Van Dyck, Workshop and copies.

DYCK, Workshop and copies.

1475 «**Pietà**» (Canvas, 114 × 100 cm). This is a copy after an original from about 1627.

1484 «**King Charles I**» (Canvas, 123 × 85 cm). This is a replica of an original kept in Windsor Castle, but not entirely done by Van Dyck. The composition recalls Ruben's portrait of the Duke of Lerma (in the Prado).

1493. Van Dyck. 'Policena Spinola.   1642. Van Dyck. Pietà.

1499   «Charles II as Prince of Wales» (Canvas, 137 × 111 cm).
1501   «Charles I of England» (Canvas, 366 × 281 cm). This is a copy after an original in the National Gallery, London.
1502   «Francisco de Moncada» (Canvas, 114 × 98 cm). The same sitter was painted on horseback by Van Dyck in an original shown in the Louvre.
2526   «The Earl of Arundel and his grandson» (Canvas, 278 × 162 cm). This is a copy after an original kept in Windsor Castle.
2556   «St. Rosalia of Palermo» (Canvas, 127 × 108 cm). This is a copy after an original in the Metropolitan Museum, New York.
2565   «The Infanta Isabella Clara Eugenia» (Canvas, 218 × 131 cm). This is a copy of an official portrait, in which she is painted in widow's weeds.
2569   «The Infanta Isabella Clara Eugenia» (Canvas, 109 × 90 cm). See No. 2565.
        ERTVELT, Andries van Ertvelt (Antwerp 1590-1652). Seascape painter.
2163   «Seascape» (Canvas, 124 × 168 cm). This painting is typical of his style.
        ES, Jacques van Es (b. ?; d. Antwerp 1666). Still-life painter with a sober style, similar to that of the Dutch masters. He concentrated on compositional unity and a homogeneous effect without excessive attention to details.
1504   «Oysters and lemons» (Wood, 27 × 32 cm).
1505   «Still life» (Wood, 27 × 37 cm). The colouring is sober and uniform.
1506   «Flowers and fruit» (Circular panel, 30 × 30 cm). The bulk and tactile quality of the fruit stand out against the dark background and the table-cloth.
        EYCK, Gaspard van Eyck (b. Antwerp, 1613; d. Brussels 1673). Seascape painter, follower of Ertvelt.
1507   «Seascape» (Canvas, 81 × 107 cm). This work resembles his style, but its attribution is not certain.
1508   «Naval battle between Turks and Maltese» (Canvas, 87 × 118 cm). Signed and dated 1649.
1509   «Seascape» (Canvas, 87 × 108 cm). The effect of the quiet waves seen against the light is particularly attractive.
        EYCK, Jan Eyck or Yck (active 1626-1633). He worked with Rubens.
1345   «The Fall of Phaethon» (Canvas, 197 × 180 cm). This work was painted for the Torre de la Parada after a sketch by Rubens. The works of this series are the only definitely known ones by this master.
1714   «Apollo and Daphne» (Canvas, 193 × 207 cm). Attribution is not certain.
        EYCK, Jan van Eyck (b. Maaseyck? c. 1390; d. Bruges 1441). He was the chief figure among the early Flemish masters and reputed to be the first to use oil paints. There is no original Van Eyck in Spain, but the Prado displays some works associated with his style.
        EYCK, School.
1510   See Mabuse.
1511   «The Fountain of Grace» (Wood, 181 × 116 cm). This is a very controversial panel; at present it is considered to be a copy after an untraceable original by Van Eyck or the work of a very close follower. It is closely related to Van Eyck's famous many-winged altar-piece The Adoration of the Lamb in St. Bavon's Cathedral in Ghent. The painting is composed like a splendid scenography where the human and divine elements are arranged on different levels; in the uppermost part 'we see God the Father with the Lamb at His feet, between the Virgin and St. John; below, the triumph of

the Church over the synagogue is depicted. Although it lacks Van Eyck's quality, this panel contains all the features of his style, such as the strictly symmetrical composition, the fullness of his figures and his concern for highly-finished detail. It belonged to the monastery of El Parral in Segovia and must have reached Spain at an early date to judge by the number of contemporary copies that exist.

1617 «The Stigmata of St. Francis» (Wood, 47 × 36 cm). This is a freely-executed copy after an original by Van Eyck, probably done by the Master of Hoogstraten.

2716 «Christ giving His Blessing» (Wood, 52 × 39 cm). This is a copy after the central figure of the Ghent altar-piece. It has been attributed to Jan van Scorel, who worked on restoring the altar-piece.

EYCK, Follower.

2696 «The Virgin and Child» (Wood, 18 × 15 cm). This picture is very clearly in the style of Van Eyck.

FINSONIUS, Louis Finsonius (b. Bruges ?; d. Amsterdam 1617). He worked in the South of France and possibly also in Naples, where he might have been in contact with Caravaggio.

3075 «The Annunciation» (Canvas, 173 × 218 cm). Here he combines Tenebrist-style illumination with a very characteristic handling which almost makes the textures appear metallic.

1511. Eyck, school. The Fountain of Grace.

FLEMALLE, Master of. The name comes from the panels of the monastery of Flémalle, near Liège, but nowadays he is considered to have been Robert Campin (c. 1375-1444), a master in Tournai and an outstanding figure in early 15th-century Flemish painting.

1513 «St. John the Baptist and the Franciscan Heinrich von Werl» (Wood, 101 × 47 cm). Dated 1438. Like No. 1514, it is a wing of a triptych, the central panel having been lost. An inscription on the lower part identifies the donor and the date. The panel is a late work and reveals the influence of Van Eyck, both in its conception of space, more coherent and ample than in other works by Campin, and in some specific details, like the convex mirror.

1514 «St. Barbara» (Wood, 101 × 47 cm). See No. 1513. The saint is identified by the tower under construction seen through the window in the background. It is one of the artist's best works and marks the culminating point in his search for tridimensional effects. The interior of a house is a usual setting for religious scenes with the early Flemish masters, as well as the habit of giving everyday objects a symbolic meaning: for example, the towel or the transparent glass flask here are allusions to the saint's virginity. The combination of the cold light from the window and the warm reddish blaze of the fire is admirably achieved and St. Barbara reveals not only Campin's accustomed skill in portraying figures, but also a special delicate effect.

1887 «The betrothal of the Virgin» (Wood, 77 × 88 cm). This work still recalls the International Gothic style, for example in the great number of secondary figures, the choice of extravagant, exotic clothes and the caricature-like expression on some of the faces. On the left we see the miracle of St. Joseph's rod in a small temple intended to appear Romanesque, and on the right the betrothal of the Virgin in a Gothic portico under construction. The juxtaposition of the different architectural styles is a reference to the difference between the Old and the New Law. On the reverse: «St. James and St. Clare». The figures in grisaille are the oldest known; their presence here presumably indicates that this panel was once part of an altar-piece. The bulk of the figures and their draperies reflect the sculpture of the time.

1915 «The Annunciation» (Wood, 76 × 70 cm). Art historians do not agree in attributing this work to the Master of Flémalle; many consider it a high-quality workshop painting. The scene takes place in a Gothic interior, as becomes the first act of the New Testament; but the angel does not enter, an allusion to the chastity of the Virgin.

FLEMALLE, Master of (?).

3144 «The Virgin and Child» (Wood, 18 × 13 cm). This is a fragment of a larger work and has been purchased recently by the Museum. It has not yet been thoroughly investigated, but should probably be considered a late version of one of the Master's models.

FLORIS, Franck de Vriendt Floris (?) (Antwerp 1516-1570).

1518 «The Death of Abel» (Canvas, 151 × 125 cm).

FRANCK. See Vrancx.

FRANKEN I, Frans Franken «the Elder».

1521 See Franken II.
1522 See Franken II.

FRANKEN II, Frans Franken «the Younger» (Antwerp 1581-1642). He was the main representative of the Franken family of painters. He studied in the workshop of his father, Frans Franken «the Elder», and although he initially received the influence of the Romanist painters, he gradually incorporated Baroque elements in his style. He specialized in cabinet pictures on religious and mythological themes, attempting to bring out their decorative possibilities. His handling is delicate, tending to over-refinement, which gave his paintings a sumptuous tone greatly appreciated by his contemporaries. He collaborated with other artists (Jan Bruegel, Neefs and Momper), painting the figures in their interiors and landscapes.

1519 «The Trial of Jesus» (Wood, 58 × 81 cm). Signed. As usual, he takes pleasure in portraying numerous little figures, which gives a lively, bustling air to the composition.

1520 «St. John the Baptist preaching» (Wood, 56 × 91 cm). Signed and dated 1623. The artist's interest in decorative effects leads him to fill the scene with figures in Oriental dress, with large turbans and sweeping robes, very characteristic of his pictures.

1521 «Ecce Homo» (Copper, 33 × 23 cm). Signed.

1522 «Jesus taken Prisoner» (Copper, 44 × 23 cm). Signed.

1523 «The Triumph of Neptune and Amphitrite» (Copper, 30 × 41 cm). Signed. This is a subject he painted many times, inspired by Italian compositions.

1525 «Christ in Abraham's bosom» (Copper, 26 × 20 cm).

2734 «The Original Sin» (Copper, 68 × 86 cm). Signed. This is the first of a series of twelve pictures on biblical subjects. All have similar compositions, often with a mass of meticulously painted trees in the centre. The figures are typical of Franken, somewhat stereotype and with characteristic features, but always elegant and distinguished in their movements.

2735 «Cain killing Abel» (Copper, 68 × 86 cm). Signed.

2736 «Noah with the animals entering the Ark» (Copper, 68 × 86 cm). Signed. He painted several versions of this subject, which was no doubt very sucessful due to the decorative possibilities of the different animals and objects put on board the Ark and must have appealed to the curiosity of his Flemish admirers.

2737 «The construction of the Tower of Babel» (Copper, 68 × 86 cm). Signed.

2738 «Abraham and Melchizedek» (Copper, 68 × 86 cm). Signed.

2739   «Hagar and the angel» (Copper, 68 × 86 cm). Signed.
2740   «Abraham and the three angels» (Copper, 68 × 86 cm). Signed.
2741   «Lot and his daughters» (Copper, 68 × 86 cm). Signed.
2742   «The sacrifice of Isaac» (Copper, 68 × 86 cm).
2743   «Rebekah and Eliezer» (Copper, 68 × 86 cm). Signed. This is one of the most beautiful paintings of the series.
2744   «Jacob's ladder» (Copper, 68 × 86 cm). Signed.
2745   «Jacob's fight with the angel» (Copper, 68 × 86 cm). Signed.
       FRANKEN III, Frans Franken. See Ludwig Neefs.
       FRANKFURT, Master of Frankfurt. See German Masters.
       FYT, Jan Fyt (Antwerp 1611-1661). He painted landscapes and animal studies. After travelling to France and Italy he returned to his native town where he spent the rest of his life. His still lifes are conceived along the lines of the innovations introduced by Snyders, which he transformed and marked with his own particular personality. He generally prefers smaller-size and often squarer canvases than Snyders; his compositions usually contain a compact mass in the centre, forming a densely interwoven structure of objects, fruit and animals. His handling is characteristic with its use of rich impasto and long brush-strokes. The intensity and depth of his colouring are unified by means of the light whose contrasts set off the bulk of the objects. He achieves astonishingly realistic effects in the representation of tactile qualities, especially when it comes to painting animal skins and feathered birds.
1526   «Hen-roost» (Canvas, 123 × 242 cm).
1527   «A glede» (Canvas, 95 × 134 cm). The collection of different species of birds does not give the impression of an inventory or an illustration out of a natural history book, as sometimes occurs with works by Snyders or Kessel; Fyt grouped the birds more closely and thus obtained a more cohesive scene.
1528   «Game with a dog» (Canvas, 72 × 121 cm). Signed.
1529   «Still life with a cat and dog» (Canvas, 77 × 112 cm). Signed. The splendid technical quality of this still life commands attention as well as the artist's mastery in painting fur, feathers and the smooth or velvety fruit-skins in such a way that we can almost guess their weight and feel prompted to stretch out a hand to touch them.
1530   «Hare chased by dogs» (Canvas, 113 × 163 cm). Signed. Fyt borrowed this kind of subject from Snyders and treated it in a similar manner.
1531   «Ducks and moor-hens» (Canvas, 127 × 163 cm). Signed.
1532   «Cocks fighting» (Canvas, 114 × 167 cm). This is also a subject used by Snyders, but Fyt's composition is more compact, unified by the light which concentrates on the main group.

1527. Fyt. A glede.

1533 «Ducks and moor-hens» (Canvas, 119 × 174 cm). Signed. This is another version of No. 1531.

1534 «Birds» (Canvas, 135 × 174 cm). Signed and dated 1661.

GHERING, Anton Gunther Ghering (active in Antwerp about 1662/3; d. Antwerp c. 1667). He painted church interiors and fantastic architectures.

1535 «The Jesuit Church in Antwerp» (Canvas, 84 × 121 cm). He painted this subject several times with absolute mastery of perspective and homogeneous colouring.

GLAUBER. See Boudewyns.

GOSART, Gossaert. See Mabuse.

GOWY, Jacob Peter Gowy (active in Antwerp 1632-37). His biography is practically unknown.

1538 «Hippomenes and Atalanta» (Canvas, 181 × 220 cm). Signed. The influence of Rubens is obvious. The painting shows the moment when Atalanta stoops to pick up the golden apples dropped by Hippomenes.

1539 See Jordaens.

1540 «The fall of Icarus» (Canvas, 195 × 180 cm). Signed.

GYSELS, Peter Gysels (Antwerp 1621-1690). A painter of landscapes, animal studies and still lifes, his style resembles that of Bruegel «de Velours».

1388 «Landscape» (Copper, 25 × 29 cm). This painting was originally attributed to Brill, but it is now considered, with certain doubts, to be by Gysels.

HAARLEM, See Cornelisz van Haarlem.

HAYE (?), Corneille de la Haye or de Lyon (The Hague c. 1500-1574?).

1958 «Portrait of a man» (Wood, 28 × 21 cm).

HEERE (?), Lucas de Heere, called «Lucas of Holland» (b. Ghent 1534; d. Paris 1584).

1949 «Philip II» (Wood, 41 × 32 cm). This portrait follows the sober line of the 16th-century Dutch masters; it is possibly a fragment of an unfinished larger composition.

HEIL, Daniel van Heil (Brussels 1604-1662?). Chiefly a landscape painter.

1458 «A town on fire and plundered» (Circular panel converted into a square one: 43 × 44 cm). This is a companion piece to the following painting.

1459 «A town on fire» (Wood, 54 × 78 cm). Like the preceding one, this painting was originally attributed to Pieter Bruegel «the Younger». Fires are a typical subject-matter in the work of Heil.

HEMESSEN, Jan Sanders van Hemessen (b. Hemixen c. 1500; d. Haarlem c. 1564/66). He was influenced by Italian painting in his compositions and in his desire to portray monumental figures, but the smooth, enamel-like surface of his pictures and the meticulous, realistic interpretation are typically Flemish. A particular feature is his manner of depicting light, producing bold contrasts and underlining the tightly drawn figures.

1541 «The surgeon» (Wood, 100 × 141 cm). Here we see, against a townscape background, the scene of the extraction of the stone reputed to cause madness, a frequent subject in Flemish painting (cf. Bosch No. 2056). The still-life objects on the table are very realistically depicted as well as the expressions of the different figures. It is an exceptional work.

1542 «The Virgin and Child» (Monogram AOD, 1543. Wood, 135 × 91 cm). This work is influenced by Raphael's Madonnas. The artist has skilfully merged the figures into a Flemish-style landscape.

HERP, William van Herp (Antwerp 1614-1677). This artist specialized in religious subjects and genre paintings, imitating Rubens.

1722 «The wedding of Cana» (Copper, 66 × 92 cm).

1986 «The freeing of prisoners» (Canvas on wood, 90 × 98 cm). The Prado's present Catalogue of Flemish Paintings does not include this work; its attribution had been questioned previously.

HUYNEN, C. van Huynen (active in 1671). His biography is unknown.

2165 «Garland of flowers and fruit with a Pietà» (Canvas, 81 × 61 cm). Like the following work, it was listed under Anonymous Dutch Masters. Both are signed and reveal excellent quality and masterly execution.

2166 «Garland of fruit with the Holy Family» (Canvas, 81 × 61 cm). Signed.

HUYS, Peeter Huys (active in Antwerp between 1545-1581).

2095 «Hell» (Wood, 86 × 82 cm). Signed and dated 1570. He was not a great creative artist, but reproduced correctly and with a good technique Bosch's fantastic compositions, which were highly appreciated by contemporary collectors. This work comes from El Escorial and must have belonged to Philip II, who was a fervent admirer of Bosch's style.

IJKENS. See Ykens.

1388. Gysels. Landscape.

ISENBRANDT, Adriaen (active after 1510; d. Bruges 1551). A follower of Gerard David, Isenbrandt's characteristic feature is a refined colour scheme with predominant use of silvery greys and blues, as well as soft, diffuse forms, especially in the faces, which are portrayed with greater sentimentalism and gentleness than by David.

1943 **«St. Gregory's Mass»** (Canvas, 72 × 56 cm). Against a background of Renaissance-style architecture, we see the scene where the Pope St. Gregory, who doubted about the Mystery of the Eucharist, saw the figure of Christ appear to him while he was celebrating Mass.

2544 **«The Virgin and Child with the infant St. John and three angels»** (Wood, 165 × 123 cm). This badly preserved work is characteristic of Isenbrandt.

2664 **«Mary Magdalene»** (Wood, 45 × 34 cm). A very delicately executed work, that represents Mary Magdalene as a young girl of Isenbrandt's time in a studio portrait.

2818 **«Christ, Man of Sorrows»** (Wood, 46 × 29 cm). This work avoids an overdramatic effect of the scene. The technique is *sfumato*.

JORDAENS, Jacob Jordaens (Antwerp 1593-1678). He studied in Antwerp with Adam van Noort; unlike Rubens and Van Dyck, Jordaens remained all his life in his native town and married his master's daugther. He collaborated with Rubens and was influenced by him, although his personal style differs considerably from that of Rubens: Jordaens conserved a popular vein and even when he painted mythological subjects his lack of contact with the classical world becomes evident. His prestige earned him many commissions from England, Sweden and Holland and he also worked for Philip IV's *«Torre de la Parada».* On Rubens' death, Jordaens was commisioned to complete his unfinished works.

1539 **«The fall of the giants»** (Canvas, 171 × 285 cm). This work was painted for the *Torre de la Parada,* like the Nos. 1551, 1634 and 1713, according to sketches by Rubens. Jordaens tried to adapt himself to Rubens' style, even to the extent of giving up his own style, which has made it difficult to determine the attribution of some of his paintings.

1544 See Van Dyck.

1545 See Van Dyck.

1546 **«Meleager and Atalanta»** (Canvas, 151 × 241 cm). The dense composition is typical of Jordaens, as well as the vigorous *chiaroscuro* and the compactly modelled figures.

1547 **«Offering to Ceres»** (Canvas, 165 × 112 cm). The goddess of Agriculture receives homage from the peasants; Jordaens seems to have taken pleasure in depicting their weather-beaten faces and rustic appearance.

1548 **«Goddess and nymphs after bathing»** (Canvas on wood, 131 × 127 cm).

1549 **«Family portrait»** (Canvas, 181 × 187 cm). This is considered a self-portrait of Jordaens with his family; the artist portrays himself with a lute, his favourite instrument; his wife, Catherine van Noort, is seated next to him and beside her is their daughter Elisabeth, bright-eyed and cheerful. The woman standing next to them is generally taken for a servant, although her prominent place in the picture, unusual in this kind of painting, and her elegant clothing do not seem appropiate to that role. The garden in the background alludes to the artist's prosperous position. The whole picture reflects the hearty, comfortable atmosphere full of solid, bourgeois virtues that so often emanate from Flemish and particularly Dutch family portraits. The spontaneity of the scene, together with its lively colouring and the pleasing effect of the light filtering through the trees make this one of the most attractive works by Jordaens in the Museum.

1550 «**Three wandering musicians**» (Wood, 49 × 64 cm). This is a preliminary sketch, but the sure execution, bold short, straight lines and unhesitating rendering of forms and light effects make it an independent and surprisingly modern work.

1550. Jordaens. Three wandering musicians.

1551 «**Apollo defeats Pan**» (Canvas, 181 × 267 cm). See No. 1539.

1634 «**The wedding of Thetis and Peleus**» (Canvas, 181 × 288 cm). See No. 1539.

1712 «**Apollo defeats Pan**» (Canvas, 181 × 223 cm). This is a copy by J. B. del Mazo.

1713 «**Cadmus and Minerva**» (Canvas, 181 × 300 cm). See No. 1539.

KESSEL «the Younger», Jan van Kessel (b. Antwerp 1654; d. Madrid 1708). This artist settled in Madrid as Court Painter to Charles II.

2525 «**Family in a garden**» (Canvas, 127 × 167 cm). Signed and dated 1680. This is a very scenographic portrait, whose lively, worldly atmosphere is far-removed from the Spanish artistic world of the time. The artist appears in a self-portrait in a window and some art critics consider the figure of the water-carrier to be a caricature of the King.

KESSEL «the Elder», Jan van Kessel (Antwerp 1626-1679). A painter of flowers and animals in particular, his style is highly detailed and reveals keen observation of reality. His works are usually very small and were possibly intended to decorate marquetry cabinets. He was a grandson of Bruegel «de Velours», whose influence is evident both in the technique and subjects of his works.

1552 «**Garland with the Infant Jesus and St. John**» (Copper, 101 × 80 cm). Signed. This is a copy after a composition by Rubens.

1553 See Crayer.

1554 «**The four corners of the world**» (Copper, 17 × 23 cm each). Signed and dated 1660. This is a series of forty pieces, which were originally sixty-eight. They illustrate the fauna of the different parts of the world. Kessel borrowed this kind of didactic subject-matter from Bruegel «de

Velours», a pioneer in this field. The animals are very precisely portrayed, but the compositions lack coherence.

2749 «**Fish and landscape**» (Copper, 14 × 19 cm). Signed and dated 1656.

2750 «**Fish and seascape**» (Copper, 14 × 19 cm). Pendant to No. 2749.

LAMEN, Christophe van der Lamen (b. Brussels (?) 1606/7; d. Antwerp before 1652). Painter of conversation pieces.

1555 «**Banquet with courtesans and peasants**» (Wood, 47 × 63 cm). This work is characteristic of his subjects, trivial but pleasant.

2586 «**Scene with soldiers**» (Wood, 44 × 33 cm). This work was previously attributed to Palamedesz.

LEGEND OF ST. CATHERINE, Master of the. This artist takes his name from a series of panels narrating the saint's life. The similarity in style to that of Van der Weyden have led art historians to identify him as the artist's son Pierre van der Weyden, born in Brussels in 1434.

2663 «**The Crucifixion**» (Wood, 100 × 71 cm). This work is a repetition of most of the central part of the Vienna Triptych by Van der Weyden.

2706 «**The Marriage of the Virgin**» (Wood, 45 × 29 cm). On the reverse: «Christ Man of Sorrows». This panel was a wing of a triptych.

LIGNIS, Pietro de Lignis (b. Mechlin (?) c. 1577; d. Rome 1627).

1556 «**The Adoration of the Magi**» (Copper, 70 × 54 cm). Signed and dated 1616. This work is very much influenced by Italian painting.

LISAERT, Pieter Lisaert (b. Antwerp; d. 1629/30).

2724 «**The wise virgins and the foolish virgins**» (Wood, 73 × 104 cm). This work is still very much Mannerist in style.

LOMBARD, Lambert (Liège 1506-1566).

2207 «**Charity**» (Wood, 163 × 105 cm). Lombard was one of the representatives of Romanist or Italian-style painting. He studied with Gossaert and travelled through Italy, returning to Liège in 1537. Some art historians find in this work echoes of Leonardo da Vinci's famous *Leda*, now lost, which Lombard may have seen in Italy or at least in copies and engravings.

LUYCK, Frans Luyck (b. Antwerp 1604; d. Vienna 1668). Court portrait painter, he worked for the Emperor in Vienna and Prague.

1267 «**Ferdinand IV, King of the Romans**» (Canvas, 214 × 218 cm). The inscription identifying him as Joseph I is incorrect.

1272 «**Maria of Austria**» (Canvas, 215 × 147 cm). This portrait is evidently influenced by Velazquez, whose work must have been familiar to Luyck from paintings sent to the Court in Vienna.

2441 «**Maria Anna of Austria**» (Canvas, 167 × 116 cm). Although the compositional scheme follows Velazquez' style, the detailed technique is typically Flemish.

LUYCKS, Christian Luycks (Antwerp 1623 c. 1653). This artist painted flowers and still lifes, in particular *«vanitas»* which he executed in Spain.

1460 «**Garland with three Cupids**» (Canvas, 102 × 72 cm). Signed.

MABUSE, Jan Gossaert of Maubeuge, called «**Mabuse**» (b. Maubeuge 1478; d. Middelborg c. 1533/34). Gossaert's painting combines the Flemish tradition of highly-finished detail with the imposing style and mythological subjects he found on his visit to Rome in 1508 as a member

2801. Massys. Christ presented
to the people.

1536. Mabuse. The
Virgin of Louvain.

of Philip of Burgundy's entourage. He painted primarily for the princes and princesses of the House of Burgundy, which explains the perfect quality of his works, intended for aristocratic patrons.

1510 «Christ between the Virgin Mary and St. John the Baptist» (Wood, 122 × 133 cm). The heads are painted on paper stuck to the wood. The half-length figures are freely copied from Van Eyck's altar-piece in St. Bavon's Cathedral in Ghent. It is a mature work which reveals the artist's perfect technique together with a harmonious serenity and fullness, thus combining the classicism of Italian art with the Northern tradition.

1536 «The Virgin of Louvain» (Wood, 45 × 39 cm). On the reverse, an inscription attributes the panel to Gossaert explaining that it was given to Philip II in 1588 by the city of Louvain. Some art critics consider that it could have been painted by Van Orley, a contemporary of Mabuse. The fantastic architecture that frames the delicate figure of the Virgin is inspired by Italian Renaissance motifs.

1930 «The Virgin and Child» (Wood, 63 × 50 cm). This is one of Mabuse's most characteristic works in the grand, monumental figures of the Virgin and Child; the latter recalls Michelangelo's child nudes which Mabuse must have seen while he was in Italy. The light plays subtly around the figures and sets off the folds in the draperies and the fine hair, depicted in perfect detail in the purest Flemish tradition.

MARINUS. See Reymerswaele.

MASSYS, Cornelis Massys or Metsys (Antwerp c. 1510-c. 1562).

1612 «Rest on the Flight into Egypt» (Wood, 63 × 112 cm). Son of the painter Quentin Massys, his landscapes have their origin in those of Patenier, like this one, in spite of the dark tones and brownish shades he used here. The forms are loose and porous, which gives the whole composition a fantastic air.

MASSYS, Jan Massys (b. Antwerp c. 1509; d. before 1575). Son of Quentin Massys, he followed his father's style, adapting it to the Italianate taste of the 16th century.

1561 «The Saviour» (Wood, 44 × 35 cm). Signed Quentin Metsys and dated 1529. See No. 1562.

1562 «The Virgin Mary» (Wood, 44 × 35 cm). This is the companion piece to the preceding panel. Although they are both signed Quentin Metsys, art critics consider them to be the work of his son Jan, whereas other historians attribute them to Marinus van Reymerswaele. They are of excellent quality, finely drawn and coloured.

2207 See Lombard.

MASSYS, Quentin Massys, Matsys or Metsys (b. Louvain 1466; d. Antwerp 1530). Massys belongs to the last generation of Early Flemish masters. Although most of his work falls within the 16th century, he did not share the prevailing taste of the Romanist artists and preferred to paint in the traditional Flemish style. His works recall Leonardo da Vinci and stress the expressive aspect of the figures. Together with Patenier he was one of the first to discover the possibilities of landscape painting as an independent branch of painting.

1615 See Patenier and Quentin Massys.

2801 «Christ presented to the people» (Wood, 160 × 120 cm). This is one of the artist's masterpieces and dates from about 1515, when Massys had reached his artistic maturity. It reveals typically Flemish depiction of rich draperies and textures, whereas the architectural elements in the background denote acquaintance with Renaissance styles. The low viewpoint places the observer among the crowd, thus making him participate in the scene. The splendid series of caricature-like heads deserve attention.

3074 «Old woman tearing at her hair» (Wood, 55 × 40 cm). This work is probably an allegory on Anger or Envy since these sins are usually represented in the shape of an old woman with expressive, distorted features.

MEDIAS FIGURAS (Master of the Half-length Figures) (1530/40).

1919 «Adoration of the Magi» (Wood, 54 × 36 cm). This work dates from about 1535 and has its origin in the style of Gerard David.

2552 «Triptych of the Nativity» (Central panel: 83 × 70; side wings: 83 × 33 cm). The side wings represent the *Annunciation* and the *Presentation in the Temple*.

MEIREN, Jan Baptist van der Meiren (Antwerp 1664?-1708?). Landscape painter.

2046 «Jacob's Journey» (Canvas, 43 × 51 cm). This work was previously attributed to the Dutch master Bloemaert.

MEMLING, Hans Memling (b. Seiligenstadt-am-Main c. 1440; d. Bruges 1494). He studied in Van der Weyden's workshop and settled in Bruges. In its formal aspect, his painting recalls that of his master, but its mood is completely different; it tends towards decorative effects, gives preference to clear, symmetrical compositions and avoids dramatizing the subject-matter, thus conveying an overall impression of gentleness and harmony.

1557 **«Nativity - The Adoration of the Kings - The Purification»** (Triptych. Central panel: 95 × 145 cm; wings: 95 × 63 cm). This work has its origin in Van der Weyden's triptych on the same theme preserved in the *Pinakothek* in Munich. Memling's version omits several elements in order to obtain a clearer impression of space, but his figures appear disconnected and somewhat aloof from the scene they are meant to portray.

1558 See Weyden, Copy by Memling.

2543 **«The Virgin and Child between two angels»** (Wood, 36 × 26 cm). The motif of the angel offering the Child a piece of fruit was used by Memling on various occasions. This panel is considered a workshop painting.

1557. Memling. Nativity.

3209. Mostaert. Portrait of a gentleman.

METSYS. See Massys.

MEULEN, Adam Frans van der Meulen (b. Brussels c. 1632; d. Paris 1690). A follower of Snayers, he specialized in battle scenes. He worked for Louis XIV and made designs for Gobelin tapestries.

1349 **«A general leaving on a campaign»** (Canvas, 69 × 80 cm). Signed and dated 1660.

1563 **«An encounter between Cavalry troops»** (Canvas, 86 × 121 cm). Signed and dated 1657.

MEULENER, Peeter Meulener or Molenaer (Antwerp 1602-1654). He specialized in battle scenes, imitating Snayers, but with less panoramic views and paler colouring.

1565 **«Defence of a convoy»** (Canvas, 52 × 79 cm).

1566 **«Battle between Cavalry troops»** (Wood, 52 × 79 cm). Signed and dated 1644.

2527 **«Cavalry attack»** (Copper, 25 × 32 cm). See No. 2528.

2528 **«Cavalry skirmish»** (Copper, 25 × 32 cm). These two works were previously attributed to Courtois, but the Museum's present Catalogue of Flemish Paintings lists them as by Meulener. They are signed P. M.

MICHAU, Theobald Michau (b. Tournai 1676; d. Antwerp 1765). He imitated Bruegel «de Velours», but his handling is freer and more pictorial.

1567 **«River with figures and cattle»** (Wood, 29 × 40 cm).

1568 **«Houses on a river-bank»** (Wood, 29 × 40 cm).

MIEL, Jan Miel (b. Beveren-Waas 1599; d. Turin 1663). Painter of outdoor *genre* pictures. He worked mainly in Rome, where he was a friend of Van Laer. He also painted landscapes and portraits.

1569 **«Guitar player»** (Canvas, 67 × 50 cm).

1570 **«The picnic»** (Canvas, 49 × 68 cm). This work is typical of his compositional schemes, with a background of simple, diagonally traced walls.

1571 **«Shack with its occupants»** (Canvas, 49 × 49 cm).

1572 **«Hunters' rest»** (Canvas, 50 × 67 cm). This work reflects his characteristic scheme, with the diagonal in the background broken by a leafless tree. The execution is extremely simplified without any attention to detail.

1573 **«Popular scenes»** (Canvas, 50 × 65 cm). These scenes came to be called *bambocciate* and were generally painted by Flemish and Dutch artists living in Rome. The inventor of this type of picture, Van Laer, was given the nickname «Bamboccio» (simpleton) because of the triviality of his subjects.

1574 **«Landscape with shepherds»** (Canvas, 43 × 37 cm).

1575 **«Conversation on the way»** (Canvas, 48 × 37 cm).

1577 **«Roman Carnival»** (Canvas, 68 × 50 cm). Signed and dated 1653.

MINDERHOUT, Hendrick van Minderhout (b. Rotterdam 1632; d. Antwerp 1696). Dutch landscape painter resident in Belgium.

2104 **«Disembarkation»** (Canvas, 70 × 167 cm). Signed and dated 1668.

2105 **«Embarking for a party»** (Canvas, 70 × 167 cm). Signed and dated 1668.

MIROU, Antoine Mirou (b. Antwerp 1570; d. after 1661). Landscapist.

1579 **«Landscape with the story of Abraham and Hagar»** (Copper, 52 × 43 cm). Signed. The work is delicately executed, with obvious taste for picturesque details.

MOL, Peeter van Mol (b. Antwerp 1599; d. Paris 1650). He followed Rubens's style, but with a heavier kind of execution and greater light contrasts.

1937 **«St. Mark»** (Wood, 64 × 49 cm).

1938 **«St. John the Evangelist»** (Wood, 61 × 49 cm).

MOMPER, Jan de Momper. A painter of landscapes with figures, his biography is practically unknown. 17th century.

1586 **«Deer-hunt»** (Canvas, 70 × 130 cm). Pendant to the following.

1587 **«Boar-hunt»** (Canvas, 70 × 130 cm). Its handling is rapid and careless.

2077 **«A quay»** (Canvas, 91 × 134 cm). Previously attributed to J. G. Cuyp.

MOMPER, Joost de Momper (Antwerp 1564-1635). A landscapist, he studied with his father, Bartolomé de Momper. He started out from traditional 16th-century patterns, notably influenced by Bruegel, but his style evolved towards a more personal concept of landscape painting, at times majestic and with touches of Romanticism.

1440 **«Country life»** (Canvas, 165 × 165 cm). This work was attributed to Bruegel «de Velours». It follows patterns of Bruegel «the Elder».

1443 **«Flemish market and washing place»** (Canvas, 166 × 194 cm). Previously attributed to Bruegel de Velours, it is now ascribed to Momper.

1588 **«Landscape with skaters»** (Wood, 58 × 88 cm). This landscape reflects Momper's style and his typical handling, with the forms set off by means of clear, straight, fine brushstrokes.

1589 **«Landscape»** (Wood, 58 × 84 cm). The figures are believed to be by Bruegel «de Velours».

1590 **«A farm»** (Wood, 42 × 68 cm). The wide landscape, formed by diagonally intersecting planes, is typical of his style.

1592 **«Landscape with sea and mountains»** (Canvas, 174 × 256 cm). Here we see Momper's most personal and characteristic style, with majestic, somewhat fantastically formed mountains and haziness in the distance.

2817 **«Crossing a river»** (Wood, 57 × 84 cm). The figure has been attributed to Bruegel «the Younger».

MOMPER and Bruegel «de Velours».

1428 **«Country excursion with the Infanta Isabella Clara Eugenia»** (Canvas, 176 × 237 cm).

1429 **«The Infanta Isabella Clara Eugenia in the Park of Mariemont»** (Canvas, 176 × 236 cm).

1591 **«Landscape»** (Wood, 42 × 68 cm).

MORO, Anthonis Moor van Dashorst, known in Spain as **«Antonio Moro»** (b. Utrecht 1517; d. Antwerp 1576). A follower of Jan van Scorel, Moro specialized in portraiture and was renowned as one of the most famous portrait painters of his time. He was protected by Cardinal Granvelle and the Duke of Alba, Governors of the Netherlands; he was Court Painter to the Queen Regent Maria of Hungary and through her to her nephew King Philip II of Spain. In Madrid he gained the King's friendship and confidence, but did not remain here long, possibly for fear of the Inquisition due to his sympathies with the Protestants. His sitters were always members of the royal family and the nobility as can be observed in the elegant, serene and often majestic air of his compositions. The influence of Titian can be recognized in the psychological studies of his sitters and during his stay in Italy he must also have come into contact with the works of Bronzino and other famous portrait painters. Moro attached importance to depicting elements that could contribute towards emphasizing the power, authority or wealth of his models, as well as the clothing and jewelry which he portrays with particular care; he also accentuated the facial expressions by putting the whole character of his sitters into a turn of the mouth or a haughty look. Moro's work is important in Spain in order to understand the development of courtly portraiture at the end of the 16th century prior to the appearance of Velazquez. The Prado possesses some of Moro's finest work, all belonging to the royal collection.

2107 **«Pejerón, the Jester of the Count of Benavente and the Duke of Alba»** (Wood, 181 × 92 cm). This figure has been identified in old court inventories as «Pejerón, the Count of Benavente's fool», «a witty, inoffensive man» according to his contemporaries; this is possibly the first portrait of a jester in history.

2108 **«Queen Mary of England (Mary Tudor), second wife of Philip II»** (Wood, 109 × 84 cm). Signed and dated 1554. Daughter of Henry VIII and Catherine of Aragon, she was born in 1516 and married Philip II in 1554, dying four years later. This is one of Moro's masterpieces, where he combines perfect technique with an interesting psychological study.

2109 **«Catherine of Austria, wife of King John III of Portugal»** (Wood, 107 × 84 cm). She was one of the daughters of Philip the Fair and Joanna of Aragon (the Mad Queen) and therefore a sister of the Emperor Charles V.

2110 **«The Empress Maria, wife of Maximilian II»** (Canvas, 181 × 90 cm). Signed and dated 1551. Daughter of Charles V, she was born in 1528 and died in 1603. She married the Emperor Maximilian II in 1548.

2111 **«Emperor Maximilian II»** (Canvas, 184 × 100 cm). Signed and dated 1550. He was the son of the Emperor Ferdinand I and was born in Vienna in 1527. This canvas is the companion piece to the preceding No.

2112 **«Joanna of Austria, mother of King Sebastian of Portugal»** (Canvas, 195 × 104 cm). She was a daughter of Charles V, born in 1535. She married Don Juan, Prince of Brasil, in 1552 and died in 1573. In Madrid she founded the Convent of Barefoot Carmelites, where she is buried. This is one of the portraits that can best convey an insight into the austerity of the Spanish Court in the 16th century.

2113 **«The lady with the jewel»** (Wood, 107 × 83 cm). The lady has not been identified. The portrait was purchased in Naples by Charles III. Some art historians consider it to portray the Empress Isabella, the wife of Charles V, whereas others regard it as a portrait of Doña Maria of Portugal when she was betrothed to Philip II.

2114 **«Metgen, the painter's wife»** (Wood, 100 × 80 cm). The portrait shows a profound psychological study of the sitter, Moro's wife.

2115 **«The Duchess of Feria»** (?) (Canvas, 95 × 76 cm). Born in 1538, she was the daughter of Sir William Dormer and a friend of Mary Tudor.

2116 **«Lady wearing a cross»** (Canvas, 94 × 76 cm). The lady has been identified, although without sufficient proof, as Margaret Harrington, the daughter of the Baron of Extor, who married Don Benito Cisneros.

2117 **«Doña Maria of Portugal, wife of Alessandro Farnese»** (Wood, 39 × 15 cm). Born in Lisbon in 1538, she was the daughter of Prince Edward, brother of King John III of Portugal. She married Alessandro Farnese, Governor of the Netherlands and captain of the Spanish Armada.

2117bis **«Margarita of Parma»** (Wood, 39 × 15 cm). She was the daughter of Charles V and Joanna van der Gheyst, born in 1521, and the mother of Alessandro Farnese.

2118 **«Philip II»** (Wood, 41 × 31 cm). This portrait of the King as a young man was used by Moro to paint other portraits now preserved in El Escorial and Vienna.

2119 **«The lady with the golden chains»** (Canvas, 112 × 97 cm).

2880 **«Portrait of a lady»** (Canvas, 96 × 76 cm).

MORO, Copies by Bartolomé González.

1141 **«Anna of Austria, fourth wife of Philip II»** (Canvas, 107 × 86 cm). Daughter of the Emperor Maximilian II, she married her uncle Philip II in 1570. This is a copy after a portrait by Moro kept in the Museum of Vienna.

1143 **«Knight of the Order of Santiago»** (Wood, 41 × 30 cm). This is a copy after a portrait by Moro dated 1558 and now preserved in Budapest.

MORO, Follower.

1516 **«48-year-old gentleman»** (Wood, 71 × 35 cm).

1517 **«35-year-old lady»** (Wood, 72 × 56 cm). Both this and its preceding companion piece were originally attributed to Franck Floris.

2881 **«Portrait of a lady»** (Canvas, 96 × 75 cm).

MOSTAERT, Jan Mostaert (Haarlem c. 1475-1555/6).

3209 **«Portrait of a young gentleman»** (Wood, 53 × 37 cm). He holds a glove in his right hand and a ring in his left. For some time this was

considered a portrait of Charles V; if so it may have been painted for his betrothal, but the features do not correspond to those of the Emperor.
NEEFS, Ludwig Neefs (b. Antwerp, 1617; d. after 1648). A brother of Neefs «the Elder», he specialized in interiors.

1598 **«Church interior»** (Wood, 28 × 25 cm). Signed and dated 1646. The figures were painted by Frans Franken «the Younger».
NEEFS, Peeter Neefs «the Elder» (b. Antwerp c. 1578; d. c. 1656/61). He specialized in architectural interiors, especially churches, with preference for the Gothic, three-nave style. His rendering of perspective is perfect and the light effects are executed with great care. Frans Franken «the Younger» painted the figures in his pictures.

1599 **«Interior of a Flemish church»** (Wood, 84 × 72 cm). Its attribution is doubtful.

1600 **«Viaticum in the interior of a church»** (Wood, 51 × 80 cm). Signed and dated 1636. The figures are by Franken.

1601 See Peeter Neefs «the Younger».

1602 **«Interior of a church with worship of relics»** (Wood, 27 × 39 cm). The light contrast is an effect he used frequently and succeeds in giving a touch of mystery to his otherwise severe perspectives.

1605 **«Church in Flanders»** (Wood, 58 × 98 cm). Signed and dated 1618.

2726 **«Interior of the Cathedral of Antwerp»** (Wood, 38 × 63 cm). Signed by Neefs and Franken, who painted the figures. Pendant to No. 2727.

2727 **«Interior of the Cathedral of Antwerp»** (Wood, 39 × 63 cm). Signed.
NEEFS II, Peeter Neefs «the Younger» (Antwerp 1620-1675). He followed the style of his father, Neefs «the Elder».

1601 **«Interior of the Cathedral of Antwerp»** (Wood, 31 × 44). Signed.
NEUFCHATEL, Nicolas de Neufchatel, called «Lucidel» (b. Mons, Belgium 1577; d. Nuremberg after 1590).

1957 **«Lady with a dog»** (Wood, 77 × 57 cm).
OOSTSANEN, Jacob Cornelis van Oostsanen (b. Oostsanen c. 1470; d. Amsterdam 1533).

2697 **«St. Jerome»** (Wood, 48 × 43 cm). Oostsanen is an example of Dutch Mannerism and possibly the first important artist of the Amsterdam School. His work reveals the influence of Dürer, which made itself felt in Dutch art from early in the 16th century onwards, although he interpreted it in a provincial tone and with an overwhelming sense of space. A particular feature is the energetically modelled head of the meditating saint.
ORLEY, Bernaerdt van Orley (Brussels c. 1491-1542). Court painter in Brussels and Antwerp, Van Orley's work follows the line of the artists who introduced Renaissance styles in the Netherlands. He probably never visited Italy, but must have been familiar with engravings of works by Italian masters and the famous cartoons by Raphael for tapestries that were woven in Flanders for the Vatican in 1517. Van Orley's work is refined and decorative, in keeping with the taste of the courtly circles he worked for.

1932. Orley. Virgin and Child.　　2692. Orley. The Holy Family.

1920 **«The Virgin of the Holy Milk»** (Wood, 54 × 30 cm). Many copies were made of this work, which comes from El Escorial.

1932 **«Virgin and Child»** (Wood, 98 × 71 cm). This work was painted about

1516. The composition is delicate and harmonious, the figures slightly blurred (*sfumato*), but draperies, objects and architectural elements are clearly outlined, in true Northern fashion.

2692 «The Holy Family» (Wood, 90 × 74 cm). Signed and dated 1522. This panel is one of the most characteristic of Van Orley's style. The Virgin and Child recall works of Raphael, whereas the other figures and objects are executed with a typically Flemish love of detail, as also the tapestry, crown and flowers, which seem like the work of a 15th-century master. **ORLEY, Copy.**

2725 «The Virgin of Carandolet» (Wood, 56 × 40 cm). This is a copy after a famous original by Van Orley, considered by some to be by Rubens. **ORLEY, Follower.**

1934 **«The Virgin and Child with Hernán Gómez Dávila and St. Francis»** (Wood, 60 × 78 cm). This work comes from the burial chapel of the Gómez Dávila family in the Cathedral of Avila. This knight, lord of Navamorcuende, died in the battle of Geldern in 1511. **PALAMEDESZ.** See Lamen.

1614. Patenier. Landscape with St. Jerome.

PATENIER, Henri de. See Massys, Cornelis.
PATENIER, Joachim Patenier (b. Bouvignes c. 1480; d. Antwerp 1524). The wonderful landscape backgrounds of the 15th-century masters acquire special significance in the work of Patenier. He was the first to invert the relationship figure-landscape, attaching more importance to the latter and relegating to a subordinate role the scenes and figures, which thus appear lost in his immense vision of nature. Patenier thereby created what was to become a new branch of painting. In his landscapes we can distinguish large expanses of vegetation, forests and quiet, green plains, hills, valleys, fantastic rock-formations, lakes and rivers, real architecture, huts and houses, together with enormous constructions invented by Patenier's imagination. His landscapes are rich and varied and with their many different elements succeed in conveying a total vision of nature, which is always placid, shady, at times melancholy, sometimes enlivened by rays of light that emphasize a particular point of the composition. The high horizon-line and skilful use of colours, brown in the foreground, green in the middle distance and bluish tones in the background, create an impression of distance and panoramic effect. Patenier worked in the prosperous city of Antwerp and collaborated with other masters such as Quentin Massys, Joos van Cleve and Isenbrandt, adding landscapes to their pictures.

1611 **«Rest on the Flight into Egypt»** (Wood, 121 × 177 cm). The central part of the composition is occupied by the Virgin and Child, exquisitely drawn and coloured, but the principal aspect of the work is the vast landscape. Probably the most interesting part is the right-hand side, with the peasants in the village and working in the fields. The fantastic architectural elements on the left represent Egypt with figures dressed in Oriental clothes and others offering sacrifices to an idol. St. Joseph approaches carrying a jug of milk.

1614 **«Landscape with St. Jerome»** (Wood, 74 × 91 cm). Signed. This is one of the artist's most complicated and characteristic landscapes. On the left, the saint is meditating in front of the crucifix with the lion by his side; in the background we see a desolate, rocky landscape with a town and on the right a vast plain near the estuary of a river brings to mind a true Dutch landscape. Small secondary, possibly symbolic scenes like the blind man and his guide or the lion attacking a peasant with his donkey, can also be distinguished.

1616 **«Charon crossing the Styx»** (Wood, 64 × 103 cm). This is one of Patenier's most famous masterpieces. The great beauty of the landscape with its horizon sharply outlined against the bright sky almost makes us forget the painting's main theme, which combines Christian and pagan beliefs about the world to come. On the left, we see Paradise with two angels accompanying those who have saved their souls towards the heavenly Jerusalem; in the foreground there are peacocks and flowers. The transparent structure of the heavenly buildings in the background clearly recall similar constructions in Bosch's works. In the centre, Charon, the mythological ferryman whose mission was to transport the souls of the dead to Hades, is seen crossing the Styx with one of them in his boat. Hell is depicted on the right with the three-headed watch-dog Cerberus guarding its entrance and with glowing fires and tormented figures that again remind us of Bosch.

PATENIER and Quentin MASSYS.

1615 **«The Temptation of St. Anthony»** (Wood, 155 × 173 cm). Signed. This work was done by Patenier and Massys in collaboration, the former painting the landscape and the latter the figures; between them they have achieved a work that reveals perfect unity. In the centre the saint is tempted by three luxuriosuly dressed beauties while a devil disguised as a monkey pulls at his cloak. The figure of the old woman on the left who is meant to remind us of the transience of beauty is typical of Massys. Two other scenes of the Temptation are virtually merged in the magnificent landscape, which again calls to mind Patenier's own native country with its rivers, villages, windmills and peasants labouring in the fields. Dutch and Flemish landscape painting in the 17th century is anticipated by Patenier's attention to light and atmospheric effects.

PATENIER, Follower.

1613 **«Rest on the Flight into Egypt»** (Wood, 63 × 112 cm). The dark shades and variety of trees and foliage differ from Patenier's orderly landscapes.

PEETERS, Bonaventura Peeters (b. Antwerp 1614; d. Hoboken 1652). Seascape painter, brother of Jan Peeters.

1618 **«Seascape»** (Wood, 18 × 24 cm).

PEETERS, Clara Peeters (Antwerp 1594-1659). Still-life painter, apparently self-trained early in life. She is masterly in the representation of objects, which she usually groups on a table parallel to the picture-plane and viewed from a raised angle.

1619 **«Still life»** (Wood, 51 × 71 cm). Signed and dated 1611.

1620 **«Table»** (Wood, 52 × 73 cm). Signed and dated 1611. The tight handling of this work that models the objects sharply against a shadowy background is typical of her exquiste style. She tried to avoid empty spaces, filling them with little flowers or other small objects, which although somewhat candid does not lack charm. She painted her own reflection on metal objects.

1621 **«Table»** (Wood, 50 × 72 cm). Signed and dated 1611.

1622 **«Table»** (Wood, 55 × 73 cm). Signed. The use here of homogeneous tones, tending towards monochrome colouring, suggests that she was in contact with the Dutch school of Haarlem.

PEETERS, Jan Peeters (Antwerp 1624-1677). Seascape painter like his brothers Bonaventura and Gilles. He lived in Holland.

2128 **«A harbour»** (Copper, 70 × 86 cm). Signed.

POURBUS, Frans Pourbus (b. Antwerp 1569; d. Paris 1622). A por-

1557. Hans Memling. The Adoration of the Kings. (detail)

trait painter, he worked at the Courts of Brussels, Mantua and Paris. His style is that of the traditional solemn, aloof portraits of the 16th century.

1624 **«Marie de Medici»** (Canvas, 225 × 115 cm). Signed and dated 1617. The widowed queen of Henry IV was at the time Regent of France.

1625 **«Elizabeth of France, wife of Philip II»** (Canvas, 193 × 107 cm). The identity of the sitter is not completely certain; if she is, indeed, Elizabeth of France, she wears mourning for the death of her father-in-law in 1611.

1977 **«Elizabeth of France»** (Canvas, 61 × 51 cm). This portrait bears witness to the Queen's beauty, for which she was famed. Here she is wearing a famous diamond purchased by Philip II.

2293 See Bartolomeus Breenbergh in Dutch Masters.

1624. Pourbus. Marie de Medici.

POURBUS, Copy by Charles Beaubrun.

2233 **«Marie de Medici»** (Canvas, 108 × 88 cm). This is a copy after an original kept in the Louvre.

PREVOST, Jan Prevost (b. Mons c. 1465; d. Antwerp 1529).

1296 **«Zacharias»** (Wood, 123 × 45 cm). This panel was originally a wing of a polyptych on the *Genealogy of the Virgin,* inciuded in the inventory of Philip II's collection, but now lost. Another of the wings, although not intact, is kept in the Louvre. The elaborately executed figure of Zacharias reveals this artist's characteristic features in the perfect arrangement of the figure in a closed space, a well-kept garden, beyond which we see a vast, bright landscape. There is something tense about the figure with his fine, vigorous hands opened in a gesture of surprise and the intense expression on his face emphasized by the light. On the reverse there is a statuesque figure of St. Bernardino of Siena in grisaille.

QUELLINUS, Erasmus Quellinus (Antwerp 1607-1678). He studied with his father and later under Rubens, with whom he collaborated on various occasions. On Rubens' death he succeeded him as city painter of Antwerp.

1627 See Rubens.

1628 **«The Rape of Europa»** (Canvas, 126 × 87 cm). Signed. Like the following works, this was painted for Philip IV's hunting lodge, *La Torre de la Parada,* according to sketches by Rubens who supervised the whole decoration. The paintings represent scenes from Ovid's *Metamorphoses.* The sketch is kept in the Prado (No. 2457).

1629 **«Bacchus and Ariadne»** (Canvas, 180 × 95 cm). Signed.

1630 **«The Death of Eurydice»** (Canvas, 179 × 195 cm). Signed.

1631 «Jason and the Golden Fleece» (Canvas, 181 × 195 cm). Signed.
1632 «Cupid on the back of a dolphin» (Canvas, 98 × 98 cm).
1633 «The Harpies pursued by Zetes and Calais» (Canvas, 98 × 99 cm).
1718 «Sleeping Cupid» (Canvas, 81 × 98 cm). This work was part of a larger composition on the subject of Psyche and Cupid.

REYMERSWAELE, Marinus Claeszon van Reymerswaele (b. Reymerswaele c. 1497; d. after 1567). Marinus was one of the inventors of a branch of painting that was to reach its height with the Dutch school in the 17th century: *genre* painting. His work has its origin in Quentin Massys and Gossaert, although in certain technical aspects it is influenced by Dürer. His draughtsmanship has been defined as aggressive and expressionist, at times bordering on caricature.

2100 «St. Jerome» (Wood, 75 × 101 cm). Signed on the lectern and dated 1551. This is one of the subjects that the artist repeated various times and is inspired by an original painted by Dürer in Antwerp in 1521. The vigorous, expressive figure of St. Jerome is characteristic with his energy-laden face and delicate hands ending in long, tapering fingers that point to the skull. The objects stand out in the harsh light and seem to become living parts of the composition. The book which the saint is meditating on is open at a page containing a miniature of the Last Judgement and the table and book-shelves are piled high with the saint's writings.

2101 «The Virgin suckling the Child» (Wood, 61 × 46 cm). Dated 1511.
2567 «The money-changer and his wife» (Wood, 83 × 97 cm). Signed and dated 1539. This is another of the scenes repeated by Marinus; in this case its origin is to be found in a painting on the same subject by Quentin Massys now kept in the Louvre. As in the preceding picture of St. Jerome, the artist reveals special skill in depicting the scene and conveying the tactile reality of objects and draperies. The figures again have long, vigorous hands and intense facial expressions.

2653 «St. Jerome» (Wood, 80 × 108 cm). Signed and dated 1547. Replica of No. 2100.

REYMERSWAELE, Follower.

2099 «St. Jerome» (Wood, 75 × 101 cm). This is a copy after the famous version of St. Jerome by Van Reymerswaele.

REYN, Jan van Reyn. See Jordaens.
RIGOULTS. See Thielen.
ROMBOUTS, Theodor Rombouts (Antwerp 1597-1637). He travelled to Italy where he joined in the Caravaggio movement. On his return, in 1625, he fell under the influence of Rubens.

1635 «The tooth-extractor» (Canvas, 119 × 221 cm). This painting is very

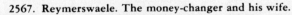

2567. Reymerswaele. The money-changer and his wife.

1588. Joost de Momper. Landscape with skaters. (detail)

2108. Anthonis Moor. Mary Tudor, second wife of Philip II. (detail)

1635. Rombouts. The tooth-extractor.

characteristic of Caravaggio's Northern followers: *genre* pictures with half-length figures illuminated by Tenebrist-style light.

1636 **«Card-players»** (Canvas, 100 × 23 cm).

RUBENS, Peter Paul Rubens (b. Siegen 1577; d. Antwerp 1640). Rubens spent his childhood in Cologne and received his artistic training in Antwerp, in the workshops of Tobias Verhaecht, Adam van Noort and Otto van Veen. Later he travelled to Italy, where he remained eight years in the service of the Duke of Mantua. On his return to Antwerp he was appointed Court Painter by the Archduke Albert and Infanta Isabella Clara Eugenia, who appreciated his talent not only as a painter, but also as a person whom they could charge with delicate diplomatic missions, for example that of trying to effect a reconciliation between England and Spain. Rubens was an optimistic, self-possessed and extremely cultured man, known and appreciated by all who met him for his good-natured character; contemporary accounts record his cordial manner, splendid qualities as a conversationalist, far-reaching knowledge of a variety of topics, in particular classical literature, and incredible vitality, which enabled him to attend to various different matters at the same time. As an artist he triumphed throughout Europe and accepted commissions from the main Courts of his time. His family life is reflected in the radiant portraits of his children and his two wives, both of whom he loved dearly. His early pictures do not differ much from the Flemish Romanist style in which he had been trained; in Italy he apparently painted little, but he must have studied enthusiastically, making a large number of sketches and copying the works of great masters, as well as learning from the two major artistic trends of the time: the Classicist movement in Bologna and Caravaggio's naturalism. Without becoming directly involved in either, Rubens learnt to portray the human figure in its heroic aspect as well as the plenitude of forms. These qualities, coupled with the vitality that underlies all Flemish art, Rubens' down-to-earth realism and frank sensuality, contributed towards creating a completely personal form of Baroque capable of satisfying all the persuasive needs of the Church in the Counter-Reformation and all the European monarchs' thirst for grandeur in extremely eloquent plastic terms. His most outstanding quality was probably his facility in arranging his compositions, tracing the movement of the figures in forceful lines that run convulsively through his pictures. His deft technique, energetic draughtsmanship and long, vibrating brush-strokes imbue his forms with palpitating vitality, making them stand out by means of loose touches of impasto that give them their particular relief. Rubens was a prodigious artist who practised all branches of painting, portraiture, religious, historical and mythological subjects, allegories and landscapes and succeeded in infusing all of them with the same buoyant liveliness, exuberant shapes and glowing colours that are so characteristic of his work. Rubens' personality had a decisive effect on the art of his time and banished from Flemish painting all sign of timidity, thus marking the beginning of its second great era, whose magnificent contributions can well be compared with those of the Primitive masters.

1543 See Rubens, School.

1627 **«The Immaculate Conception»** (Canvas, 198 × 124 cm). This work was previously ascribed to Quellinus; although its existence was documented, its recognition was made difficult because its appearance had been altered (originally it finished in a semi-circular arch) and it had been repainted, although by such an expert hand that some critics consider Velázquez to have been responsible for the finishing touches. Instead of the traditionally devout attitude of the Virgin, here Rubens has brought movement into her pose, opening her hands and turning her body to obtain a more dynamic silhouette. The work was commissioned in 1628.

1638 «The Adoration of the Magi» (Canvas, 346 × 438 cm). Dated 1610. This work was presented to Don Rodrigo Calderón by the City of Antwerp. During his second visit to Spain, in 1628, Rubens repainted it adding new strips of canvas at the top and on the right, so that what we now see corresponds to Ruben's more mature, fluent and pictorial style. The original composition ended with the Virgin and Child and the figures of the half-naked servants in the foreground, but Rubens later opened it in such a way that a diagonal crosses the whole work from the upper right-hand corner, so that the figures are placed in the form of a cascade focusing the beholder's attention on the Virgin and Child in the opposite corner. The total effect is overwhelming. Rubens had no doubt learnt from Veronese to obtain the best decorative effects from the subject, transforming it into a dazzling ceremony with the Kings and their numerous entourage resplendent in silks, brocades and jewels.

1639 «The Holy Family with St. Anne» (Canvas, 115 × 90 cm). This work dates from about 1626/30.

1640 «Rest on the Flight into Egypt» (Wood, 87 × 125 cm). Dating from about 1632/35, this is one of Rubens' mature works, which he kept in his own house and in which he repeated models and poses from *The Garden of Love*. As on other occasions, he has reproduced the features of his second wife, Helene Fourment, in the Virgin.

1642 See Van Dyck.

1639. Rubens. The Holy Family with St. Anne.   1644. Rubens. St. George.

1643 «The Supper at Emmaus» (Canvas, 143 × 156 cm). It dates from 1635/38.
1644 «St. George» (Canvas, 304 × 256 cm). Dating from about 1606, this painting belongs to his early work in Italy; his handling is smooth and enamel-like with bold brushwork that adds a sense of vibration to the surface. The tightly modelled figures, intense colouring and decorations on the saint's armour (the helmet is copied from a portrait by Leonardo) are all typical of this period. The composition is now entirely Baroque and the tension of the struggle is represented by intersecting diagonals and in the attitudes of the opponents. This is one of the most impassioned versions made of the traditional medieval theme so popular with Italian artists.

1645 See Rubens and Jan Wildens.
1646 «St. Peter» (Wood, 108 × 84 cm). This is the first of a series (now incomplete due to the loss of the Saviour) of the Apostles that Rubens painted for the Duke of Lerma. The date is unknown. The technique corresponds to his youthful style, with high surface-finish and thick brushwork, firm modelling and the accent on colouring. Some Apostles are more conventional, while others reveal strong individuality.

1647 «St. John the Evangelist» (Wood, 108 × 84 cm). See No. 1646.

1616. Joachim Patenier. Charon crossing the Styx.

1638. Peter Paul Rubens. The Adoration of the Magi. (detail)

1648   **«St. James the Elder»** (Wood, 108 × 84 cm). One of the most vigorous of the series, he is portrayed in an arrogant attitude; the intense look on his face reveals personality. See No. 1646.

1649   **«St. Andrew»** (Wood, 108 × 84 cm). See No. 1646.

1650   **«St. Philip»** (Wood, 108 × 84 cm). See No. 1646.

1651   **«St. James the Younger»** (Wood, 108 × 84 cm). See No. 1646.

1652   **«St. Bartholomew»** (Wood, 108 × 84 cm). See No. 1646.

1653   **«St. Matthias»** (Wood, 108 × 84 cm). See No. 1646.

1654   **«St. Thomas»** (Wood, 108 × 84 cm). The aged saint with the light falling on his head and splendid beard commands attention. See No. 1646.

1655   **«St. Simon»** (Wood, 108 × 84 cm). See No. 1646.

1656   **«St. Matthew»** (Wood, 108 × 84 cm). This model was used by Rubens on several occasions. See No. 1646.

1657   **«St. Paul»** (Wood, 108 × 84 cm). This model was also used on other occasions; he stands out among the Apostles with his lively face and striking hair and particularly due to the penetrating look he directs at the spectator.

1658   **«The Rape of Deidamia»** (Canvas, 182 × 290 cm). This work was painted about 1636/38 for the *Torre de la Parada,* the hunting lodge built by Philip IV in El Pardo. The decoration was a very ambitious project which the King supervised personally and with great interest. Rubens was appointed to direct the whole undertaking; he painted many of the pictures himself and prepared the sketches for those that were to be painted by his followers. Velazquez also contributed with portraits of huntsmen and some mythological subjects. The pictorial project comprised hunting and mythological scenes; the latter are based on Ovid's *Metamorphoses* and constitute an unprecedented attempt to illustrate this classical work on such a large scale. Rubens spent the last years of his life on this enterprise, working without a break in spite of his attacks of gout, pressed by the King's impatience, and when he died it was still unfinished. *The Rape of Deidamia* is an example of the aesthetic feeling with which Rubens went about this project; Baroque violence reaches its height here in this tensely dramatic scene where Theseus wrenches Deidamia from the arms of the Centaur. The poses of the different figures are linked in such a way that each movement seems to be the effect of the preceding and cause of the following one, thus achieving a tremendously dynamic composition.

1659   **«The Rape of Proserpine»** (Canvas, 180 × 270 cm). This work is also from the *Torre de la Parada* (see No. 1658). It shows Proserpine being carried off by Pluto while Minerva, Venus and Diana try to prevent it. Here again the poses are subordinated to the general effect of movement.

1660   **«Tereus' Banquet»** (Canvas, 195 × 267 cm). See No. 1658. Here Philomele and Procne present Tereus the decapitated head of his son whom he has unwittingly eaten. Although unusual in his works, Rubens does not avoid the gruesome aspect of the legend and portrays the scene here at its most dramatic height.

1662   **«Atalanta and Meleager»** (Canvas, 160 × 260 cm). This work dates from before 1636. In his later years Rubens felt himself particularly attracted by landscapes; this setting deep in the woods where the rays of light scarcely penetrate seems to come to life and vibrate, as everything that

1656. Rubens. St. Matthew.   **1670. Rubens. The Three Graces.**

Rubens touched with his brush. The figures make an excellent hunting scene as they pursue the boar which defends itself with all its strength.

1663 «Perseus and Andromeda» (Canvas, 265 × 160 cm). Rubens left this work unfinished when he died and it was completed by Jordaens. It shows Perseus about to free Andromeda after killing the monster; her face is expressive and the eyes of both figures speak for themselves. Rubens was an expert narrator and here he described perfectly the feeling of relief and serenity after the danger had passed.

1665 «Diana and her nymphs discovered by satyrs» (Canvas, 136 × 165 cm). Wildens and Snayers collaborated on this work painting the landscape and the animals respectively. It was a frequent habit of Rubens to lay the weight of the composition on the right, thus availing of the natural direction from left to right, like in reading, to represent and accelerate the movement of the painting.

1666 «Nymphs and satyrs» (Canvas, 136 × 165 cm). Nymphs and satyrs are a much-used theme in Rubens' works. Here he reveals himself as a worthy follower of Titian presenting us a happy world where nature showers her gifts, fresh water and the inviting shade of her forests in a golden age where children play with wild beasts and nymphs need not escape from the satyrs. The work transmits a quiet sensuality common to other paintings of the same time (1635) and could be interpreted as an allegory of abundance.

1667 «Orpheus and Eurydice» (Canvas, 194 × 245 cm). See No. 1658.

1668 «The creation of the Milky Way» (Canvas, 181 × 244 cm). See No. 1658.

1669 «The Judgement of Paris» (Wood, 199 × 379 cm). This work dates from about 1639. Paris has to hand the apple to the goddess he considers most beautiful. Rubens painted this work for Philip IV a year before his death, in spite of his gout, which however did not prevent him from painting with all the technical perfection of his mature age.

1670 «The Three Graces» (Wood, 221 × 181 cm). This work probably dates from about 1636. Rubens kept it at his own home and it was acquired by Philip IV at the auction of the artist's estate. It is justifiably famous for its delicate execution. Rubens obviously took pleasure in rendering the texture of the Graces' translucent skin, the flowers and draperies behind them and harmonious landscape. The Graces' beauty is of the opulent kind so typical of Rubens; their arrangement in almost linked poses forms an undulating rhythm and the subtle play of curvilinear outlines enlivens the flowing design, thus producing an impression of vital vibration. It is a gay, lively scene and expresses admirably the great master's direct, wholesome sensuality.

1671 «Diana and Callisto» (Canvas, 202 × 323 cm). The work represents the moment when the nymphs show Diana that Callisto is pregnant. The golden lighting effect brings the whole composition into harmony.

1673 «Mercury and Argus» (Canvas, 179 × 297 cm). See No. 1658. Mercury is preparing to kill Argus, who guards Io transformed into a cow.

1674 «Fortuna» (Canvas, 179 × 95 cm). See No. 1658.

1676 «Vulcan» (Canvas, 181 × 97 cm). See No. 1658.

1677 «Mercury» (Canvas, 180 × 69 cm). See No. 1658.

1678 «Saturn» (Canvas, 180 × 87 cm). See No. 1658. Here Saturn is seen devouring his son. Rubens succeeded in achieving one of the most dramatic versions of the subject, which later no doubt impressed Goya.

1679 «The Rape of Ganymede» (Canvas, 181 × 87 cm). See No. 1658.

1680 «Heraclitus» (Canvas, 181 × 63 cm). See No. 1658.

1681 «Satyr» (Canvas, 181 × 64 cm). See No. 1658. This work was previously erroneously listed as Democritus.

1682 «Democritus» (Canvas, 179 × 66 cm). See No. 1658.

1685 «Marie de Medici» (Canvas, 130 × 108 cm). This work dates from before 1622. It is an unfinished portrait which Rubens possibly made as a preliminary sketch for an allegorical series commissioned by the Queen Mother of France. Rubens knew his sitter well and she held him in high esteem; something of this attitude is reflected in the Queen's face.

1686 «Philip II on horseback» (Canvas, 314 × 228 cm). This is an allegorical portrait based on the studies that Titian had made of King Philip II.

1687 «The Cardinal-Infante» (Canvas, 335 × 258 cm). This portrait was painted to commemorate the Battle of Nordlingen (1634) and is presided over by Fame and the Habsburg eagle.

1688 «Sir Thomas More» (Wood, 105 × 73 cm). This is a copy with some variations of the portrait of Sir Thomas More by Holbein (Frick Collection).

1689 «Anne of Austria» (Canvas, 129 × 106 cm). About 1622. The sitter was the daughter of Philip III of Spain and wife of Louis XIII of France.

1690. Peter Paul Rubens. The Garden of Love.

1800. David Teniers. The old man and the maidservant. (detail)

1690 «The Garden of Love» (Canvas, 198 × 283 cm). This work has been known under different titles: *Conversation à la mode, The party, School of Love* and *Garden of the Graces*. It was considered at the time to portray Rubens' own family and the artist painted several versions of the same subject. The painting was greatly admired and Philip IV hung it in his bedchamber. It probably represents an allegory on conjugal love. The scene takes place in a garden next to a house which appears to be an idealized version of Rubens' own house. On the right, a fountain symbolizes Juno, the goddess who protected marriage; some Cupids fly around with symbols of love (arrows, flowers of pleasure, Hymen's torch, doves of fertility and marriage yoke), while others entertain the couples. The central group has been interpreted in different ways: in other versions of the same subject the composition varies slightly and indicates more clearly that the theme is the punishment of Cupid, who is seen being hit by a lady with her fan, but in this version the meaning is more ambiguous. The picture as a whole is probably intended as a tribute to Helene Fourment, Rubens' second wife, whose features appear with variations in all the female figures. The technique shows Rubens' mature style at its best, with loose vibrant brushwork; the dense, golden-tinged atmosphere that floods the whole scene unifying the colouring is once again reminiscent of Titian and his vital hedonism and transforms the painting into an invitation to the senses.

1691 «Peasants' Dance» (Wood, 73 × 106 cm). This work dates from about 1630 and is one of the most perfect examples of Rubens' ability to construct his compositions in a continuous line that embraces the whole scene in its movement. This subject, which is frequent in Flemish art, acquires here Italian touches in the landscape and peasants' costumes, while some details appear to contain an allegorical significance beyond the mere anecdotic content of the peasants dancing.

1692 «Adam and Eve» (Canvas, 237 × 184 cm). This work dates from 1628/29 and is a copy after an original by Titian kept in the Prado (No. 429).

1693 «The Rape of Europa» (Canvas, 181 × 200 cm). This is a copy after an original by Titian which belonged to Philip II. It dates from about 1628. This and the preceding copy were painted by Rubens during his second visit to Spain and reveal an interest in the Venetian master that remains evident in all his later work.

1695 «St. Clare among the doctors of the Church» (Wood, 65 × 68 cm). Together with the Nos. 1696-1700 this work belongs to a series of models for tapestries commissioned by the Infanta Isabella Clara Eugenia on the general subject of the Triumph of the Eucharist, possibly as a votive offering for the victory of Breda. The tapestries are kept in the Convent of the Barefoot Carmelites in Madrid.

1696 «Abraham paying tithes to Melchizedek» (Wood, 87 × 91 cm). See No. 1695. The theme is a prefiguration of the Eucharist: Abraham offers bread and wine to Melchizedek, priest-king of Salem.

1697 «The triumph of the Eucharist over heresy» (Wood, 68 × 91 cm). See No. 1695. Time and Truth triumph over the heretics, among whom Luther and Calvin can be distinguished.

1698 «The triumph of the Church over fury, discord and hatred» (Wood, 86 × 91 cm). See No. 1695. Presented like a Roman victory, this work is one of the most elaborate compositions of the series and expresses perfectly the religious spirit of the Counter-Reformation.

1699 «The triumph of the Eucharist over idolatry» (Wood, 69 × 91 cm). See No. 1695.

1700 «The Triumph of Divine Love» (Wood, 87 × 91 cm). See No. 1695. At the feet of Charity we see a pelican, which according to a legend feeds its young with its own flesh and therefore traditionally symbolized the Eucharist.

1701-2 See Rubens, Copies.

1703 «The Virgin surrounded by saints» (Copper, 64 × 29 cm). This work dates from about 1628 and is a smaller version of a canvas preserved in the Museum of Antwerp. Rubens adapts the Renaissance subject of the Holy Conversation and transforms it with a clearly Baroque spirit to convey a realistic depiction of the dialogue. The composition flows cascade-like forming a wide curve linking the figures in an imposing stage-like setting.

1727 «Diana as a huntress» (Canvas, 182 × 194 cm). It dates from about 1620.

1731 «The Judgement of Paris» (Wood, 91 × 114 cm). This is an early work and still reveals Mannerist elements.

2038 See Rubens, Copies.

2039 See Rubens, Copies.

2040 **«Apollo and the serpent Python»** (Canvas, 27 × 42 cm). This is the sketch for Cornelis de Vos' painting for the *Torre de la Parada.*

2041 **«Deucalion and Pyrrha»** (Wood, 25 × 17 cm). This is the sketch for a painting by Jean Cossiers for the *Torre de la Parada,* now lost.

2042 **«Prometheus»** (Wood, 25 × 17 cm). This is the sketch for Jean Cossiers' painting for the *Torre de la Parada* (Prado No. 1464).

2043 **«Hercules and Cerberus»** (Wood, 28 × 31 cm). This is a sketch for an untraceable painting for the *Torre de la Parada.*

2044 **«Vertumnus and Pomona»** Wood, 26 × 38 cm). This is a sketch for the decoration of the *Torre de la Parada.*

2454 **«The education of Achilles»** (Wood, 110 × 80 cm). Together with Nos. 2455 and 2566, this was one of a series of tapestry designs on the life of Achilles. They have architectonic borders with caryatids. Here we see Achilles riding the centaur Chiron, entrusted with his education.

2455 **«Achilles discovered by Ulysses and Lycomedes»** (Wood, 107 × 142 cm). Disguised as a woman, Achilles is discovered when he takes the arms offered to him by Ulysses and Lycomedes, disguised as merchants.

2456 **«The death of the consul Decius Mus»** (Wood, 99 × 138 cm). This work is inspired by Leonardo's *Battle of Anghiari* which Rubens copied when he was in Italy. In spite of the density of its design, the composition is clear and perfectly organized in its play of intersecting diagonals. As usual, Rubens represents the most dramatic moment of the story.

2457 **«The Rape of Europa»** (Wood, 18 × 14 cm). This is the sketch for

1691. Rubens. Peasants' Dance.

Quellinus' painting for the *Torre de la Parada* (Prado No. 1628).

2458 **«The pursuit of the Harpies»** (Wood, 14 × 14 cm). This is a sketch for Quellinus' painting for the *Torre de la Parada* (Prado No. 1633).

2459 **«Cephalus and Procris»** (Wood, 26 × 28 cm). This is a sketch for a painting for the *Torre de la Parada,* now lost.

2460 See Rubens, Copies.

2461 **«The Death of Hyacinth»** (Wood, 14 × 14 cm). This is a sketch for a painting for the *Torre de la Parada.*

2566 **«Briseis restored to Achilles»** (Wood, 106 × 162 cm). See No. 2454.

2811 See Rubens, School.

3048 See Rubens, Workshop.

3137 **«The Duke of Lerma»** (Canvas, 283 × 200 cm). Signed, but the date is incomplete; the work was painted during Rubens' first visit to Madrid (1603). The artist, who was at the time in the service of the Duke of Mantua, travelled to Madrid on a diplomatic mission, accompanying a consignment of paintings and gifts for the King of Spain. Rubens made a favourable impression on Lerma, who asked to be portrayed by him. The painting constitutes an important innovation in the field of equestrian portraits since it breaks with the tradition of the classical pose which placed the horse in profile; here the horse advances towards the spectator

2825. Rogier van der Weyden. The Deposition.

as if it wants to break out of the picture. The refined execution, with a touch of preciosity in the rendering of the Duke's clothes and armour, is still a Mannerist feature in a painting otherwise Baroque in its conception. **RUBENS and Jan Bruegel.**

1418 **«Garland with the Virgin and Child»** (Canvas, 79 × 65 cm). This work dates from about 1614/18.

1683 **«The Archduke Albert»** (Canvas, 112 × 173 cm).

1684 **«The Infanta Isabella Clara Eugenia»** (Canvas, 102 × 173 cm). This is the companion-piece to No. 1683. **RUBENS and Van Dyck.**

1661 **«Achilles discovered by Ulysses and Lycomedes»** (Canvas, 246 × 267 cm). As usual when working in collaboration with his assistants, Rubens provided the designs and at the end added the finishing brushwork, so that it is difficult to distinguish between the contributions of each of them. **RUBENS and Frans Snyders.**

1420 **«Garland of flowers and fruit»** (Canvas, 174 × 56 cm).

1664 **«Ceres and two nymphs»** (Canvas, 223 × 162 cm).

1672 **«Ceres and Pan»** (Canvas, 177 × 279 cm). **RUBENS and Jan Wildens.**

1645 **«Act of devotion of Rudolf I of Habsburg»** (Canvas, 198 × 283 cm). **RUBENS, Copies.**

1701 **«Triumph of the Eucharist over Science, Philosophy and Nature»** (Wood, 86 × 91 cm). This is a copy after an original kept in Brussels that was one of a series of tapestry designs on the *Apotheosis of the Eucharist.*

1702 **«The four Evangelists»** (Wood, 86 × 91 cm). See the preceding No.

1706 **«Democritus»** (Canvas, 119 × 47 cm). This is a copy of No. 1682.

1708 **«Mercury»** (Canvas, 108 × 49 cm). This is a copy of No. 1677.

1709 **«The four Evangelists»** (Wood, 86 × 91 cm). This is a copy of No. 1702.

1710 **«Hercules killing the Lernaean Hydra»** (Canvas, 117 × 49 cm). This is a copy after an untraceable original by Rubens for the *Torre de la Parada.*

1711 **«Hercules killing the dragon of the Hesperides»** (Canvas, 65 × 156 cm). This is a copy after an untraceable original.

1715 **«Andromeda»** (Canvas, 193 × 104 cm). Copy after an original in Berlin (Dahlem).

1725 **«Diana as a huntress»** (Canvas, 119 × 49 cm). This is a copy after an untraceable original.

1744-P **«Dido and Aeneas»** (Canvas, 146 × 145 cm). This is a copy after an original by J. B. del Mazo, now lost.

2038 **«The giant Polyphemus»** (Wood, 27 × 14 cm). This is a copy after an original by Cossiers from a sketch by Rubens for the *Torre de la Parada.*

2039 **«Atlas bearing the world»** (Wood, 25 × 17 cm). This is a copy after a sketch for the *Torre de la Parada,* previously considered an original.

2460 **«The Rape of Dejanira»** (Wood, 18 × 13 cm). See the preceding No. **RUBENS, Workshop.**

1675 **«Flora»** (Canvas, 167 × 95 cm).

3048 **«The death of Seneca»** (Wood, 128 × 121 cm). **RUBENS, School.**

1543 **«The Judgement of Solomon»** (Canvas, 184 × 217 cm).

1713 See Jordaens.

1716 **«Aeolus»** (Canvas, 140 × 126 cm).

1717 **«Vulcan»** (Canvas, 140 × 126 cm). Pendant to the preceding No.

1718 See Quellinus.

1961-2 See Sustermans, School.

2811 **«St. Augustine meditating»** (Canvas, 209 × 159 cm). **RYCKAERT, David Ryckaert** (Antwerp 1612-1661). *Genre* painter, expert in still lifes. He used a kind of night-lighting effect borrowed from Dutch painters.

1730 **«The alchemist»** (Wood, 58 × 86 cm). **RYCKAERT, Martin Ryckaert** (Antwerp 1587-1631). Landscape painter, in the line of Paul Brill. He studied in Italy.

2002 **«Rocky mountain landscape»** (Copper, 43 × 66 cm). **SANTA SANGRE (Master of the Holy Blood).** (active in Bruges in the first third of the 16th century). This artist, a follower of Quentin Massys, is known by this name due to a *Pietà* Triptych that he painted for the chapel of the Holy Blood Brotherhood in Bruges. Together with a series of other similar works, this triptych reveals the artistic personality of the unknown master.

1559 **«Triptych of the Ecce Homo»** (Central panel: 109 × 89 cm; side wings: 109 × 39 cm). This is one of the master's finest works; it is based on a panel by Quentin Massys now kept in the Doge's Palace in Venice.

A salient feature is the characteristic expressionism of this artist, who used bright colouring and precise design; the heads and expressions of his figures are all highly detailed, from the brutal, caricature-like faces of the soldiers to the delicate, serene head of Christ. In the foreground of the left-hand wing we see the donor, a perfect portrait of a contemporary burgher.

2494 «**Triptych of the Annunciation**» (Central panel: 39 × 33; side wings: 43 × 15 cm). The central panel represents the Annunciation and the side wings St. Jerome and St. John the Baptist against a landscape background. It is not a high-quality work and contains errors in the proportions and grouping of the figures. Its attribution should probably be revised.

SANTA SANGRE (Master of the Holy Blood), Style.

2694 «**The Virgin and Child with angels making music**» (Wood, 121 × 87 cm).

SCOREL, Jan van Scorel (b. Schoorl 1495; d. Utrecht 1562). He was one of the Dutch artists who travelled to Italy at the beginning of the 16th century. He visited Venice in 1519, went to the Holy Land later and in 1522 Pope Adrian VI appointed him conservator of the antiquities of the Belvedere, a post that had previously been held by Raphael. In Scorel's art the Flemish tradition is combined with the study of Italian models painted by Raphael, Michelangelo and some of the Venetian masters like Giorgione and Palma Vecchio. The outlines of his figures are well defined, the sense of bulk is clear and strong, set off by light effects. Towards the end of his life Scorel fell under the influence of Mannerism, his compositions became crowded with dramatic figures and Michelangelo-type nudes; the artist lost the balance and harmony that characterized his early years.

1515 «**The Universal Deluge**» (Wood, 109 × 178 cm). This work belongs to the artist's Mannerist period. The clear-cut forms and highly-detailed depiction are typical of a Northern artist.

2580 «**A humanist**» (Wood, 67 × 52 cm). This portrait is characteristic of Scorel, with the half-length filling part of the composition against a landscape backdrop of extremely delicate design. The effect of the light focused on the man's face sets off its bulk and intensifies its expression.

SCHOEVAERTS. See Bruegel «de Velours», Workshop.

SEGHERS, Daniel «the Jesuit» (Antwerp 1590-1661). He specialized in flower studies in the line of Bruegel «de Velours», his master, but introduced innovations in the composition. Seghers grouped the flowers in large bouquets and linked them by means of ivy branches or thorny stalks around a space which was usually filled with a religious motif by another artist.

1905 «**Garland with the Virgin and Child**» (Canvas, 86 × 62 cm). The flowers are typical of Seghers, very fresh-looking and full of buds. The figures are possibly by Schut or Diepenbeek.

1906 «**Garland surrounding the Virgin and Child**» (Copper, 88 × 67 cm). Signed and dated 1644. The figures are by Schut «the Elder».

1907 «**Garland with the Virgin and Child**» (Wood, 76 × 53 cm). Roses and tulips are the favourite flowers of this artist, who preferred to paint the species of his native country. The figures have been ascribed to Schut.

1906. D. Seghers. Garland.

1737. Snayers. Hunting scene with Philip IV.

1908 «Garland surrounding St. Francis Xavier» (Canvas, 109 × 80 cm). Signed.

1909 «Garland with the Virgin and Child and St. John» (Wood, 76 × 60 cm). The figures are by Schut.

1910 «Garland surrounding the Virgin and Child» (Copper, 84 × 55 cm).

1911 «Garland of roses» (Wood, 39 × 65 cm). Segher's execution is, as usual, delicate and meticulous and he has avoided over-compactness of the groups by means of loose branches that encircle them in various directions.

1912 «Garland» (Canvas, 93 × 70 cm).

1991 «Garland with Jesus and St. Teresa» (Canvas, 130 × 105 cm). This work, together with the following, was previously ascribed to Catharina Ykens.

1994 «Garland of flowers with the Virgin and Child and St. John» (Canvas, 130 × 105 cm). See No. 1991.

SEGHERS, Copies.

2729 «The Virgin and Child in a garland» (Canvas, 87 × 62 cm).

SEGHERS, Style.

2730 «Garland of flowers and fruit with a painter» (Wood, 73 × 53 cm).

SEGHERS, Gerard Seghers (Antwerp 1591-1651). During his stay in Italy (1611-20) he was influenced by Caravaggio; on his return to Antwerp he joined the group of artists around Rubens.

1914 «Jesus in the house of Martha and Mary» (Canvas, 205 × 215 cm).

1746. Snayers. The Relief of the Fortress of Lérida.

SNAYERS, Peeter Snayers (b. Antwerp 1592; d. Brussels c. 1666). He specialized in battle scenes in the manner of Sebastian Vrancx and was imitated by a number of artists. He worked for the Habsburgs and reproduced numerous episodes of the Thirty Years' War, but also painted hunting scenes, processions and official events.

1733 «Hunting scene with the Cardinal-Infante» (Canvas, 195 × 302 cm). Signed.

1734 «Hunting scene with Philip IV» (Canvas, 181 × 576 cm). This picture was commissioned by the Cardinal-Infante in 1638. It represents a contemporary Spanish-style hunt in an enclosure like in some of Velazquez' and Mazo's paintings. The panoramic view is typical of his style, with a darker foreground where the figures are situated.

1735 «Clash of Cavalry troops» (Canvas, 79 × 104 cm). Signed and dated 1646. In this kind of painting Snayers comes closest to the style of Vrancx.

1736 «Hunting scene with Philip IV» (Canvas, 180 × 149 cm). Signed. The King, on foot, is killing a wild boar. The event was widely commented on due to the danger involved in killing a boar in this fashion.

1737 «Hunting scene with Philip IV» (Canvas, 126 × 145 cm). Signed.

1738 «The Siege of Gravelines» (Canvas, 188 × 260 cm). This work, together with all the following ones, belongs to a type of painting widely cultivated by Snayers, which gives his pictures an important historic value. They are panoramic depictions of battles and sieges, painted in light and silvery tones with the high horizon-line drawn out to make the episode clearer and the figures kept on a small scale. Snayers is known to have worked on these pictures with the aid of maps.

1739 «Night attack on Lille» (Canvas, 181 × 267 cm). Signed and dated 1650.
1740 «The surrender of Yprès» (Canvas, 184 × 263 cm). Signed.
1741 «The siege of Bois-le-Duc» (Canvas, 184 × 263 cm).
1742 «The surrender of Saint-Venant» (Canvas, 184 × 263 cm).
1743 «The surrender of Breda» (Canvas, 184 × 263 cm). Signed and dated 1650.
1744 «The relief of Saint-Omer» (Canvas, 184 × 263 cm). Signed.
1745 «The siege of Aire-sur-la-Lys» (Canvas, 184 × 263 cm). Signed and dated 1653.
1746 «The relief of the fortress of Lerida» (Canvas, 195 × 288 cm). Signed.
1747 «The Infanta Isabella Clara Eugenia in the siege of Breda» (Canvas, 200 × 265 cm).
1748 «The siege of Breda» (Canvas, 140 × 226 cm). Signed. Velazquez is thought to have taken this picture into account when he painted the landscape of *Las Lanzas* («The Surrender of Breda»).
2022 See Anonymous Flemish Masters.

SNYDERS, Frans Snyders (Antwerp 1579-1657). He painted still lifes and hunting scenes. Initially he was influenced by Pieter Bruegel II, who was his master, and Bruegel «de Velours», but his style changed on contact with Rubens, with whom he collaborated frequently. In his pictures we find the typical Flemish still life with its characteristic decorative profusion and Baroque exuberance.

1749 «The boar-hunt» (Canvas, 109 × 192 cm). Snyders painted this subject on several occasions, always with the same sense of motion; the figures seem to be cut off at the edges of the painting, thus producing the impression that the picture continues into space.
1750 «The pantry» (Canvas, 99 × 145 cm). This picture is an example of the Baroque desire to breathe life into the painted scene by transforming the «still life» into a kind of «true-life» study, where living animals approach the tempting display of foodstuffs scattered over floor and tables.
1751 «Dog with game» (Canvas, 105 × 174 cm).
1752 «Fox-hunt» (Canvas, 111 × 82 cm). The scene takes place in a wide landscape painted in the manner of Wildens.
1753 «The fable of the hare and the tortoise» (Canvas, 112 × 84 cm). Signed.
1754 «Water-fowl and stoats» (Canvas, 181 × 79 cm). Signed. This type of painting, which was also popular with other Flemish artists like Van Kessel, reveals an intellectual kind of curiosity in the different species of birds and animals, which are presented here with a scanty anecdotic pretext, while the general composition is held together by the landscape.
1755 «The cat and the fox» (Canvas, 181 × 103 cm). Signed.
1756 «The fable of the lion and the mouse» (Canvas, 112 × 84 cm).
1757 «The fruit-seller» (Canvas, 153 × 214 cm). The still life with figures is a *genre* introduced by the Flemish masters in the 16th century that came to its height in the 17th century.
1758 «Birds» (Canvas, 98 × 137 cm).
1759 «Wild boar at bay» (Canvas, 98 × 101 cm).
1760 See Paul de Vos.
1761 «Birds» (Canvas, 79 × 151 cm).
1762 «Wild boar at bay» (Canvas, 79 × 145 cm). Signed. The composition is perfectly designed here and the combining movements of the animals produce a very dynamic effect.
1763 «Bull attacked by dogs» (Canvas, 98 × 100 cm).
1764 «Cock-fight» (Canvas, 158 × 200 cm).
1766 See Paul de Vos.
1767 «Table» (Canvas, 154 × 186 cm).
1768 «Still life» (Canvas, 121 × 183 cm). This picture with its composition set on a diagonal and the live bird pecking at the grapes is an example of the richness and abundance of the typical Flemish still life, presented here with pyramids of fruit and game overflowing dishes and table.
1770 «Poultry-yard» (Canvas, 99 × 144 cm).
1771 «Fruit» (Canvas, 70 × 102 cm). The manner of representing fruit is typical of Snyders: fresh and juicy-looking, with full forms and intense colouring set off against the dark table-cloth and the contrast of the delicate porcelain.
1772 «Stag-hunt» (Canvas, 58 × 112 cm).
1851 «Philopoemenes recognized by an old woman» (Canvas, 201 × 311 cm). This work was previously attributed to Utrecht; most critics agree

that the figures are by Rubens. The still life acquires capital importance in the picture with the large pieces of game linked on a diagonal producing an extraordinarily decorative effect.

1877 See Paul de Vos.
      SNYDERS, Workshop.
1765 «A cook in the pantry» (Canvas, 188 × 254 cm).
      SOMER, Paulus van Somer (b. Antwerp c. 1576; d. London 1621). Portrait painter.
1954 «James I of England» (Canvas, 196 × 120 cm).
      SON, Joris van Son (Antwerp 1623-1667). Still-life painter in the manner of Davidsz de Heem, he also painted garlands of flowers and fruit grouping them around a central theme in lavish clusters generally connected by cherry branches, all with an intense, harmonious colouring.
1774 «Still life» (Canvas, 48 × 33 cm). Signed and dated 1664.
1775 «Still life» (Canvas, 48 × 33 cm). Signed and dated 1664. This is the companion-piece to the preceding No.
1776 «Garland of fruit surrounding St. Michael» (Canvas, 119 × 88 cm). Signed and dated 1657. This type of garland framing a grisaille relief or central space with a religious subject was invented by Bruegel «de Velours» and copied by many 17th-century Flemish artists.
2728 «The Virgin and Child in a garland of fruit» (Canvas, 120 × 84 cm).
      SON, School.
1779 «Basket of grapes» (Canvas, 28 × 35 cm).
      SPIERINCK, Peeter Spierinck (b. Antwerp 1635; d. England 1711?). Landscape painter who worked in Italy and was influenced by Salvator Rosa.
1780 «Landscape with tavern and Roman aqueduct» (Canvas, 81 × 114 cm).
1781 «Italian landscape» (Canvas, 81 × 114 cm). Pendant to the preceding No.
      STALBENT, Adriaen Stalbent (Antwerp 1580-1662). He worked in the group around the Bruegels collaborating on occasions with Pieter «the Younger».
1405 «The Sciences and the Arts» (Wood, 93 × 114 cm). This allegorical subject is presented like a typical collectors' cabinet with an assemblage of objects pertaining to the arts and science.
1437 «Interior» (Wood, 40 × 41 cm).
      STALBENT and Pieter Bruegel «the Younger».
1782 «David's victory over Goliath» (Wood, 88 × 216 cm). Signed by both artists.
      STEVENS, Peeter Stevens (b. Mechlin 1567; d. after 1624). Landscape painter. He was Court Painter to Rudolf II in Prague.
2024 «Leafy landscape» (Wood, 33 × 48 cm).
      STOCK, Ignatius van der Stock (active in Brussels in 1660). Landscape painter in the manner of d'Arthois.
1360 «Landscape» (Canvas, 70 × 84 cm). Signed and dated 1660.
      SUSTERMANS, Justus Sustermans (b. Antwerp 1597; d. Florence

1761. Snyders. Birds.

1681). Court portrait painter. Renowned in his time, he worked in Paris and later in the service of the Medicis in Florence.

9 «**Maria Magdalena of Austria, Grand-Duchess of Tuscany**» (Canvas, 77 × 63 cm). The smooth surface of the face and the refined handling recall Bronzino.

10 «**Ferdinand II, Grand-Duke of Tuscany**» (Canvas, 77 × 63 cm).
SUSTERMANS, School.

1961 «**Eleanor of Mantua**» (Canvas, 112 × 96 cm).

1962 «**Ferdinand II**» (Canvas, 111 × 96 cm).
SYMONS, Peter Symons (master in Antwerp in 1629).

1971 «**Cephalus and Procris**» (Canvas, 174 × 204 cm). Signed. This work was painted for the *Torre de la Parada* after a sketch by Rubens.
TENIERS, Abraham Teniers. See Teniers, David.

1797. Teniers. «Le Roi boit».

TENIERS, David Teniers (b. Antwerp 1610; d. Brussels 1690). *Genre* painter in the manner of Brouwer; he also painted other subjects, such as portraits and landscapes. His approach is more superficial than that of Brouwer; he takes pleasure in describing his still lifes in great detail and underlining their picturesque aspects. His technique is excellent, rapid and precise, his colouring delicate.

1391 «**Music in the kitchen**» (Wood, 33 × 55 cm). Previously attributed to Brouwer, art critics now ascribe this work to Teniers.

1392 «**The conversation**» (Wood, 33 × 56 cm). The same applies as to No. 1391.

1785 «**Peasants merry-making**» (Canvas, 69 × 86 cm). This is a typical theme; Teniers contrasts the revelry of the peasants with the presence of several burghers watching the scene.

1786 «**Country fête**» (Canvas, 75 × 112 cm). Signed and dated 1647. As usual, Teniers takes pleasure in depicting anecdotic details in this composition, full of life and motion, thus forming different points of interest in the scene.

1787 «**Country fête**» (Copper, 77 × 99 cm). Signed.

1788 «**Peasants feasting**» (Canvas, 120 × 188 cm). Signed and dated 1637.

1789 «**A game of bowls**» (Wood, 42 × 71 cm). Signed.

1790 «**Shooting with the crossbow**» (Wood, 54 × 88 cm). Signed.

1791 «**The merry soldier**» (Wood, 47 × 36 cm). Teniers represented this subject-matter several times and critics have considered the main figure to be a self-portrait of the artist. The soldier's vivacious expression, the charm of the dense atmosphere enveloping the figures and the delicate light effects contribute towards making it one of Teniers' most attractive works.

1793 «**A tavern**» (Wood, 52 × 65 cm). Signed.

1794 «**Smokers and drinkers**» (Wood, 34 × 48 cm). Signed. The theme recurs frequently in works by Teniers, who shows his masterly treatment of light effects here in a smoke-filled, half-dark room; as usual, he combines various different scenes.

1795 **«Drinkers and smokers»** (Canvas, 40 × 50 cm). Signed.

1796 **«Smokers»** (Wood, 40 × 62 cm). Signed.

1797 **«Le roi boit»** (Copper, 58 × 70 cm). Signed. This picture illustrates a popular custom.

1798 **«The kitchen»** (Wood, 35 × 50 cm). Signed. It is characteristic of Teniers to use subjects like this to accumulate details for a still life, arranged in pyramid-form, as was the custom with contemporary still-life painters.

1799 **«The old man and the maidservant»** (Wood, 55 × 90 cm). Piquant scenes are also frequent in Teniers' works; here the flirtations between the old man and the maidservant are observed by the wife from a window.

1800 **«The old man and the maidservant»** (Copper, 49 × 64 cm). This could be a copy by Abraham Teniers.

1801 **«Peasants' feast»** (Wood, 42 × 58 cm). The landscape is by Lucas van Uden.

1802 **«A surgical operation»** (Wood, 38 × 61 cm). Signed. A satirical approach to doctors and quacks was traditional in Flemish art. The facial expressions are very vivaciously portrayed.

1803 **«A surgical operation»** (Wood, 33 × 25 cm). Signed.

1804 **«The alchemist»** (Wood, 32 × 25 cm). This is the companion piece of the preceding No. The satirical intention of associating the doctor with the alchemist is obvious.

1805 **«The monkey painter»** (Copper, 23 × 32 cm). Signed. The Nos. 1805-1810 constitute a series in which Teniers painted the usual scenes of his *genre* pictures interpreted by monkeys.

1806 **«The monkey sculptor»** (Copper, 32 × 32 cm). Signed.

1807 **«The monkey in a wine-cellar»** (Copper, 21 × 30 cm). Signed.

1808 **«Monkeys at school»** (Copper, 25 × 34 cm). Signed.

1809 **«Monkeys as drinkers and smokers»** (Wood, 21 × 30 cm). Signed.

1810 **«The monkeys' banquet»** (Wood, 25 × 34 cm). Signed.

1811 **«The bivouac»** (Wood, 68 × 89 cm). Signed. A large still life with arms occupies most of the scene which takes place in one of Teniers' favourite settings, a cellar with light from the windows illuminating part of the scene.

1812 **«The guard»** (Copper, 67 × 52 cm).

1813 **«The Archduke Leopold William in his picture gallery»** (Copper, 100 × 129 cm). Signed. Teniers was the Archduke's Court Painter and conservator of his art collection. This type of picture was very popular in the 17th century and has a great documentary interest. A number of famous works can be recognized here, most of them by Italian masters. The scene represents the Archduke (with a hat) showing his collection.

1814 **«Shepherds' talk»** (Canvas, 75 × 89 cm). Signed.

1815 **«Villagers talking»** (Wood, 41 × 63 cm). Signed.

1816 **«Country house»** (Canvas, 136 × 179 cm). Signed.

1817 **«Landscape with hermits»** (Canvas, 177 × 230 cm). We can appreciate Teniers' mastery as a landscape painter at its best in this extensive somewhat grandiose landscape that reveals the influence of Joost de Momper.

1818 **«Landscape with gypsies»** (Canvas, 177 × 239 cm). Signed.

1819 **«Landscape with a hermit»** (Canvas, 95 × 143 cm). Signed. The land-

1803. Teniers. A Surgical Operation   **1804. Teniers. The Alchemist.**

scape is rather fantastic and the opening of the grotto provides a pretext for contrived lighting effects.

1820 «The Temptation of St. Anthony Abbot» (Wood, 51 × 71 cm). This was a favourite subject in Flemish art since Bosch and provided an occasion to portray a motley array of fantastic creatures.

1821 «The Temptation of St. Anthony Abbot» (Canvas, 79 × 110 cm). Signed.

1822 «The Temptation of St. Anthony Abbot» (Copper, 55 × 69 cm). Signed. The hermit is harassed by the capital sins; the scene is crowded with freakish beings that no doubt symbolize different kinds of vice.

1823 «St. Paul, the first hermit, and St. Anthony Abbot» (Canvas, 63 × 94 cm). Signed. The calm atmosphere is rather unusual in Teniers' pictures. The wide grotto overlooks a lovely landscape in the manner of Momper.

1825 «Armida before Godfrey of Bouillon» (Copper, 43 × 37 cm). Signed. This is the first of a series of paintings (Nos. 1825-36) which illustrate the story of Armida and Rinaldo as narrated in Tasso's «*Jerusalem Delivered*». They were previously attributed to David Teniers the Elder (1582-1649), but art historians have recently ascribed them to Teniers the Younger.

1826 «Godfrey and the Council listen to Armida's request» (Copper, 27 × 39 cm).

1827 «The search for Rinaldo» (Copper, 27 × 39 cm). Signed.

1828 «Rinaldo on the island of Oronte» (Copper, 27 × 39 cm). Signed.

1829 «Rinaldo sleeping in Armida's carriage» (Copper, 27 × 39 cm). Signed.

1830 «Carlo and Ubaldo on the Fortunate Islands» (Copper, 27 × 39 cm). Signed.

1831 «Armida's garden» (Copper, 28 × 39 cm). Signed.

1832 «Armida and Rinaldo separated» (Copper, 27 × 39 cm). Signed.

1833 «Rinaldo flees from the Fortunate Islands» (Copper, 27 × 39 cm). Signed.

1834 «Rinaldo's feats against the Egyptians» (Copper, 27 × 39 cm). Signed.

1835 «Armida in the battle against the Saracens» (Copper, 27 × 39 cm). Signed.

1836 «Rinaldo and Armida reconciled» (Copper, 27 × 39 cm). Signed.

2732 «The smokers» (Wood, 18 × 17 cm).

TENIERS, Copies and Workshop.

1783 «The guard» (Copper, 49 × 68 cm).

1784 «The guard» (Copper, 49 × 68 cm).

1839 «Villagers talking» (Canvas, 66 × 88 cm).

THIELEN, Jan Philips van Thielen, van Rigoults or van Couwenberg (b. Mechlin 1618; d. Boisschot 1667).

1843 «St. Philip in a niche» (Copper, 126 × 96 cm).

THOMAS, Jan Yprès Thomas (b. Yprès 1617; d. Vienna 1678). Follower of Rubens.

1496 «The Virgin of the Roses» (Canvas, 111 × 86 cm).

THULDEN, Theodore van Thulden (Bois-le-Duc 1606-1669). He collaborated with Rubens, from whom his style is derived, but his general tone is calmer.

1844 «Orpheus» (Canvas, 195 × 432 cm). This work was painted for Philip IV's *Torre de la Parada*. Paul de Vos probably collaborated on the animal figures.

1845 «The discovery of the purple dye» (Canvas, 189 × 212 cm). This work was painted for the *Torre de la Parada*.

TIEL, Justus Tiel or Tilens (active in 1593). His biography is unknown, but he is believed to have worked for the Spanish Court.

1846 «Allegory on the education of Philip III» (Wood, 158 × 105 cm). Signed. This is an allegorical portrait in a very Mannerist style.

UDEN, Lucas van Uden (Antwerp 1595-c. 1672/3). Landscape painter, who often collaborated with figure-painters. He was influenced by Momper and Rubens.

1848 «Landscape» (Wood, 49 × 68 cm). This is an example of the characteristic composition of his landscapes, with a promontory on one side and a valley on the other.

UTRECHT, Adriaen van Utrecht (Antwerp 1599-1653). He painted all types of landscapes, garlands, farmyard scenes, etc. He usually arranged his subjects horizontally and in a space with an impression of depth. He often collaborated with other painters.

1851 See Snyders.

1852 «A pantry» (Canvas, 222 × 307 cm). Signed and dated 1642. The contrasting light and unifying colouring are typical of Utrecht.

1853 «Festoon of fruit and vegetables» (Canvas, 186 × 60 cm). Signed and dated 1638.

VALCKENBORGH, Lucas van Valckenborgh (b. Mechlin 1540; d. Frankfurt 1597). His work underwent various changes in style. His early paintings recall Patenier's extensive, panoramic landscapes; later he was influenced by Bruegel, especially in subject-matter; in his late works he achieved unity in his landscapes by means of an elaborate technique of changing shades whereby a greyish tone covered the whole surface of the picture like a haze allowing the other colours to show through.

1446 «Landscape with the casting out of devils» (Wood, 37 × 58 cm). On the seashore Jesus and his disciples are casting out evil spirits from a group of people possessed by devils; the spirits rush into the sea transformed into pigs.

1854 «Landscape with ironworks» (Wood, 41 × 64 cm). Signed and dated 1595. See No. 1855.

1855 «Landscape with ironworks» (Wood, 41 × 60 cm). Signed. Both works belong to the last period of the artist's activity. They are highly-detailed, descriptive landscapes that still recall Bruegel.

1857 «The Royal Palace in Brussels» (Wood, 168 × 257 cm). The detailed description of the architecture makes this a very attractive work.

VEEN, Otto van Veen or **Venius** (b. Leyden 1558; d. Brussels 1629). Romanist artist and a highly cultured man; Rubens studied in his studio.

1858 «Don Alonso de Idiáquez, Duke of Cività Reale» (Wood, 119 × 37 cm). Like the following No., this was one wing of a triptych; on the reverse, St. Ildefonso in grisaille. Its attribution is not quite certain.

1859 «Doña Juana de Robles, Duchess of Cività Reale» (Wood, 119 × 37 cm). See the preceding No. On the reverse, St. John the Baptist in grisaille.

VEERENDAEL, Nicholas van Veerendael (Antwerp 1587-1661). Painter of flowers.

1419 «Garland with the Virgin Mary» (Copper, 81 × 65 cm). The exuberance of the garland is typical of his style. The work was previously ascribed to Bruegel «de Velours».

VERHAECHT, Tobias Verhaecht (Antwerp 1561-1631). Landscape painter. His work still reflects the conventional styles of the 16th century. He spent some time in Italy.

3057 «Alpine landscape» (Canvas, 170 × 267 cm). This work is an example of his type of landscapes, fantastic and decorative, full of picturesque details.

VIRGO INTER VIRGINES, Master of the Virgo inter Virgines. This anonymous master worked between 1470-1500. His name comes from a work with this title now kept in the *Rijksmuseum* in Amsterdam.

2539 «Pietà» (Wood, 84 × 78 cm).

VOS, Cornelis de Vos (b. Hulst c. 1584; d. Antwerp 1651). Chiefly a portraitist, although here he is represented with mythologies, he worked with Rubens.

1623 «Portrait of an unknown lady» (Canvas, 109 × 87 cm). This work was previously listed under Anonymous Flemish Masters and is ascribed here to Vos with certain doubts.

1860 «The Triumph of Bacchus» (Canvas, 180 × 295 cm). Signed. Together with the following works, this was painted for the *Torre de la Parada* after

1860. Cornelis de Vos. The Triumph of Bacchus.

sketches by Rubens. The general tonalities are typical of Vos, who preferred light, almost pastel shades.

1861   **«Apollo and the serpent Python»** (Canvas, 188 × 265 cm). Signed. Rubens used the figure of the Apollo Belvedere for his sketch, which is also preserved in the Prado.

1862   **«The birth of Venus»** (Canvas, 187 × 208 cm). Signed. See No. 1860.

VOS, Paul de Vos (b. Hulst 1595; d. Antwerp 1678). Painter of animal studies and hunting scenes in the manner of Snyders, his brother-in-law; he was more talented than the latter in his compositions and his scenes are more dynamic. He worked on the decoration of Philip IV's hunting lodge, *Torre de la Parada,* in El Pardo.

1760   **«A lion and three wolves»** (Canvas, 158 × 195 cm). This work was previously ascribed to Snyders.

1766   **«The goat and the wolf cub»** (Canvas, 214 × 212 cm). This work was previously ascribed to Snyders.

1865   **«Running fox»** (Canvas, 84 × 81 cm). Signed.

1866   **«Cats fighting in a pantry»** (Canvas, 116 × 172 cm). The compositional scheme is reminiscent of Snyders, who also used live animals to add motion to his still lifes.

1867   **«A dog»** (Canvas, 116 × 82 cm). Signed.

1868   **«The dog and the magpie»** (Canvas, 115 × 83 cm). Signed.

1869   **«Deer-hunt»** (Canvas, 212 × 347 cm). Signed. The tenseness of the struggle is stressed by the composition: the figures of the dogs trace diagonals that converge on the figure of the harassed deer.

1870. Paul de Vos. Stag held at bay by a pack of dogs.

1870   **«Stag held at bay by a pack of dogs»** (Canvas, 212 × 347 cm). Signed. Vos proves himself superior to his master Snyders here in the compositional scheme relating the movements of the animals and making them converge on the stag, who tries dramatically to throw off his pursuers.

1871   **«Greyhound lying in wait»** (Canvas, 116 × 84 cm). Signed.

1872   **«Bull attacked by dogs»** (Canvas, 157 × 200 cm).

1875   **«The fable of the dog and its prey»** (Canvas, 207 × 209 cm). This work illustrates one of Aesop's Fables.

1876   **«A white greyhound»** (Canvas, 105 × 105 cm).

1877   **«Provisions»** (Canvas, 177 × 291 cm). Signed. This work is very similar in style to Snyders, to whom it was attributed.

1879   See Boel.

1880   **«Heaven on earth»** (Canvas, 156 × 196 cm).

VOS, Copy by Mazo.

1873   **«Wild boar»** (Canvas, 68 × 47 cm).

VRANCX, Sebastian Vrancx (Antwerp, 1573-1647). He painted scenes of pillage, plundering and other episodes that he must have witnessed frequently during the Thirty Years' War. He also painted *genre* pictures and collaborated with Bruegel and Momper.

1882   **«The Siege of Ostend»** (Canvas, 73 × 111 cm). The Prado's present Catalogue of Flemish Paintings does not include this picture among Vrancx's works.

1884 «A convoy ambushed» (Wood, 48 × 86 cm).

1885 See Bruegel «de Velours».

WEYDEN, Rogier van der Weyden (b. Tournai c. 1399/1400; d. Brussels 1464). He worked from 1427 to 1432 in Robert Campin's workshop. In 1435 he was already in Brussels, where he was appointed official city painter and remained, except for a few interruptions, until his death. Elements from both Campin and Jan van Eyck can be recognized in his compositions, but his style is fundamentally different. Van der Weyden was primarily a narrative artist and tried to emphasize the human and sentimental content of the religious scenes he painted. He constantly renewed his artistic formulas in orden to obtain greater dramatic effects and an entirely new, intenser expressiveness in the gestures and facial traits of his figures. In the same way he avoided the exact symmetry of Van Eyck's compositions and arranged his figures in rhythmical groups, discarding the sense of depth that Van Eyck had discovered and using instead a stratified space where the outlines are more sharply silhouetted. His style was highly admired throughout Europe and contributed notably towards the creation of Hispano-Flemish painting.

1888
1889 «The Redemption» (Triptych. Central panel: 195 × 172 cm. Side
1891 wings: 195 × 77 cm). The attribution of this work has been questioned. The general concept, the type of figures and the manner of framing the scenes in Gothic arches correspond to Van der Weyden's style, but the quality of this triptych does not come up to his standard and the golden tones are an archaic feature which he did not use. At present the work is ascribed to one of his followers, Franck van der Stock, born in Brussels around 1420, who was his successor in the post of city painter.

1890
1892 «Caesar's penny» (Wood, 195 × 77 cm each). These two works are the exterior of the wings belonging to the triptych mentioned above (see Nos. 1888, 1889 and 1891). The figures in grisaille imitate sculptures. These kind of figures used to decorate the outside of the side wings and could therefore only be seen when the triptych was closed.

2540 «Pietà» (Wood, 47 × 35 cm). Three other variants of this subject by Van der Weyden are known. Van der Weyden was a true master in portraying the most moving passages of the Gospel, where he tried to discover the deeper meaning of the scenes and interpret them in a new, more emotive manner. Here he added a human note to the traditional *Pietà* pose when he represented the Virgin embracing the lifeless body of her Son while St. John tries to pull her away. Portraying the donor as a participant in the scene was Van der Weyden's invention and later became a custom.

2722 «The Virgin and Child» (Wood, 100 × 52 cm). The idea of representing painted images as statues is frequent in Van der Weyden. It should be kept in mind that the artists of the time did not shun doing «lesser» works such as gilding or painting religious images and that this familiarity with statuary art contributed to their desire of giving their painted figures a

2540. Weyden. Pietà.

solid three-dimensional, almost tangible effect. Observe the charmingly realistic detail of the Child crinkling the pages of the Virgin's book while she looks on with a melancholy expression that seems to foresee her Son's Passion.

2825 «**Deposition**» (Wood, 220 × 262 cm). This panel is of capital importance in Van der Weyden's work and one of the most representative masterpieces of early Flemish art. The outstanding technique common to Van der Weyden and other great Flemish masters reaches an amazingly high level here in representing draperies, brocades and skin textures and specially in rendering the different shades of flesh. The artist does away with a background and concentrates on the figures, giving them the solid appearance of a sculptural group and arranging them with perfect mastery in such a reduced space. St. John and Mary Magdalene close the group like brackets on either side and in front of the upright figures the bodies of Christ and the Virgin in parallel postures break the symmetrical arrangement of the surrounding figures. The sorrowing faces of the three Marys and the other saints surround them like a tragic chorus. This *«Deposition»* is one of the best examples of Van der Weyden's exceptional narrative gift and his ability to give traditional themes a fresh interpretation, filling every gesture and figure with new meaning.

WEYDEN, Copy by Memling.
1558 «**The Adoration of the Magi**» (Wood, 60 × 55 cm). This is a copy with several variations after the central panel of the Munich Triptych.

WEYDEN, Anonymous copy.
1894 «**Deposition**» (Wood, 200 × 263 cm). This is a 16th-century copy.

WEYDEN, Follower.
1886 «**The Crucifixion**» (Wood, 47 × 31 cm). This is a freely executed copy, of fine quality, after an original by Van der Weyden kept in the Museum of Vienna. It bears an apocryphal signature of Dürer and the date 1513.

2663 See Legend of St. Catherine, Master of.

WOLFORDT, Arthur Wolfordt (Antwerp 1581-1641). Two works signed with the monogram A. W. have been ascribed to him in this Museum. However, the recent Catalogue of Flemish Paintings prefers to designate the artist as «Monogramist A. W.» thus questioning his identification with Wolfordt.

1900 «**The flight into Egypt**» (Copper, 58 × 77 cm). Signed.
1901 «**Rest on the flight into Egypt**» (Copper, 58 × 77 cm). Signed.

YKENS, Catharina Ykens (b. Antwerp 1659; d. ?). Painter of flowers in the manner of Seghers.
1991 See Seghers, Daniel.
1994 See Seghers, Daniel.

YKENS, Frans Ykens or **Ijkens** (Antwerp 1601-1693). Still-life painter, who also painted garlands of flowers and fruit. He followed the general line of his time, without making new contributions, but his work reveals excellent quality.
1904 «**Provisions**» (Canvas, 107 × 175 cm). The influence of Fyt is evident.
2757 «**Table**» (Wood, 74 × 105 cm). This work reveals masterly execution and remarkable naturalistic effects.

ANONYMOUS FLEMISH MASTERS
56 «**Unknown child**» (Wood, 81 × 68 cm). This work was attributed to Bronzino and later to Pourbus. 16th century.
1361 «**The Adoration of the Magi**» (Triptych. Central panel: 58 × 30 cm; side wings: 58 × 12 cm). This work represents the Epiphany with scenes of the Magi's visit to Herod (on the left) and the Queen of Sheba before Solomon (on the right). It was done by the same artist who painted another Epiphany kept in the *Pinakothek* in Munich, which bears an apocryphal signature of Henricus Blesius (Herrimet Bles); for this reason the anonymous artist has been designated «Pseudo Bles». In the present work we even find the owl (over the arch in the central scene) which the real Bles frequently painted in his works. «Pseudo Bles» shows a predilection for extravagant decoration and pageantry which was typical of the Antwerp Mannerists; his elongated figures, well-proportioned with regard to the architectonic elements that frame them, reveal a typical terseness, which seems to be transmitted to their draperies, moulded to their bodies in extremely fine, fragile-looking folds. 16th century.
1383 «**Landscape with a lake**» (Wood, 55 × 98 cm). 17th century. Previously ascribed to Paul Brill, the Prado's present Catalogue of Flemish Paintings considers this work to be by S. Vrancx.

2722. Weyden. Virgin and Child.

1361. Anonymous Master.
Adoration of the Magi.

1386 «**Landscape with a river**» (Copper, 25 × 29 cm). 17th century.

1445 «**Harbour**» 17th century.

1451 «**The Palace in Brussels**» (Canvas, 150 × 228 cm). 17th century.

1593 «**Landscape with a crag and trees**» (Canvas, 52 × 81 cm). 17th century.

1596 «**Sheepfolds**» (Canvas on wood, 106 × 148 cm). 17th century.

1857 «**The Royal Palace in Brussels**» (Canvas, 168 × 257 cm). 17th century. This work was ascribed to Valckenborgh. The Museum's present Catalogue of Flemish Paintings considers it close to the style of S. Vrancx.

1916 «**The mystic betrothal of St. Catherine**» (Triptych. Central panel: 93 × 62 cm; side wings: 93 × 26 cm). 16th century. This is the work of an anonymous master who worked in Bruges about 1520.

1917 «**Miracle of St. Anthony of Padua in Tolosa**» (Wood, 121 × 80 cm). 16th century.

1918 «**The devout man and the inattentive man in Mass**» (Wood, 61 × 32 cm). 16th century.

1924 «**The Circumcision**» (Wood, 52 × 42 cm). 16th century.

1953 «**Count Mansfeld and his son**» (Canvas, 76 × 122 cm). 16th century. The sitter (1520-1604) was Governor-General of the Netherlands.

1959 «**Unknown lady**» (Wood, 32 × 23 cm). Late 16th century.

1995 «**The Holy Family in a garland**» (Canvas, 54 × 72 cm). 17th century.

1997 «**Valour and abundance, garland**» (Wood, 84 × 59 cm). 17th century. Previously this work was attributed, with doubts, to Davidsz de Heem.

1999 «**Festoon of fruit and vegetables**» (Canvas, 182 × 42 cm). 18th century.

2022 «**Goose-hunters**» (Canvas, 156 × 246 cm). 17th century. This work is at present ascribed to Peter Snayers.

2035 «**Landscape with a temple ruin**» (Canvas, 145 × 215 cm). 17th century.

2217 «**The Adoration of the Magi**» (Triptych. Central panel: 105 × 71 cm; side wings: 105 × 34 cm). This work is by the Master of 1518. See No. 2702.

2635 «**Birth and childhood of Christ**» (Triptych. Central panel: 135 × 87 cm; side wings: 135 × 33 cm). 16th century.

2636 «**The Saviour**» (Wood, 34 × 27 cm). 16th century.

2648 «**Cleopatra**» (?) (Wood, 85 × 64 cm).

2699 «**St. Christopher**» (Wood, 62 × 36 cm). This is the side wing of a triptych. On the reverse: *The Annunciation of the Virgin*. 16th century.

2701 «**St. Monica**» (Wood, 35 × 24 cm). About 1500. It could be a *Mater Dolorosa*.

2702 «**Crucifixion**» (Wood, 83 × 132 cm). This work is probably by the so-called Master of 1518, like the Nos. 2217 and 2718. The master is known by this name due to the predella and wings of an altar-piece in the *Briefkapelle* of St. Mary's Church in Lubeck, which he signed with the date 1518. His style is very personal and he used a rich, bright palette. His figures have very particular faces with broad foreheads and straight noses; they are boldly foreshortened and wear wide robes modelled with vigorous *chiaroscuro*.

2704 «**Still life**» (Wood, 24 × 20 cm). 17th century.

2718 «**The Holy Family**» (Wood, 38 × 33 cm). 16th century. This is a work by the Master of 1518 (see No. 2702).

2746-7 See Arthois, School.

2884 «**Judith with the head of Holofernes**» (Wood, 98 × 120 cm). 16th century.

ITALIAN MASTERS

The collection of Italian paintings is another of the Prado's great treasures, ranking behind the Spanish and on the same level as the Flemish collection. The quantity and quality of these works make them a constant source of attraction for art scholars and visitors alike. The majority belonged to the royal collections; they were brought to Spain as gifts or purchases and can be regarded as a result of the political interests of the Spanish kings, always closely linked with Italy, but also of the personal taste of the individual monarchs who all showed a marked preference, at different periods of history, for one or another Italian master or for a definite school of Italian painting.

14th-century Gothic art is scantily represented in the Prado and the works displayed are recent purchases, like the two small panels by Taddeo Gaddi.

During the 15th century the Spanish kings imported primarily works of art from Flanders, so that Italian paintings by the fine and important early Renaissance artists were also missing. However, during the past century the Prado acquired Fra Angelico's outstanding *Annunciation* and in the present century the series of works by Botticelli, Mantegna's *Death of the Virgin* and Antonello da Messina's *Dead Christ,* an excellent recent purchase.

Philip IV took the decision to buy works by Raphael which are now some of the Prado's chief treasures, including such paintings as *Christ falls on the way to Calvary, Portrait of a Cardinal* and some of his famous *Madonnas.* The figure of Raphael opens the fine collection of 16th-century Italian paintings in the Prado. The most outstanding artists of the first half of the century represented here are Andrea del Sarto, Parmigianino, Correggio and Bernardino Luini and of the late 16th century Barocci. Andrea del Sarto's portrait of his wife, *Lucrezia di Baccio,* Correggio's *Noli me tangere* and Barocci's *Nativity of Christ* are some of the most famous Italian works in the Prado. However, the most important group of Italian paintings is that of 16th-century Venetian masters, which was started by the Emperor Charles V, continued by his son Philip II and later enlarged on by Philip III and Philip IV and cannot be surpassed by any other collection of Venetian art. Giorgione, Titian, Tintoretto and Veronese fill several rooms of the Prado with their colouring, richness and vitality. Veronese's *Christ with the doctors in the Temple* and *Moses rescued from the Nile,* Tintoretto's *Christ washing the disciples' feet,* Titian's portraits and mythological scenes and the Bassanos' biblical paintings reveal all the wealth of the Venetian School and anticipate the Spanish masters of the 17th century who studied these works in the king's collection.

In recent years a renewed interest in Baroque art and the various Italian schools during that period has contributed towards drawing attention to the exceptional value of the Prado's large collection of Baroque paintings. It includes examples of works by Caravaggio and his Tenebrist followers. The Bolognese Classicists are represented by masterpieces by Guido Reni, the Carracci, Guercino, Lanfranco, Domenichino and Albani; many of these works were originally commissioned by Philip IV for the decoration of the Buen Retiro Palace. The Neapolitan School derived from the work of the Spanish artist Ribera is not only interesting in itself, but also as a point of reference to study the latter's art. But the characteristic features of Neapolitan art such as colouring, decorativeness and naturalistic depiction can best be appreciated in the work of Luca Giordano.

18th-century Italian painting is not so well represented in the Prado, possibly due to the arrival of the French Bourbons, who showed more interest in the art of their native country. There are nonetheless some interesting portraits, like those by Batoni and Amigoni, and also some large-scale decorative works by Giaquinto and the Tiepolos. Lesser-known artists like Conca and Trevisani have also left some interesting works. The 18th century closes the extraordinary collection of Italian paintings in the Prado, which numbers some six hundred works, excluding those which belong to this museum but are at present on loan to other national institutions.

ALBANI, Francesco (Bologna 1578-1660). Bolognese School. He was a pupil of the Carracci, with whom he collaborated in his early years on their large-scale projects to decorate palaces in Bologna. Albani owes his fame as a painter mainly to his small pictures on mythological subjects with idyllic, pastoral settings, in which he arranged his scenes and executed his figures with a grace and delicacy that anticipate Rococo art. His works were particularly appreciated by 17th-century collectors.

1 **«The toilet of Venus»** (Canvas, 114 × 171 cm). See No. 2.

2 **«The Judgement of Paris»** (Canvas, 113 × 171 cm). This is the companion piece to the preceding No.; both have the same measurements and pictorial subject, the goddess Venus. These are frequent themes in Albani's work and there are similar versions in other collections, for example in the Academy of San Fernando in Madrid. The beautiful landscape, painted in the Bolognese tradition of the Carracci, and perfect technique are remarkable.

ALLORI, Alessandro (Florence 1535-1607). Florentine School.

6 **«The Holy Family and Cardinal Ferdinand of Medici»** (Canvas, 263 × 201 cm). Signed and dated 1583. A pupil of Bronzino and influenced by Michelangelo and Raphael, Allori was an important painter at the court of the Medici in Florence. In this work, with its orderly composition and cold colouring including Mannerist-style crimsons and blues, the artist introduces realistic details that anticipate 17th-century pictorial patterns.

ALLORI, Cristofano (Florence 1577-1621). Florentine School.

8 **«Christine of Lorraine, Duchess of Florence»** (Canvas, 218 × 140 cm). A son of the preceding artist, Cristofano Allori belonged fully to the 17th century and combined early Florentine naturalism, which arose at the end of the 16th century, with elements of Venetian colouring as is reflected in this very expressive portrait.

AMIGONI, Jacopo (b. Venice c. 1682; d. Madrid 1752). Venetian School. Possibly of Neapolitan origin, but trained in the Venetian School, Amigoni already belonged to the *Fraglia* of Venetian artists in 1711. He travelled widely and worked in various Italian cities and European courts before settling definitively in Spain in 1747 as Court Painter to Ferdinand VI. His work consists mainly of very refined courtly portraits and mythologies in the Rococo style of his time.

12 **«The Holy Face»** (Canvas, 121 × 156 cm). Signed. The inherent dramatic element of this kind of composition is attenuated here by the child-like gracefulness of the tearful little angels.

14 See Solimena.

2392 **«The Infanta Maria Antonia Fernanda»** (Canvas, 103 × 84 cm). Clear colouring and highly-detailed depiction of the dress and flowers are the key-notes of this portrait of one of the daughters of Philip IV and Elizabeth Farnese which was mistakenly considered a portrait of her sister, the Infanta Maria Teresa Antonia.

2477 **«A garden party»** (Canvas, 69 × 48 cm). This work was mistakenly attributed to Amigoni and is now considered to belong to the Neapolitan school.

22. Bassano. The Animals entering the Ark.

2792 «Portrait of a lady» (Canvas, 79 × 65 cm). The attribution of this work to Amigoni is uncertain; it could be of French origin.

2939 «The Marquis of La Ensenada» (Canvas, 124 × 104 cm). The luxurious clothing and the Orders of the Golden Fleece, granted to the Marquis in 1750, and of St. Januarius, together with the massive architectural background by the sea give this portrait a very lavish air which makes it the most remarkable work by Amigoni in the Prado.

ANGELICO, Fra Giovanni da Fiesole, called **Fra Angelico** (b. Vicchio di Mugello c. 1400; d. Rome 1455). Florentine School. He was a monk in the Dominican convent at Fiesole, near Florence, where he became prior in 1449. He began his artistic career early in the field of miniature painting. His work reveals from the start an interest in Renaissance discoveries with regard to the treatment of space, volume and figure proportions. However, at the same time his painting shows traces of late 14th-century Gothic elements which combine with his own character, deeply religious and sometimes verging on mysticism. His works are full of light, clear colouring and idealized forms of beauty, which all make him one of the most outstanding artists of the first half of the 15th century in Italy. He was commissioned to do a large number of important works in Florence and in 1446 he was sent for by Pope Nicholas V to decorate the Niccolini Chapel in the Vatican.

15 «The Annunciation» (Wood, 194 × 194 cm). The predella contains scenes from the life of the Virgin: Birth and Betrothal, Visitation, Epiphany, Purification and Death. It was painted for the Dominican convent in Fiesole between 1430 and 1432; it is one of Fra Angelico's best works and one of the treasures of the Prado. Both in the large central panel and in the smaller scenes of the predella, Fra Angelico found many solutions to the problems of representing space in his search for perspective. The subtle and fragile architectural settings that frame the scenes are related to real works by the Renaissance architect Michelozzo, a contemporary of Fra Angelico. The clear lighting brings out the chromatic values with highly naturalistic detail, like the flowers, which reveal the meticulous technique of a miniaturist. The frame is original.

ANGUISCIOLA, Lucia (Cremona c. 1540-1565). Lombardic School.

16 «Pietro Maria, the doctor of Cremona» (Canvas, 96 × 76 cm). Signed. Lucia was the sister of the more famous Sofonisba Anguisciola, who worked at the Spanish Court, and like her sister she belonged to the artistic circle of the Campi. Sober colouring and an intense psychological study are the salient features of this portrait, which contains some imperfections, such as the arrangement of the hands, which denote the artist's youth.

ANTONIAZZO ROMANO, Antonio Aquili, called «Antoniazzo Romano» (in Rome between 1461 and 1508). Roman School. He worked in Rome on the decorations for the Vatican Library together with Ghirlandaio and Melozzo da Forli and later assisted Perugino on the frescoes of the Sistine Chapel. His painting combines elements of the Florentine and Umbrian Schools.

577 «Virgin and Child» (Fresco on wall, 130 × 110 cm). The upper part of this work was lost and repainted. The central part with the Virgin and Child stands out against the Renaissance-style architectural backdrop.

577a «Triptych. Side wings: St. John the Evangelist and St. Colomba, St. John the Baptist and St. Peter. Central panel: Head of Christ». (Central panel: 87 × 62 cm; side wings: 94 × 35 cm). The figures reflect a solemn, calm mood and serene beauty; the work reveals meticulous draughtsmanship and rich colouring.

ARPINO, Giuseppe Cesari, called «the Gentleman from Arpino» (b. Arpino 1568; d. Rome 1640). Roman School. He received important commissions in Rome in his youth, so that by the turn of the century he was already a renowned artist. His style is related to late Mannerism and also recalls Michelangelo and Raphael, all interpreted with solemn gracefulness that made him popular in official circles. However, Arpino's creative capacity was curbed by the rise of Caravaggio's naturalism on the one hand and by the Classicist movement prevailing in Rome after 1610 on the other; his painting could not keep up with the artistic trends of the time and began to decline during the last period of his life.

555 «The mystic betrothal of St. Catherine» (Wood, 54 × 41 cm). This work does not come up to Arpino's usual standard.

556 «The Holy Family with the infant St. John» (Canvas, 89 × 67 cm). This work was previously attributed to Vanni, but current opinion among

15. Fra Angelico. The Annunciation.

art scholars ascribes it unanimously to Arpino. The graceful child figures are characteristic of his style. The Virgin is portrayed majestically and very elegantly, as can be appreciated in the noble stylization of her hands and the harmonious positioning of her legs.

ASSERETO, Giovacchino (Genoa 1600-1649). Genoese School.

1134 «**Moses striking water out of the rock**» (Canvas, 245 × 300 cm). Assereto was a pupil of Ansaldo and his early work was related to the Lombardic Mannerist style of the Procaccini. This *Moses* is a masterpiece executed with a colouristic, succulent technique that sets off the numerous realistically portrayed figures. The painting was kept in Seville in the 17th century and exerted an undeniable influence on Spanish artists like Murillo.

BADILE, Antonio (Verona (?) c. 1517-1560). Venetian School.

485 «**Unknown lady**» (Canvas, 110 × 93 cm). This painter was the master of Veronese and his portraits reveal him as belonging to the Venetian School. The richly dressed figure is silhouetted against a dark background.

BARBALONGA, Antonio Alberti, called «**Barbalonga**» (Messina 1600-1649). Roman School.

17 «**St. Agueda**» (Canvas, 104 × 127 cm). Of Sicilian origin, Barbalonga worked in Rome in the workshop of the Classicist artist Domenichino. In this work he has combined the decisive influence of his master with knowledge of Neapolitan painters like Vaccaro.

BARBIERI. See Guercino.

BAROCCI, Federigo Fiori, called «**Barocci**» (Urbino 1535-1612). Umbrian School. Barocci belonged to a family of artists and grew up in the extremely rich cultural atmosphere of the Court of Urbino. From a young age he frequented artistic circles in Rome where he became a renowned painter. Ill health or, according to contemporary accounts, an attempt at poisoning him due to envy over his success, made him decide to return to his native city. Barocci's works, both his small pictures and his numerous large-scale altar-pieces, follow lines that would not be fully developed on until almost a hundred years later in Baroque painting. The most characteristic features of his art are the brilliant, variegated colouring, iridescent illumination which produces plastic and moving effects, clever positioning of the figures in space and an obsessive insistence on their sentiments.

18 «**The Nativity of Christ**» (Canvas, 134 × 105 cm). This work was painted in 1597 for the Duke of Urbino and sent as a gift to Margaret of Austria, the wife of the Spanish King Philip III, in 1605. It is one of the artist's late works and represents a new and personal interpretation of the often repeated theme of the Nativity, in accordance with the guiding lines of the Counter-Reformation. The divine power of the artificial light focussing on the Child sets off the central figure of the composition, the Virgin, who commands the spectator's attention with her brilliant, clear colouring against the dark background.

18a «**Christ on the Cross**» (Canvas, 374 × 240 cm). Dating from 1604, this work was painted for the Duke of Urbino who bequeathed it to the Spanish King Philip IV in his will. Its fullness of form, pious expressiveness and soft technique are all characteristic of Baroque sensibility. The dark, mysterious landscape in the lower part of the picture shows the city of Urbino and its surroundings.

BASSANO, Francesco da Ponte «the Younger», called «**Francesco Bassano**» (b. Bassano 1549; d. Venice 1592). Venetian School. He was one of the sons of Jacopo Bassano and worked with his brothers in his father's workshop, painting the same themes and biblical scenes as the latter with refined colouring.

33 «**Adoration of the Magi**» (Canvas, 86 × 71 cm). Signed. This is a sober composition, with rich twilight effects and extremely realistic details in the animal figures.

34 «**The Last Supper**» (Canvas, 151 × 214 cm). Signed. The anecdotic details are pleasing and the colouring very attractive, but there is something slightly awkward about the grouping of the figures and the execution of the draperies.

36 «**Peasants at work**» (Canvas, 119 × 171 cm). The scene and landscape bring to mind late 16th-century Flemish painting and the style is closer to that of the circle around Tintoretto.

BASSANO, Jacopo da Ponte, called «**Jacopo Bassano**» (Bassano c. 1515-1592). Venetian School. He was the founder of the family of painters known as the Bassanos and began his artistic career as a follower of Titian. Around 1550 his work reflects the style and manner of other artists, but the decisive influence came from his contact with Tintoretto, whose art made itself felt in his figures, technique and lighting effects, a development that ran parallel to that of the young Greco. In his last period Bassano returned to his native town where he painted for private collectors; his studio, where his sons worked with him, produced series of biblical paintings, treated like pastoral scenes set in wide landscape backgrounds depicted with great attention to realistic detail which was to play a decisive role in the development of Baroque *genre* painting.

21 «Adam reproached» (Canvas, 191 × 287 cm). Reproached by God after the Fall, Adam and Eve are lost in a wide landscape in which the artist's main preoccupation seems to be a precise and realistic portrayal of the different species of animals in Paradise, which thus become the central subjects of the composition.

22 «The animals entering the Ark» (Canvas, 207 × 265 cm). This work was purchased by Titian for the Emperor Charles V and reiterates Bassano's pattern in which secondary or anecdotic elements almost supersede the main subject. The light effects and colouring are very attractive. In some parts of the painting the artist has achieved extremely naturalistic effects.

23 See Leandro Bassano.

25 «The Adoration of the Shepherds» (Wood, 60 × 49 cm). This is a delicate and brilliantly coloured work with nocturnal light effects and models that are related to the art of Tintoretto.

26 «The Adoration of the Shepherds» (Canvas, 128 × 104 cm). As in the preceding panel, the artist has represented the scene at night with the Child and the little angels in the upper part flooded in light.

27 «The traders cast out of the Temple» (Canvas, 150 × 184 cm). The scene from the Gospel is presented in a monumental architectural setting which recalls works by Tintoretto. The warm, variegated tones underline the composition's vivaciousness and naturalistic details.

28 «The traders cast out of the Temple» (Canvas, 149 × 233 cm). The artist shows evident pleasure in depicting naturalistic and anecdotic elements which almost fill the scene leaving the main subject of the painting more or less hidden in the background.

BASSANO, Leandro da Ponte, called «Leandro Bassano» (b. Bassano 1557; d. Venice 1622). Venetian School. He was another of the sons of Jacopo Bassano and worked with his father in his native town until he moved to Venice in 1592, where he became an important portrait painter.

23 «Noah after the Deluge» (Canvas, 80 × 113 cm). This work was previously attributed to Jacopo Bassano, but is now considered to be a youthful work by Leandro.

29 «The rich man and the beggar Lazarus» (Canvas, 150 × 202 cm). See No. 39.

30 «Spring» (Canvas, 68 × 80 cm). See No. 31.

31 «Winter» (Canvas, 79 × 95 cm). These two works were possibly part of a series on the Seasons, treated in this case like *genre* scenes. They were ascribed to Jacopo Bassano, but the style is closer to that of his son.

32 «Portrait of a man» (Canvas, 64 × 50 cm). The salient features of this work are its sober colouring and the intenseness of the man's expression.

39 «The return of the Prodigal Son» (Canvas, 142 × 200 cm). This work is the companion piece to No. 29 and both are very characteristic of Bassano's style. They are very attractive works with their abundance of naturalistically depicted elements, rich colouring and masterly light effects.

40 «The Flight into Egypt» (Canvas, 86 × 71 cm). The light is admirably treated and sets off details of the figures and vegetation in this nocturnal scene.

41 «The Crown of Thorns» (Slate, 54 × 49 cm). The style of this work is more related to that of Francesco Bassano's workshop.

43 «The Virgin Mary in Heaven» (Canvas, 175 × 140 cm). This is a copy on a reduced scale of a painting by Jacopo Bassano kept in the Museum of Bassano.

44 «Venice: the embarkation of the Doge» (Canvas, 200 × 597 cm). This work is in line with the tradition of Venetian artists who took pleasure in representing their city and events occurring in it.

45 «A magistrate or clergyman with a crucifix» (Canvas, 98 × 80 cm). The sobriety and colouring of this work make it a traditional composition.

s.n. «Orpheus and the animals» (Canvas, 98 × 108 cm). This work reveals the artist's characteristic style.

18. Barocci. The Nativity of Christ.

248. Andrea Mantegna. The Death of the Virgin. (detail)

BASSANTE, Bartolomeo Bassante or **Passante** (b. Brindisi (?) c. 1616; d. Naples 1656). Neapolitan School.

47 **«The Adoration of the Shepherds»** (Canvas, 99 × 131 cm). Signed. According to biographical references, Bassante was a pupil of Ribera, but the style of this work is more closely related to that of other, more refined Neapolitan artists, for example Cavallino.

BATONI, Pompeo Gerolamo (b. Lucca 1708; d. Rome 1787). Roman School. Batoni was of Tuscan origin, but settled in Rome at an early age, where he was attracted by Classicist painting. He studied Classic statuary and the painting of Raphael and his 17th-century followers: the Carracci, Reni and Maratti. These influences, together with his own artistic sensibility, determined the characteristics of his mature work. He was one of the founders of Neo-Classical painting, together with his contemporary Mengs and the German art scholar resident in Rome, Winckelmann. The beauty and serenity of his compositions, his orderly, precise draughtsmanship and a somewhat Caravaggesque softness and sensuality contributed to the success of his paintings. He was an important portraitist and the portraits he made of foreign visitors to Rome spread his fame throughout Europe.

48 **«A traveller in Italy: Sir William Hamilton»** (?) (Canvas, 127 × 100 cm). Signed and dated 1778. This sober, elegant portrait reveals a keen psychological approach that is typical of the Classicist School. The Roman bust on the table alludes to the sitter's intellectual environment and the renewed interest in Classical Antiquity prevailing at the time.

49 **«A gentleman in Rome: Charles Cecil Roberts»** (Canvas, 221 × 157 cm). Signed and dated 1778. The sitter's elegant pose and the atmospheric effects of the landscape relate this work to contemporary portraits by Reynolds or Gainsborough. In the background St. Peter's and the Castle of Sant'Angelo can be seen.

BATTAGLIOLI, Francesco (b. Modena c. 1725; d. Venice c. 1790). Battaglioli studied in Venice and specialized in townscapes, following the Venetian tradition of Canaletto or Guardi. He worked at the Spanish Court after 1754, where he also prepared theatre and opera decorations.

4180 **«The guests arriving at the Palace of Aranjuez for the St. Ferdinand's Day celebrations»** (Canvas, 86 × 112 cm). This is the companion piece to the following work.

4181 **«King Ferdinand VI and Queen Barbara of Braganza with their guests in the gardens of the Palace of Aranjuez»** (Canvas, 86 × 112 cm). Signed and dated 1756. This work has been acquired by the Prado recently and is an example of the painting of the Venetian *veduttisti*.

BATTISTELLO. See Caracciolo.

BELLINI, Giovanni (Venice c. 1432-1516). Venetian School. In the late 15th century Bellini was one of the artists who renovated Venetian painting, departing from the prevailing Gothic style in his search for new Renaissance ideals. His brother-in-law Mantegna's influence can be perceived in the firm draughtsmanship of the figures and clearly defined forms, somewhat mellowed in his later period by rich colouring and study of light and *chiaroscuro* effects, which he no doubt learnt from works by the young Giorgione. He was Titian's master.

50 **«The Virgin and Child with two Saints»** (Wood, 77 × 104 cm). Signed. This work probably belongs to the artist's late period, about 1490. The sharply illuminated half-length figures are silhouetted against a dark background forming a «Holy Conversation» group. The reduced range of colours is broken up into an exquisite variety of shades.

576 **«The Saviour»** (Wood, 44 × 34 cm). This is a replica of an original kept in the Academy of San Fernando in Madrid.

BELVEDERE, Abate Andrea (Naples c. 1646-1732). Neapolitan School.

549 **«Flowers»** (Canvas, 151 × 100 cm). Signed. See No. 550.

550 **«Flowers»** (Canvas, 151 × 100 cm). Signed. This is the companion piece to the preceding work and they are both examples of the finest work by this artist, one of the last still-life painters of the Neapolitan School. He worked in Madrid at the end of the 17th century and collaborated on some works of his fellow-Neapolitan Luca Giordano. His work reveals an almost Northern kind of exuberance. His style derives from that of Ruoppolo, who is also represented in the Prado, although the influence of the Flemish artist Abraham Bruegel, who was in Naples about 1671, can also be felt.

BERNINI, Gian Lorenzo (b. Naples 1598; d. Rome 1680). Roman School.

2476 **«Self-portrait»** (Canvas, 46 × 32 cm). Although Bernini was primarily known for his work as a sculptor and architect, he also left some notable paintings. They are all small-size works, chiefly portraits, executed with a vigorous, outlined technique, like this *Self-portrait,* where the artist has eliminated any superfluous elements. It should be dated about 1640.

BERRETTINI. See Cortona, Pietro da.

BIAGIO. See Catena, Vicenzo.

BIANCHI, Isidoro (?) (b. Campione 1581; d. Milan 1662). Lombardic School.

141 «Charity» (Canvas, 156 × 118 cm). Bianchi worked with Morazzone in Milan and also carried out some important commissions for Turin. In this work, which is doubtfully attributed to Bianchi, he has combined a composition inspired by Raphaelesque motifs with a technique that is typically Lombardic, with the characteristic intense lighting that sets off the main scene, leaving the rest in the shade.

BILIVERTI, Giovanni (Florence 1576-1644). Florentine School.

53a «The gratitude of Tobias» (Canvas, 171 × 148 cm). Biliverti was descended from a Flemish goldsmith and received his training in Florence with Cigolli at a time when the late Mannerist movement was searching for a renewal along naturalistic lines. In 1604 he visited Rome and came into contact with the newest trends prevailing in that city. He painted numerous religious pictures for Florence. This work is a replica of a painting kept in the Pitti Gallery in Florence; the figures are depicted in somewhat affected poses in a reduced space, which is attenuated by the beautiful technique and the half-darkness that diffuses the forms.

BONINI, Gerolamo (Ancona, 17th century). Bolognese School.

4 «The Nativity of the Virgin» (Canvas, 93 × 51 cm). Bonini was a pupil of Albani in Bologna and imitated his style. In this work he has copied a famous painting by Annibale Carracci now kept in the Louvre.

BONITO, Giuseppe (b. Castellammare di Stabia 1707; d. Naples 1789). Neapolitan School.

54 «The Turkish embassy to the Court of Naples» (Canvas, 207 × 170 cm). Signed and dated 1741. Bonito was a pupil of Solimena and mainly known as a portraitist. In this original and exotic canvas he has portrayed the Turkish ambassador Hagi Hussein and his entourage, who visited King Charles of Naples, later Charles III of Spain, in 1741. The figures are realistically depicted in the best Neapolitan tradition, which still reflected the influence of Ribera in the 18th century.

2838. Botticelli. The Story of Nastagio degli Onesti.

BONZI, Pietro Paolo, called «il Gobbo dei Carracci» (b. Cortona 1576; d. Rome 1636). Roman School.

1226 «Head of an old man» (Canvas, 39 × 31 cm). This work was attributed for a time to Velázquez, but is now unanimously considered to be by Bonzi, who was a pupil of the Carracci in Rome and a still-life painter in the early 17th-century Tenebrist manner. It may have been a preparatory sketch to judge by the rapid, energetic technique and unfinished forms.

BORDONE, Paris (b. Treviso 1500; d. Venice 1570). Venetian School.

372 «Self-portrait» (Canvas, 104 × 76 cm). Bordone was a student of Titian and one of the most important representatives of the Venetian School.

The apparent age of the artist makes us date this portrait between 1530 and 1540.

BORGIANNI, Orazio (Rome c. 1578-1616). Roman School.

877 «**Self-portrait**» (Canvas, 95 × 71 cm). This artist worked in Spain around 1600. His technique reveals Venetian influence and is evidently reminiscent of El Greco. On his return to Rome he was attracted by the Caravaggesque movement. This expressive portrait illustrates the artist's restless personality.

BOTTICELLI, Sandro Filipepi (Florence 1445-1510). Florentine School. Botticelli was one of the great figures of the Renaissance; he was a pupil of Fra Filippo Lippi, who painted delicate Madonnas, and later fell under the influence of Leonardo's master, Verrocchio. From an early age he was in contact with the intellectual and humanist environment of the Court of Lorenzo de' Medici and his work reflects the literary and philosophical trends of his time. His fondness for ideal beauty, the melancholy mood of his models and his perfect technique are salient features of his work, which also reveals his sensitive, restless character. He is famous for works like *Spring* and *The Birth of Venus* and was sent for by Pope Sixtus IV to collaborate on the decoration of the Sistine Chapel. Towards the end of his life a religious crisis made him destroy a large number of his works which he considered pagan.

2838 «**The story of Nastagio degli Onesti**» (3 panels of approx. 82 × 140 cm
2839 each). This series originally consisted of 4 panels (the fourth is now in an
2840 American collection) and was commissioned by Lorenzo de' Medici as a wedding gift for members of two important Florentine families, the Pucci and the Bini, whose coats-of-arms appear on the frames. It represents a story from Boccaccio's *Decamerone;* the young Nastagio degli Onesti is walking through a forest deep in melancholic thoughts after being rejected by his beloved, when he sees a knight pursuing a young girl (No. 2838), whom he kills, throwing her heart to the dogs (No. 2839). The knight explains to Nastagio that he has been condemned to repeat this scene every Friday as an eternal punishment for the young girl's disdain and his own suicide. Nastagio conceives the idea of celebrating a banquet in this spot with his beloved and her family so that they may witness the scene and accede to his love (No. 2840). The happy end is portrayed in the missing panel. The colouring and beauty of the composition and its figures command attention.

BRONZINO, Agnolo di Cosimo, called «**Bronzino**» (Florence 1503-1572). Florentine School.

5 «**Don Garzia de' Medici**» (Wood, 48 × 38 cm). Bronzino was a Mannerist artist and pupil of Pontormo; his work as a portraitist is important, as can be appreciated in this portrait, dating from about 1550, which reveals great attention to detail and delicate colouring.

BUONACCORSI. See Perino del Vaga.

CALIARI. See Veronese, Paolo.

CAMASSEI, Andrea (b. Bevagna 1602; d. Rome 1649). Roman School.

122 «**Lupercalia**» (Canvas, 237 × 365 cm). This scene shows the ancient Roman festival held in honour of Lupercus, considered the god of fertility and equivalent to the Greek Pan, and Lucine, the goddess who presided over birth. On this day the priests ran through the streets striking women with thongs in the belief that this would make them fertile. The colouring is attractive and the free technique denotes Venetian influence.

2315 «**Gladiators fighting**» (Canvas, 182 × 235 cm). This work was attributed to Lanfranco but is now unanimously ascribed to Camassei. Compare the type of figures, identical with those of the preceding work.

CAMBIASO or **Cangiaso, Luca** (b. Moneglia 1527; d. El Escorial 1585). Genoese School.

60 «**Holy Family**» (Canvas, 131 × 103 cm). This work is characteristic of Cambiaso, a Genoese painter who worked in El Escorial. The soft technique with which he envelops his figures in a gentle *sfumato* does not prevent him from producing clearly-defined forms which are set off by well-balanced colouring and varying light effects.

61 «**Cupid sleeping**» (Canvas, 64 × 72 cm). The scene is emphasized by brownish tones and intense *chiaroscuro.*

62 «**Lucretia**» (Canvas, 123 × 120 cm). This is a very attractive work with its Venetian colouring and loose technique that brings out the female nude and mitigates the dramatic effect of the scene.

CAMPI, Antonio (Cremona 1524-1587). Lombardic School.

59 «**St. Jerome meditating**» (Wood transferred to canvas, 183 × 122 cm).

2840. Sandro Botticelli. The story of Nastagio degli Onesti (III). (detail)

Signed. This work was painted for Philip II; the intense expression of the elongated figure of the Saint commands attention. There are some extremely realistic details like the table with the meticulously depicted cloth that makes it resemble a still-life composition.

CAMPI, Vicenzo (Cremona 1536-1591). Lombardic School.

59a «Crucifixion» (Canvas, 210 × 141 cm). Signed and dated 1577. The reduced space that gives the scene an impression of tension is typical of the Mannerist style. The fondness of Lombardic artists for hard modelling gives the work an enamel-like surface finish which is combined with the colours and almost metallic sheens of the textures.

2715 «A merry table» (Canvas, 78 × 100 cm). The popular figures and profane subject-matter relate this work to the Flemish tradition.

CANALETTO, Antonio Canale, called **«Canaletto»** (Venice 1697-1768). Copies. Venetian School.

2465 «The Grand Canal and Rialto Bridge in Venice» (Canvas, 37 × 54 cm). See No. 2478.

2466 «The church of San Giorgio Maggiore and the Venetian toll-house» (Canvas, 32 × 48 cm). See No. 2478.

2478 «St. Mark's Square in Venice» (Canvas, 32 × 48 cm). These are not very high-quality works; they were considered in the past to be by Canaletto and later connected with the name of Battaglioli, an Italian artist who worked in Spain. They are, however, copies after originals by Canaletto now kept in other collections.

CANTARINI, Simone (Pesaro 1612-1648). Bolognese School.

63 «The Holy Family» (Canvas, 75 × 55 cm). This work is characteristic of Cantarini who combines here a keen sense of reality with the idealization and elegance found in models by Guido Reni, who was his master.

CARACCIOLO, Giovanni Battista, called **«Battistello»** (Naples c. 1570-1637). Neapolitan School.

2759 «St. Cosme and St. Damian» (Canvas, 96 × 121 cm). A follower of Caravaggio, Caracciolo uses here the latter's Tenebrist style; however, his naturalism is attenuated by the almost noble elegance of the Saints' poses.

CARAVAGGIO, Michelangelo Merisi, called **«Caravaggio»** (b. Caravaggio 1573; d. Porto Ercole 1610). Roman School. A revolutionary artist in his time, Caravaggio represents the beginning of one of the most important artistic trends of the 17th century, Tenebrism, that influenced not only Italian painting but also other European schools like the French, Dutch and Spanish. His work was inspired by reality, which he interpreted with the aid of strong light contrasts which sometimes emphasize the mysterious mood of his compositions and at other times heighten the dramatic effect of a scene. The life of this artist, who was born in Northern Italy and moved to Rome at an early age, was full of violent events and his uncompromising character earned him the miscomprehension of friends and patrons until finally he had to flee from Rome faced with a charge of homicide. He painted in Naples, Malta and Sicily; when he received the Pope's pardon and intended to return to Rome he had to interrupt his journey due to an attack of fever and died alone on the beach at Porto Ercole.

65 «David victorious over Goliath» (Canvas, 110 × 91 cm). This work dates from about 1600 and its salient features are the intensely realistic figure and tight handling which sets off the almost sculptured modelling of the young David. The expressiveness of the scene is heightened by the play of focusing light.

CARBONI, Giovanni Bernardo (?) (Genoa 1614-1683). Genoese School.

2564 «Portrait of a child» (Canvas, 172 × 111 cm). Its attribution to Carboni is not completely certain, but the work is related to the style of the Genoese artists influenced by Van Dyck.

CARDUCCIO, Bartolomeo (b. Florence 1554; d. El Pardo 1608). Florentine School. Carduccio was a pupil of the sculptor Ammannati and belonged to the late Mannerist tradition. He used vivid colouring and Michelangelesque models which he interpreted with a naturalistic touch that anticipated Baroque painting. He came to Spain with other painters to decorate El Escorial and settled at the Spanish Court. His work had an important influence on early 17th-century painting in Madrid, one of whose representatives was his brother Vicente Carducho (see Spanish Masters).

66 «The Deposition» (Canvas, 263 × 181 cm). Signed and dated 1595. This is the artist's masterpiece and was painted for a church in Madrid. The

composition reflects perfect harmony and balance and is limited to the essential figures, which are treated with a delicately sentimental touch characteristic of the Florentine School in the late 16th century.

68 «The Last Supper» (Canvas, 256 × 244 cm). Signed and dated 1605. This is a traditional composition in which Carduccio combines the figures' elegant poses with a certain naturalistic approach as can be appreciated in the faces of the Apostles or the still-life details.

CARLETTO. See Veronese, Carletto.

CARPI, Girolamo da (Ferrara 1501-1556). Ferrarese School.

69 «Alfonso II d'Este» (?) (Wood, 101 × 64 cm). This work was ascribed to Bronzino for a time, but is now considered closer to the style of Carpi.

5. Bronzino. Don Garzia de' Medici.   65. Caravaggio. David and Goliath.

CARRACCI, Agostino (b. Bologna 1557; d. Parma 1602). Bolognese School. Together with his brother Annibale and his cousin Ludovico he founded a famous Fine Arts Academy in Bologna and was the artist who did most to renew painting at the end of the 16th century, creating the Classicist movement, which had its roots in Raphael, but drew on the Venetians for its technique and Correggio for its solution of space. Due to his humanistic education Agostino was the Academy's theorist, although he did not give up painting and engraving.

404 «The Holy Supper» (Canvas, 172 × 237 cm). There are various versions of this composition, which dates from about 1595. It reveals extreme care in the distribution and poses of the different figures. Prominent features are the beauty of the draperies, painted in the Venetian manner, the highly realistic still-life details and the addition of anecdotic elements like the two small dogs playing.

CARRACCI, Annibale (b. Bologna 1560; d. Roma 1609). Bolognese School. He was one of the artists who renewed Italian painting in the 17th century, along with his brother Agostino and his cousin Ludovico. He worked on frescoes for many palaces in Bologna, where Baroque Classicism appears for the first time, based on Raphael but mainly centred on a constant study of nature. He was called to Rome in 1595 to decorate the Farnese Gallery and in the frescoes of the main gallery he left one of his major works, Loves of the gods, which was a model for future artists. His full and vital sense of colouring influenced Rubens, whereas French artists were impressed by his perfection and formal beauty; the standards he set up remained valid down until 18th-century Neo-Classicism.

72 «Madonna and Child with St. John» (Circular panel, 29 cm in diameter). This is a small, but extremely delicate work which appears to be taken directly from motifs by Raphael.

75 «The Assumption of the Virgin» (Canvas, 130 × 97 cm). This work dates from about 1590 and reveals knowledge of Venetian models in the positioning of the figures, the monumental architectural elements and the sense of colouring. The landscape in the background is extremely attractive.

Decorations from the Herrera Chapel: (see No. 2910 below).

76 «Apotheosis of St. Francis.»

77 «Apotheosis of St. James.»

288. Giorgione. The Virgin and Child between St. Anthony and St. Roch. (detail)

2843. Melozzo da Forlí. Angelic musician. (detail)

78 «**Apotheosis of St. Lawrence**» (3 ovals, 155 × 105 cm each).

132 «**Landscape with bathers**» (Canvas, 47 × 56 cm). This work is typical of Annibale Carracci's landscape painting: nature is perfectly ordered, as corresponds to the painter's classical ideal, without losing its vibrating sense.

2631 «**Venus, Adonis and Cupid**» (Canvas, 212 × 268 cm). This work dates from about 1595 and is the most important painting by Annibale Carracci in the Prado. It shows Venus falling in love with Adonis after being hit by one of Cupid's arrows. It is an example of the artist's most Venetian style and has reminiscences of Titian and Veronese, although with ample Baroque forms.

2908 «**St. Diego receiving the Franciscan habit.**»

2909 «**The miraculous meal.**»

2910 «**The miracle of the child in the oven**» (4 trapezoids, 125 × 220 cm each). The Prado preserves seven of the frescoes, transferred to canvas, that Carracci painted to decorate the Herrera Chapel of the Spanish Church of St. James in Rome. They were brought to Spain in 1850 and the remaining nine are kept in the Museum of Barcelona. Carracci worked on them during the time he spent in Rome, between 1602 and 1607, with the collaboration of some of his best pupils, such as Albani and Domenichino, who followed the master's preparatory drawings. They narrate scenes from the life of St. Diego of Alcalá, patron of the chapel, and although they are not well preserved, Carracci's characteristic features can be observed in the orderly arrangement of the compositions and the ample, majestic figures.

s.n. «**St. Diego receiving alms.**»

CARRACCI, Ludovico (Bologna 1555-1619). Bolognese School. He was the eldest of the Carracci and a cousin of Agostino and Annibale; together with them he worked for a renewal of painting along Baroque lines. He adapted his art to the rules dictated by the Council of Trent, trying to bring the ideals of the Counter-Reformation closer to the people by means of his naturalism and deep-felt religiosity.

70 «**Franciscan jubilee**» (Canvas, 200 × 147 cm). This work represents the apparition of Christ and the Virgin to St. Francis of Assisi in ecstasy, interpreted with the formal beauty typical of Ludovico Carracci's mature period.

74 «**Agony in the Garden**» (Canvas, 48 × 55 cm). This work dates from 1590/1600. The beautiful colouring is enhanced by a play of light that anticipates the following style of the Bolognese School (cf. Guercino).

CARRACCI, Follower.

2631. A. Carracci. Venus, Adonis and Cupid.

84 «The Virgin and Child with St. John» (Wood, 43 × 33 cm). This is a very delicate work that bears relation to the circle around the Carracci.

CARRUCCI. See Pontormo.

CASTIGLIONE, Giovanni Benedetto (b. Genoa 1610; d. Mantua 1670). Genoese School. He was a widely travelled artist; trained in Genoa and also well acquainted with Roman Classicism and the Neapolitan realism derived from Ribera, he was above all a vital colourist. He cultivated all branches of painting, but showed preference for allegories, mythological and *genre* scenes, which he interpreted with a fully naturalistic touch and vibrating, succulent technique.

88 «Diogenes» (Canvas, 97 × 145 cm). The theme of Diogenes searching for an honest man but finding only animals, satyrs and drunkards is related to the moralizing allegories of the 17th century. This work dates from his last period, in which he combined his naturalistic approach with an extremely Classical arrangement of the scene; some of the figures are taken directly from Roman sculptural groups.

89 «Still-life with a sheep's head» (Canvas, 41 × 58 cm). This work has traditionally been attributed to Castiglione; it is not a particularly good work, but is related to his style.

3152. Cavallino. Tobias' betrothal.

CATENA, Vincenzo di Biagio, called «Vincenzo Catena» (Venice c. 1480-1531). Venetian School.

20 «Christ presenting the keys to St. Peter» (Wood, 86 × 135 cm). The perfect, clear-cut delineation of the forms is related to Bellini's style and was already an archaism in these early years of the 16th century, when the prevailing technique was Giorgione's and Titian's light, loose touch.

CAVALLINO, Bernardo (Naples 1616-1654). Neapolitan School.

3151 «The healing of Tobias» (Canvas, 76 × 103 cm). See No. 3152.

3152 «Tobias' betrothal» (Canvas, 76 × 103 cm). This is the companion piece to the preceding work; they both illustrate the story of Tobias as related in the Apocrypha, which Cavallino painted on several occasions. The artist transforms Neapolitan Caravaggesque realism into more refined pictorial forms, using rich colouring and stressing the elegance of the figures, like the angel in *The healing of Tobias*.

CAVAROZZI, Bartolomeo (b. Viterbo c. 1590; d. Rome 1625). Roman School.

146 «The Holy Family with St. Catherine» (Canvas, 256 × 170 cm). This work is characteristic of Cavarozzi, a painter who interpreted the Caravaggesque realistic tradition with sweetened forms and pleasing compositions that are related to the style of Guido Reni and Gentileschi. Cavarozzi was important for Spanish painting because he spent two years in Madrid.

CAVEDONE, Giacomo (b. Sassuolo 1577; d. Bologna 1660). Bolognese School.

3092. Antonello da Messina. Dead Christ supported by an angel. (detail)

95 «The Adoration of the Shepherds» (Canvas, 240 × 182 cm). This very attractive work by Cavedone, who was a pupil of the Carracci, is a replica of one of his most famous pictures, painted for Bologna. He has combined realistic models, like the shepherds, with a serenely Classicist composition, all interpreted with rich Venetian colouring.

CECCO DEL CARAVAGGIO (known to have been in Rome in the first half of the 17th century).

148 «Woman with a dove» (Canvas, 66 × 47 cm). Previously attributed to Artemisa Gentileschi, art critics are now unanimous in ascribing it to Cecco del Caravaggio. It reveals an almost surrealistic fondness for textures, draperies, animals and flowers, which is characteristic of this artist, who belonged to the circle of Caravaggio's followers, but whose biography and real name are unknown. This is the companion piece to a portrait of a man, kept in the Royal Palace in Madrid.

CELEBRANO, Francesco (Naples 1729-1814). Neapolitan School.

2496 «A hunt» (Canvas, 121 × 154 cm). This work was attributed in the catalogues to the French artist Charles de La Traverse, but current opinion among art critics considers it to be by Celebrano, a Neapolitan artist who was a pupil of Solimena and only left works of minor importance. In this painting he has depicted many highly-detailed scenes that enliven the composition.

CERQUOZZI, Michelangelo, called «Battles Cerquozzi» (Rome 1602-1660). Roman School.

96 «Hut» (Canvas, 51 × 41 cm). This work is typical of Cerquozzi, who painted in the circle of the *bamboccianti,* the Northern artists in Rome who used an attenuated form of Caravaggesque realism to portray scenes from popular, everyday life full of colour and animation.

CERRINI, Giovanni Domenico (b. Perugia 1609; d. Rome 1681). Roman School.

97 «Time destroying Beauty» (Canvas, 258 × 229 cm). This is a frequent allegory in Baroque painting and alludes to the transience of beauty. The old man Time, identified by the water-clock and scythe, destroys Beauty as he passes rapidly by. Attractive colouring and draperies billowing in the wind are characteristic features of this artist from the Roman Classicist circle around Reni.

CESARI. See Arpino.

CIGNAROLI, Giambettino (Verona 1706-1770). Venetian School.

99 «The Madonna and Child with saints» (Canvas, 314 × 171 cm). This work, which was commissioned by the Spanish Queen Elizabeth Farnese for one of the chapels of the Riofrío Palace in Segovia, is an example of the style of Cignaroli, whose rich colouring and magnificent composition belong to the best Veronese tradition.

CIMA, Giovanni Battista Cima da Conegliano (Conegliano c. 1460-1516/18). Venetian School.

2638 «The Madonna and Child» (Wood, 63 × 44 cm). Signed. Although the attribution of this work to Cima is doubtful, it is related to the style of the early 16th-century Venetian artists whose archaic manner was a late imitation of Bellini. The abstract, almost geometrically dry forms are characteristic of Cima's style.

CODAZZI, Viviano (b. Bergamo 1603; d. Rome 1672). Roman School.

510 «St. Peter's in Rome» (Canvas, 168 × 220 cm). Codazzi was a painter of architectural settings and perspectives who studied in Neapolitan naturalistic circles and later came into contact with the *bamboccianti* in Rome (see Cerquozzi); here he paints a highly-detailed description of the square in front of St. Peter's with the façade of the basilica as it was before it was renovated in the mid-17th century. The attractive light contrasts and sense of space are noteworthy. The figures were painted by Aniello Falcone.

COLOMBO, Giovanni Battista (Arogno, Lugano 1717-1793). Lombardic School.

3194 «Scenes in a garden» (Canvas, 122 × 92 cm). Signed. Colombo was a painter of theatrical decorations who travelled to various European Courts and settled in London for a long time. In this landscape he portrays a typical 18th-century courtly context in a brilliant, decorative and highly-detailed kind of painting with a somewhat scenographic sense. The Prado possesses another work by this artist, but its state of preservation is poor.

COLONNA. See Mitelli.

CONCA, Sebastiano (Gaeta 1680-1764). Roman School.

101 «**Alexander the Great in the Temple at Jerusalem**» (Canvas, 52 × 70 cm). This is a preparatory sketch for one of the large-scale works of the Throne Room at the La Granja Palace. The scene is an allusion to Philip V's religious virtues and represents Alexander offering a sacrifice to the God of Israel. This is a sample of the style of Conca, who studied in Naples in the circle around Giordano and Solimena and whose work also reflects his contacts with Roman Classicism.

102 «**The idolization of Solomon**» (Canvas, 54 × 71 cm). This work shows more finish than the preceding one and is characterized by a spacious composition, carefully poised figures, beautiful draperies and attractive, Rococo-style colouring.

s.n. «**Thetis presents Achilles to Chiron**» (Canvas, 57 × 73 cm). This mythological work was painted to commemorate the birth of Philip V's youngest son, Luis Antonio Jaime, and represents an event in the childhood of the Greek hero Achilles.

CONTE, Jacopino del (?) (b. Florence 1510; d. Rome 1598). Florentine School.

329 «**The Holy Family**» (Wood, 105 × 100 cm). This work is considered by some art historians to be by Salviati, while others ascribe it to Jacopino del Conte. It is without doubt derived from Parmigiano's elegant models, interpreted with Florentine fondness for sculptural modelling of the forms and clear colouring.

CORREGGIO, Antonio Allegri, called «il Correggio» (Correggio 1489-1534). Parmese School. Although he only lived 45 years, he had a clearly-defined creative personality and exerted an influence on Italian painting; his work is reminiscent of Mantegna and influenced by Leonardo and Raphael. His large-scale fresco decorations contain novelties in pictorial expression which would not be fully developed until the height of the Baroque. His altar-pieces and smaller religious and mythological pictures, like these works in the Prado, which are very frequent in his production, are characterized by the psychological tenseness of the figures, mellow modelling, exquisite changes in colouring and refined light contrasts, combined with a naturalistic touch, which all anticipate the painting of the 17th century.

111 «**Noli me tangere**» (Wood transferred to canvas, 130 × 103 cm). The date of this work is doubtful since some art critics believe it to be a youthful work while others assign it a later date. However it is unanimously considered one of Correggio's masterpieces. A moist, shady landscape, full of green and bluish tones, is the setting for the figures of Christ and Mary Magdalene, whose emotions are concentrated in the intensity of their expressions. The warm tones of Mary Magdalene's clothes provide a contrast to the cool colouring of Christ's skin and mantle.

112 «**The Madonna and Child with the infant St. John**» (Wood, 48 × 37 cm). This work dates from about 1516. It is clearly derived from works by Leonardo, for example in the rocks seen against the light in front of a *sfumato* landscape background or in the Virgin's mysterious, melancholy smile. There is a certain naturalistic touch about the children's gracefulness.

CORREGGIO, Copies by Eugenio Caxes.

119 «**The rape of Ganymede**» (Canvas, 175 × 72 cam). This is a copy after an original kept in the Vienna Museum.

120 «**The legend of Leda**» (Canvas, 165 × 193 cm). This is a copy after an original kept in the Dahlem Museum in Berlin.

CORREGGIO. Anonymous copies.

115 «**Rest on the Flight into Egypt or the Madonna della Scodella**» (Canvas, 211 × 140 cm). This is a copy after an original kept in the Parma *Pinacoteca*.

117 «**The Fifth Sorrow**» (Wood, 39 × 47 cm). This is a smaller-scale copy after an original kept in the Parma *Pinacoteca*.

118 «**Martyrdom of SS. Placidus, Flavia, Eutychius and Victorinus**» (Wood, 39 × 47 cm). This is a copy after an original kept in the Parma *Pinacoteca*.

CORTONA, Pietro Berrettini, called «Pietro da Cortona» (b. Cortona 1596; d. Rome 1669). Roman School. Cortona was one of the most famous artists in Rome in the 17th century and was appointed Director of St. Luke's Academy at an early age. On his arrival in Rome he immediately made contact with the cultural and intellectual circles of the city and was protected in his career by important families, such as the Barberini, who took pleasure in decorating their palaces with Cortona's spectacular works, based on complicated compositions with numerous figures, rich colouring and perspective, which mark the beginning of full Baroque painting, spread throughout Italy by his followers.

121 **«Nativity»** (Red agate and oil, 51 × 40 cm). This very attractive work, representative of Cortona's style in the models used, was a gift from the Barberini family to Philip IV.

1969 **«David crowned»** (Canvas, 147 × 213 cm). This work bears relation to Cortona's youthful style.

CRESPI, Daniele (b. Busto Arsizio 1597; d. Milan 1630). Lombardic School.

128 **«Pietà»** (Canvas, 175 × 144 cm). Signed. This work is characteristic of Crespi, whose treatment of light and naturalistic approach have been compared with that of Spanish artists. The majestic, almost Michelangelesque nude is moulded by direct lighting that stresses its anatomical perfection and the sober compositional scheme. The technique is light, slightly *sfumato*.

129 **«The Flagellation»** (Wood, 129 × 100 cm). The technical and stylistic characteristics of this work are similar to those of the preceding one, but the oil paint on wood gives a brilliant, terse surface finish that produces plastic qualities and tactile values highly appreciated by Crespi.

111. **Correggio. Noli me tangere.**   112. **Correggio. Madonna and Child.**

CRESPI, Giovanni Battista, called «il Cerano» (b. Cerano 1575; d. Milan 1633). Lombardic School.

547 **«St. Carlo Borromeo before the dead Christ»** (Canvas, 109 × 156 cm). The Lombardic painter, sculptor and architect «il Cerano» was the master of Daniele Crespi and painted deeply religious scenes in the same naturalistic manner with strong light contrasts. The realistic depiction of the Saint's ecstasy is the keynote of this work.

1965 **«Rest on the Flight into Egypt»** (Copper, 43 × 31 cm). This is a very attractive and delicate work that probably dates from the artist's early period still close to Mannerist styles in its strange, fantastic manner of representing space and fondness for cold colouring, with iridescent tones both in the landscape and the figures.

DOMENICHINO, Domenico Zampieri, called «il Domenichino» (b. Bologna 1581; d. Naples 1641). Bolognese School. In Bologna he was a pupil of Ludovico Carracci, but moved to Rome when he was still in his prime and worked as an assistant to Annibale Carracci. He soon became an independent artist and the success of his rigorously Classicist painting, orderly and harmonious, with a certain naturalistic touch, gained him official protection and the admiration of younger artists who copied his compositions. Towards the end of his life, in Naples, he was unable to depart from the beaten path and adapt his style to the Baroque trends of the following generation of artists.

130 See Masari.

131 **«The sacrifice of Isaac»** (Canvas, 147 × 140 cm). This work is representative of the artist's late period. It is an orderly composition with very serene models among whom Abraham stands out with his rhetoric and affected air.

540 **«Arch of Triumph»** (Canvas, 70 × 60 cm). This is an allegorical work dedicated to the memory of Giovanni Battista Agucchi, Domenichino's friend and patron and a theorist of the Roman Classicist movement.

542 «The martyrdom of St. Andrew (Canvas, 102 × cm). This is one of Domenichino's youthful works and still contains strong light contrasts reminiscent of Caravaggio combined with Raphaelesque Classicist figures.

2926 «Funeral rites for a Roman Emperor» (Canvas, 227 × 363 cm). This work was painted as part of a series of paintings on Roman customs and events to decorate the Buen Retiro Palace (see Lanfranco, Camassei, Romanelli and Stanzione). Domenichino has attempted an almost archeological reconstruction of Ancient Rome and depicted monuments and buildings as he imagined them.

DUGHET, Gaspard or Gaspard Poussin (Rome 1615-1675). Roman School. Although he was of French extraction, Dughet was born and grew up in the artistic environment of Rome, becoming a brother-in-law of the great French artist Poussin, by whose name he is sometimes known. He mainly painted landscapes of the Roman countryside, combining them with Classical ruins, which made him famous and influenced 17th-century landscape painting.

134 «The storm» (Canvas, 49 × 66 cm). This work reveals the artist's almost Romantic fondness for depicting nature during a storm. It dates from about 1650, when his style began to evolve gradually away from that of his master Poussin.

135 «A hurricane» (Canvas, 74 × 98 cm). This work resembles the preceding one in its atmospheric effects.

136 «Landscape with the repentant Mary Magdalene» (Canvas, 76 × 130 cm). This work belongs to the artist's late period. It is an elaborately Classicist composition in which Dughet takes pleasure in depicting an ordered vision of nature, rich in detail and with subtle atmospheric and light effects which make it one of the finest examples of his work.

137 «Landscape» (Canvas, 73 × 96 cm). See No. 138.

138 «Landscape» (Canvas, 74 × 98 cm). This is possibly a companion piece to the preceding No. and is also a very elaborate work with small figures of shepherds and sheep, buildings bathed in sunlight and attractive atmospheric effects.

2305 «Landscape with a hermit preaching to animals» (Canvas, 159 × 233 cm). This is a high-quality work, which led art critics to attribute it to Poussin, but the style corresponds to Dughet's early period, with a highly-detailed description of the vegetation and an infinite range of greenish tones.

DUGHET and Maratti.

552 «Repentant Mary Magdalene» (Canvas, 71 × 75 cm). The landscape is by Dughet and the figures by Maratti, a Roman Classicist painter with whom Dughet collaborated on several occasions (see Maratti).

DUPRA, Domenico (Turin 1689-1770). Piedmontese School.

2250 «Doña Bárbara de Braganza» (Canvas, 75 × 60 cm). Dupra worked in Lisbon, where he painted this portrait of the future wife of Ferdinand VI and Queen of Spain. The colouring is light, in accordance with French taste, and the work does not reveal very high artistic quality.

FALCONE, Aniello (Naples c. 1607-1656). Neapolitan School. Falcone specialized in battle scenes, which were highly appreciated by 17th-century art collectors; through Ribera he applied Caravaggio's style, light contrasts and naturalistic approach, adapting them to his own artistic sensibility and profane subject-matter, which he interpreted with great vivaciousness. In his later works he used more serene and Classical forms, possibly influenced by the great French painter resident in Rome, Poussin.

87 «A concert» (Canvas, 109 × 127 cm). This work belongs to his mature style; the scene is keenly realistic, indeed it seems like a «snapshot» view of the singers and musicians concentrating on their work. It is one of Falcone's most attractive paintings with its refined colouring, warm tones and the sensitive lighting effects that play around the still-life details, draperies and fruit.

91 «Elephants in a circus» (Canvas, 229 × 231 cm). This work has been ascribed to many different artists, such as Pietro Testa, Castiglione and Andrea di Leone, but art critics are now inclined to attribute it to Falcone. The subject-matter is taken from the history of Rome, although possibly without a very definite meaning, and was probably part of the decoration of the Buen Retiro Palace.

92 «Gladiators» (Canvas, 186 × 183 cm). The anatomical studies show perfect and realistic execution. Reminiscences of Ribera in the figures are combined with knowledge of Roman Antiquity, as can be appreciated in the statues, reliefs and architectonic elements.

93 «**Roman soldiers in the circus**» (Canvas, 92 × 183 cm). This work also belonged to the decoration of the Buen Retiro Palace. It dates from the period when Falcone was most directly influenced by Poussin. The interpretation of the scene is very personal, with its foreground in the form of a Classic frieze which contrasts with the bustling activity on the steps in the background. The rich colouring is set off by direct lighting.

94 «**Jesus driving the traders out of the Temple**» (Canvas, 101 × 135 cm). The style of this work is related to that of the *Concert;* the details are realistically depicted, the colouring is warm and the lighting intense. The biblical scene is treated in an almost profane manner.

139 «**Roman battle**» (Canvas, 133 × 215 cm). This is an example of Falcone's work as a specialist in battle scenes. All the tension of the battle has been captured in this painting.

2314 «**Noah after the Deluge**» (Canvas, 100 × 127 cm). Although this work has traditionally been attributed to Falcone, it is also considered by some critics to be the work of his pupil, Andrea di Leone. The subject-matter was very popular with Poussin's followers.

FIESOLE. See Angelico.

FIORI. See Barocci.

FRACANZANO, Cesare (b. Brisceglie, Apulia c. 1612; d. Naples 1653). Neapolitan School.

142 «**Two wrestlers**» (Canvas, 156 × 128 cm). This work is reminiscent of Ribera, although within a rigorous compositional scheme that relates it to the Bolognese tradition. It is considered to represent Hercules and Antaeus.

FRANCIA, Giacomo and **Giulio** (both active in Bologna in the first half of the 16th century). Bolognese School.

143 «**St. Jerome, St. Barbara and St. Francis**» (Wood, 156 × 145 cm). Signed by both brothers, it is not an exceptionally good work, but serves as an example of their style, with harmonious and attractively coloured compositions, inherited from the somewhat cool Classicism of their father, Francesco Francia, a representative of the first Bolognese Renaissance School.

FURINI, Francesco (Florence 1600-1646). Florentine School.

144 «**Lot and his daughters**» (Canvas, 123 × 120 cm). This work is characteristic of Furini who painted biblical and mythological subjects in a refined style; he tried to convey sensual effects with a *sfumato* technique which in the present picture underlines the mellow forms of the female nudes which he used profusely in his works and account for much of his fame.

GADDI, Taddeo (Florence 1300-c. 1366). Florentine School.

2841 «**St. Eloi before King Chlotar**» (Wood, 35 × 39 cm). See No. 2842.

2842 «**St. Eloi in his goldsmith's workshop**» (Wood, 35 × 39 cm). Gaddi studied under Giotto and inherited his workshop. Here he represents his brilliant master who renewed Italian painting in the 14th century. These two panels (art historians are not unanimous in attributing them to Gaddi) are very characteristic of the work of Giotto's followers, who introduced decorative elements and anecdotic details, without departing from their master's monumental forms, and emphasized their compositions with rich colouring in which the gilded background is an essential element.

GAGLIARDI, Filippo (active between 1640-59). Roman School.

145 «**Interior of St. Peter's in Rome**» (Canvas, 210 × 156 cm). Signed and

202. Guercino. St. Augustine meditating. 144. Furini. Lot and his daughters.

dated 1640. This painting shows the interior of the basilica before Bernini began to work on the high altar. Little is known about Gagliardi, who was an architect and painter of perspectives. He uses a highly-detailed technique to describe the decorative beauty and impressive interior of the basilica, peopled with small, lively figures of clergymen, beggars and gentlemen.

GARGIULO, Domenico, called «Mico Spadaro» (Naples 1612-c. 1675). Neapolitan School.

237 «**The triumphal entry of Vespasian in Rome**» (Canvas, 155 × 363 cm). See No. 238.

238 «**The triumphal entry of Constantine in Rome**» (Canvas, 155 × 355 cm). This is the companion piece to the preceding work; in both the artist depicts with his characteristic vivaciousness scenes of Roman triumphs, with a large variety of slender, elongated figures and anecdotic elements, that try to bring Antiquity to life in a naturalistic manner.

GENTILESCHI, Artemisa (b. Rome 1597; d. Naples 1652). Roman School. Artemisa was the daughter and pupil of Orazio Gentileschi and one of the most outstanding woman painters in history. She was famous as an artist at an early age. Her life was by no means a quiet one. Her law-suit against Agostino Tassi, one of her father's assistants, who tried to rape her as a child, is well-known. She married early, but later separated from her husband. After residing in Florence, she moved to Naples in 1630, where she re-married. On her father's death she stayed in London for a year before returning to Naples. Artemisa's painting assimilates various trends, including her father's attenuated Caravaggesque style and Bolognese Classicism, but always bears the mark of her personal approach.

149 «**Birth of St. John the Baptist**» (Canvas, 184 × 258 cm). Signed. This work is characteristic of Artemisa and considered by art critics the finest interior scene of 17th-century Italian painting. It is part of Stanzione's series on the life of St. John the Baptist, whose birth is portrayed here with extreme realism and intimate feeling.

147. O. Gentileschi. Moses rescued from the Nile.

GENTILESCHI, Orazio (b. Pisa 1563; d. London 1639). Roman School. Of Tuscan origin, Gentileschi settled in Rome in his youth, where he came into contact with Caravaggio and became one of his first and most faithful followers. He travelled through Italy (the Marche, Tuscany and Genoa) and in 1623 he was in Paris, from where he went to England in 1630, remaining there until his death. The realism of his early style gradually evolved towards more sensual and idealized forms, executed with clear colouring and light. His fondness for rich, brilliant draperies, which he depicted with great mastery, is possibly accounted for by the courtly and aristocratic circles he frequented during the last years of his life.

147 «**Moses rescued from the Nile**» (Canvas, 242 × 281 cm). Signed. This work was painted in England and sent as a gift to Philip IV in 1633. It is an important work and represents the daughter of the Pharoah and her entourage with all the brilliance and colouring of a contemporary scene at the English Court. For a time the work was attributed to Veronese due to the beauty of the draperies and Venetian-style landscape.

1240 «**The Infant Jesus sleeping on the Cross**» (Canvas, 75 × 100 cm). This theme, foreshadowing the death of Christ, was frequent in 17th-century art.

3122 «**St. Francis supported by an angel**» (Canvas, 126 × 98 cm). This work belongs to his Roman period and is still close to the Caravaggesque Tenebrism of his early years.

3188 «**Executioner with the head of John the Baptist**» (Wood transferred to canvas, 82 × 61 cm). Signed. The figure is realistically portrayed and the technique highly-detailed.

GIAQUINTO, Corrado (b. Molfetta 1703; d. Naples 1766). Neapolitan School. Giaquinto studied in Naples under Solimena, who painted large-scale Baroque decorations, but when he moved to Rome, still very young, he came into contact with the Rococo style prevailing there at the time. He collaborated with Sebastiano Conca, from whom he took over the rich colouring and 18th-century refinement. In 1753 he came to Madrid as Court Painter to Ferdinand VI and later he was appointed Director of the Academy of San Fernando. He carried out important commissions for the Spanish Court, including frescoes for the Royal Palace in Madrid and the Palace of Aranjuez, as well as a large number of religious, historical and mythological paintings, of which the works in the Prado are fine examples.

103 «**Birth of the Sun and Triumph of Bacchus**» (Canvas, 168 × 140 cm). This was the preparatory sketch for the fresco on the same subject for the stair-case of the Royal Palace in Madrid. It dates from 1762. It is one of the artist's most attractive works for its colouring and imaginative wealth. In the upper part of the painting Apollo, symbolizing the Sun, arises in his chariot illuminating the triumph of the god Bacchus, surrounded by nymphs.

104 «**Justice and Peace**» (Canvas, 216 × 325 cm). Signed. This is an allegorical painting which illustrates the effects of Justice and Peace in producing abundance and banishing war.

105 «**The sacrifice of Iphigenia**» (Canvas, 75 × 123 cm). Signed. This is a very attractive work related to the artist's Roman period. He has used a light technique, which gives it the air of a sketch. The figures have Classical reminiscences, but are treated with Rococo delicacy. The daughter of the Greek king Agamemnon, Iphigenia, was about to be sacrificed by her father to ensure his good fortune in the Trojan War when the goddess Diana appeared and ordered that a deer should be sacrificed in her place.

106 «**The battle of Clavijo**» (Canvas, 77 × 136 cm). This was a sketch for the decoration of the cupola of the Royal Palace chapel. It is related to the battle pieces which were so popular in 17th-century Neapolitan art.

107 «**Agony in the Garden**» (Canvas, 77 × 136 cm). See No. 3132.

108 «**Deposition**» (Canvas, 147 × 109 cm). See No. 3132.

109 «**St. Lawrence in Glory**» (Canvas, 97 × 137 cm). This was a preparatory sketch for the decoration of the cupola of the Palace chapel. Together with St. Lawrence a large number of biblical figures and other saints can be seen. The keynotes of the work are the beauty of its iridescent tones and the light technique with which the artist produces atmospheric effects.

110 «**The triumph of St. John of God**» (Canvas, 213 × 98 cm). This was a preparatory sketch for a fresco painted by Giaquinto in the church of San Giovanni Calabita in Rome. It is a very finished composition with serene, monumental figures which come closer to full Baroque than to Rococo delicacy. The draperies, which are important for their colouristic effects in all the artist's works, are particularly harmonious.

582 «**Justice and Peace**» (Canvas, 210 × 320 cm). Giaquinto painted this work for the conference room of the Fine Arts Academy of San Fernando in Madrid. The composition resembles that of No. 104. The beauty of the female figures contrasts with the unpleasant presence of Death on the pedestal, which recalls full Baroque allegories.

2424 «**The Holy Face**» (Canvas, 65 × 175 cm). See No. 3132.

2640 «**Moses in the Sinai**» (Canvas, 148 × 60 cm). This work is not by Giaquinto, but possibly by an 18th-century Spanish artist close to the style of Bayeu.

3131 «**The Crown of Thorns**» (Canvas, 141 × 97 cm). See No. 3132.

3132 «**Christ on the way to Calvary**» (Canvas, 141 × 97 cm). Together with the Nos. 107, 108, 2424, 3131 and others on loan to various Spanish museums, this work belongs to a series on Christ's Passion which Giaquinto painted for the King's oratory in the Buen Retiro Palace about 1754. They are executed with his characteristic sketch-like style, with rich tones and unreal light effects, which led art critics in the past to attribute some of them, for example the *Deposition*, to Goya.

3192 «**Landscape with a cascade and shepherds**» (Canvas, 156 × 229 cm).

3193 «**Landscape with huntsmen**» (Canvas, 152 × 226 cm). This is a pendant to the preceding work; in these works Giaquinto combines the Arcadic, serene style of Roman landscapes, like those of Dughet, with the brighter, livelier Neapolitan kind of landscape with its emphasis on light effects.

3204 «**The Holy Trinity**» (Oval canvas, 80 × 68 cm). This composition was repeated several times by Giaquinto. Here the majestic beauty of the nude body of Christ commands attention.

GIAQUINTO, Copy by José del Castillo.

s.n. «**The death of Absalom**» (Canvas, 403 × 618 cm). This was a cartoon for a tapestry done by José del Castillo after a composition by Giaquinto.

GIORDANO, Luca, known in Spain as «**Lucas Jordán**» (Naples 1634-1705). Neapolitan School. Giordano was trained in Naples in the studio of the Spanish artist Ribera, whose intense realism and striking contrasts of light and shade he adopted; in fact he imitated his master's style so perfectly that in many art collections works by Giordano were considered originals by Ribera. The astonishing ease and rapidity with which he worked earned him the nickname «Luca fa presto» among his contemporary colleagues. He moved to Rome, attracted by the art of the great Renaissance masters, whose works he copied enthusiastically, and at the same time participated in the artistic trends of his time, showing particular interest in Pietro da Cortona's imposing frescoes. However, the most decisive factor in forming his style was his stay in Venice. From then on his work, mainly religious and mythological scenes, was characterized by colouring, bright lighting effects, Baroque emphasis, spaciousness and vitality. His fame spread abroad and the Spanish King Charles II called him to Madrid to be his Court Painter. He decorated the cupolas at El Escorial and in the Royal Palace in Madrid with enormous frescoes full of imagination, spaciousness and atmospheric feeling; he also left a large number of canvases which reveal his evolution towards clearer colouring with greys and blues that recall Velázquez. After 10 years' work in Madrid he returned to Naples in 1702 and the last works he painted there paved the way for the rich, decorative Neapolitan painting of the 18th century.

151 «**Abraham listening to the Lord's promises**» (Canvas, 66 × 180 cm). See No. 153.

152 «**Abraham and the three angels**» (Canvas, 65 × 168 cm). See No. 153.

153 «**Lot made to drink wine by his daughters**» (Canvas, 58 × 154 cm). These three works belong to a series on the lives of Abraham and Isaac, along with many others now kept in other collections. They date from about 1694. The figures are portrayed in flowing draperies that produce a very decorative effect with their colouring and contrasts of light and shade.

157 «**Jacob's journey to Canaan**» (Copper, 54 × 84 cm). See No. 159.

159 «**The song of the prophetess Maria**» (Copper, 58 × 84 cm). This is the pendant to the preceding work. The animals are realistically depicted and the figures, whom the artist has grouped skilfully, making a lively, bustling composition, are portrayed in an idealized and elegant manner.

160 «**The defeat of Sisera**» (Canvas, 102 × 130 cm). See No. 161.

161 «**Victory of the Israelites and song of Deborah**» (Canvas, 102 × 154 cm). Like the preceding work, this is a preparatory sketch for the decorations of the church of Santa Maria Donnaromita in Naples, which Giordano completed soon before coming to Spain, in 1692. Its lightness, together with the striking and at times enveloping movement of the figures, reveal Giordano's creative power at its best and at the same time anticipate the work of Neapolitan artists like Solimena and Giaquinto. The technique consists of broad brushstrokes that are extraordinarily expressive. Only a few spots of colour break the general dark-toned colouring.

162 «**Hercules on the pyre**» (Canvas, 224 × 91 cm). This is one of a series of mythologies (Nos. 193-195), which date from the artist's last years in Spain.

163 «**Samson and the lion**» (Canvas, 224 × 142 cm). This is one of a series of scenes on Samson's life now preserved in various different collections.

165 «**Bathsheba in her bath**» (Canvas, 219 × 212 cm). This work, dating from about 1700, is one of Giordano's best works in the Prado. A serene, classical air pervades the composition and the scene is arranged in a way that sets off the female nude, which is strongly illuminated. This work was used as a model by the Royal Tapestry Factory in Madrid.

166 «**The prudence of Abigail**» (Canvas, 216 × 362 cm). This is an excellent work, painted about 1700, in which Giordano combines fondness for naturalistic details, like the dog or the dwarf, with serene elements and refined poses in the principal figures. It represents the biblical scene of

Abigail offering David victuals for the Israelite army. It is an example of Giordano's mastery in painting large canvases full of figures.

167 «St. Joseph's dream» (Wood, 62 × 48 cm). The angels are somewhat reminiscent of Correggio, whose works Giordano must have seen on his travels. In the lower part, full of strong light contrasts, the Virgin praying next to the sleeping cat commands attention with her homely and intimately devotional mood.

168 «The Holy Family» (Circular panel, 104 cm in diameter). In this work Giordano imitates Raphael, including his monogram. In his youthful period he frequently painted in the manner of the Renaissance masters.

171 «The kiss of Judas» (Canvas, 43 × 66 cm). See No. 172.

172 «Pilatus washing his hands» (Copper, 43 × 66 cm). This is a companion piece to the preceding work; both are now considered workshop paintings.

178 «St. Anthony of Padua» (Canvas, 121 × 93 cm). This is an early work.

179 «St. Rosalia» (Canvas, 81 × 64 cm). The Saint in ecstasy is given an intensely expressive air and interpreted according to the rules of Classicist elegance. The work is decorative and somewhat superficially religious.

181 «St. Francis Xavier» (Canvas, 97 × 71 cm). This work belongs to the school of Giordano.

182 «A (female) saint saved from a shipwreck» (Canvas, 62 × 77 cm). This work dates from about 1700. The very light, almost sketch-like technique heightens the dynamic effect of the composition.

183 «Capture of a stronghold» (Canvas, 235 × 343 cm). This is an imposing work painted in Giordano's most dynamic style; he continues the Baroque tradition of battle pieces, but portrayed here on a grand scale. The beauty and energetic, high-spirited air of the galloping horse are noteworthy. The scene has not been identified.

184 «The Battle of St. Quentin» (Canvas, 53 × 168 cm). See No. 185.

185 «The Battle of St. Quentin» (Canvas, 53 × 168 cm). These two works were sketches for frescoes to decorate the ceiling of the monumental staircase in the Monastery of El Escorial. They are very attractive works.

186 «The Battle of St. Quentin» (Canvas, 53 × 168 cm). This is another of the sketches for frescoes for the grand staircase in El Escorial. They commemorate Philip II's victory over the French at St. Quentin in 1557.

187 «The French High Constable Montmorency taken prisoner» (Canvas, 53 × 168 cm). See No. 188.

188 «The Admiral of France taken prisoner» (Canvas, 53 × 168 cm). Like the preceding sketches, this work was also for the decoration of El Escorial; they represent different scenes of the same battle.

3179. Giordano. Solomon's Dream.

189 «King Philip II visiting the works of El Escorial with his architects» (Canvas, 53 × 168 cm). This was a sketch for another of the frescoes, on a different subject, for the staircase of El Escorial.

190 «Rubens painting: Allegory on Peace» (Canvas, 337 × 414 cm). This

work dates from 1660/70, a time when Giordano was particularly interested in the work of Rubens, to whom he pays tribute in this picture. Seated on Discord, Rubens is painting a figure who makes Fury withdraw. In the upper part Minerva and Abundance hover above the artist. A little Cupid playing with soap bubbles symbolizes the vanity of worldly things. On the right a cavalcade of attractive figures repel War. Giordano's light technique, with loose brushstrokes and colourful *impasto,* bears direct relation to the Flemish artist's work, which is also well represented in the Prado.

191 «Air» (Canvas, 194 × 77 cm). The subject is allegorical. The technique recalls that of the School of Madrid.

193 «The death of the centaur Nessus (Canvas, 114 × 79 cm). See No. 162.

194 «Perseus defeating Medusa» (Canvas, 223 × 91 cm). See 162.

195 «Andromeda» (Canvas, 78 × 64 cm). Giordano painted this work in the manner of Titian.

196 «Aeneas on the flight from Troy» (Canvas, 279 × 125 cm). The subject is taken from Homer's *Iliad* and represents the hero Aeneas fleeing from Troy after the fall of the city. The scene is tensely dramatic with the reddish blaze of the city on fire in the background.

197 «Charles II on horseback» (Canvas, 81 × 61 cm). See No. 198.

198 «Doña Mariana of Neuburg on horseback» (Canvas, 81 × 61 cm). These are two portraits of the King and Queen of Spain. The technique is light and sketch-like, indicating that they were intended as preparatory sketches for larger works. They evidently derive from Velázquez' courtly portraits, although interpreted by Giordano in a more rhetoric tone.

2211a «Orpheus» (Canvas, 198 × 311 cm). Its attribution is uncertain.

2761 «Charles II on horseback» (Canvas, 68 × 54 cm). See No. 197.

2762 «Charles II on horseback» (Canvas, 80 × 62 cm). See No. 197.

2763 «Doña Mariana of Neuburg» (Canvas, 80 × 62 cm). This is the pendant to the preceding portrait and repeats the same composition as No. 198.

2993 «St. Carlo Borromeo» (Canvas, 126 × 104 cm). There is another version of this work in an Italian collection.

3178 «The Judgement of Solomon» (Canvas, 250 × 360 cm). See No. 3179.

3179 «Solomon's dream» (Canvas, 245 × 361 cm). Together with the preceding picture, this work belongs to a series of eight paintings on David and Solomon; the other six are kept in the Royal Palace in Madrid. They repeat compositions from the frescoes on the cupola at the Monastery of El Escorial. With their upward perspective they reveal a feeling for scenographic and theatrical effects, stressed by the rhetoric gestures of the figures. The brilliant colouring, with clear shades and predominance of greys, blues and golden tones, is characteristic of Giordano's Spanish period.

3195 «Struggle between Isaac and Ishmael» (Canvas, 175 × 84 cm). The scene is depicted with a naturalistic, almost popular touch.

GIORDANO, Copy.

573 «Self-portrait» (Canvas, 58 × 44 cm).

GIORGIONE, Giorgio da Castelfranco, called «Giorgione» (b. Castelfranco, Veneto 1477/78; d. Venice 1510). Venetian School. Giorgione received a humanistic education in the philosophical, artistic and literary circles of Renaissance Venice; he was also a musician and poet and probably received an independent artistic training. He possibly worked in Bellini's studio, whom he influenced in the last years of his life; his contact with Leonardo's art can be observed in his characteristic *sfumato.* Very little is known about his life and only few works can be attributed to him with complete certainty, so that the figure of Giorgione continues to be surrounded by a certain air of mystery. The few works that have been handed down to us reveal him as one of the great geniuses of the Italian Renaissance, whose painting, with its relationship of light and colouring and its constant fusion between Man and nature, marked a renewal in Venetian art.

288 «The Virgin and Child between St. Anthony and St. Roch» (Canvas, 92 × 183 cm). Opinion among art historians is divided over whether this canvas should be attributed to Giorgione or Titian's early period; it is, however, one of the finest religious works in the Museum with its intimate, restrained and mysterious air. Its delicate, *sfumato* technique, iridescent tones, *chiaroscuro* and atmospheric feeling will be further developed in the works of the Venetian *Cinquecento* here in the Prado.

GRAMMATICA, Antiveduto (b. Tuscany c. 1571; d. Rome 1626). Roman School.

353 «St. Cecilia» (Canvas, 128 × 100 cm). Antiveduto Grammatica was a friend

of Caravaggio, but his works reveal pronounced Classicist elements, like in this *St. Cecilia,* where the sheens of the draperies are depicted with an extremely delicate subtlety which sets off the Saint's beauty. This work was attributed in the past to Lionello Spada.

GRIMALDI, Gian Francesco (b. Bologna 1606; d. Rome c. 1680). Bolognese School.

80 «**Landscape**» (Canvas, 119 × 168 cm). Grimaldi was a Bolognese landscape painter whose work derives from that of the Carracci; in this picture he has copied a famous landscape by Domenichino kept in the Louvre. It is a serene, Classical work that comes up to the standard of the original and was attributed in the past to Annibale Carracci.

81 «**Landscape**» (Canvas, 112 × 149 cm). This landscape was ascribed to Carracci or Domenichino, but its style is similar to that of No. 80.

GUERCINO, Gian Francesco Barbieri, called «**il Guercino**» (b. Cento 1591; d. Bologna 1665). Bolognese School. Guercino was one of the most personal artists in 17th-century Italian painting. He trained in Bologna under Ludovico Carracci, adopted Venetian colouring and technique and Ferrarese fondness for metallic effects. His painting was successful in Rome, where he was influenced by the prevailing Classicist style without losing his vigorous touch. He was admired by Velázquez, who visited him in Cento, where he had retired in 1623. His painting evolved gradually towards serene, well-balanced forms, with delicate colouring and attractive, idealized models. His nickname «Guercino», «squint-eyed» in Italian, came from an eye defect.

200 «**St. Peter freed by the angel**» (Canvas, 105 × 136 cm). This work dates from his Roman period and is related to the monumental forms of Roman Classicism, but painted with the light contrasts and striking colouring characteristic of his early years.

201 «**Susannah and the Elders**» (Canvas, 175 × 207 cm). This work dates from 1617 and therefore belongs to his early period. The landscape and light, porous technique remind us that he was well acquainted with 16th century Venetian painting, although his naturalistic touch cannot be denied in his treatment of the figures, the old men's faces and the female nude underlined by light effects that bring out some parts and leave others in the shade.

202 «**St. Augustine meditating on the Holy Trinity**» (Canvas, 185 × 166 cm). The majestic figure of the Saint, interrupted in his work by the Child, commands attention. This is a fine example of a mid-17th century altar painting for a Roman church.

203 «**Mary Magdalene in the desert**» (Canvas, 121 × 141 cm). This work dates from Guercino's later years and reveals a perfectly arranged composition with refined, almost monochrome colouring.

JOLI, Antonio (b. Modena 1700; d. Naples 1777). Bolognese School.

232 «**Charles III embarking in Naples**» (Canvas, 128 × 205 cm). Signed and dated 1759.

233 «**Charles III embarking in Naples**» (Canvas, 128 × 205 cm). Signed and dated 1759. This is the companion piece to the preceding work and characteristic of Joli's style; he was an 18th-century representative of the

3091. Lanfranco. Gladiators at a banquet.

traditionally Venetian and Bolognese branch of perspectives, fantastic architectural settings and townscapes. Joli worked in Spain on theatrical decorations and these two pictures were painted here; they are highly detailed and full of decorative motifs, as appealed to Neapolitan artists.

LANFRANCO, Giovanni (b. Terenzano, Parma 1582; d. Rome 1647). Bolognese School. Lanfranco started to work in Parma in his youth with Agostino Carracci and from there went to Rome to assist Annibale Carracci on the frescoes for the Farnese Gallery. In Parma he had familiarized himself with Correggio's imposing decorations, which had a decisive influence on his mature style, when he broke with the Classical Bolognese tradition in his search for new formulas that were to pave the way for the full Baroque towards the end of the 18th century. His artistic style is characterized by figures in motion, foreshortened and underlined by intense colouring and changing light effects, executed with long brush-strokes applied directly on the reddish primed canvas. The Prado has a series of works by Lanfranco on the history of Rome commissioned by Philip IV for the decoration of the Buen Retiro Palace about 1639.

234 **«Funeral rites for a Roman emperor»** (Canvas, 335 × 488 cm). This is a spectacular composition with scenes of nude gladiators fighting violently in the foreground around the emperor's funeral pyre. The technique used is concise, light and energetic.

235 **«Naumachy (mock sea fight)»** (Canvas, 181 × 362 cm). See No. 236.

236 **«Auspices in Rome»** (Canvas, 181 × 362 cm). This is the companion piece to the preceding work; it is more Classical in its composition and recalls antique Roman reliefs with its frieze-shaped arrangement. The keynotes of the *Naumachy* are its full Baroque exuberance and tenseness of the fighting figures. The *Auspices* contains extremely delicate, almost Mannerist-style elements, like the nude young man on the right.

2315 See Camassei.

2943 **«Scene of triumph»** (Canvas, 230 × 362 cm). This is the companion piece to the following No. 3091 and represents a victorious Roman emperor distributing laurel wreaths to his soldiers. The rapid execution makes the work appear modern in the background and contrasts with the tender, delicate scene of the child playing with the dogs oblivious of what is going on around him. It is a very expressive work and one of the best by Lanfranco in the Prado.

3091 **«Gladiators at a banquet»** (Canvas, 232 × 355 cm). This is a masterpiece with its ambitious arrangement of space where the cold tones of the fighting gladiators alternate with the rich colouring which Lanfranco brings out with his play of light and shade in the banquet scene.

LEONARDO DA VINCI (b. Vinci 1452; d. Cloux, France 1519), Copy. Florentine School.

504 **«La Gioconda»** (Wood, 76 × 57 cm). This is an old copy after Leonardo's famous painting in the Louvre. Art historians do not agree whether the copy is Spanish or Flemish. It differs from the original in several points, the most noteworthy being the landscape background, which has been substituted here by a dark background, as appealed to Flemish artists.

LEONARDO DA VINCI, Old imitation.

349 **«St. Anne with the Virgin and Child»** (Canvas transferred to wood, 105 × 74 cm). This work is inspired by one of Leonardo's paintings kept in Milan; it was done in the 16th century, possibly by an Italian artist.

LEONARDONI, Francesco (b. Venice 1654; d. Madrid 1711). Venetian School.

3043 **«Self-portrait»** (Canvas, 60 × 46 cm). Signed and dated 1701. This artist studied in Venice and came to Madrid when he was still in his prime. He was Court Painter to the Queen, Doña Mariana of Neuburg. This portrait reveals a keen sense of reality and a highly-detailed technique.

LEONE, Andrea di (Naples 1610-c. 1685). Neapolitan School.

86 **«Jacob's journey»** (Canvas, 99 × 123 cm). See No. 239.

239 **«Jacob wrestling with the angel»** (Canvas, 99 × 125 cm). The measurements, subject-matter and importance attached to the landscape in both works probably indicate that they are companion pieces. Andrea di Leone was a follower of Aniello Falcone and maintained contact with Salvator Rosa. The scenes portrayed are full of bustling movement, depicted with a refined taste for colour.

LICINIO, Bernardino (b. Poscante di Bergamo 1489; d. Venice 1560). Venetian School.

289 **«Agnese, the painter's sister-in-law»** (Canvas, 98 × 70 cm). Licinio stu-

died in Venice in the Giorgionesque tradition; here he has painted a traditional Venetian portrait in a range of cold colours.

LOTTO, Lorenzo (b. Venice c. 1480; d. Loreto 1556). Venetian School. Lotto received his training in Venice in the circle of artists around Bellini and Giorgione; in 1508 he was in Rome painting for Pope Julius II. Later his style changed and the apparently calm character of his early works gave way to a fondness for disturbing, nervous compositions which he painted in cold colours and changing light effects that reflected the artist's own personality, restless, sensitive, constantly travelling from one city to another, impetuous and subject to religious crises which finally led him to withdraw as a lay brother to the Monastery of Loreto, where he died.

240. Lotto. Master Marsilio and his wife.

240   «Master Marsilio and his wife» (Canvas, 71 × 84 cm). Signed and dated 1523. This work belongs to Lotto's most fruitful and quiet period, when he was living in Bergamo. It is a wedding portrait, with a mischievous, smiling Cupid putting the marriage yoke on the bride and bridegroom. The perfectly harmonious colours and lavish clothes somehow produce an uneasy feeling in the spectator, possibly due to the absent, mysterious looks of the sitters, who seem lost in thought.

448   «Penitent St. Jerome» (Canvas, 99 × 90 cm). This work dates from about 1544, during the last decade of Lotto's activity as an artist. It was previously attributed to Titian, whose influence is obvious in the shady, reddish-tinged landscape. The nude body of the Saint is reminiscent of Michelangelo.

LUINI, Bernardino (b. Luino, Lombardy 1480/90; d. Milan 1532). Lombardic School. Little is known about the life of Luini. He might have studied in the circle of artists around Bramante, the great Milanese painter and architect; but the novelties introduced by Leonardo are the chief influences to be found in his easel paintings. In his technique we find the *sfumato* outlines, soft modelling, extremely subtle effects of light and shade and the mysterious Leonardesque smile. All this is combined in Luini's works with Flemish-style detail and realism in depicting draperies, hair and still-life elements.

242   «The Holy Family» (Wood, 100 × 84 cm). This work was presented to Philip II as a gift in Florence; it was believed to be an original by Leonardo, from whose style it obviously derives. The technique with which the artist has portrayed the delicate, highly-detailed figures is perfect.

243   «Salome with the head of John the Baptist» (Wood, 62 × 78 cm). This is a harmonious composition centred around John the Baptist's head. The *sfumato* treatment of the forms is highly attractive.

LUINI, Copy.

241 **«The Infants Jesus and St. John embracing»** (Wood, 30 × 37 cm). This is a copy after a drawing by Luini kept in Paris and repeats almost exactly the children's figures from the *Holy Family*.

MAGNASCO, Alessandro, called **«il Lissandrino»** (Genoa 1677-1749). Genoese School.

3124 **«Christ attended by angels»** (Canvas, 193 × 142 cm). This work dates from about 1730; Magnasco was chiefly known for his satirical and *genre* pictures, in which he depicted different aspects of 18th-century society, like monks and soldiers, scenes inside lunatic asylums and prisons; his work as a landscapist was also noteworthy. In this scene of Jesus after the Temptation, he has portrayed his characteristic small, vigorous figures in an elaborate, fantastic landscape with evident fondness for decorative effects.

3124. Magnasco. Christ attended by angels.

MAINIERI DA PARMA, Gian Francesco (active between 1489 and 1504). Ferrarese School.

244 **«The Virgin and St. Joseph adoring the Child»** (Wood, 63 × 48 cm). This work is an example of the expressionist style of the Ferrarese School, where Mainieri da Parma received his training and worked for the Duke of Ferrara. The linear aspect of the composition is set off by its clear colouring. It contains secondary scenes, like that which shows the stigmata of St. Francis in the upper part, whose size and subject-matter mark a contrast with the main theme of the painting and break its unity.

MALOMBRA, Pietro (Venice 1556-1618). Venetian School.

245 **«The hall of the Doge's Palace in Venice»** (Canvas, 170 × 214 cm). Malombra specialized in this kind of decorative picture; here he portrays the Venetian Doge Leonardo Donato receiving a Spanish ambassador. The hall is depicted in great detail with its marble, works by Veronese and Tintoretto and gilded caissoned ceiling, which reflect all the magnificence of the Venetian Court.

MANETTI, Rutilio (Siena 1571-1639). Sienese School.

2688 **«The vision of St. Bruno»** (Canvas, divided in two; upper part
2689 120 × 84 cm, lower part 66 × 84 cm). Trained in Tuscany and still related to the delicate and colouristic Sienese Mannerist style, Manetti was influenced in Rome by Caravaggio's naturalism, which marked the rest of his work and can be observed here in the realistic portrayal of the monks, sharply illuminated by Tenebrist-style light; their ascetic aspect brings them close to Spanish painting.

MANFREDI, Bartolomeo (b. Ostiano, Mantua, c. 1587; d. Rome c. 1620). Roman School.

247 **«Soldier with the head of John the Baptist»** (Canvas 133 × 95 cm). Manfredi was a close follower of Caravaggio and painted the latter's deeply religious subjects in the manner of *genre* pictures, which made him popular among the Northern artists studying in Rome. In this work the metallic

glow of the soldier's armour seems to be the central part of the scene, in which it is difficult to find any religious meaning.

MANTEGNA, Andrea (b. Isola di Cartura, Padua 1431; d. Mantua 1506). Paduan School. Mantegna was one of the great Renaissance masters in Northern Italy. He studied in the cultured atmosphere of his native town, Padua, where the sculptor Donatello was working at the time, and soon became acquainted with the discoveries of the Renaissance in Tuscany: centralized perspective, light and correct anatomical proportions. He travelled to Rome, where he studied ancient Roman ruins. His work combines the beauty and monumental character of Classical sculpture with the plasticity and brilliant colouring characteristic of the Paduan School; the result is Mantegna's ideal and heroic kind of painting. In his use of perspective he went to the extent of creating imaginary spaces which anticipate Baroque solutions in his large fresco decorations.

248 **«Death of the Virgin»** (Wood, 54 × 42 cm). This painting is considered by some art critics the finest work in the Prado. Its clear, rigorous arrangement of space and the beauty and expressiveness of the figures certainly make it one of this Museum's most outstanding works. The landscape is realistically depicted and interpreted with simple, cubic forms that make it appeal to our modern sensibility. A skilful positioning of the figures and the colouring of their clothes achieve the spacious impression of the room. There are eleven Apostles around the Virgin's bed because St. Thomas, who was preaching in India, did not return in time for the Virgin's death, although he was present at her Assumption.

MARATTI, Carlo (b. Camerano, Ancona 1625; d. Rome 1713). Roman School. Maratti holds an important place in Roman painting in the second half of the 17th century since he was the link between the Classicist style of the Carracci and the Neo-Classical movement of the mid-18th century. He had many followers throughout Italy and his works were also appreciated abroad, especially in France and England, where private collectors were proud to own his attractive, harmoniously colourful paintings.

53 **«Repentant Mary Magdalene»** (Canvas, 14 × 20 cm). In spite of its small size, this work is a good example of the artist's style.

327 **«The painter Andrea Sacchi»** (Canvas, 67 × 50 cm). The sitter was Maratti's master; it is a sober portrait with a psychological study of the sitter.

543 **«The Flight into Egypt»** (Canvas, 69 × 54 cm). This work repeats Maratti's painting for the Chigi Chapel in the Cathedral of Siena.

2769 **«Pope Clement XI»** (Canvas, 30 × 24 cm). This work is not by Maratti, but by one of his pupils, possibly A. Masucci.

MARATTI and **Dughet.** See Dughet No. 552.

MASARI, Lucio (Bologna 1568-1633). Bolognese School. A follower of the Carracci and Domenichino, Masari's works are inspired in their models, but his paintings do not come up to their standards.

130 **«St. Jerome»** (Canvas, 184 × 129 cm). This work was attributed to Domenichino, but old inventories list it under Masari's name and current opinion among art historians considers it to be by him.

472 **«Women fighting»** (Canvas, 175 × 199 cm). The subject-matter is not clear, possibly a struggle between Amazons. The style comes closer to that of the Neapolitan artists than to the Bolognese.

566 **«Gifts for the Tabernacle»** (Canvas, 119 × 171 cm). This work was previously considered anonymous.

MAZZOLA. See Parmigianino.

MAZZUCHELLI. See Morazzone.

MELOZZO DA FORLI, Melozzo degli Ambrogi, called **«Melozzo da Forlì»** (Forlì 1438-1494). Umbrian School.

2843 **«Angelic musician»** (Fresco, 63 × 52 cm). A follower of Piero della Francesca, Melozzo da Forlì chiefly painted large-scale fresco decorations. His most important work, in the apse of the church of the Apostles in Rome, was separated from the wall and divided up; this fresco in the Prado is possibly one of the fragments. The angel's expression is captured with naturalistic detail.

MERISI. See Caravaggio.

MESSINA, Antonio, called **«Antonello da Messina»** (Messina c. 1430-1479). Venetian School. He received his training in Naples, which accounts for the originality of his art. The city of Naples, at that time under the domination of the Crown of Aragon, was the cross-roads where several different artistic trends met, in particular the realistic styles of Spanish and Flemish origin and the spacious, monumental tendency of

Italian art; Messina fused these different elements in a masterly fashion. On a visit to Flanders he learnt the technique of preparing oil paints and when he returned and settled in Venice about 1475 he was one of the artists who contributed to generalizing the use of oil paint in Italy, where tempera was still being used. He was influenced by Giovanni Bellini and his style in turn had a decisive influence on Venetian painting towards the end of the 15th century. The plastic quality of his forms, rich colouring, fine delineation and atmospheric effects, combined with his realistic, penetrating vision of nature, all go to making him one of the most outstanding Renaissance artists in the North of Italy.

3092 **«Dead Christ supported by an angel»** (Wood, 74 × 51 cm). This is one of Antonello's masterpieces, dating from the last years of his life when he was working in Venice. It is a recent acquisition and one of the most outstanding works in the Prado. The realistic details are attenuated by the monumental character of the dying Christ's nude body surrounded by a bright, transparent Venetian-style atmosphere. The desert-like foreground contrasts symbolically with the green landscape background, which makes nature reflect the Redemption by means of Christ's Crucifixion.

MICHELANGELO (b. Caprese 1475; d. Rome 1564), Follower.

57 **«Scourging of Christ»** (Wood, 99 × 71 cm). Although this work was ascribed to Michelangelo for some time, art historians later considered it to be by one of his followers.

MITELLI, Agostino (b. Bologna 1609; d. Madrid 1660). Bolognese School.

2907 **«Model for a ceiling»** (Canvas, 187 × 281 cm). The style of Mitelli cannot be separated from that of his collaborator Angelo Michele Colonna (b. Como 1600; d. Bologna 1686) since they always worked together on the large frescoes they executed. They represent the Bolognese tradition of large decorations and false architectonic perspectives (quadrature) like this one shown in the Prado, which was a model for the Buen Retiro Palace, painted about 1659, with imaginary marble entablatures and bronze medallions connected by garlands of fruit and flowers.

MOLA, Pier Francesco (b. Colderio, Como 1612; d. Rome 1666). Roman School.

537 **«St. John the Baptist as a child»** (Canvas, 13 × 17 cm). This work is characteristic of Mola and the only example of his style in the Prado. He was important in mid-17th century artistic circles in Rome as he combined various different trends, attaching special importance to the landscape.

MORAZZONE, Pier Francesco Mazzuchelli, called **«Morazzone»** (Morazzone 1573-1626). Lombardic School.

3153 **«Betrothal of the Virgin»** (Paper on canvas, 31 × 41 cm). This is a grisaille sketch in monochrome grey oil paint for one of the frescoes of the church of the Santo Monte di Varallo between 1602/5. Elongated figures reminiscent of Mannerist forms and light contrasts are its keynotes.

MORONI, Giovanni Battista (b. Albino c. 1529; d. Bergamo 1578). Lombardic School.

262 **«A soldier»** (?) (Canvas, 119 × 91 cm). In this portrait Moroni has combined Venetian-style colouring and rich draperies with the psychological keenness and realistic precision characteristic of German artists. This sober, naturalistic work is a good example of his art.

MUTTONI. See Vecchia.

NANI, Mariano (b. Naples ?; d. Madrid 1804). Neapolitan School. Nani was a still-life painter from Naples who worked at the Spanish Court and also designed models for the Royal Porcelain Factory.

263 **«A hare and two partridges»** (Canvas, 67 × 43 cm).
264 **«A partridge, a goose and other birds»** (Canvas, 72 × 48 cm). Signed.
265 **«A dead hare and various birds»** (Canvas, 72 × 48 cm). Signed. The animals and birds are very realistically depicted, but with a decorative intention. These works were attributed to Mariano's father, Giacomo Nani, whose style can be recognized here, according to the latest opinion of art historians.

NICCOLO DELL'ABATE (b. Modena c. 1509; d. Fontainebleau 1571). Bolognese School.

416 **«The lady with the green turban»** (Canvas, 64 × 50 cm). This work was ascribed in the past both to Titian and to Dosso Dossi, but current opinion among art critics considers that it was painted by Niccolo dell'Abate at the time he was closest to the Venetian tradition, evident here in the colouring and technique, which Niccolo must have known through his contacts in Modena with the art of Correggio and Dossi.

296. Raphael. Holy Family with a lamb. (detail)

NOGARI, Giuseppe (Venice 1669-1763). Venetian School.
51 «**Old woman with a crutch**» (Canvas, 54 × 43 cm). This is an example of the naturalistic style of Nogari, who specialized in this kind of painting, similar to *genre*, with popular, half-length figures, related to the subjects of more important artists of the same period, like Piazzetta.

NOVELLI, Pietro, called «**il Monrealese**» (b. Monreale 1603; d. Palermo 1647). Neapolitan School.
471 «**The Resurrection of Christ**» (Canvas, 163 × 181 cm). Novelli is unmistakably a representative of the Neapolitan School influenced by Ribera and introduced in his paintings the elegance of the models of Van Dyck, whose works he must have known when he was studying in Palermo. This work is cold, exceedingly contrived, but redeemed by its colouring and attractively modelled nude body of Christ.

NUZZI, Mario, called «**Mario dei Fiori**» (Rome 1603-1673). Roman School. Nuzzi specialized in flower pieces, which he painted in a highly detailed, masterly style reminiscent of some of the Flemish artists who worked in Rome; he was very successful in this kind of painting and collaborated with important artists, carrying out the flower motifs in their works.
252 «**Flowers on a cloth**» (Canvas, 84 × 157 cm).
3239 «**Flowers and onions**» (Canvas, 83 × 154 cm). These are definitely works by Nuzzi listed in old inventories. Their exceedingly sober, realistic character and the play of light contrasts show that they still belong to the style of early 17th-century flower still lifes.

ORIZZONTE. See Van Bloemen in Flemish Masters.

PADOVANINO, Alessandro Varottari, called «**Padovanino**» (Padua 1588-1648). Venetian School.
266 «**Orpheus**» (Canvas, 165 × 108 cm). Attributed to Titian in the past, this work is directly related to the Classical and slightly affected style of early 17th-century Venetian painting, inspired in compositions by 16th-century masters.

PALMA GIOVANE, Jacopo Negretti, called «**Palma Giovane**»« (Venice 1544-1628). Venetian School. He was a nephew of Palma Vecchio and went to Rome early in life to study the works of Raphael and Michelangelo. On his return to Venice he entered Titian's studio where he served as an assistant until the master's death. Although Palma Giovane lived and worked until well into the 17th century, he did not adapt his art to Baroque naturalism; he clung to the forms learnt from Titian and Tintoretto, which he rendered with imaginative deftness and attenuated colouring, although they remain purely decorative.
271 «**David victorious over Goliath**» (Canvas, 207 × 235 cm). This scene of David being received by the Israelite women is portrayed by Palma with a sense of space, warm colouring and light technique that derive from the 16th-century Venetian School.
272 «**The conversion of St. Paul**» (Canvas, 207 × 335 cm). This is the companion piece to the preceding scene. The composition and sheen of the draperies recall Tintoretto. However, the figures reveal full forms that relate them to the Baroque.
380 «**A Venetian senator**» (Canvas, 65 × 58 cm).
402 «**Pietà**» (Canvas, 136 × 183 cm). The artist has centred the composition around the nude body of the dead Christ, portrayed in a masterly fashion, and relied on the emphasis of the colouring and varying light for his dramatic effects.

PALMA VECCHIO, Jacopo Negretti, called «**Palma Vecchio**» (b. Serina, Bergamo c. 1480; d. Venice 1528). Venetian School.
269 «**The Adoration of the Shepherds**» (Wood, 118 × 168 cm). Its attribution to Palma Vecchio is controversial; some critics consider it the work of Bonifacio Veronese. It is related to the Venetian style of the early 16th century. The arrangement of the scene is attractive and varied and the artist has adopted the light, colouristic technique used by the followers of Giorgione.

PANINI, Giovanni Paolo Panini or **Pannini** (b. Piacenza 1691/2; d. Rome 1765). Roman School. Panini was trained in Bologna, where he came into contact with the painters of imaginary architectural elements («*quadraturisti*»), whose kind of painting and style he used for his decorations in palaces during his early years in Rome, about 1715. After entering Benedetto Luti's Drawing Academy he became interested in landscape painting, particularly fantastic townscapes of the city of Rome and its Classical ruins, for which he was renowned throughout Europe.

273 «Ruins with the pyramid of Caius Cestius» (Canvas, 48 × 64 cm). Signed. The picture surface is enlivened by a technique consisting of small, light brushstrokes.

275 «Ruins with an Apostle preaching» (Canvas, 63 × 48 cm). See No. 276.

276 «Ruins with a Sibyl preaching» (Canvas, 63 × 48 cm). This is a companion piece to the preceding work and they are both characteristic of Panini's late style.

277 «Jesus among the doctors» (Canvas, 40 × 62 cm). Signed. See No. 278.

278 «Jesus driving the traders out of the Temple» (Canvas, 42 × 62 cm). Signed. This is the companion piece to the preceding work; they are preparatory sketches for two paintings commissioned from Panini for the decoration of the Palace of La Granja about 1725. The artist shows an interest in monumental interiors and large-scale perspectives as a setting for his crowd of excited figures arranged in a variety of different poses. PARMIGIANINO, Francesco Mazzola, called «il Parmigianino» (b. Parma 1503; d. Casalmaggiore 1540). Parmese School. This artist was trained in the manner of Correggio's sensual, chromatic painting, but from the start his own restless and refined character invested his works with a formal elegance that exceeded his master's style. In 1524 he visited Rome, which was to prove decisive for his art, since he made the acquaintance of artists who were evolving towards Mannerism, the style that was to prevail in the mid-16th century and responded to the political, religious and social crisis which was convulsing the whole of Europe with an intellectual kind of art, of difficult symbolic contents, elegant and aristocratic in its forms, far-removed from nature. Parmigianino was one of the major exponents of Mannerism, which led to very different results in the various Italian schools. His art is characterized by extremely elongated forms, pleated draperies moulded to sculpturally modelled figures and harmonious, variegated colouring; it exerted an important influence on the French School of Fontainebleau.

279 «Pedro Maria Rossi, Count of San Segundo» (Wood, 133 × 98 cm). For some time this portrait was considered the companion piece to No. 280, an opinion no longer held by art critics. The sitter was a soldier who fought both on the side of Charles V and on that of his enemy, the French king Francis I. It is a typical example of a Mannerist portrait with its severe composition and the aloof, elegant pose of the sitter. The small statue of a warrior, maybe Perseus, on the right also shows the artist's characteristic elongated forms.

280 «A lady with three children» (Wood, 128 × 97 cm). This is an example of a 16th-century group portrait. The lady's serene, proud and imposing presence is disturbed by the nervous poses of the children who seem intent watching a scene out of the spectator's sight and whose expressions break the calm atmosphere of the composition.

281 «Cupid» (Wood, 148 × 65 cm). This is a replica or repetition of a work in the Museum of Vienna.

282 «St. Barbara» (Wood, 48 × 39 cm). This is an example of the height of Parmigianino's elegant, stylized and refined art.

282. Parmigianino. St. Barbara. 280. Parmigianino. Lady with three children.

298. Raphael. Christ falls on the way to Calvary.

299. Raphael. Portrait of a Cardinal. (detail)

283 «The Holy Family with an angel» (Wood, 110 × 89 cm). This is probably the clearest example of the artist's Mannerist style. The reduced space obliges him to group the figures in the foreground, in precarious and affected poses. The forms are treated with extreme *sfumato,* to the extent of losing their consistency and becoming almost tissue-like in their structure.

PARRASIO, Micheli or **Michieli** (Venice c. 1516-1578). Venetian School. Having been a pupil of Titian and a follower of Veronese, his style is a faithful reflection of that of his masters.

284 «Dead Christ adored by Pope St. Pius V» (Copper, 42 × 30 cm). It is not a first-rate work, but contains some interesting realistic details.

479 «The birth of the Infante Ferdinand, son of Philip II» (Canvas, 182 × 223 cm). This is an interesting and very decorative work in the manner of Veronese, although in a minor key. It is an allegory of the birth of one of Philip II's sons, who is being received by the provinces of the kingdom, symbolized by richly dressed female figures. In the upper part of the painting, Fame spreads the news.

PENNI, Gianfrancesco, called «il Fattore» (b. Florence 1488; Naples 1528). Roman School.

315 See Raphael.

323 See Romano.

PENSIONANTE DI SARACENI (active in Rome in the first third of the 17th century).

2235 «The bird-seller» (Canvas, 95 × 71 cm). Pensionante di Saraceni is the name art critics have given to an unknown artist who painted a number of works, nearly all of them fine *genre* pictures, related to the style of Saraceni, a Venetian Caravaggist, who was possibly Pensionante's teacher. This work is painted in a satirical vein: the young man is paying the bird-seller and at the same time stealing his chickens. The technique is delicate and soft, set off by the lighting.

PERINO DEL VAGA, Pietro Buonaccorsi, called «Perino del Vaga» (b. Florence 1501; d. Rome 1547). Roman School. Perino represents the Mannerist style derived from Raphael, whose pupil and assistant he was in Rome. His pictures, full of bustling movement, are the link between the Roman and Tuscan tradition and on his travels he did much to spread Mannerism throughout Italy.

523 «Noli me tangere» (Wood, 61 × 47 cm). This is a very attractive work which is not far removed from Flemish painting, especially in the figures of Christ and Mary Magdalene or in the highly-detailed landscape.

PERUZZI, Baldassarre (?) (b. Siena 1481; d. Rome 1536). Roman School. Although he is better known as an architect, Peruzzi also left important pictorial works. He was trained in Siena in the tradition inherited from Pintorricchio, a decorative painter of Umbrian origin; after settling in Rome his painting comes closer to the style of Raphael, although he shows greater fondness for large imaginary spaces.

524 «The Rape of the Sabines» (Wood, 47 × 157). See No. 525.

525 «The temperance of Scipio» (Wood, 46 × 157 cm). This is the companion piece to the preceding work; both were ascribed to Pintorricchio, but art historians have now attributed them definitively to Peruzzi. With their various different scenes, bustling activity and colouring they are good examples of his work. The artist has portrayed an idealized kind of beauty and emphasized the very decorative landscape. These works were possibly front pieces of Florentine *cassoni* (chests) intended as wedding gifts and often decorated with paintings.

PINO, Marco dal, called «Marco da Siena» (b. Siena c. 1525; d. Naples 1587/8). Roman School. He received his training in his native town, but soon moved to Rome to work in the rich cultural environment of this city, where he tried to fuse the art of Raphael and Michelangelo, creating a strong, pathetic style related to Mannerism.

58 «Dead Christ supported by angels» (Wood, 43 × 28 cm). This work derives directly from compositions by Raphael, although both the technique and composition evidently lack quality.

PIOMBO, Sebastiano Luciani, called «Sebastiano del Piombo» (b. Venice c. 1485; d. Rome 1547). Roman School. Sebastiano studied under Giovanni Bellini in Venice and probably worked with Giorgione in the early years of the 16th century. When he arrived in Rome in 1511 he already had his own personal style which consisted of soft, colouristic technique, use of *sfumato* and monumental forms; he was fully accepted in

Roman artistic circles, where he almost became a rival of Raphael. Sebastiano's style was better adapted to the plastic, monumental character of works by Michelangelo, who even gave him preliminary sketches to paint. In his mature period Sebastiano evolved towards abstract and geometric forms and simpler compositions. The religous crisis he went through towards the end of his life is reflected in his paintings, pervaded by a melancholy and deeply emotional mood, which also reflects the crisis of Renaissance values around the middle of the 16th century.

345 «Jesus carrying the Cross» (Canvas, 121 × 100 cm). Dating from about 1528/30, after a visit to Venice, this work reveals the influence of Titian on his technique and colouring. It is intensely dramatic.

346 «Christ descending into Limbo» (Canvas, 226 × 114 cm). This work dates from about 1532 and is one of Sebastiano's masterpieces. It is inspired in drawings by Michelangelo; the harmonious arrangement of the scene and its deep devotional feeling are admirable.

348 «Christ carrying the Cross» (Slate, 43 × 32 cm). This work is tense and dramatic; the forms are clearly delineated.

569. Porpora. Flowers.   345. Piombo. Jesus carrying the Cross.

PONTE. See Bassano.

PONTE, Giovanni di Marco di Santo Stefano, called «Giovanni dal Ponte» (active in Florence between 1376 and 1437). Florentine School.

2844 «The seven liberal Arts» (Wood, 56 × 155 cm). This panel was the front of a *cassone* or Florentine chest decorated with paintings on the front and sides. The liberal Arts that formed the basis of Medieval knowledge are grouped against a gilded background. They hold symbols identifying them and are accompanied by famous philosphers and wise men of Antiquity. In the centre we see Astronomy with Ptolomy, surrounded by Geometry with Euclid, Arithmetic with Pythagoras and Music with Tubalcain on one side and Rhetoric with Cicero, Dialectics with Aristotle and Grammar with Donatus on the other. The gilded 13th-century style background gives the work a rather archaic air; the figures are delicate and elegant with their varying poses and emphasis on details.

PONTORMO, Jacopo Carrucci, called «il Pontormo» (b. Pontormo 1494; d. Florence 1557). Florentine School.

287 «The Holy Family» (Wood, 130 × 100 cm). This is an interesting and attractive work from the Florentine School, but its interest lies more in its relation to Pontormo's followers than to his own painting. He received his training in the tradition of Leonardo and Michelangelo, but later evolved towards forms that departed from the pure Classicist style of his early years, influenced by the art of Dürer which he had seen in engravings. The clear light, cold tones and precise sense of mass relate this work to the Tuscan Mannerist style derived from Pontormo, but the comparatively serene figures of the Virgin and St. Joseph have little in common with the anguished, almost deranged expressions painted by the master.

PORPORA, Paolo (Naples 1617-1673). Neapolitan School.

332. Andrea del Sarto. Lucrezia di Baccio del Fede, the painter's wife. (detail)

363. Giambattista Tiepolo. The Immaculate Conception.

569 «Flowers» (Canvas, 77 × 65 cm). Porpora was one of the most important still-life painters of the Neapolitan School and specialized in flower pieces. He combined Neapolitan exuberance with Dutch realism, which he had probably became acquainted with in Rome, and achieved a high degree of technical mastery in depicting flowers and drops of water.

PORTELLI, Carlo (b. Loro c. 1510; d. Florence 1574). Florentine School.

476 «Charity» (Wood, 151 × 115 cm). Portelli was a follower of the Florentine Mannerists Pontormo and Vasari and developed an eclectic style which tended towards affected and complicated scenes, like the one depicted in this panel. The clear-coloured figures are kept within a rigorously geometric scheme.

3146. Preti. Christ in Glory with Saints.

PRETI, Mattia, called «il Cavalier Calabrese» (b. Taverna, Calabria 1613; d. La Valetta 1699). Neapolitan School. After studying in Naples Preti travelled throughout Italy, Rome, Modena, Venice, and possibly in Spain before settling in Malta in 1672, where he became official painter to the Order. His art evolved from his early style which was influenced by Caravaggesque Naturalism and Tenebrism towards more serene and monumental forms with evident reminiscences of the Classicist style of Domenichino or Lanfranco. His compositions, full of richly-dressed figures, brilliant cloth textures and a showy sense of space, were specially appreciated by 18th-century Italian artists.

290 «The water from the rock» (Canvas, 176 × 209 cm). This is possibly a replica of an untraceable original by Preti.

3146 «Christ in Glory with saints» (Canvas, 220 × 253 cm). This was possibly a ceiling decoration, to judge by the forced perspective. It dates from about 1660, when Preti's style was fully developed. It is difficult to perceive the realistic elements like the heads of the saints, almost Riberesque in their intensity, among the movement and brightness of the Venetian-coloured composition.

PROCACCINI, Andrea (b. Rome 1671; d. La Granja 1734). Roman School.

2882 «Cardinal Carlos de Borja» (Canvas, 245 × 174 cm). A pupil of Carlo Maratti, Procaccini was Court Painter to Philip V and must have painted this interesting portrait of the King's chaplain, who was appointed Cardinal in 1721, in Madrid. The movement, intensity and colouring of the portrait are completely Baroque.

PROCACCINI, Camillo (b. Bologna 1550; d. Milan 1629). Lombardic School. Camillo and Giulio Cesare Procaccini belonged to a family of painters from Bologna who worked in Milan from the last decade of the 16th century on. Their style still derives from late Bolognese Mannerism, but it is interpreted with soft, diffused forms and melancholy figures pervaded by the rich, refined and bright colourfulness of the preceding period.

292 **«The Holy Family with a bunch of grapes»** (Wood, 135 × 108 cm). This is an attractive work that emphasizes the figure of the Child, but it does not resemble the style of Camillo Procaccini, although it is a typically Lombardic work.

PROCACCINI, Giulio Cesare (b. Bologna 1574; d. Milan 1625). Lombardic School.

293 **«Madonna with a sparrow»** (Wood, 93 × 75 cm). This work belongs to the Lombardic School, but does not correspond to Procaccini's style, although it has traditionally been attributed to him.

3974 **«Samson destroying the Philistines»** (Canvas, 263 × 263 cm). The composition of this tensely dramatic scene is extremely geometric, with the warriors marking horizontal and vertical lines.

1417 **«The Virgin and Child with angels in a garland»** (Copper, 48 × 36 cm). The garland is by the Flemish painter Jan Bruegel «de Velours», whereas the central group is a fine example of Procaccini's most refined style, steeped in melancholy.

PULIGO, Domenico di Bartolomeo Puligo (Florence 1492-1527). Florentine School.

294 **«The Holy Family»** (Wood, 130 × 98 cm). Puligo specialized in paintings of the Madonna and Child. He used a mellow technique with *sfumato* which had its origin in Andrea del Sarto, but he applied it to such a degree of formal sophistication that his works, like this one in the Prado, can be related to the Mannerist style.

RAPHAEL, Raffaello Santi or **Sanzio,** called **«Raphael of Urbino»** (b. Urbino 1483; Rome 1520). Roman School. Together with Leonardo and Michelangelo, Raphael is one of the geniuses of Italian Renaissance painting and one of the great masters of universal art. His artistic vocation manifested itself early in life. He learnt the rudiments of his art from his father, who was also an artist, although of minor importance, in the rich Court of Urbino, and when he was still a child he was apprenticed to the workshop of the famous artist Perugino. Raphael adopted his master's spacious scenes, brightness, serenely delicate landscapes and idealized, elegant female models. He was scarcely twenty years old when he went to Florence where Leonardo and Michelangelo were working at the time. There he was primarily attracted by Leonardo's art with its *sfumato,* colouring and harmonious compositions. Already a famous artist himself, Raphael was summoned to Rome by Pope Julius II to decorate the Vatican chambers with magnificent frescoes that were to be the centre of admiration of his colleagues and a source of inspiration for many generations of artists. In Rome Raphael's interest was also aroused by the art of Michelangelo who had completed the decorations of the Sistine Chapel in 1512; his works began to reflect tenseness, dramatic effects and sometimes an-

292. Procaccini. The Holy Family.

300. Raphael. The Visitation.

2824. Tintoretto. Jesus washing the disciples' feet.

407. Titian. Self-portrait. (detail)

guish, factors that were to be developed on by his pupils and assistants. Raphael was a sensitive, impassioned character, an elegant, refined and cultured man, something of a poet, who enjoyed luxury and died young, leaving behind him the reputation of his artistic fame, his wealth and a love-affair with the mysterious Fornarina, whose features art historians have tried to recognize in the female faces he painted in his pictures and portraits. The Prado's collection of paintings by Raphael is important and includes some of his most famous works. Spain was on the point of losing them when the French took them to France to be installed in the Napoleon Museum in Paris during the Peninsular War, but fortunately the collection returned to Spain in 1818. It has undergone some restoration work, for example some of the works painted on wood have been transferred to canvas.

296 «The Holy Family with a lamb» (Wood, 29 × 21 cm). Signed and dated 1507. Raphael signed this small panel on the golden braid of the Virgin's dress; it is one of the most delicate works painted by Raphael while he was in Florence. It contains obvious references to the style of Leonardo da Vinci, for example in the triangular form of the composition, as well as in the models he has used and the typical *sfumato* technique of the landscape. However, the artist's careful attention to detail reminds us that he learnt his craft in the studio of Perugino.

297 «Madonna with a fish» (Wood transferred to canvas, 215 × 158 cm). This work dates from about 1513 and therefore belongs to Raphael's Roman period. The ordered, serene and richly-coloured composition is a fine example of his Classicism. The work takes its name from the fish that Tobias is offering the Virgin, an allusion to the episode from the Apocrypha in which the Archangel Raphael, who also appears in this picture, ordered the young Tobias to catch a miraculous fish in the river to heal his father's blindness. The painting might have been a votive offering for the cure of some important personality or a petition to the Virgin to heal our ailments.

298 «Christ falls on the way to Calvary» (Wood transferred to canvas, 318 × 229 cm). Signed. This work was painted for the church of Santa Maria dello Spasimo in Palermo, Sicily, from where it gets its popular name «il spasimo di Sicilia», or in Spanish «el pasmo de Sicilia», which means something like the Sicilian wonder, thus expressing the admiration this work produced in Spain. According to contemporary historians, it almost went down with the ship that transported it from Rome to Sicily. When it was purchased by Philip IV in 1661 it was already considered «the costliest gem in the world». It is indeed one of Raphael's finest works; it dates from 1517, his most purely Classicist period. The varying poses and feelings expressed by the participants in the scene, ranging from the indifferent onlookers to the lamenting women, are interesting to observe. Thanks to a recent cleaning, the work can be seen in all its splendour and doubts about the authenticity of Raphael's signature have been dismissed.

299 «Portrait of a Cardinal» (Wood, 79 × 61 cm). Although this is one of Raphael's most famous portraits, the sitter has not yet been identified. Many names have been put forward, among others those of Giulio de' Medici, Luis de Aragón, Ippolito d'Este, Scaramuccia-Trivulzio, who were all cardinals at the time of Pope Julius II; more recently the name of Bandinello Sauri has been suggested, a restless man who was imprisoned in 1517. Raphael has made a fine psychological study of his sitter with his intense, intelligent expression and cold, almost haughty look. The Cardinal's brilliant silk garments are depicted in a perfect, realistic manner.

300 «The Visitation» (Wood transferred to canvas, 200 × 145 cm). By relation to other works painted in the last few years of Raphael's life, this one should be dated about 1519; some critics consider it one of his finest creations (cf. Longhi), in which he was assisted by his best students.

301 «The Holy Family» (Wood, 144 × 115 cm), called «The Pearl»; this denomination dates from the time of Philip IV, who called it the pearl of his collection. Classical buildings can be seen in the landscape, which also shows an interesting play of light and shade. The artist seems interested in offering us an image of the stages of life, childhood, youth and old age, in the figures of the Holy Family. The scene is contained in a perfectly triangular composition.

302 «Madonna with a rose» (Canvas, 103 × 94 cm). Dating from about 1518, this is one of Raphael's most famous compositions; it again repeats

the group of the Holy Family with the infant St. John, a favourite theme during Raphael's last years of which there are various examples in the Prado.

303 «**The Holy Family under an oak-tree**» (Wood, 144 × 110 cm). This work is related in style to the two preceding ones and therefore belongs to the last period of Raphael's artistic activity. It is also a well-known work and has been reproduced in a variety of copies and different versions in other collections. References to Classical Antiquity are evident in the temple ruins and the capital the Virgin and St. Joseph are leaning against. In the background a splendid landscape with the Tiber Valley can be seen.

302. Raphael. Madonna with a rose. 220. Reni. St. Paul.

RAPHAEL, Copies.

304 «**Andrea Navaggero**» (Canvas, 68 × 57 cm). This is a copy after a work in the Doria Gallery in Rome.

305 «**Agostino Beazzano**» (Canvas, 79 × 60 cm).

313 «**The Holy Family dell'Impannata**» (Wood, 164 × 128 cm). This is a copy after a work in the Pitti Gallery in Florence.

315 «**The Transfiguration**» (Wood, 236 × 263 cm). This is a copy by Penni, one of Raphael's pupils, after an original kept in the Vatican Museum that dates from Raphael's last years, as can be perceived in the figures' tense, dramatic mood.

RECCO, Giuseppe (b. Naples 1634; d. Alicante 1695). Bolognese School.

319 «**Still life with fish and a tortoise**» (Canvas, 75 × 91 cm). Signed. Giuseppe Recco is the most famous member of a family of painters specialized in *genre* painting. This still-life is a typical example of the pictures of fish, shellfish and other species of sea animals that made him famous. The details are depicted with great technical mastery.

RENI, Guido (Bologna 1575-1642). Bolognese School. Reni studied in Bologna under the Carracci, together with Albani and Domenichino, and is one of the principal representatives of the Roman-Bolognese Classicist style. His work is based on a thorough study of Raphael, whose elegance, serene, harmonious mood and ideal sense of beauty he adopted, but transforming them into delicate refined forms that correspond to his own sensitive, somewhat weakly personality. He conveyed feelings like no other artist of his time. Towards the end of his life his painting evolved, giving his pictures an unfinished appearance; he used long, loose brush-strokes with which he only roughly modelled his figures, thus giving them a decidedly modern air. His work has been compared to that of Renoir, but it was not understood by his contemporaries.

150 «**Cupid**» (Canvas, 101 × 80 cm). Several versions exist of this *Cupid,* which is considered an original due to its fine handling.

208 «**Lucretia**» (Canvas, 70 × 57 cm). This was previously considered a studio work; it is a subject that was often represented in Reni's paintings.

209 «**Cleopatra**» (Canvas, 110 × 94 cm). This work dates from Reni's late period; the brushwork is loose and the very reduced range of colours verges on monochrome. These two works reveal the somewhat languid, sentimental mood of Reni's paintings.

410. Titian. The Emperor Charles V at Mühlberg. (detail)

210 **«Madonna with a chair»** (Canvas, 212 × 137 cm). Directly based on compositions by Raphael, this work is an example of Reni's Classicist style.

211 **«St. Sebastian»** (Canvas, 170 × 133 cm). This is one version of a subject that Reni interpreted on several occasions. It is a very attractive work with the mellowness of the Saint's nude body and the shady, late-afternoon landscape that heightens the impression of the martyr's loneliness.

212 **«St. James the Elder»** (Canvas, 135 × 89 cm). Deep religious feeling is revealed in this interpretation of the Saint in ecstasy; the range of warm tones derives from Venetian colouring.

213 **«The Assumption and Coronation of the Virgin»** (Wood, 77 × 81 cm). This work belongs to Reni's early period. He avoids monotony or stiffness in this symmetrical composition by portraying the angels in a variety of different poses. The small size of the picture obliged the artist to use a very delicate, meticulous technique. The rich colouring is accentuated by the orange-tinged clouds in the background.

214 **«The Martyrdom of St. Apollonia»** (Copper, 28 × 20 cm). See No. 215.

215 **«St. Apollonia praying»** (Copper, 28 × 20 cm). This is the companion to the preceding work and dates from about 1602/3; they reveal the strong *chiaroscuro* that Reni used in his early years under the influence of Caravaggio.

216 **«Mary Magdalene»** (Canvas, 75 × 62 cm). This is a repetition of part of a famous painting by Reni in the Museum of Old Art in Rome.

218 **«Girl with a rose»** (Canvas, 81 × 62 cm). This is characteristic of the models used by Reni in his late period, with a delicate technique and refined colour.

219 **«St. Peter»** (Canvas, 76 × 61 cm). See No. 220.

220 **«St. Paul»** (Canvas, 76 × 61 cm). This is a companion to the preceding work; the loose technique relates it to the Venetian School, whose style reached Rome through the Bolognese Classicists. These two paintings are examples of Reni's interest in expressing feelings.

3090 **«Hippomenes and Atalanta»** (Canvas, 206 × 297 cm). Here Reni narrates the Greek myth in which Hippomenes, in order to outstrip the agile and speedy Atalanta on the racecourse and win her hand, drops golden apples in front of her, which she stoops to pick up, thus losing the race. It is one of the artist's most famous works and the beauty of the models and vital impression of the windblown draperies make us overlook its rigorously geometric scheme with its interweaving triangles.

RENI, Copy.

226 **«Judith»** (Canvas, 220 × 135 cm). This is a copy after an original by Reni kept in the Spada Gallery in Rome.

ROBUSTI. See Tintoretto.

ROMANELLI, Gian Francesco (Viterbo c. 1610-1662). Roman School. He studied in Rome under Pietro da Cortona, but interpreted the latter's grandiose compositions full of movement with a more tempered and Classicist touch, inspired in the works of Sacchi and Poussin (both represented in the Prado). He decorated some of the galleries of the Louvre in Paris, where he was greatly admired and acted as a link between Italian and French Classicism.

229 **«St. Peter and St. John in front of the Holy Sepulchre»** (Copper, 47 × 39 cm). This work is characteristic of Romanelli. For a time it was ascribed to Sacchi, but the exceedingly ample, billowing draperies and the figures' lively eyes are typical of Romanelli's style.

2968 **«Gladiators fighting»** (Canvas, 235 × 356 cm). This work was part of a series of paintings on the history of Ancient Rome for the decoration of the Buen Retiro Palace, of which there are other examples in the Prado (see Lanfranco, Camassei, Poussin).

ROMANO, Giulio Pippi, called **«Giulio Romano»** (b. Rome c. 1499; d. Mantua 1546). Roman School. Romano was a painter and architect and one of Raphael's favourite pupils and assistants. He collaborated with his master on his most important works and followed his style faithfully, although he introduced elements of tension in his imposing, muscular figures which derive from Michelangelo.

322 **«The Adoration of the Shepherds»** (Wood, 48 × 37 cm). This is a refined work from Romano's early period, which is characterized by harmonious arrangement of the scene and a fondness for iridescent colouring.

323 **«Noli me tangere»** (Wood, 220 × 160 cm). Romano painted this work in collaboration with Gianfrancesco Penni, another of Raphael's pupils. The beautifully modelled, extremely plastic figures command attention.

ROSA, Salvator (Naples 1615-1673). Neapolitan School. Rosa studied in Naples under Ribera and Falcone, but moved to Rome when he was still young. He was an interesting, at times eccentric personality, who engaged in both literary and artistic pursuits and attracted the attention of Roman intellectual circles. With his original subject matter, allegories, satires, battles and other wild scenes, he developed one of the most personal styles of the whole 17th century. In his landscapes he shows interest in atmospheric contrasts, which reflect a tense, almost Romantic-style image of nature.

324 «**The Gulf of Salerno**» (Canvas, 170 × 260 cm). This work from about 1640 is an example of Rosa's landscapes; it is a sea-piece with striking contrasts and a variety of scenes.

ROSSI. See Salviati.

3090. Reni. Hippomenes and Atalanta.

RUOPPOLO, Giovanni Battista (Naples 1620-1685). Neapolitan School.
1990 «**Still life**» (Canvas, 78 × 151 cm). Ruoppolo was one of the most outstanding representatives of Neapolitan *genre* painting, of which there are interesting examples in the Prado (see Recco, Porpora, Belvedere). This still life is extremely realistic, with striking light contrasts.

SACCHI, Andrea (b. Nettuno, Rome 1599; d. Rome 1661). Roman School. Sacchi continued in Rome the Classicist style of the Carracci and their followers. His extremely sensitive and harmonious painting evolved in the 1630s towards a Neo-Venetian style that brought colour and a freer touch to the painting of this period.

3 «**The birth of St. John the Baptist**» (Canvas, 262 × 171 cm). This is another version of a work painted by Sacchi for the Baptistry of the church of St. John Lateran; the perfect arrangement of the scene and refined beauty of the models and poses are an example of the artist's Classicist style.

83 «**Ecce homo with two executioners**» (Canvas, 50 × 67 cm). This is a copy after a work by Annibale Carracci in the Pinacoteca in Bologna.

326 «**The painter Francesco Albani**» (Canvas, 73 × 54 cm). This is a portrait of Sacchi's master, painted in a sober tone and with a keen psychological study.

328 «**The hermits St. Anthony and St. Paul**» (Canvas 114 × 141 cm). This masterly composition, with the Saints' calm, serious mood, reveals Sacchi at his most Venetian moment.

3189 «**St. Rosalia**» (Canvas, 140 × 140 cm). This is a companion piece to the preceding work and also reflects the artist's pure Classicist style. It represents the patron saint of Sicily with the vulcan Etna in the background.

SALVIATI, Francesco de' Rossi, called «**il Salviati**» (b. Florence 1510; d. Rome 1563). Florentine School.

477 «**The Madonna and Child with two angels**» (Wood, 114 × 99 cm). This work reflects the varied training of Salviati, who studied under Andrea del

Sarto, but was also familiar with the style of Raphael through the works of his followers, with whom he made contact when he went to Rome. This work reveals Salviati's most monumental style in the figures of the Virgin and Child, but the anguished expressions and complicated arrangement of space place it within the Tuscan Mannerist style. The perfect technique, tight modelling and clear tones are characteristic of Salviati.

SANI, Domenico Maria (b. Cesena 1690; d. La Granja 1773).

330 «**The village charlatan**» (Canvas, 105 × 126 cm). See No. 331.

331 «**A beggars' gathering**» (Canvas, 105 × 126 cm). These two companion pieces have recently been attributed to Francesco Sasso (b. Genoa 1720; d. Madrid c. 1776). They reflect the 18th-century fondness for popular scenes.

SARTO, Andrea del (Florence 1486-1530). Florentine School. Andrea del Sarto was one of the outstanding figures in early 16th-century painting in Italy. His work is related to that of Raphael in its calm, ordered Classical mood, which he interprets to the utmost perfection, but he uses a soft technique with *sfumato* derived from Leonardo and colouring from the Venetian artists, although his religious paintings have a much stronger emotional content. He may have travelled to Rome and Venice; in Florence he left a large number of frescoes and his fame reached the Court of the French King Francis I, who called him to Paris in 1518, where he was able to appreciate directly the last works Leonardo da Vinci painted there. The Prado possesses a series of paintings by Andrea del Sarto that are good examples of his style.

332 «**Lucrezia di Baccio del Fede, the painter's wife**» (Wood, 73 × 56 cm). The sitter has been identified as the wife of Andrea del Sarto. The work belongs to his fully-developed style and portrays the beauty of Lucrezia, who, according to the artist's contemporary biographer Vasari, was unfaithful and cruel to him, although neither in this portrait nor in any of his other works where he used her features for his Madonnas, is this supposed cruelty reflected; on the contrary, she appears to be his inspiring Muse. The apparent simplicity of the composition, which recalls Leonardo's famous *Gioconda* in her smile and pose, is the result of del Sarto's particular skill; he has combined in a masterly fashion the simple, soft-coloured dress and the mysterious woman's indefinable expression. The old frame with inlaid ivory is noteworthy.

334 «**Mystic subject**» (Wood, 177 × 135 cm). This is one of Andrea del Sarto's masterpieces and reveals all his ordered, rigorous Classicism in a triangular composition, with monumental figures pervaded by a vaguely melancholy air. The colouring is refined.

335 «**The Holy Family**» (Wood, 140 × 112 cm). The cold colouring and a certain nervous tension in the figures probably indicate that this work dates from the last years of the artist's life, when he came close to the Mannerist style.

336 «**The sacrifice of Isaac**» (Wood, 98 × 69 cm). Andrea del Sarto has turned the biblical scene into a perfect psychological study of the subtle expressions on the faces of the figures, the agony of the youthful Isaac, whose body is a model of classic beauty, and the calmly resigned expression of Abraham obeying God's command to sacrifice his son.

337 «**Madonna and the infant Jesus**» (Wood, 86 × 68 cm). This work is strongly influenced by Leonardo in its composition and technique.

338 «**Madonna and Child with the infant St. John and two angels**» (Wood, 106 × 79 cm). The Leonardesque *sfumato* in the forms causes a mysterious impression in the heads that emerge from the shadows.

579 «**St. John the Baptist with a lamb**» (Wood, 23 × 16 cm). Attributed with doubts to Andrea del Sarto, this work comes closer to the style of the Milanese artists derived from Leonardo da Vinci.

SASSOFERRATO, Giovanni Battista Salvi, called «Sassoferrato» (b. Sassoferrato 1605; d. Rome 1685). Roman School. The style of Sassoferrato is based on a close study of Domenichino and Reni and consists of a very personal interpretation of these Bolognese artists. His numerous compositions of the Virgin and Child are characterized by extremely pure forms, clear colouring and deep devotional feeling.

341 «**Meditating Madonna**» (Canvas, 48 × 40 cm). He repeated this theme, taken from one of Dürer's engravings, on several occasions.

342 «**Madonna with the sleeping Child**» (Canvas, 48 × 38 cm). This composition derives from an engraving by Guido Reni.

SCARSELLINO, Ippolito Scarsella, called «**lo Scarsellino**» (Ferrara c. 1550-1620). Ferrarese School.

344 «**Madonna and Child**» (Wood, 20 × 28 cm). This lovely small work is characteristic of Scarsellino, who combines a Venetian-style landscape with the intense, almost metallic colouring of the Ferrarese School. The scene of the Virgin playing with the Child is portrayed with a great sense of naturalistic depiction, a specifically Baroque feature.

SELLITO, Carlo, called «**Carlo Napolitano**» (Naples 1581-1614). Neapolitan School.

563 «**The Assumption of Mary Magdalene**» (Canvas, 61 × 45 cm). This is an exact copy after a work by Lanfranco known in various different versions.

SERODINE, Giovanni (b. Ascona 1594; d. Rome 1631). Roman School.

246 «**St. Margaret raising a young man from the dead**» (Canvas, 141 × 104 cm). This is a characteristic work by Serodine, who was trained in the Caravaggesque realistic style, but the influence of Northern, particularly Dutch and French, artists working in Rome is obvious in his thick brushwork and the brownish tones of his colouring.

342. Sassoferrato. Madonna and Child. 341. Sassoferrato. Meditating Madonna.

SOLIMENA, Francesco, called «**Abate Ciccio**» (b. Nocera 1657; d. Barra, Naples 1747). Neapolitan School. Solimena was a painter and architect in Naples. His painting is the link between the full Baroque style of his friend Luca Giordano and the refined Rococo of his pupils Conca and Giaquinto. His large compositions have something theatrical about them, they are flamboyantly Baroque and filled with scores of vividly coloured figures that become more subdued and darker in colour in his old age, when he abridged his technique and modelled his figures on the reddish priming with bright, energetic brushstrokes.

14 «**The Infanta Maria Isabella of Naples**» (Canvas, 75 × 63 cm). This work was attributed in the past to Amigoni, but recently art critics have pointed out its Neapolitan style and related it to other portraits by Solimena.

351 «**St. John the Baptist**» (Canvas, 38 × 34 cm). This work is characteristic of Solimena's late period and dates from about 1730. The Saint's look is intensely expressive.

352 «**Self-portrait**» (Canvas, 38 × 34 cm). There are several different versions of this small portrait of Solimena drawing in an elegant, almost aloof pose. The play of light that sets off the rich costume is very attractive.

2660 «**St. Joachim, St. Anne and the Virgin**» (Canvas, 43 × 38 cm). This is an example of Solimena's most decorative style, in which the models and puffed-up draperies are related to Luca Giordano's fullest Baroque.

STANZIONE, Massimo (b. Orta di Antella 1585; d. Naples 1656). Neapolitan School. He was trained under the Neapolitan Tenebrist influence derived from Caravaggio, but his visits to Rome brought him into contact with Classicism, leading him to incorporate the Classicist ideals of strict compositional schemes, variegated colouring and idealized models into his naturalistic style, thus exerting a considerable influence among other Neapolitan artists. The series of paintings on the *Life of John the Baptist* in the Prado, on which he was assisted by Artemisa Gentileschi (see Gentileschi, Artemisa), dates from about 1634 and belonged to the decoration of the Buen Retiro Palace in Madrid. It illustrates Stanzione's style and the evolution of mid-17th century painting in Naples towards Classicism prior to the appearance of Luca Giordano, who changed the course of Neapolitan art.

256 **«The birth of John the Baptist foretold to Zacharias»** (Canvas, 188 × 337 cm). Together with Nos. 257, 258 and 291, this work is one of the series on the life of John the Baptist. It is possibly the most Classical and restrained of the series.

257 **«John the Baptist preaching in the desert»** (Canvas, 187 × 335 cm). The taut figure of the Baptist dominates the scene, which is illuminated from different angles and centres around the different poses and expressions of those who are listening to him.

258 **«The beheading of John the Baptist»** (Canvas, 184 × 258 cm). Of the whole series on John the Baptist, this is the work that comes closest to Caravaggio with its ample space and strong contrasts of *chiaroscuro,* although Stanzione is a more decorative artist and here he puts aside the devotional aspect of the Baptist's martyrdom in order to achieve more dramatic effects.

259 **«Sacrifice to the god Bacchus»** (Canvas, 237 × 358 cm). This work dates from about 1634 like the others and is one of Stanzione's most beautiful paintings, with figures that seem to come directly out of old Roman reliefs, like the woman with the pitcher. The composition is unified by deep colouring, with rich golden, green and reddish tones, that contrast with the pale, brightly illuminated areas of nude flesh.

291 **«John the Baptist taking leave of his parents»** (Canvas, 181 × 263 cm). Signed. This also belongs to the series on the life of John the Baptist and is probably the most realistic of these four works. The beauty and devout mood of the scene on the left, with St. Elizabeth weeping while Zacharias gives his blessing to his departing son, are particularly admirable.

STROZZI, Bernardo (b. Genoa 1581; d. Venice 1644). Genoese School.

354 **«St. Veronica»** (Canvas, 168 × 118 cm). Strozzi represents the painting of the rich 17th-century Genoese School. He was familiar with Caravaggio's naturalism, whose striking play of light and shade he adopted, and came into contact with the art of Rubens, who passed through Genoa at the beginning of the 17th century leaving the influence of his exuberant, colouristic painting with its thick brushwork underlining textures and rich surface finish. These are the features of this *Veronica* which Strozzi painted shortly before 1630, the year he went to Venice.

SUSTRIS, Lambert (b. Amsterdam c. 1515; d. Venice 1580). Venetian School.

581 **«Baptism of Christ»** (Wood, 125 × 165 cm). Although he was of Dutch extraction, Sustris studied in Venice under Titian and in the circle around Tintoretto, whose elongated, nervous and extremely elegant figures are reflected in this work. Its salient features are paler and more monotonous tones than those used by his Venetian contemporaries and *impasto* at times applied with small, light touches.

TIEPOLO, Giambattista (b. Venice 1696; d. Madrid 1770). Venetian School. Tiepolo is the grand finale of Venetian decorative painting that

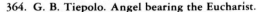

364. G. B. Tiepolo. Angel bearing the Eucharist.

had originated with the great 16th-century masters. He soon became famous for his illusionistic frescoes with their imaginary spaces full of light and colour and peopled with lavishly dressed figures that reflect the luxury of 18th-century Venice. His frescoes and canvases with religious and allegorical subjects filled churches and palaces, aristocrats' country villas and art collections; in his works Baroque exuberance blends with Rococo over-refinement while the expressions on his figures' faces reflect a melancholy mood which seems to foreshadow the decadence and end of a society that will be swept away towards the end of the century by the French Revolution. Tiepolo's fame spread throughout Europe; in 1750 he decorated the *Kaisersaal* of the *Residenz* at Würzburg and in 1762 he arrived in Spain with his sons Domenico and Lorenzo to carry out one of his masterpieces, the ceiling of the Throne Room in the Royal Palace in Madrid, commissioned by Charles III.

363 **«The Immaculate Conception»** (Canvas, 279 × 152 cm). Signed. This work was part of the decoration of the church of San Pascual in Aranjuez, which was divided up and is now kept in the Prado. It dates from 1769 and was one of Tiepolo's last works, since he died immediately after finishing the series. It is one of his most sober paintings and centres on the devout figure of the Virgin surrounded by angels; it is obviously related to Murillo's *Immaculate Conceptions*, which Tiepolo must have seen in Madrid.

364 **«Angel bearing the Eucharist»** (Canvas, 185 × 178 cm). This fragment is the upper part of the painting of San Pascual Baylon from the high altar of the church of the same name in Aranjuez. Tiepolo's technique here consists in outlining the forms lightly with black brushstrokes, using a rich variety of tones later in the colouring.

364a **«San Pascual Baylon»** (Canvas, 153 × 112 cm). This is part of the lower section of the preceding work from the church in Aranjuez.

365 **«Olympus or the Triumph of Venus»** (Canvas, 86 × 62 cm). This was a preparatory sketch for an untraceable work painted for the Imperial Palace in St. Petersburg. It is a fine example of the delicacy and open, atmospheric sense of space of Tiepolo's large-scale decorations.

365a **«The stigmata of St. Francis of Assisi»** (Canvas, 278 × 153 cm). This work also belonged to the church of San Pascual in Aranjuez; it is the one in which the aging Tiepolo reveals most devotional feeling.

583 **«Angel with a wreath of lilies»** (Canvas, 40 × 53 cm). This is another small fragment from the church in Aranjuez.

2464 **«Abraham and the three angels»** (Canvas, 197 × 151 cm). This is one of Tiepolo's late works and recalls the models and sober compositions of the series from the church in Aranjuez. Next to the realistic portrayal of Abraham the heavenly appearance of the angels commands attention, especially the one in the centre whose features, frequently repeated in Tiepolo's works, have been identified by some art historians as those of the artist's mistress, who accompanied him to Spain.

3007 **«St. Anthony of Padua with the Infant Jesus»** (Oval canvas, 225 × 176 cm). This work belonged to the decoration of the church in Aranjuez; it had an influence on 18th-century Spanish painting, including some of Goya's early works.

3243 **«The temperance of Scipio»** (Canvas, 250 × 500 cm). This is one of Tiepolo's early works, dating from about 1722/23, and has been purchased recently by the Prado. It narrates an episode from the Punic Wars when Scipio lets a young girl free who was part of his share in the spoils. The very expressive technique comes to its best when viewed from a distance.
TIEPOLO (?).

2691 **«The freeing of St. Peter»** (Wood, 25 × 18 cm). The technique of this sketch comes close to that of Tiepolo.

2900 **«San Pascual Baylon»** (Canvas, 39 × 26 cm). This might possibly have been Tiepolo's first idea for the central painting for the church in Aranjuez.
TIEPOLO, Gian Domenico (Venice 1727-1804). Venetian School. Domenico was his father's pupil and assistant and also had an independent activity as a painter; although his style was based on that of his father, it had its own characteristic features and he received numerous commissions from all over Italy. The keynote of his work is its satirical vein, sometimes reaching the extreme of popular caricatures, which he uses to portray contemporary Venetian society with biting humour. He accompanied his father to Germany and later also worked for the Spanish Court, returning to Venice after his father's death. His work as an engraver was also important.

356. G. D. Tiepolo. Christ at the Column.

355 **«Agony in the Garden»** (Canvas, 125 × 142 cm).
356 **«Christ at the column»** (Canvas, 124 × 144 cm).
357 **«Christ crowned with thorns»** (Canvas, 124 × 144 cm).
358 **«Christ falls on the way to Calvary»** (Canvas, 124 × 144 cm).
359 **«The Disrobing of Christ»** (Canvas, 124 × 144 cm).
360 **«The Crucifixion»** (Canvas, 124 × 144 cm).
361 **«The Descent from the Cross»** (Canvas, 124 × 142 cm).
362 **«The Entombment of Christ»** (Canvas, 124 × 144 cm). Signed and
dated 1772. These eight works were painted for the church of St. Philip
Neri in Madrid. They are fine examples of Domenico Tiepolo's style,
more expressive and dramatic than that of his father; in his range of
colours he avoids brilliant shades, limiting the strong colours to a few areas
and using almost monochrome tones for the rest.
TINTORETTA, Marietta Robusti, called **«Tintoretta»** (Venice 1560-
1590). Venetian School. A daughter of Jacopo Tintoretto, she followed
her father's style, although without attaining his degree of mastery. She
specialized in small works and portraits like these in the Prado, which lack
the vigour and colouring of Tintoretto's portraits.
381 **«Self-portrait»** (Canvas, 60 × 51 cm).
383 **«Young Venetian lady»** (Canvas, 77 × 65 cm).
400 **«Venetian lady»** (Canvas, 77 × 65 cm). These three portraits belong to
the tradition of Venetian portraiture, characterized by great simplicity.
TINTORETTO, Domenico (Venice c. 1556-1635). Venetian School.
He was the son of Jacopo Tintoretto and his style is a faithful repetition of
his father's, without offering anything novel since he was unable to adapt
his art to the new Baroque trends.
387 **«Prosperity or Virtue routing Evil»** (Canvas, 207 × 140). In this allegorical scene Prosperity or Virtue is represented armed in the shape of the
goddess Minerva. The technique is smooth and draughtsmanslike, the
colouring cold.
TINTORETTO, Jacopo Robusti, called **«il Tintoretto»** (Venice
1518-1594). Venetian School. Together with Titian and Veronese, Tintoretto was one of the great masters of Venetian painting in the 16th century, his principal merit being that he introduced in Venice the Mannerist
style prevailing in the rest of Italy. In sharp contrast with the poise, full
colouring, serene forms and vivaciousness of works by Titian and Veronese, Tintoretto painted ample compositions full of dramatic tenseness,
cold light that sets off the draperies with almost metallic sheens and elongated forms that are not intended to represent an ideal of beauty but

greater expressive power. He probably adopted these characteristics from Michelangelo, whose work he had studied directly and who influenced him at an early stage, as well as from the Bolognese Mannerists and their wide imaginary spaces and sharply foreshortened figures. Tintoretto was also an excellent portraitist in line with the Venetian tradition of simple compositions, naturalistic portrayal and psychological studies of the sitters. He portrayed the Venetian bourgeoisie, whereas Titian painted royalty and aristocratic circles, which accounts for the great difference between the portraits painted by the two artists. He lived a quiet life in Venice, where he carried out a large number of decorations, including the magnificent paintings for the School of St. Roch. His son and daughter, Domenico and Marietta, assisted him in his workshop. Tintoretto exerted a decisive influence on El Greco, whose style is directly related to that of the great Venetian master. The Prado's collection of Tintorettos is one of the finest and contains examples of all the subjects he painted during his lifetime.

366   «Venetian general» (Canvas, 82 × 67 cm). This is an excellent work and characteristic of Tintoretto's style. The brushwork is soft and light; the shining armour is rendered in a masterly manner.

369   «The Archbishop Pietro» (Canvas, 71 × 54 cm). The sitter has been identified as the archbishop of Pisa, Pietro Jacopo of Bourbon.

370   «A jesuit» (Canvas, 50 × 43 cm).

371   «A Venetian senator or secretary» (Canvas, 104 × 77 cm). This is an excellent work, sober in colour and with a keen psychological study.

373   «Venetian magistrate» (Canvas, 54 × 43 cm).

374   «Venetian magistrate» (Canvas, 54 × 43 cm). In the case of these two portraits art critics have raised doubts about their attribution to Tintoretto since their naturalistic style brings them closer to works by Jacopo Bassano.

377   «A Venetian patrician» (Canvas, 78 × 65 cm).

378   «The nobleman with the golden chain» (Canvas, 103 × 76 cm). This work, which dates from about 1550, is one of Tintoretto's finest portraits. Some art scholars consider the sitter to be the painter Veronese. The study of the light that moulds the expressive head and hands is particularly notable. Tintoretto uses a very limited range of colours, although with extreme refinement, so that the work gives the impression of a «black and white» portrait.

379   «A procurator of the Republic of Venice» (Canvas, 77 × 63 cm). The cloth textures are set off with loose, light brushstrokes.

382   «Lady revealing her bosom» (Canvas, 61 × 55 cm). This is one of the finest female portraits in the Prado. Some critics consider the sitter to have been Tintoretto's daughter Marietta, and others the famous Venetian courtesan Veronica Franco. In the colouring the artist has departed from his usual dark tones and the whole composition is interpreted with clear, pearl-like shades from the infinite range of greys and mauves.

384   «Marietta Robusti» (?) (Canvas, 65 × 51 cm).

385   «Portrait of an unknown lady» (Canvas, 61 × 55 cm).

386   «Susannah and the elders» (Canvas, 58 × 116 cm). See No. 396.

388   «Esther and Ahasuerus» (Canvas, 59 × 203 cm). See No. 396.

389   «Judith and Holofernes» (Canvas, 58 × 119 cm). See No. 396.

390   «The death of Holofernes» (Canvas, 98 × 325 cm). This is one of the outstanding works by Tintoretto in the Prado; the dramatic aspect of the scene is brought out by means of nocturnal lighting effects that throw some areas into thick shadow whereas others are illuminated and richly coloured. The figures have a precarious appearance; the technique is rapid.

391   «Judith and Holofernes» (Canvas, 188 × 251 cm). See No. 392.

392   «The violence of Tarquinius» (Canvas, 188 × 271 cm). This work is considered the companion piece to the preceding one; both belong to Tintoretto's early period, to judge by the clear colouring and the figures, whose bodies and poses are reminiscent of Michelangelo. The artist's interest centres around the play of light and shade.

393   «The purification of the Midianite virgins» (Canvas, 295 × 181 cm). This work belongs to the same series of biblical paintings commented on under No. 396, this being the centre of the ceiling decoration. It represents an episode from the Old Testament in which Moses, seen in the upper part, receives God's command to purify in the river the Midianite virgins who had been taken prisoner and were to be consecrated to the Lord. It is a very attractive composition, in which the artist takes pleasure in portraying feminine beauty.

394 «**The visit of the Queen of Sheba to Solomon**» (Canvas, 58 × 205 cm). See No. 396.

395 «**Joseph and the wife of Putiphar**» (Canvas, 54 × 117 cm). See No. 396.

396 «**Moses rescued from the Nile**» (Canvas, 56 × 119 cm). This is a companion piece to the other six biblical scenes, which must have been a ceiling decoration. They were purchased by Velazquez in Venice. The *di sotto in su* perspective is noteworthy, as well as the vivaciousness of the scenes which are rendered in clear colouring, similar to that of Veronese, which indicates that the work dates from Tintoretto's early period.

397 «**The Baptism of Christ**» (Canvas, 137 × 105 cm). The subject was painted several times by Tintoretto. The scene is set in a modern-style landscape.

398 «**Paradise**» (Canvas, 168 × 544 cm). This work was purchased by Velazquez in Venice. It is a large composition full of figures distributed in an ordered and clear manner, but with foreshortenings and tenseness that situate this work in a very Mannerist period of Tintoretto's life.

399 «**Battle between Turks and Christians**» (Canvas, 186 × 307 cm). This is another work purchased by Velázquez in Venice, which indicates how much Tintoretto's art interested the Spanish artist. The technique is modern in that the background is only summarily rendered.

393. Tintoretto. Midianite Virgins.   382. Tintoretto. Lady revealing her bosom.

2824 «**Christ washing the disciples' feet**» (Canvas, 210 × 533 cm). This is one of Tintoretto's masterpieces. It was originally painted for a church in Venice, but was acquired by King Charles I of England, upon whose death it was purchased by the Spanish king Philip IV. It is a large-scale, spacious work which appears a continuation of the natural space, thus giving the spectator the impression of being able to enter the scene. Velázquez probably studied the rendering of air between the figures for his own works. The subject is treated in a Mannerist style, placing the main scene on one side and highlighting other scenes of secondary importance.
TINTORETTO (?).

367 «**Pietro de' Medici**» (?) (Canvas, 68 × 56 cm). The attribution of this work is doubtful.

484 «**Portrait of a young lady**» (Canvas, 114 × 100 cm). Opinion among art critics is divided about this work: some attribute it to Veronese, others to Tintoretto or Bassano.
TINTORETTO, Follower.

401 «**Cardinal Andrea of Austria**» (Canvas, 112 × 96 cm). He was Governor of Flanders.
TITIAN, Tiziano Vecellio, called «**Titian**» (b. Pieve di Cadore c. 1490; d. Venice 1576). Venetian School. Titian was the most outstanding representative of Venetian painting in the 16th century and also one of the great masters of universal art. He gained the admiration of his contemporaries; the success he achieved with his art made him rich and enabled him to lead a life of luxury in his palace in Venice. He was the favourite painter of the Emperor Charles V, at that time master of the world, who, according to a well-known anecdote, deigned to stoop to pick up one of Titian's brushes that had fallen on the floor. Although this supposed gesture of admiration is probably only a traditional anecdote, it is however true that the Emperor

honoured Titian with his friendship and confidence. In his early years Titian's work is related to that of his master, Giovanni Bellini, and particularly to that of Giorgione, from whom he took the light, colouristic technique and *sfumato,* as well as a fondness for shady landscapes as a background for his paintings. Titian's style soon evolved towards solemn, imposing forms in his religious works, which do not lack a certain degree of pathos but are interpreted with very rich colouring in warm, variegated tones, that comes out still stronger in his many mythological pictures where joy of living, sensuality and vitality are the keynotes. Towards the end of his life Titian's colouring turned darker and his technique consisted in applying briefly extremely modern and expressive patches of paint directly on the reddish priming. The noble lineage of his sitters played a role in giving his portraits a solemn, aristocratic air and extremely lavish colouring. Titian was of capital importance for the painters who came after him. Rubens and the Italian Baroque artists like the Carracci and their followers were all directly influenced by him, as well as the Spanish artists who had the opportunity of seeing his works in the royal collection. Titian's works became a constant source of inspiration; wherever artists seek for colour rather than design the name of Titian stands out among all others.

408. Titian. The Duke of Mantua.   415. Titian. The Empress Isabella.

407 «Self-portrait» (Canvas, 86 × 65 cm). This is Titian's late masterpiece, probably painted shortly before the outbreak of the plague in Venice which put an end to his life in 1576. With its sober colouring and light, blurred technique, which leaves the outlines unfinished, this is one of Titian's most suggestive works and anticipates the Impressionist movement almost 300 years later.

408 «Federigo Gonzaga, 1st Duke of Mantua» (Wood, 125 × 99 cm). This magnificent portrait, which dates from about 1530, was probably painted for his betrothal to Margherita Paleologus. It is a fine psychological study of the duke and the technical accomplishment with which Titian depicts the brilliant blue velvet or the naturalistically portrayed dog are also admirable. It is a typical example of the way in which Titian gives an enhancing touch to the noble aspect of his courtly sitters.

409 «The Emperor Charles V» (Canvas, 192 × 111 cm). This is possibly the portrait painted by Titian in Bologna in 1532, for which the Emperor granted him the title of Count of the Lateran Palace and Royal Adviser.

410 «The Emperor Charles V at Mühlberg» (Canvas, 332 × 279 cm). This portrait represents the Emperor victorious after the Battle of Mühlberg, where he defeated the Protestants and took the Saxon Elector Frederick prisoner on April 24, 1547. Charles V is portrayed on horseback, as in the traditional Classical Roman equestrian portraits; the work is considered one of the finest and most original portraits in the history of painting. The horse's impulsiveness and the tense figure of the monarch are attenuated by a calm, lonely evening landscape and by the Emperor's melancholy air, which seems to forebode his withdrawal from the throne to the monastery of Yuste and the decline of his empire.

411 «Philip II» (Canvas, 193 × 111 cm). This portrait, which did not meet

with Philip II's approval, was sent to the king's future wife, Mary Tudor. It is important for its impressive technical mastery and variety of shades.

412 «The nobleman with a watch» (Canvas, 122 × 101 cm). This is a portrait of an unidentified knight of the Order of Malta.

413 «A gentleman with an ermine collar» (Canvas, 81 × 68 cm). Signed and dated 1537.

414 «Daniello Barbaro, Patriarch of Aquileia» (Canvas, 81 × 69 cm).

415 «The Empress Isabella» (Canvas, 117 × 98 cm). Doña Isabella of Portugal was the wife of Charles V and although she died young she left an unforgettable memory in the Emperor's mind. He had this portrait painted in Augsburg in 1548, many years after her death, and Titian used an old portrait of her as a model. The wonderful, naturalistically depicted landscape seen through the window and the figure's delicate, noble features are outstanding.

417 «The Marquis del Vasto addressing his troops» (Canvas, 223 × 165 cm). This work was painted about 1540 and is a very original painting that caused admiration at the time due to the novelty of rendering this scene with its impression of a silent crowd in the area of the soldiers, multiplied in number by the blurred technique and vertical lances, which almost anticipate the lances that Velázquez was to paint a hundred years later in his famous *Surrender of Breda*. The shiny armour and draperies attract attention to the figure of the general, who is accompanied by his eldest son Ferrante Francisco.

418 «Bacchanal» (Canvas, 175 × 193 cm). This is a youthful work by Titian, dating from about 1518 and together with his *Garden of Loves* (No. 419) and *Bacchus and Ariadne* (in the National Gallery, London) was part of a series on subjects from Greek mythology and Roman literature painted for the Duke of Ferrara, Alfonso d'Este. This painting represents the arrival of Dionysos on the island of Andros where the inhabitants receive him in a state of drunkenness. This work with the perfect rhythm of its figures, full, vital forms, exquisite colouring and landscape was considered a model to be followed by the 17th-century Classicist artists, who put up a staunch resistance, in particular Domenichino, against its exportation when it was embarked, together with other works, in the port·of Naples to be transported to Spain. The figure in red in the centre of the picture has been identified as Titian's love, Violante.

409. Titian. Emperor Charles V.

419 «Garden of Loves» (Canvas, 172 × 175 cm). Signed. This is the companion piece to the preceding work and represents a theme by the Greek writer Philostratus, in which Cupids in a variety of playful poses offer flowers and fruit of the goddess of Love. The painting was copied by

419. Titian. Garden of Loves.

Rubens, which shows his interest in Titian's art. The landscape is particularly beautiful, as in the preceding work.

420 **«Venus and the organ-player»** (Canvas, 136 × 220 cm). This is one
version of a theme that was repeated several times by Titian. The Prado
also possesses an earlier version (No. 421). Both are very attractive works
in which the mature Titian blends the sensual aspect of the female nude
with an ample, bright landscape and exceptional rendering of draperies.
The whole composition is pervaded by an air of subtle mystery.

421 **«Venus and the organ-player with Cupid»** (Canvas, 148 × 217 cm).
Signed. Titian painted this work for Charles V and introduced in this version a Cupid playing with Venus.

422 **«Venus and Adonis»** (Canvas, 186 × 207 cm). This work represents the
mythological scene from the Roman poet Ovid's *Metamorphoses* when
Adonis takes leave of Venus before departing for the hunt where he will
be killed by the boar. It was painted for Philip II in 1553 and contains an
intense study of light and atmosphere.

425 **«Danaë receiving the shower of gold»** (Canvas, 129 × 180 cm). This
work, painted in 1553 for Philip II, is one of Titian's masterpieces in the
Prado. It reveals the artist's mature style in the wonderful way in which
the forms dissolve in space with a naturalistic vibration admired by his
contemporaries, including Michelangelo. The splendid beauty of the female nude is set off by the rich range of white and crimson tones around
her, by the threatening colour of the sky from where Zeus is falling in the
form of a shower of gold, and by the dark, distorted body of the servant.

426 **«Sisyphus»** (Canvas, 237 × 216 cm). See No. 427.

427 **«Tityus»** (Canvas, 253 × 217 cm). These two works were commissioned
by Queen Mary of Hungary when Titian was in Augsburg in 1549. They
are conceived on a grand scale and represent two mythological figures
condemned in Hell; the inspiration of Michelangelo in the two nudes cannot
be denied.

428 **«Salome with the head of John the Baptist»** (Canvas, 87 × 80 cm). The
young woman has been identified as Titian's daughter Lavinia. The work
was painted about 1549; its salient features are the loose technique, the
colouring and the fleeting and somewhat cruel look of the young girl.

429 **«Adam and Eve»** (Canvas, 240 × 186 cm). Signed. This work was also copied by Rubens (see Rubens No. 1692); it dates from about 1570 and is therefore one of Titian's late works. The artist takes pleasure in portraying the different male and female nudes and the luminous, spatial and atmospheric aspects of the scene.

430 **«Spain coming to the aid of Religion»** (Canvas, 168 × 168 cm). Signed. This is an allegorical work in which Titian represents Spain saving Religion threatened by the power of the infidels. It is an allusion to the Battle of Lepanto where the Spaniards won a decisive victory over the Turks in 1571.

431 **«Philip II offering Prince Ferdinand to God after the victory of Lepanto»** (Canvas, 335 × 247 cm). Signed. This work dates from about 1573/75. It is related to the preceding one in its allusion to the Battle of Lepanto, symbolized by an allegorical figure of Victory and a Moslem prisoner in chains in the lower part.

432 **«Gloria»** (Canvas, 346 × 240 cm). This work was commissioned by Charles V in 1551. The Emperor can be seen praying in the right-hand upper part accompanied by various members of his family and surrounded by a choir of angels. The sharp *di sotto in su* perspective transports the spectator up into the vision of heaven. Charles V took this canvas with him when he retired to Yuste and died contemplating it.

433 **«The Adoration of the Magi»** (Canvas, 141 × 219 cm). Some critics consider this to be a workshop copy or replica of an original Titian.

434 **«The Virgin and Child with St. George and St. Catherine»** (?) (Wood, 86 × 130 cm). This work is representative of Titian's youthful style, directly inspired by Bellini, also in the way in which the subject is treated, like a «Holy Conversation»; but the figures' oppulent forms and perfectly studied expressions, as well as the rich draperies and shiny armour, foreshadow his later and more characteristic works.

436 **«Agony in the Garden»** (Canvas, 176 × 136 cm). This is one of Titian's late works and contains very attractive light effects caused by the artificial light from the lower part that contrasts with the dazzling divine light from above.

437 **«Ecce Homo»** (Slate, 69 × 56 cm). Signed. This is another deeply religious work that the Emperor Charles V took with him to Yuste.

438 **«Christ and the Cyrenian»** (Canvas, 67 × 77 cm). Signed. This is one of Titian's late works.

439 **«Jesus and the Cyrenian»** (Canvas, 90 × 116 cm). Art historians are not unanimous in ascribing this work to Titian.

440 **«The Entombment of Christ»** (Canvas, 137 × 175 cm). Signed. In this work, which dates from 1559 and reveals deep devotional feeling, the first signs of the unfinished technique of Titian's old age can be observed. It is one of the artist's most impressive paintings in which the whole tragedy of death is reflected in the figures with their sorrowing, devout or anguished

425. Titian. Danaë receiving the shower of gold.

gestures, which are not exaggerated or theatrical but an example of tense, restrained sorrow.

441 «The Entombment of Christ» (Canvas, 130 × 168 cm). This is another version of the preceding work.

442 «The Redeemer as the gardener» (Canvas, 68 × 62 cm). This is a fragment of a painting of Christ and Mary Magdalene.

443 «Mater Dolorosa» (Wood, 68 × 61 cm). This was also one of the works taken by Charles V to the monastery of Yuste. The Virgin's intensely dramatic expression and restrained sorrow are admirably rendered.

444 «Mater Dolorosa» (Marble, 68 × 53 cm). This is the companion piece to the *Ecce Homo* (No. 437).

445 «St. Margaret» (Canvas, 242 × 182 cm). Signed. This is a beautiful work from Titian's old age, in which the Saint's sentimental and dramatic expression clearly anticipates Baroque painting. The splendidly modelled female figure is silhouetted against a blurred dark landscape rendered with a masterly technique.

533 «The Elector Frederick, Duke of Saxony» (Canvas 129 × 93 cm). He was taken prisoner by Charles V at the Battle of Mühlberg. Titian portrayed him in Augsburg in 1548.

429. Titian. Adam and Eve.   443. Titian. Mater Dolorosa.

TITIAN (?)

42 «Ecce Homo» (Canvas, 100 × 100 cm). This is possibly an imitation of Titian's prototypes by one of his followers.

447 «St. Catherine» (Canvas, 135 × 98 cm).

TITIAN, Workshop.

446 «St. Margaret» (Canvas, 116 × 91 cm). A canvas similar to this one kept in the Uffizi Gallery in Florence is attributed there to Palma Giovane.

452 «Philip II» (Canvas, 103 × 82 cm).

TITIAN, Copies by Juan Bautista del Mazo (?).

423 «Diana and Actaeon» (Canvas, 96 × 107 cm).

424 «Diana discovers Callisto's offence» (Canvas, 98 × 107 cm). These two works are copies of original Titians that were in Spain, but were sent as gifts to the French marshal De Gramont in 1704 by Philip V.

TORRESANI, Andrea (Brescia ? - c. 1760). Venetian School.

457 «Landscape with cows» (Canvas, 60 × 76 cm). Torresani was a North Italian landscape painter related to the Venetian School; his work reflects an idyllic, beautiful aspect of nature, with calm, shady forms, characteristic of 18th-century Venetian landscapes.

TRAINI, Francesco (active in Pisa between 1321/63). School of Pisa.

2944 «Madonna and Child» (Wood, 48 × 42 cm). This is one of the few examples of 14th-century Italian painting in the Prado. Traini used delicate forms and was in contact with the Sienese School as is indicated by his rich range of colours that contrast with the golden background.

TREVISANI, Francesco (b. Capodistria 1656; d. Rome 1745). Roman School. Trevisani was of Venetian origin and studied in Venice before settling in Rome, where his refined style and Rococo sensibility, together with his rich colouring and attractive light contrasts, brought him success and many commissions for private collectors and the most important churches in Rome.

458 «**Virgin with the sleeping Child**» (Canvas, 76 × 68 cm). This work dates from 1708/10 and is characteristic of the artist's most delicate style.

459 «**Penitent Mary Magdalene**» (Canvas, 99 × 76 cm). This is another version of the numerous paintings of Mary Magdalene left by Trevisani.

TRONO, Giuseppe (b. Turin 1739; d. Lisbon 1810). Piamontese School.

2416 «**Carlota Joaquina, Queen of Portugal**» (Canvas, 172 × 128 cm). Signed and dated 1787. Trono was a Court portraitist, travelled to many Italian cities and spent several years in Lisbon. This portrait is painted in the Neo-Classical manner and with great attention to detail.

TURCHI, Alessandro, called «**l'Orbeto**» (b. Verona 1578; d. Rome 1650). Venetian School.

461 «**The Flight into Egypt**» (Canvas, 284 × 200 cm). This is a very attractive work painted about 1633 for the Oratory of St. Romualdo in Rome. The elegant poses, in particular that of the angel, are outstanding and were already admired by his contemporaries. The landscape, a fondness for billowing draperies and the solemnity of the scene possibly indicate that this artist received his training in Venice.

VACCARO, Andrea (Naples c. 1598-1670). Neapolitan School. In Neapolitan art the name of Vaccaro goes hand in hand with that of Stanzione. Like the latter, Vaccaro combined the naturalistic Caravaggesque style with the Classicism of the Bolognese artists; in his painting he attached importance to orderly, sometimes rather monotonous compositions and he enjoyed fame in Naples until the appearance of Luca Giordano.

462 «**St. Cajetan offered to the Virgin by his mother**» (Canvas, 123 × 76 cm). See No. 465.

463 «**St. Cajetan offered to the Virgin as a child**» (Canvas, 123 × 76 cm). See No. 465.

464 «**The selflessness of St. Cajetan**» (Canvas, 123 × 76 cm). See No. 465.

465 «**Death of St. Cajetan**» (Canvas, 123 × 176 cm). These four works together with six others kept in the Royal Palace belong to a series on the life of St. Cajetan. They are interesting for their realistic portrayal, some of the scenes revealing a devout and almost popular character, like the one representing *St. Cajetan offered to the Virgin as a child;* in others the artist has adopted a more Classicist style in his search for greater formal elegance.

466 «**Penitent Mary Magdalene**» (Canvas, 179 × 128 cm). Signed. This work seems to be derived from one of Titian's models.

468 «**Meeting of Rebekah and Isaac**» (Canvas, 195 × 246 cm). Signed. This is possibly the most elaborate of Vaccaro's works in the Prado; the harmonious arrangement of the figures and the beauty of the female models derive from classic prototypes.

469 «**Death of St. Januarius**» (Canvas, 207 × 154 cm). Signed. This work represents the patron saint of Naples and the city can be seen in the lower part of the composition. The upward surge of the figure and his mystic, realistically portrayed expression are noteworthy.

470 «**St. Rosalia of Palermo**» (Canvas, 228 × 179 cm). Signed. This work is over-orderly, verging on lack of expressiveness.

475. Vanvitelli. View of Venice from the island of San Giorgio.

VACCARO (?).

472 See Masari.

473 **«Cleopatra taking her life»** (Canvas, 199 × 150 cm). This is a very Classical model derived from Guido Reni.

VAGA. See Perino del Vaga.

VANNI, Francesco (Siena 1563-1610).

474 **«St. John and the three Marys»** (Canvas, 58 × 25 cm). Although it is not of particularly high quality, this work is characteristic of the style of this Sienese artist acquainted with the painting of Barocci, whose naturalism and expressive sensibility he adopted.

VANVITELLI, Gaspar van Wittel, called **«Vanvitelli»** (b. Amersfoort 1653; d. Rome 1736). Roman School. This artist was of Dutch extraction but settled in Rome at an early age and is considered of the Roman School. He was above all a landscapist and his works were very successful due to his realistic depiction of townscapes, light effects, clear-cut forms and variegated colouring. He had an important influence on 18th-century townscape painting.

475 **«View of Venice from the island of San Giorgio»** (Canvas, 98 × 174 cm). Signed and dated 1697. This work anticipates more naturalistic and pictorial views of Venice painted by Canaletto or Guardi.

2462 **«Surroundings of Naples»** (Canvas, 32 × 37 cm). See No. 2463.

2463 **«The grotto of Posilipo in Naples»** (Canvas, 32 × 37 cm). This is a companion piece to the preceding work; both date from the artist's late period and can be considered among his finest and most delicate paintings.

VASARI, Giorgio (b. Arezzo 1511; d. Florence 1574), Follower. Florentine School.

98 **«Agony in the Garden»** (Wood, 120 × 125 cm). This is the work of a pupil or follower of Vasari, who was the biographer of the Italian masters and a painter and architect himself. He painted in the manner of Michelangelo, although attenuating the latter's monumental forms. In this work the evening landscape is outstanding.

VECCHIA, Pietro Muttoni, called **«Pietro della Vecchia»** (Venice 1605-1678). Venetian School.

478 **«Dionysius of Syracuse teaching Mathematics»** (Canvas, 103 × 120 cm). Pietro della Vecchia's style is based on that of the great masters of the *Cinquecento,* but evolved towards Caravaggesque Tenebrism. This work is an example of his non-religious and *genre* painting, in which he used striking *chiaroscuro* and thick surface finish applied with long brushstrokes.

VERONESE, Paolo Caliari, called **«Paolo Veronese»** (b. Verona 1528; d. Venice 1588). Venetian School. Together with Titian and Tintoretto, Veronese was one of the great masters of Venetian painting in the 16th century. Early in life he settled in Venice, where the cultural and artistic life was more interesting than in his native town. There he began to decorate churches and palaces and became famous. His enormous stage-like works include backgrounds with monumental architectonic elements which resemble those of the Venetian architect Palladio, with whom he sometimes collaborated. Veronese went further than merely depicting illusions of space; he used them as a setting for his pictures in which a rich range of colours brings out in a brilliant manner silken textures, brocades and armour and represents mythological, historical, religious and allegorical scenes with a feeling for theatrical effects. All of Veronese's work is pervaded by a vital, naturalistic character and a full, joyful sense of life that make him one of the most attractive artists of his time. In his mature period the keynotes of his work were vibrating rendering of air and atmospheric feeling which were to be an object of study for following generations of artists and can be found in the origins of the Baroque.

482 **«Venus and Adonis»** (Canvas, 212 × 121 cm). This work was purchased by Velazquez in Venice. It dates from about 1580, Veronese's late period, and reveals admirable mastery in representing air and vibrating atmospheric effects, which undoubtedly had an influence on the Spanish artist. The scene abounds in foliage that filters the sunlight on Venus' nude body in a realistic fashion.

483 **«Susannah and the elders»** (Canvas, 151 × 177 cm). This work is interesting for its naturalistic touch and deep colouring.

486 **«Livia Colonna»** (?) (Canvas, 121 × 98 cm). This portrait dates from Veronese's late period, so that it is not very probable that the sitter was Livia Colonna, who was assassinated in 1552. The texture of the draperies is depicted with great mastery.

487 «**Lavinia Vecellio**» (Canvas, 117 × 92 cm). This is regarded as a portrait of Veronese's daughter, since the sitter's features correspond to those of other portraits.

491 «**Christ with the doctors in the Temple**» (Canvas, 236 × 430 cm). Dating from 1548, although some critics date it about 1558/60 due to features of its style and technique, it is related to the works Veronese painted during his early years in Venice; it also reveals knowledge of Palladio's style of architecture, which forms the framework of this painting. The naturalistic positioning of the figures in an upward perspective with the imposing series of heads and varied expressions is particularly attractive.

492 «**Jesus and the centurion**» (Canvas, 192 × 297 cm). This is one of the most beautiful works by Veronese in the Prado; it entered the royal collection in the 18th century and was possibly purchased in England on the death of Charles I. It is a tempered, structured work, but does not lack Veronese's typical dynamic approach.

494 «**The marriage feast at Cana**» (Canvas, 127 × 209 cm). Art critics are

492. Veronese. Jesus and the Centurion.

doubtful about ascribing this work definitively to Veronese, but it is a high-quality painting; the figures dressed according to 16th-century fashion are possibly all portraits of Venetian personalities.

497 «**The Martyrdom of St. Mennas**» (Canvas, 238 × 182 cm). Some critics regard this as a workshop painting, whereas others consider it to be totally by Veronese's hand. It is an interesting work and the dramatic effect is heightened by the movement of the draperies and the flashes of light.

498 «**Penitent Mary Magdalene**» (Canvas, 122 × 105 cm). Dated 1583. In this work from his late period Veronese shows interest in varying light effects; his technique is light and full of nuances.

499 «**Youth between Vice and Virtue**» (Canvas, 102 × 153 cm). This is a frequent subject in painting from the 16th century on, based on Roman literature; it represents Hercules as a child deciding which path to follow.

500 «**Abraham's sacrifice**» (Canvas, 129 × 95 cm). This is regarded as one of the masterpieces of Veronese's old age. The diagonal composition was adopted by Baroque artists (see Domenichino No. 131). It is characterized by light and atmospheric effects.

501 «**Cain as a fugitive with his family**» (Canvas, 105 × 153 cm). The most interesting aspect of this work is possibly the poetic and melancholy landscape in the background.

502 «**Moses rescued from the Nile**» (Canvas, 50 × 43 cm). This work, painted in his mature period, is probably one of the finest examples of Veronese's art in the Prado. Several versions are known, of which this is the best; its small size does not detract from the impressiveness of the composition. Veronese's technical mastery catches and holds the spectator's attention from the silvery background with its landscape and architectural elements to the foreground with the dwarf and the Negress, figures that reveal the artist's fondness for exotic types. The brilliant silk draperies

418. Titian. Bacchanal. (detail)

420. Titian. Venus and the organ-player. (detail)

underline the elegance of the figures shaped by the vibrating air and light and the eye is led into the background following the small, impressionistically portrayed figures dancing on the left.

VERONESE (?).

490 «**The Virgin and Child with St. Lucia and a martyr**» (Canvas, 98 × 137 cm). Most critics consider it a workshop painting, although some regard it as a youthful work by Veronese.

VERONESE, Copy.

489 «**The Adoration of the Magi**» (Canvas, 160 × 140 cm). This is a copy after an original by Veronese kept in the National Gallery, London.

VERONESE, Carlo Caliari, called «**Carletto Veronese**» (Venice 1570-1596). Venetian School. He was the son of Paolo Veronese and also his assistant; he did not become very famous as an independent artist and painted in the manner of his father.

480 «**St. Agueda**» (Canvas, 115 × 86 cm). This is a serene and ordered composition; the naturalistic details and intense study of the light are interesting.

502. Veronese. Moses rescued from the Nile.

VOLTERRA, Danielle Ricciarelli, called «**Danielle da Volterra**» (b. Volterra 1509; d. Rome 1566). Roman School.

522 «**The Annunciation**» (Wood, 186 × 125 cm). Volterra painted in the manner of Michelangelo, imitating him faithfully without attaining his heroic grandeur. Here he has produced a moderated and well-balanced composition, but there are some elements of spatial tension and forced forms.

VOLTERRA (?), Copy.

511 «**The Deposition**» (Copper, 70 × 54 cm). This is a copy with some variants after Volterra's fresco in the Santa Trinità dei Monti church in Rome.

ZANCHI, Antonio (b. Este, Padua 1631; d. Venice 1722). Venetian School.

2711 «**Penitent Mary Magdalene**» (Canvas, 110 × 90 cm). Although Zanchi is an artist of secondary importance, the interest of this work lies in the fact that it is an example of 17th-century Venetian painting, which is not very well represented in the Prado. This beautiful Magdalene is a sample of the sensual, colourful trend which derived from the German artist Johann Liss, who settled in Venice in the first half of the 17th century and whose works were highly appreciated by collectors and other artists; his influence lingered on into the 18th century.

ZELOTTI, Gian Battista (b. Verona 1526; d. Mantua 1578). Venetian School.

512 «**Rebekah and Eliezer**» (Canvas, 219 × 270 cm). This work bears an apocryphal signature by Veronese. Zelotti was one of Veronese's assistants and painted this work completely in the manner of his master.

ZUCCARO, Federigo (b. Sant'Angelo del Vado, Urbino 1542; d. Ancona 1609), Follower. Roman School.

513 «**The Resurrection**» (Canvas, 137 × 71 cm). This work is by one of the pupils of Zuccaro, a painter, architect and art theoretician who lived in Spain for some time training the group of artists who decorated El Escorial. It is a cold, rather affected work and lacks creative power.

ANONYMOUS ITALIAN MASTERS. The Prado possesses a large number of works that cannot be attributed to definite artists, although they can be classified according to schools. Some of them are excellent works. In recent studies on Italian painting in the Prado several of the works previously listed as anonymous have been identified and are now included under the name of the corresponding artist.

7 «Cosme II, Grand-duke of Tuscany» (Canvas, 200 × 108 cm). He belonged to the Medici family and was Duke of Tuscany from 1609 until his death.

11 «Venetian lady» (?) (Canvas, 222 × 140 cm). 17th-century Venetian work.

55 «Viola-player» (Wood, 77 × 59 cm). This excellent portrait from about 1540 was attributed in the past to Bronzino. It is an example of Mannerist portraiture.

85 «The communion of St. Teresa» (Canvas, 160 × 121 cm). This work is related to the early 17th-century Lombardic School.

100 «Repentant Mary Magdalene» (Canvas, 191 × 121 cm). 17th-century Florentine or Roman School.

270 «The mystic betrothal of St. Catherine» (Canvas, 117 × 151 cm). 16th-century Venetian School, related to the style of Palma Giovane or Tintoretto.

368 «Colonel Francisco Verdugo» (?) (Canvas, 54 × 37 cm). 16th-century Venetian School.

406 «Paolo Contarini» (Canvas, 117 × 91 cm). 16th-century Venetian School.

519 «An ecclesiastic» (Wood, 54 × 42 cm). Possibly early 16th-century Florentine School.

535 «The Universal Deluge» (Canvas, 58 × 75 cm). 16th-century Lombardic School.

566 See Masari.

580 «Christ shown to the people» (Wood, 78 × 53 cm). Possibly Venetian School.

1985 «Old woman» (Canvas, 106 × 77 cm). Previously ascribed to the Neapolitan Stanzione, this excellent and realistic work is possibly by a Flemish artist.

2551 «Penitent St. Jerome» (Wood, 82 × 62 cm). North Italian School, about 1550.

2585 «Head of a woman» (Canvas, 36 × 31 cm). 17th-century work.

2589 «Young man with curly hair» (Canvas, 62 × 52 cm). This work has been ascribed to the Spanish School. 18th century.

2659 «Hagar and Ishmael in the desert» (Canvas, 57 × 76 cm). This is a copy after a work by the 17th-century Roman artist Andrea Sacchi.

2708 «The Coronation of the Virgin» (Canvas, 152 × 62 cm). This was a sketch for a ceiling decoration, dating from the end of the 17th century.

2758 «Head of an old man» (Canvas, 45 × 42 cm). Late 16th-century Venetian work.

2760 «Garden with flowers and fruit» (Canvas, 175 × 226 cm). 17th-century Roman work.

2764 «The Gate of Capua in Naples» (Canvas, 30 × 51 cm). 18th century.

2765 «View of the market-place del Carmine in Naples» (Canvas, 31 × 52 cm) 18th century.

2766 «Street in Naples» (Canvas, 30 × 51 cm). 18th century.

2767 «Avenue of the gardens of Capodimonte» (Canvas, 32 × 52 cm). This and the three preceding works are examples of 18th-century Neapolitan townscapes.

2810 «Seaside walk» (Canvas, 18 × 22 cm). Early 18th century.

2989 «St. Agueda healed by St. Peter in prison» (Canvas, 109 × 88 cm). 17th-century Tuscan work.

3259 «Portrait of a clergyman». Early 16th-century Florentine School.

482. Veronese. Venus and Adonis. (detail)

FRENCH MASTERS

In number and quality, the French school forms the third group of foreign artists represented in the Prado after the Italian and Flemish masters. It comprises 200 works and although they cannot be regarded as an overall survey of French art because they were purchased in accordance with the prevailing taste of the Kings, whose prime interest lay with Italian and Flemish art, they do nonetheless compose a numerous collection of very attractive and interesting paintings which include magnificent examples by the best French artists of the 17th and 18th centuries.

The collection begins with a portrait by a follower of Clouet as representation of 16th-century painting. As a result of the peace between France and Spain and the marriage alliances between the two royal houses, the Habsburgs and Bourbons, during the 17th century many portraits of important personalities at the Court of Versailles reached the Spanish Court, in particular works by fashionable artists such as Beaubrun, Mignard and Bourdon, the latter being represented here by a fine portrait of Christina of Sweden. Two splendid works by French followers of Caravaggio, Valentin and Tournier, can be seen, as well as a small, recently acquired still life by Linard and the important works that Philip IV commissioned Poussin and Claude Lorrain to paint for the Buen Retiro Palace.

When the Bourbon dynasty acceeded to the Spanish throne in the person of Philip V, at the beginning of the 18th century, many French artists found their way to Spain, especially court portraitists like Ranc and Van Loo. Houasse, an extremely refined painter, is an interesting artist as his influence made itself felt among his Spanish colleagues towards the end of the century. The lack of outstanding Rococo works in the Prado is partly compensated by two excellent paintings by Watteau, fine examples of his style, and another two by Jean-Baptiste Pierre, recently purchased to enhance the collection. Several works by lesser-known 18th-century landscape painters such as Vernet, Pillement and Hubert Robert are shown to illustrate this important branch of French art.

BEAUBRUN, Charles (b. Amboise 1604; d. Paris 1692). He was a renowned portrait painter during the reigns of Louis XIII and Louis XIV and worked with his cousin, Henri Beaubrun, also a portraitist. Their style was restrained and sober, highly-detailed in depicting draperies and characterizing their sitters, but it reflected a certain courtly coolness and always remained within the established limits of early 17th-century portraiture without ever reaching the somewhat bombastic, decorative eloquence characteristic of the full Baroque style.

2409 **«Maria Theresa, Queen of France»** (?) (Canvas, 102 × 88 cm). The dark tones relate this work to contemporary Dutch portraits.

BEAUBRUN, Henri (b. Amboise, 1603; d. Paris, 1677) and **Charles Beaubrun.**

2231 **«Anne Marie Louise of Orleans»** (Canvas, 109 × 88 cm). She was a granddaughter of the French King Henry IV. This is the finest of all the Beaubruns' portraits.

2232 **«The Dauphin, father of Philip V»** (Canvas, 129 × 98 cm). Signed and dated 1663. This is a courtly portrait which lacks the vivaciousness of Spanish portraits on the same theme.

2234 **«Anne of Austria, Queen of France»** (Canvas, 112 × 88 cm). Daughter of the Spanish King Philip III and wife of the King of France Louis XIII, she was the mother of Louis XIV.

2292 **«Maria Theresa of Austria, Queen of France»** (Canvas, 105 × 87 cm). There are certain doubts about ascribing this portrait to the Beaubruns.

BOUCHER, François (?) (Paris 1703-1770).

2854 **«Cupids playing with pigeons»** (Canvas, 67 × 81 cm). See No. 2855.

2855 **«Cupids gathering grapes»** (Canvas, 67 × 81 cm). These two works have been attributed to Boucher without sufficient proof.

BOUCHER, Copy.

2236 **«The toilet of Venus»** (Canvas, 128 × 96 cm). This is a copy after an oval painting kept in the Rotschild Collection in London.

BOULOGNE, Jean de Boulogne, called «Valentin» (b. Coulommiers, Brie, 1591; d. Rome, 1632).

2346 **«The martyrdom of St. Lawrence»** (Canvas, 195 × 261 cm). Valentin was one of the French artists who studied in Rome, together with Vouet and Manfredi, and fell under the influence of Caravaggio, interpreting the latter's themes in the strictest naturalistic manner. This is one of his mature works. His earlier realism of almost popular origin, is attenuated here by a Classical, geometrically arranged composition in which light plays an important part in emphasizing sharply the body of the central figure, the martyr. The use of dark shades, browns and reddish ochres, is characteristic of the Northern-born followers of Caravaggio who worked in Rome.

2788   See Tournier.

1503. Bourdon. Christina of Sweden on horseback.

BOURDON, Sébastien (b. Montpellier 1616; d. Paris 1671). Bourdon studied in Rome in close contact with the last followers of the naturalistic, Caravaggesque movement, the *bamboccianti* or artists who painted *genre* pictures on trivial, popular scenes. After his return to Paris, his style changed when he found himself obliged to paint in accordance with the prevailing, deeply Classicist fashion. From 1652-1654 he was Court Painter to Queen Christina of Sweden in Stockholm, where he worked primarily as a portraitist.

1503   **«Christina of Sweden on horseback»** (Canvas, 383 × 291 cm). This is a portrait of an interesting woman, a Queen who gave up her crown to lead a freer life. She settled in Rome and was an important figure in the city's cultural and artistic life at the end of the 17th century. Many of the Classical sculptures in the Prado belonged to her collection and were purchased from her heirs by Philip V. This portrait is one of the best of Bourdon's works; it was commissioned by Philip IV and painted in 1653. The clever-minded and somewhat overbearing Queen is portrayed in masterly fashion, in a very novel composition with magnificent colouring interrupted by the brilliant dress of the page with the falcon.

2237   **«St. Paul and St. Barnabas in Lystra»** (Canvas, 47 × 36 cm). This work relates a passage from the Acts of the Apostles interpreted in the Classicist style of Bourdon's later period. There are constant references to Classical Antiquity.

BOURGUIGNON. See Courtois.

CALLET, Antoine François (Paris 1741-1825).

2238   **«Louis XVI»** (Canvas, 275 × 193 cm). This work is full of courtly pageantry and represents the King of France during the ceremony of his consecration. The artist only shows interest in details that enhance the monarch's majesty and pomp.

CHAMPAIGNE, Philippe de (b. Brussels 1602; d. Paris 1674). Of Flemish origin, Champaigne settled in Paris in his youth and became famous for his religious scenes and portraits, which gave him access to courtly circles. Soon after 1640 he came into contact with the Jansenist movement whose devout and austere character was to exert an influence on his later works, leading him to discard Baroque sentimentalism and pompousness and adopt a sober, intimate tone, full of deep religious feeling.

2240   **«Louis XIII of France»** (Canvas, 108 × 86 cm). Although this work is considered by some art historians to be a copy by a follower, it is very typical of Champaigne's sober style.

2365   **«The Christian soul accepting its Cross»** (Canvas, 70 × 64 cm). This work must be seen in relation with the severe religious allegories of the

Jansenists. Its pure, clear-cut forms and highly-detailed representation of the subject-matter make one overlook the possible monotony of the scene, in which the artist's interest centres on the geometric perspective of the crosses. Some critics ascribe the work to Jacques Stella.

CLOUET, Anonymous follower of François Clouet (b. Tours 1522; d. Paris 1572).

2355 **«Lady with a yellow carnation»** (Wood, 61 × 47 cm). This interesting work belongs to the circle of followers of the famous French portraitist Clouet, who combined the Northern taste for meticulous detail and psychological study with the monumental forms of Italian tradition. It is the only example of 16th-century French painting in the Prado.

COURTILLEAU.

2241 **«The Princess of Savoy»** (Canvas, 72 × 63 cm). Signed: Courtilleau fecit 1702. Nothing more is known about this artist, presumably French to judge by his name and style.

COURTOIS, Jacques, called **«Bourguignon»** (b. St. Hippolyte, 1621; d. Rome, 1676). He was a French painter who lived in Rome; he was famous for his stirring battle scenes where he concentrated on depicting figures in movement, but within a strict compositional scheme. He achieved masterly effects in representing dust raised by horses' hoofs and gunpowder explosions.

2242 **«Battle between Christians and Moslems»** (Canvas, 96 × 152 cm). Here he combined a landscape including Classical ruins in the manner of Claude Lorrain with a violent battle scene.

2243 **«Struggle to capture a stronghold»** (Canvas, 76 × 155 cm). This is one of the most attractive works of its kind in the Museum.

2527-8 See Meulener in Flemish Masters.

COYPEL, Antoine (Paris 1661-1722).

2247 **«Susannah accused of adultery»** (Canvas, 149 × 204 cm). Together with Le Brun, La Fosse and Jouvenet, Coypel was one of the representatives of the decorative Baroque style in France. He studied in Rome and travelled through Northern Italy, where he familiarized himself with the striking decorations of Correggio and the 16th-century Venetian artists, which influenced his sense of colouring, making it airier and more refined in his later works, tending towards the Rococo style. The salient features of this work are the dramatic expressions, although within a very moderate composition, and the beauty of the draperies, which the artist used as a study of Classical Antiquity.

2355. Clouet, follower. Lady with a yellow carnation.

DORIGNY, Michel (b. St. Quentin 1617; d. Paris 1665).

2249 **«The Triumph of Prudence»** (Canvas, 257 × 295 cm). Dorigny was a French Baroque artist whose style is related to that of Vouet; here he represents an allegory on Prudence accompanied by other virtues such as Charity, seen on the left with the children, and Justice, blindfolded and

2254. Claude Lorrain. Landscape with the embarkation of St. Paula Romana at Ostia.
(detail)

2313. Nicolas Poussin. Parnassus.

with the scales in her hand. It is a rich, varied composition in which the artist emphasizes light contrasts and the elegant poses of the figures.

DROUAIS (?), François Hubert (Paris 1727-1775).

2467 «**Madame de Pompadour**» (Canvas, 54 cm in diameter). See No. 2468.

2468 «**Madame du Barry**» (Canvas, 62 × 52 cm). Signed and dated 1770. François Hubert is the best-known of a family of portraitists. These two works are painted in the manner appreciated at the Court of Louis XVI, with generous *sfumato* in the refined forms and pastel shades in the colouring.

FLAUGIER, Joseph Bernat (b. Martigues 1757; d. Barcelona 1813).

2646 «**Unknown young man**» (Canvas, 67 × 27 cm). Flaugier was a French artist who settled in Tarragona and Barcelona, where he was the director of an art school. The origin of his painting is to be found in that of the great Neo-Classical artist David. This work is a fragment of a larger composition.

FLEMALLE, Bertholet (Liège 1614-1675).

2239 «**The Virgin and St. Anne**» (Canvas, 145 × 185 cm). Born in Flanders, Flémalle travelled to Italy about 1640, where he came in touch with the newest developments of the Baroque movement. In Paris he painted numerous works for churches and worked on decorations for the Palace of Versailles. This canvas shows the influence of Poussin's strict Classical style, although Flémalle's taste is more decorative and includes a number of elements that distract the observer's attention; the exquisitely realistic touches denote his Flemish origin.

FLIPART, Charles Joseph (b. Paris 1721; d. Madrid 1797).

13 «**The surrender of Seville to St. Ferdinand**» (Canvas, 72 × 56 cm). Flipart was a French painter and engraver who studied in Venice with the Tiepolos and Amigoni; this work was originally attributed to the latter. It represents a historical event, the conquest of Seville from the Moslems. Flipart painted it in Madrid.

GOBERT, Pierre (b. Fontainebleau 1662; d. Paris 1744). He was one of the best portrait painters of his time and left countless works, mainly portraits of French royalty and nobility. In many of them he follows the custom of presenting the sitter in the shape of one of the gods of Classical mythology, surrounded by Cupids. These portraits were very successful and became popular throughout Europe in the 18th century.

2262 «**Louis XV as a child**» (Canvas, 129 × 98 cm). This is a typical court portrait in which the artist is more concerned with decorative effects than with the sitter's personality. The technique is masterly.

2274 «**Mademoiselle de Blois in the figure of Leda**» (Canvas, 216 × 268 cm). She was the legitimated daughter of Louis XIV and Madame de Montespan. She is represented here as Leda loved by Jupiter in the form of a swan. This is a typical example of a Baroque allegorical portrait.

2297 «**Girl with a cage**» (Canvas, 82 × 65 cm). This was previously considered an anonymous work, but has now been attributed by art critics to Gobert; it is characteristic of the style of his child portraits, in which he usually portrayed children with animals.

GOBERT (?).

2263 «**The Duchess of Bouillon**» (?) (Canvas, 128 × 95 cm). This work has been ascribed by some art historians to Gobert and by others to Mignard; it is an example of an aristocratic portrait with its magnificent, lavish setting.

2296 «**The Princess Mademoiselle de Blois, Princess of Conty**» (Canvas, 80 × 66 cm). She was the legitimated daughter of Louis XIV and Madame de La Vallière.

GREUZE, Jean Baptiste (b. Tournus 1725; d. Paris 1805).

2590a «**Young man looking over his sholder**» (Canvas, 46 × 38 cm). Greuze was an interesting 18th-century artist who specialized in painting domestic scenes, both in town and rural houses, which he interpreted in a sentimental manner that at times made them monotonous. His work as a portrait painter is more interesting as can be appreciated in this fragment with its vivacious expression and delicate technique and colouring.

HOUASSE, Michel-Ange (b. Paris 1680; d. Arpajon 1730). Houasse received his artistic training in Rome, where he lived during the time his father was director of the Academy of France in Italy (1699-1705). About 1716 Houasse came to Spain and was appointed Court Painter to Philip V. He painted a wide range of subjects including mythologies and historical motifs, large-scale religious compositions and small pictures with scenes of everyday life; his portraits reveal interest in naturalistic effects combined with a taste for decorative details such as the sheen of smooth draperies.

2264 «**The Holy Family with St. John**» (Canvas, 63 × 84 cm). Signed and dated 1726. This is a very delicate work, related in its combination of Classicism and refinement with the early 18th-century Roman Rococo. Houasse takes obvious pleasure in describing the decorative pleated folds.

2267 «**Bacchanal**» (Canvas, 125 × 180 cm). Signed and dated 1719. This subject has been interpreted time and again since the Renaissance, but here we find it in a Rococo version, where nature is a garden and the figures have become so delicate that they have lost their vitality and Baroque robustness.

2268 «**Sacrifice to Bacchus**» (Canvas, 125 × 180 cm). Signed and dated 1720.

2269 «**View of the Monastery of El Escorial**» (Canvas, 50 × 82 cm). This is possibly the most interesting of Houasse's works in the Prado; it belongs to a series of views of royal seats and palaces that he painted in Spain. The scene appears truly copied from nature with its atmospheric effects and palpitating landscape rendered with an almost impressionistic technique.

2387 «**Louis I**» (Canvas, 172 × 112 cm). Signed and dated 1717. This is a portrait of one of Philip V's sons, born in 1707. It is an example of Rococo portraiture with its extremely delicate manner of reproducing details, the light shading and the child's affected pose, although this does not detract from the naturalistic portrayal of the youthful figure. The texture of the clothing is superbly rendered.

4195 «**St. Francis Regis distributing clothing**» (Canvas, 158 cm. in diameter). See No. 4196.

4196 «**St. Francis Regis preaching**» (Canvas, 158 cm in diameter). These two works were painted about 1720 for the Noviciado church in Madrid.

HUTIN, Charles François (b. Paris 1715; d. Dresden 1776).

2270 «**Saxon villager in her kitchen**» (Canvas, 83 × 55 cm). See No. 2271.

2271 «**A villager**» (Canvas, 83 × 57 cm). Signed and dated 1756. Hutin was more important as a sculptor, but some examples of his pictorial work have been handed down to us. These two works reveal a taste for popular, rural scenes that marked French art in the second half of the 18th century.

JOUVENET, Jean Baptiste (b. Rouen 1644; d. Paris 1717).

2272 «**The Magnificat**» (Canvas, 103 × 100 cm). Jouvenet studied with Le Brun, whose classical, decorative style he imitated, and collaborated with Charles de La Fosse. His painting is based on his knowledge of Raphael and Poussin, whose colouring is reflected in his pictures, together with a certain Flemish-style naturalism. This *Magnificat* is a sketch for a painting made for the high altar of Notre Dame in Paris, which is now preserved in the Louvre and was one of the artist's last works. It is an example of his large-scale decorative compositions which made him one of the most important French representatives of this kind of painting.

LA FOSSE, Charles de (Paris 1636-1716).

2251 «**Acis and Galatea**» (Copper, 104 × 90 cm). He studied with Charles

2278. Le Brun, Follower. The Triumph of Caesar.

Le Brun, the most important of Louis XIV's Court painters and a true dictator in matters of art, and then travelled to Italy; all the trends of late 17th-century French art can be found in his painting, from the Venetian-style colouring to the fully Baroque forms around 1690 and the refined Rococo of his last years, to which this work undoubtedly belongs with its dramatic landscape emphasizing the emotions of the lovers discovered by Polyphemus. The first indications of a change in style and departure from the academic, grandiloquent tradition can be discerned here.

LAGRENEE, Louis Jean François «the Elder» (Paris 1724-1805).

2273 **«The Visitation»** (Wood, 49 × 58 cm). Signed. Known primarily for his historical paintings, Lagrenée was a pupil of Carle van Loo. He travelled to Italy, as was traditional for all artists of his time, and on his return settled in Paris, where he received commissions from aristocratic and wealthy bourgeois circles. This small picture is a sample of his style: very much classicist, almost to the point of appearing cold, but compensated by its vivid colouring and perfect, harmonious shapes.

LARGILLIERE, Nicolas de (Paris 1656-1746).

2277 **«Maria Ana Victoria de Borbón»** (Canvas, 184 × 125 cm). Signed and dated 1724. Largillière received a varied training since he first lived in Flanders and later worked in London in the studio of Sir Peter Lely, the distinguished German-born portrait painter resident in England, who exerted an important influence on Largillière's work. His paintings are elegant, somewhat affected and reveal Flemish elements in the fondness for texture and quality of the draperies, which he depicted with very rich colouring.

LE BRUN, Charles. Follower of Le Brun (Paris, 1619-1690).

2278 **«The Triumph of Caesar»** (Canvas, 49 × 64 cm). Le Brun studied in Paris and Rome, following the example of Vouet and Poussin. On his return to Paris he was protected by Richelieu and Colbert and became the most important artist at the Court of Louis XIV. This *Triumph of Caesar* lacks quality to be considered by Le Brun's own hand, but it undoubtedly comes from his circle of followers and is painted in the master's showy, somewhat affected and rhetoric manner. The vagueness of the figures probably indicates that it was intended as a preliminary sketch.

LEUDEL, Andreas (active in the late 17th century).

2280 **«Masinissa mourning over the death of Sophonisba»** (Canvas, 232 × 353 cm). Signed. Nothing is known about this artist, who is presumed French and whose only signed work is this one, without doubt very attractive and of high quality and which seems to be related to Flemish art in its highly-detailed and naturalistic effects.

LINARD, Jacques (Paris (?) c. 1600-1645).

3049 **«Vanitas»** (Canvas, 31 × 39 cm). Linard represents here in the Prado an aspect of 17th-century French painting far-removed from the world of the Court. When he painted his small, allegorical still lifes he was addressing himself more to intellectual than to aristocratic circles. This recently purchased *Vanitas* is a good example of his style; it reveals a great chromatic sensibility, although within the Tenebrist-style colouring of the early 17th century, and a delicate technique reminiscent of Flemish art. The skull on the book alludes to the vanity of Science and the fading carnation to the transience of all things.

LOO, Louis-Michel van (b. Toulon 1707; d. Paris 1771). Louis-Michel was one of the most important members of a family of painters of Dutch extraction settled in France. He studied with his uncle, Carle van Loo, a famous artist in his time, whom he accompanied to Rome when he was awarded the Grand Prize of the French Academy in Italy, where he subsequently stayed from 1727-1733. Later Louis-Michel was appointed Court Painter to Philip V as successor to Jean Ranc, who had died in 1735. Van Loo did not return to France until 1752. He was renowned at the Spanish Court for his portraits, in which he combined a masterly technique in depicting luxurious draperies with a perfect psychological study of his sitters; his compositions are skilful, often magnificent and decorative; he used pale shades in his colouring in the Rococo manner.

2281 **«Louise Elizabeth of Bourbon, wife of the Duke of Parma»** (Canvas, 142 × 112 cm). Signed and dated 1745. She was the daughter of Louis XV, born in 1727 and married to the Infante Philip, Duke of Parma. This is one of Van Loo's masterpieces and a good example of his most Baroque style in the great importance he attached to the decorative aspect of the draperies.

2353. Antoine Watteau. The marriage contract. (detail)

2282   «The Infante Philip of Bourbon, Duke of Parma» (Canvas, 90 × 73 cm). He was the son of Philip V, born in 1720 and married to one of the daughters of Louis XV of France. The style resembles that of the preceding portrait.

2283   «The Family of Philip V» (Canvas, 406 × 511 cm). Signed and dated 1743. This is Van Loo's masterpiece in the Prado. With its ostentatious concept of space and composition it differs from Spanish versions of the same theme, such as Velazquez' *Meninas* or Goya's *Charles IV and his family*. The richly dressed family group is presented in a variety of poses and attitudes. In spite of a certain attempt at enhancing his subject, the artist stresses the psychological study of his sitters. The magnificent architecture of the spacious hall with its opulent red velvet hangings half-covering the musicians' stand is a product of the artist's imagination and does not correspond to any of the royal palaces of the time; the garden seen in the background recalls that of the palace of La Granja in its clear light effects.

2284   «Isabella Maria Louisa of Bourbon, the Archduchess of Austria» (Canvas, 84 × 68 cm). She was a granddaughter of Philip V and a daughter of the Duke Philip of Parma, born in 1741. This is an allegorical portrait in which the child is presented as Venus in a carriage drawn by two doves.

2285   «Philip V» (Canvas, 148 × 110 cm). This is a magnificent portrait of the Spanish king in military dress, wearing the Order of the Golden Fleece. The artist reveals an almost surrealistic interest in depicting materials.

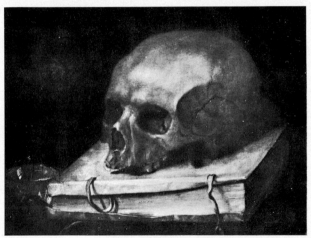

3049. Linard. Vanitas.

LORRAIN, Claude Gellée, called «Lorrain» (b. Chamagne 1600; d. Rome 1682). Lorrain was probably the most outstanding representative of 17th-century landscape painting. However he started his artistic activity very late in life; he was first a shepherd in his native region, later he became a pastry cook and was employed in the house of the painter Agostino Tassi in Rome, which is possibly where he discovered his artistic inclination. Around 1630 he began to work as an independent painter and already showed perfect command of perspective and close observation of nature as well as light and atmospheric effects. Claude Lorrain created a kind of idealized landscape, devised in the painter's mind, although directly inspired by nature, where Antiquity is reproduced in the form of Roman temples and ruins or fantastic constructions that evoke the bygone glory of the Classical world. Claude was the master of light nuances ranging from the rose-tinged clearness of a dawn sky to the calm golden hues that transfigure the Roman landscape at sunset.

2252   «Landscape with the burial of St. Seraphia» (Canvas, 212 × 145 cm). See No. 2253.

2253.   «Landscape with the finding of Moses» (Canvas, 209 × 138 cm). Claude Lorrain frequently painted pairs of pictures with practically identical measurements, where the horizon-line is at the same level and the compositions are slightly asymmetrical when viewed separately and only become completely symmetrical when put together; the light, coming from different angles in each case, is what unifies the two works. The subjects of these two paintings are taken from the Old Testament and the life of a saint and are intended to represent the contrast between life and death, the discovery of Moses and the burial of a saint. They were painted for Philip IV in 1639.

2254 «**Landscape with the embarkation of St. Paula Romana at Ostia**» (Canvas, 211 × 145 cm). This is the companion piece to No. 2255 with *Tobias and the Archangel;* they were painted for Philip IV and are considered Claude's masterpieces. In this one we see how he imagined the ancient Roman port of Ostia, full of monumental architectural elements. The light from the horizon at sunset shines right into the foreground of the picture, through the arches of the building on the left and through the trees, emphasizing the lines of the temple or palace on the right. The seldom-portrayed scene represents St. Paula leaving her children in order to embark for the Holy Land.

2255 «**Landscape with Tobias and the Archangel Raphael**» (Canvas, 211 × 145 cm). Signed. The companion piece to the preceding No., this work is simpler in the representation of the scene, set in a splendid landscape where the artist has avoided architectural elements and secondary scenes and thus depicted nature illuminated by the late-afternoon sun, evoking a mood of deep calm produced by the wide horizon-line and the enormous pine-tree in the foreground.

2256 «**Landscape with an anchorite**» (Canvas, 158 × 237 cm). See No. 2259.

2257 «**The ford**» (Canvas, 68 × 99 cm). Signed and dated. This work belongs to the artist's earliest period and is based on one of his own engravings. Various different versions are known. Its technical quality is excellent.

2258 «**Landscape with the Temptation of St. Anthony**» (Canvas, 159 × 239 cm). See No. 2259.

2259 «**Landscape with the repentant Magdalene**» (Canvas, 162 × 241 cm). Together with Nos. 2256 and 2258, this work forms part of a series of scenes with hermits commissioned by Philip IV for the Buen Retiro Palace. Apart from Claude's mentioned characteristics they reveal a fondness for shady nature which at times (cf. No. 2256) is somewhat disturbing, whereas in the *Temptation of St. Anthony* mysterious light effects anticipate the Romantic landscape of the 19th century.

2260 «**The homing flock**» (Canvas, 98 × 130 cm). See No. 2261.

2261 «**A ford in a river**» (Canvas, 98 × 131 cm). These two works were also painted for Philip IV. The figures are by an Italian artist who collaborated with Claude Lorrain, Filippo Lauri. The pictures date from Claude's early period, about 1636. Although the style is similar to that of his later works, it is still related to landscapes by Carracci (see Italian Masters) in the positioning of the large masses of dark foliage which do not yet reveal the transparent quality of his mature works.

LOUTHERBOURG, Jacques Philippe de (b. Strasbourg 1749; d. London 1813).

2799 «**Landscape with sheep and cattle**» (Canvas, 36 × 46 cm). Signed. He was an artist of secondary importance, a pupil of Carle van Loo, who specialized primarily in idealized landscapes with shepherds and their flocks or hunting scenes, which were very popular at the time; he followed the Dutch tradition in this kind of pictures, but with the addition of dramatic elements that already anticipate the Romantic style.

MALAINE, Joseph Laurent (Tournai 1745-1809).

2286 «**Flowers**» (Wood, 38 × 28 cm). Signed. See No. 2287.

2287 «**Flowers**» (Wood, 48 × 33 cm). Signed. Malaine was one of the artists of the Gobelin tapestry factory in Paris and worked almost exclusively on cartoons for tapestries or designs for woven fabrics. These two panels in the Prado are a sample of his delicate, highly-refined style and detailed technique which aimed at an exact, realistic representation of flowers, animals and insects.

MIGNARD, Pierre (b. Troyes 1612; d. Paris 1695). Mignard studied in Paris in Vouet's studio and later completed his training in Italy, where he lived from 1634 to 1657. He was therefore directly acquainted with the Classicist movement led by Poussin, as well as the Venetian, Bolognese and other schools of painting. On his return to Paris he received important commissions, to the extent of causing the envy of the most important official artist of the time, Le Brun. Mignard excelled as a portraitist and the numerous works he left bear witness to the splendour and magnificence of the Court of Versailles; however, he did not overlook the psychological aspect of his portrait studies.

2288 **«Philip of Orleans, Regent of France»** (Canvas, 105 × 87 cm). The Duke of Orleans is represented dressed as a Roman, a favourite costume for military portraits at the time, against a barely outlined landscape background so that all the observer's attention is centred on the figure.

2289 **«St. John the Baptist»** (Canvas, 147 × 109 cm). This is an example of Mignard's religious works; it clearly reveals the artist's debt to Italian models, especially in the Venetian-style twilight landscape or the saint's idealized kind of beauty. However, the rigorous, almost cold arrangement of the figure reminds us that this is the work of a French artist.

2291 **«Maria Theresa of Austria, Queen of France, with the Dauphin»** (Canvas, 225 × 175 cm). Daughter of Philip IV of Spain, she married Louis XIV of France. The severe style of the portrait and the rigid technique relate this work to the style of the Beaubruns.

2369 **«Philip of France, Duke of Orleans»** (Canvas, 105 × 86 cm). He was a son of Louis XIII and sat for Mignard in 1659. The work's salient features are the severely arranged composition, the naturalistic effect of the sitter's expression and the beautiful colouring.

2400 **«Henrietta Maria of England, Duchess of Orleans»** (Canvas, 75 × 60 cm). She married Philip of France, portrayed in the preceding picture, in 1661. This is the companion piece to the portrait of the Duke of Orleans ascribed to Nocret (see No. 2380).

MIGNARD, Follower.

2299 **«Louis XIV»** (Canvas, 105 × 90 cm). This work was previously attributed to Jean Nocret, but is now considered a copy after an untraceable portrait by Mignard.

NATTIER, Jean-Marc (Paris, 1685-1766).

2591 **«Maria Leszcynska, Queen of France»** (?) (Canvas, 61 × 51 cm). Nattier was one of Louis XV's court portrait painters who painted primarily allegorical portraits in which the sitter appears in the form of a pagan god. This is considered to be Maria Leszcynska due to the sitter's likeness to the wife of Louis XV. It is one of the artist's most sober portraits.

NOCRET, Jean (b. Nancy 1615; d. Paris 1672). Nocret's training was similar to that of Mignard; after studying in Paris he was awarded a scholarship by the French Academy in Rome, where he studied with Poussin. He is, however, a less-important artist than Mignard; he used a soft technique, slightly *sfumato,* in his portraits, which do not come up to the standard of the latter's.

2298 **«Philip of France, Duke of Orleans»** (Canvas, 105 × 86 cm). This is a portrait of the second son of the French king Louis XIII.

2380 **«Philip of France, Duke of Orleans»** (Canvas, 75 × 60 cm). This is the companion piece to No. 2400, ascribed to Mignard.

OUDRY, Jean Baptiste (b. Paris 1686; d. Beauvais 1755).

2793 **«Lady Maria Josepha Drumond, Countess of Castelblanco»** (Canvas, 137 × 105 cm). Signed. See No. 2794.

2304. Poussin. Landscape with St. Jerome.

2794 **«Don José de Rozas y Meléndez de la Cueva, 1st Count of Castel-blanco»** (Canvas, 137 × 105 cm). Oudry specialized mainly in landscapes, *genre* pictures and animal studies, but he also did some portraits following the style of his master, Largillière, in his search for elegance and mastery. Here he has portrayed the Count of Castelblanco, who was born in Lima and served the cause of the English Pretender James, and his second wife, the daughter of Lord Drumond. Both works are pompously decorative.

PIERRE, Jean-Baptiste-Marie (Paris 1714-1789).

3217 **«Diana and Callisto»** (Canvas, 178 × 114 cm). See No. 3218.

3218 **«Jupiter and Antiope»** (Canvas, 178 × 114 cm). Together with its companion piece, this work is representative of Rococo painting at the Court of Louis XVI. Pierre was a pupil of Natoire; in 1734 he was awarded the Grand Prize of Rome. He was one of the outstanding artists of his time, being appointed Director of the French Academy in Rome and First Court Painter. He specialized in historical scenes and large-scale decorations, but these two mythologies reveal his most refined Rococo style, in the manner of Boucher, although in a comparatively cooler, more elegant and stylized way; he appears to be striving for greater sobriety based on beauty of form and enamel-like colouring.

PILLEMENT, Jean (Lyon 1728-1808). He painted landscapes, flowers and *genre* pictures in a manner derived from Dutch art and at the same time directly related to the Rococo style. His work at various European courts contributed to his fame; his style was inspired by Oriental decorative motifs.

2302 **«Landscape»** (Canvas, 56 × 76 cm). Signed and dated 1773. See No. 2303.

2303 **«Landscape»** (Canvas, 56 × 76 cm). This is a companion piece to the preceding work; both represent nature and trees in all their decorative beauty by means of an almost pointillist-style technique that makes the bright touches stand out against a suggestive background suffused in haze and light.

2795 **«Landscape with a castle and warriors»** (Wood, 47 × 66 cm). See No. 2796.

2796 **«Landscape with soldiers on a river-bank»** (Wood, 48 × 65 cm). This is possibly a companion to the preceding landscape; they both reveal a somewhat more rigid style than the other two, but reflect Pillement's fondness for decorative effects.

POUSSIN, Nicolas (b. Les Andelys 1594; d. Rome 1665). Poussin was the most outstanding artist of his time in France and after making Rome his adopted home town continued to exert an important influence on 17th-century painting. He first studied in his native town and later collaborated with Philippe de Champaigne in Paris; however, what determined his artistic future was his friendship with the Italian poet Marino. On his advice Poussin travelled to Rome where Marino introduced him to progressive intellectual circles and art patrons. During an early stage Poussin's style came close to that of Lanfranco (see Italian Masters) in its expressive power and dramatic tenseness, but later it evolved towards pure Classicism, based on Raphael, his studies of Classical Antiquity and a close

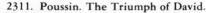

2311. Poussin. The Triumph of David.

observation of nature. The Venetian influence was strong in Rome in these years (around 1630) and affected the majority of artists (cf. Sacchi, Cortona, Testa, Mola, etc. in Italian Masters); it filled Poussin's intellectual works with rich colouring and prevented him from losing the palpitating vitality of his earlier years. Poussin is a perfect example of the philosopher-painter, who understood each of his works as a model or symbol of a human action. He lived more or less in retirement in his house in Rome, held nothing of official honours and addressed his painting to intellectual and literary circles, with whom he maintained constant correspondence. In his later period Poussin departed from his accustomed biblical and mythological subjects and his interest in landscapes became almost obsessive; the real central theme of his pictures came to be nature in all its beauty, at times passive and at others disturbing, but always indifferent to the activities of the mortals portrayed in it.

2304   «Landscape with St. Jerome» (Canvas, 155 × 234 cm). This work, the companion to No. 2305, is now attributed to Dughet and originally formed part of a series of paintings on hermits commissioned by Philip IV for the Buen Retiro Palace in Madrid. It dates from about 1636/37. It is an important work to understand the technique of Poussin's landscape painting with its abundance of elements which almost make the figure of the anchorite merge with his surroundings.

2305   See Dughet in Italian Masters.

2307   «Landscape» (Canvas, 72 × 95 cm). See No. 2309.

2308   «Landscape with ruins» (Canvas, 72 × 98 cm). See No. 2309.

2309   «Landscape» (Canvas, 72 × 95 cm). Art critics have recently decided to exclude these three landscapes from the catalogue of Poussin's works on the basis of their inferior quality and they are therefore now considered to be by one of Poussin's imitators, Jean Lemaire (1598-1659). The three works belonged to the collection of the Roman painter Carlo Maratti.

2310   «Landscape with buildings» (Canvas, 120 × 187 cm). All Poussin experts agree that this is an original, painted around 1650, at a time when the artist was increasingly inclined towards portraying nature. This work has been identified with a *Time of calm and serenity*, the companion piece to a now untraceable *Storm* which Poussin painted in 1651 for his French friend Félibien. The rigorous arrangement of the landscape, abundance of elements and wonderful atmospheric and light effects make it one of the best works by Poussin in the Prado.

2311   «The Triumph of David» (Canvas, 100 × 130 cm). This is an interesting work from Poussin's earlier period, about 1630, when his admiration for the Venetian artists was strongest; it was highly praised by contemporary biographers. The theme of David's victory is interpreted here as a meditation on Triumph. The winged female figure of Victory crowns the hero, who instead of pride in his feat reflects deep melancholy as he looks at his defeated adversary. The group of Cupids and the landscape in the background show Poussin at his most delicate.

2308. Lemaire. Landscape with ruins.

2312. Poussin. Bacchanal.

2312 «Bacchanal» (Canvas, 122 × 169 cm). This work dates from about 1632/36. The surface is so darkened that it is difficult to ascribe the work to Poussin with absolute certainty, but the figures and the scene as a whole correspond to his style.

2313 «Parnassus» (Canvas, 145 × 197 cm). This early work by Poussin (about 1626) is clearly a tribute to Raphael, whose compositions have obviously inspired it. The harmonious representation of space is limited in the background by the vertical lines of the tree-trunks and graduated towards the front by the steps of the fountain of Castalia, personified here by the nude girl sitting in the centre of the group; Apollo is seen accompanied by the Muses, one of whom is crowning Homer, while groups of poets and writers approach. The colouring and light effects are typically Venetian, as well as the two Cupids who offer the poets water from the fountain and who could have come straight out of Titian's *Garden of Loves* (see No. 419).

2316 «Hermit among ruins» (Canvas, 162 × 240 cm). Current opinion among art historians attributes this work to Jean Lemaire. It is without doubt a masterpiece in the field of fantastic Roman ruins, which were to become so popular in the 18th century.

2317 «St. Cecilia» (Canvas, 118 × 88 cm). Recently Poussin experts have suggested that this work could have been painted by Charles Mellin (1587-1649). He was one of Poussin's rivals, but fell under the master's influence; although somewhat cool in their arrangement, his delicate compositions once again show the Venetian influence in their colouring.

2318 «Bacchic scene» (Canvas, 74 × 60 cm). The subject is frequent in Poussin's work; various versions are known, all of better quality.

2320 «Meleager's hunt» (Canvas, 160 × 360 cm). This work has finally been accepted by art experts as an original by Poussin. It represents a scene from the Latin poet Ovid's *Metamorphoses:* the departure for the hunt of the wild boar sent by Diana to devastate Caledonia which was killed by Meleager and Atalanta. They both appear on the right of the group, which is remarkable in its arrangement, as in the horses' movements and the vital, happy mood prevailing among the young horsemen.

2322 «Landscape with Polyphemus and Galatea» (Canvas, 49 × 63 cm). This is a simplified, smaller-scale replica, possibly by Poussin's hand, of the famous painting in the Leningrad Hermitage which represents the splendid symbiosis of man and nature, the constant obsession of Poussin's old age. POUSSIN (?).

2306 «Noli me tangere» (Wood, 47 × 39 cm). This is one of the best versions of Poussin's theme, known from old engravings.

2323 «Ruins» (Canvas, 92 × 110 cm). This work is of excellent quality and was probably done by one of Poussin's followers, possibly Lemaire. POUSSIN, Gaspard. See Dughet in Italian Masters.

PRET, François (active in the 17th century).

2325 «Flowers» (Canvas, 130 × 97 cm). This artist's biography is unknown, but the painting, which comes from the Roman artist Carlo Maratti's collection, where it was listed as by «Mosu de Pre», seems to be the work of one of the French artists resident in Rome. It is a highly attractive painting with its exuberance and colouring, which derives from the style of the Flemish artists who worked in Rome.

RANC, Jean (b. Montpellier 1674; d. Madrid 1735). He was the son of Antoine Ranc and a pupil of Rigaud, who introduced him at Court as a portraitist. His style resembles that of his master in its fondness for showy decorativeness, draperies and monumental scenes; he used a masterly technique to bring out the most subtle effects of materials, silken sheens, different qualities of textiles and colouring, all set off by striking light contrasts. Ranc never lost sight, however, of his sitter's personality, despite the decorative aspect and the need for enhancing courtly portraits.

2265 «The Infante-Cardinal Don Luis Antonio of Bourbon» (Canvas, 105 × 84 cm). He was a son of Philip V and Elizabeth Farnese, born in 1727, and became Archbishop of Toledo.

2266 «María Theresa Antonia of Bourbon, Dauphiness of France» (Canvas, 105 × 84 cm). She was a daughter of Philip V and Elizabeth Farnese, born in 1726 and married to the French dauphin, the son of Louïs XV. This portrait is the companion piece to the preceding one; both are examples of Ranc's delicate style, formal perfection and mastery in depicting details, which acquire almost modern, abstract qualities.

2326 «Philip V on horseback» (Canvas, 335 × 270 cm). This is one of Ranc's most grandiloquent portraits; it follows Rigaud's courtly style in the general composition of the scene, with a battle in the background, a feature introduced by Rigaud, and the figure of Victory in the upper part. It also contains, however, some exquisitely realistic details, like the gentleman accompanying the King who adds a more convincing note to the scene.

2329 «Philip V» (Canvas, 144 × 115 cm). See No. 2330.

2330 «The Queen Elizabeth Farnese» (Canvas, 144 × 115 cm). This is the companion piece to the preceding portrait and represents Philip V's second wife, a daughter of the Duke of Parma Odoardo Farnese, whom the Spanish King married in 1714. They are both conventional court portraits, but are made interesting by Ranc's masterly touch, which gives them an almost surreal meaning.

2320. Poussin. Meleager's Hunt.

2332 «Louise Elizabeth of Orleans, Queen of Spain» (Canvas, 127 × 98) cm). Daughter of the French Regent, Philip of Orleans, she married the son of Philip V, Louis I, who was King of Spain for less than a year in 1724.

2333 «Ferdinand VI as a child» (Canvas, 144 × 116 cm). He was a son of Philip V and his first wife, María Louisa of Savoy, born in 1713, and became King of Spain in 1746. The elegant portrait is reminiscent of Van Dyck.

2334 «Charles III as a child» (Canvas, 142 × 115 cm). He was the son of Philip V and his second wife, Elizabeth Farnese, born in 1716; first Duke of Parma, later King of Sicily, he became King of Spain in 1759. The work is extremely attractive and also original in its arrangement of space, as well as in its decorative and anecdotic elements, such as the leafless flowers in the vase or the parrot. The forms are profusely decorated, for example the child's tunic or the furniture.

2335 **«Ferdinand VI when he was Prince of Asturias»** (Canvas, 75 × 62 cm). Signed and dated 1725.

2336 **«Maria Ana Victoria of Bourbon as a child»** (Canvas, 76 × 62 cm). She was a daughter of Philip V, born in 1718 and betrothed to Louis XV of France when she was four years old; however, the agreement was cancelled and she later married Joseph I of Portugal. The portrait is full of Rococo elegance and delicacy.

2376 **«The Family of Philip V»** (Canvas, 44 × 65 cm). Ranc must have prepared this sketch soon after his arrival in Madrid in 1722 for a painting which has been lost. It is an interesting work, sober in its composition and very different from Van Loo's monumental and ambitious *Family of Philip V*.

2394 **«Maria Theresa Antonia of Bourbon»** (Canvas, 93 × 68 cm). See No. 2266. The draperies have an almost metallic sheen.

2414 **«Barbara of Braganza, Queen of Spain»** (Canvas, 103 × 84 cm). She was the daughter of the King of Portugal and wife of Ferdinand VI, who became King of Spain in 1746. It is one of Ranc's most overladen works.

RIGAUD, Hyacinthe (b. Perpignan 1659; d. Paris 1743). Rigaud was considered the best painter of courtly portraits during the reign of Louis XIV. He studied in the South of France, in Montpellier, under Antoine Ranc and moved to Paris when he was still young. He started working for bourgeois circles, but in 1688 gained access to the Court and from then on his sitters were members of the royal family, nobility and distinguished foreign visitors to the Court of Versailles. Rigaud succeeded in incorporating the showiest and most exuberant Baroque novelties in his otherwise extremely elegant portraits, which almost recall those of Van Dyck, and in an exquisitely realistic representation of textiles, armour and still-life elements; his style reveals his firm footing in the best tradition of French portraiture, which also accounts for the psychological studies of his sitters.

2294 **«A Prince»** (Canvas, 70 × 50 cm). Although this work was originally attributed to Nattier, the artist's realistic portrayal and the child's vivacious expression make it appear closer to Rigaud's style.

2337 **«Philip V»** (Canvas, 130 × 91 cm). This is one of the first portraits of Philip V dressed in the typical Spanish manner, in black and with a ruff collar. It is one of Rigaud's most severe works, although he does show interest in depicting the silk and velvet fabrics.

2343 **«Louis XIV»** (Canvas, 238 × 149 cm). This portrait, painted in 1700, is important in Rigaud's work because in it he applies new ideas in portraying military personalities, in this case Louis XIV; Rigaud departs from the fashion of presenting the sitter dressed as a Roman and introduces the idea of painting a battle scene in the spacious landscape. In this work the background was painted by Charles Parrocel (Paris 1688-1725), a specialist in battle scenes, and only the figure is by Rigaud, although without doubt the whole conception of the scene is his. The Sun King is seen here in all his military splendour, with a haughty, somewhat disdainful air that creates a barrier between him and the beholder.

2658 **«Unknown man»** (Canvas, 58 × 56 cm).

RIGAUD, Copies.

2381 **«Francis Louis of Bourbon-Conty, King of Poland»** (Canvas, 69 × 55 cm).

2390 **«Louis, Dauphin of France»** (Canvas, 103 cm in diameter).

2391 **«Louis XIV»** (Canvas, 103 cm in diameter). This is a pendant to the preceding portrait and a partial copy of Rigaud's portrait of the King in the Louvre.

2597 **«Louis XIV in old age»** (Canvas, 42 × 34 cm).

ROBERT, Hubert (Paris 1733-1808).

2883 **«The Colosseum in Rome»** (Canvas, 240 × 225 cm). Robert studied in the French Academy in Rome and was a friend of Fragonard. He painted in the manner of the Italian artist Panini (see Italian Masters) in his somewhat fantastic portrayal of Roman ruins, a subject that came into fashion in the 18th century due to the advance in arqueological studies, thus anticipating the interest in ruins shown by Romanticism in the 19th century. In this splendid work the magnificent Roman architecture serves as a setting for decorative, anecdotic contemporary figures.

SILVESTRE, Louis de Silvestre «the Younger» (b. Sceaux 1675; d. Paris 1760).

2358 **«Maria Amalia of Saxony, Queen of Spain»** (Canvas, 260 × 181 cm). The itinerant artist Silvestre has painted an elegant, refined portrait of the daughter of the King of Poland and wife of Charles III.

STELLA, Jacques (b. Lyon 1596; d. Paris 1657).

3202 **«Rest on the Flight into Egypt»** (Canvas, 74 × 99 cm). Signed and dated 1652. Stella began his artistic career as an engraver in Florence, but later moved to Rome, where he became a friend and follower of Poussin, whose style he imitated. In this work Poussin's influence can be discerned in the models used, as well as in the arrangement of the scene, but Stella's technique is less refined and some elements are purely decorative, like the little angels, some offering, others holding the curtains, another fetching water from the stream, all of whom break the unity of the composition.

TOURNIER, Nicolas (b. Montbéliard (?) 1590; d. Toulouse after 1657).

2788 **«St. Peter denying Christ»** (Canvas, 171 × 252 cm). Tournier worked in Rome in the circle of French artists around Caravaggio and Manfredi (see Italian Masters) and his style is related to that of Vouet and Valentin, to whom this work was ascribed in the past. However, current opinion among art critics considers it to be Tournier's style, although possibly inspired by one of Valentin's compositions, now lost, whose restrained, melancholy mood is reflected in this work. The Gospel scene is represented like a *genre* painting with more than half of the composition occupied by soldiers playing dice. The superbly realistic figures and draperies are unified by the colouring and the rigorously arranged composition.

TRAVERSE, Charles de la. See Celebrano in Italian Masters.

TROY, Jean François de (b. Paris 1679; d. Rome 1752), Copy.

2367 **«Louis, Dauphin of France»** (Canvas, 105 × 87 cm). This is a subtle copy after an untraceable original known thanks to engravings. De Troy was a court portraitist and his sober manner of representing his sitters is closer to Mignard's circle than to Rigaud's more ostentatious style.

VALENTIN. See Boulogne.

VERNET, Claude Joseph (b. Avignon 1714; d. Paris 1789). Vernet was the son of a carriage-decorator and specialized in landscapes and particularly seascapes. He studied and worked in Rome, where his paintings were sought after by collectors, both colleagues and members of the French colony or foreign visitors. His work is principally inspired by Claude Lorrain's and Salvator Rosa's landscapes, but also reveals the influence of Dutch artists. Vernet's success is due to a skilful blend of realism and Romantic taste. The works on show in this Museum were commissioned by Charles IV, who was a great admirer of Vernet, and are fine examples of his style.

2347 **«Landscape with a cascade»** (Canvas, 155 × 56 cm). Signed and dated 1782. This work was commissioned by Charles IV together with Nos. 2348 and 2349 for the *Casita del Príncipe* in El Escorial.

2348 **«Roman landscape at sunset»** (Canvas, 155 × 57 cm). This work recalls landscapes by Panini (see Italian Masters) or Hubert Robert in its fondness for portraying Roman remains.

2349 **«The kite»** (Canvas, 155 × 34 cm). This work could be considered a precursor to the tapestry cartoons painted by Goya when he was young.

2350 **«Seascape: view of Sorrento»** (Canvas, 59 × 109 cm). This is possibly one of the seascapes that the French King Louis XVI gave to Charles IV while he was still a prince. It is an example of Vernet's most characteristic style, decorative and Rococo as can be observed in the fantastic rocks.

VOUET, Simon (Paris 1590-1649). Vouet was an important personality in 17th-century French art; he lived in Italy from 1613-1627, which enabled him to study all the latest artistic trends, which he introduced in France on his return. In his early years his work reflected the influence of Caravaggio's Tenebrist naturalism, but he changed his style on contact with Bolognese Classicism. He began to use lighter tones and Venetian colouring made its appearance in his paintings. Vouet interpreted the Italian Classicist trend in his own way, with moderation, calm and a perfectly clear arrangement in his compositions, as was characteristic of French artists and contributed to their success in Paris. He accepted numerous commissions from courtly and aristocratic circles and many of the artists of the next generation passed through his studio before producing the grandiloquent, decorative Baroque style of the reign of Louis XIV.

539 **«The Virgin and Child with St. Elizabeth, the infant St. John and St. Catherine»** (Canvas, 182 × 130 cm). This work dates from the time Vouet lived in Rome and reveals a strictly realistic approach to some of the figures, like St. Elizabeth, and a naturalistic representation of textures and the lamb, whereas the composition is perfectly geometric, that is triangular, thus recalling purest early 16th-century Renaissance art; this is accentuated by the poses of the two children, who could have come straight out of a work by Leonardo da Vinci.

2322. Poussin. Landscape with Polyphemus and Galatea.

2987 «**Time overcome by Youth and Beauty**» (Canvas, 107 × 142 cm). Signed and dated 1627. This allegorical work dates from Vouet's last year in Rome and can be considered a forerunner of his mature style. It reflects a very vital and joyful mood and this impression is further underlined by the clear colouring of the windblown draperies and Venetian-style landscape.

WATTEAU, Antoine (b. Valenciennes 1684; d. Nogent-sur-Marne 1721). Watteau's artistic training had a decisive influence on his future style. His native town, Valenciennes, was far removed from the contemporary cultural centre which was the French Court, where the prevailing style was Classicist, decorative Baroque imported from Italy. Where Watteau grew up artists looked towards the simpler, homelier Flemish or Dutch art for inspiration. In 1702 Watteau arrived in Paris, where he made contact with extra-official circles and the world of art dealers. The two most famous antique dealers of the time, Mariette and Gersaint, appreciated his works and he in turn found inspiration studying their collections of old engravings and drawings, making the acquaintance of works by French artists of the past such as Callot and Bellange, full of imagination and creativeness, or of small coloured sketches by Rubens. In contrast with the grand historical and mythological compositions, laden with complicated allegories, which the fashionable artists at Versailles were painting, Watteau produced his small easel-pictures on gallant scenes, performances of the Italian *Commedia dell'Arte,* country gatherings in delicate, hazy settings nearly always pervaded by an air of melancholy. Watteau's works were reproduced by means of engravings, but did not really bring him fame until after his early death when his followers carried on his ideas.

2353 «**The marriage contract**» (Canvas, 47 × 55 cm). See No. 2354.

2354 «**Gathering in a park**» (Canvas, 48 × 56 cm). Although these two works were not considered a pair in the past, their style is very similar. In both we find Watteau's characteristic elegant and stylized figures; the artist delights in describing their clothes and the sheen of the silks with a mastery that brings to mind 17th century Dutch artists. The airy, bright landscape of the *Gathering in a park,* with its iridescent shades, is a good example of the kind of landscape he painted in his most famous works.

ANONYMOUS FRENCH MASTERS. The Prado possesses a number of works, mainly portraits of members of the French royal family, whose origin has not been ascertained. They will be examined in future scientific catalogues of the Prado's French works.

1940 «**St. John the Baptist beheaded**» (Canvas, 280 × 952 cm). This is an important work, which it has not yet been possible to ascribe to any definite artist with certainty. It is considered to be the work of one of the followers of Jacques Callot, possibly Claude Deruet; an interest in caricature-like, weird and fantastic features is evident in this enormous canvas and derives from the late French Mannerist movement. It probably dates from around 1650. Many of the faces are obviously portraits.

2279 **«Lady dressed as Diana»** (Canvas, 103 × 80 cm). Late 17th century.

2295 **«Marie-Louise of Orleans, Duchess of Berry»** (Canvas, 138 × 105 cm). She married a brother of Philip V. The style is related to that of Gobert.

2297 See Gobert.

2345 **«Philip of France, Duke of Orleans»** (Canvas, 70 × 56 cm).

2352 **«Elizabeth Charlotte, Princess of the Palatinate»** (Canvas, 107 × 84 cm). It is an excellent work, the style resembling that of Mignard.

2359 **«Bacchanal»** (Wood, 100 × 251 cm). This was the panel of a clavichord, a musical instrument that was frequently decorated with paintings. It was originally ascribed to Poussin, but is now considered to be closer to the style of Gerard de Lairesse (b. Liège 1640; d. Amsterdam 1711).

2371 **«Victor Amadeus II of Savoy and his family»** (Canvas, 299 × 300 cm). He was the father-in-law of Philip V. It is an extremely overladen and candid courtly portrait.

2372 **«Portrait of an unknown lady»** (Canvas, 118 × 93 cm). The style resembles that of Beaubrun or Mignard.

2375 **«Maria Theresa of Bourbon»** (?) (Canvas, 76 × 60 cm).

2396 **«Portrait of a prince»** (Canvas, 126 × 105 cm). 18th century.

2417 **«Louis XIV as a child»** (Canvas, 125 × 105 cm).

2420 **«Louise Elizabeth of Orleans, Queen of Spain»** (?) (Canvas, 105 × 86 cm).

2435 **«Marie de Medici, Queen of France»** (Canvas, 68 × 56 cm). Early 17th century.

2437 **«Maria Josepha of Austria, Queen of Poland»** (Canvas, 121 × 91 cm). 18th century.

2469 **«Anne of Austria, Queen of France»** (Wood, 35 × 26 cm). Mid-17th century.

2592 **«A French princess»** (Canvas, 72 × 59 cm). The sitter is represented as Diana, with a bow in her hand; the work was attributed to de Troy.

2651 **«The musician Guetry»** (Canvas, 57 × 46 cm). This work was attributed to Greuze.

2789 **«Self-portrait»** (Canvas, 22 × 16 cm). Early 18th century.

2791 **«The Czarina Catherine II»** (Canvas, 83 × 67 cm). Some art historians consider this the work of a Russian artist.

2885 **«Spring»** (Canvas, 196 × 110 cm).

2886 **«Summer»** (Canvas, 196 × 110 cm). This is a companion piece to the preceding work and probably formed part of a series on the seasons. They were attributed to the painter Claude Vignon (1593-1670).

3142 **«Portrait of a lady»** (Canvas, 98 × 72 cm). 18th century.

3524 **«Woman between two ages»** (Wood, 75 × 105 cm). This is a magnificent anonymous work from the School of Fontainebleau, recently purchased for this Museum to compensate the gap of this important period of French art. The subject is taken from the Italian *Commedia dell'Arte* and is known in various versions and engravings.

3524. School of Fontainebleau. Woman between two ages.

DUTCH MASTERS

In the late 15th and during the 16th centuries all of the Low Countries formed a single nation under Spanish rule. But that does not mean that there were no differences between the Northern and Southern provinces; these existed and made themselves felt in the prevailing artistic trends from the start. The artists from the North, which soon adhered to the new Protestant movement, were more sober and austere in their outlook and their art revealed a more symbolic and moralizing character than that of Flanders, which remained Catholic. However, the style of artists born in the Northern Netherlands, which was later to become Holland, derived from that of the Flemish masters and in this period they formed a single school of painting. For this reason artists such as Bosch, Marinus, van Scorel and the portraitist Mor are included among the Flemish masters.

The Protestant Reformation accentuated the national differences within the Netherlands and finally in 1580 the rebellion broke out in the North, which succeeded in throwing off Spanish rule and forming a new nation, Holland. This is when Dutch art appears as such, with its own characteristic features which correspond to a new type of society made up of burghers and merchants with a strict, austere sense of Protestant morals that had been taking shape in the Northern provinces during the whole of the 16th century.

Spain broke off all political ties with Holland, which became her declared enemy and an ally of the rest of the Protestant countries of Europe. That is why none of the very fine and varied works of 17th-century Dutch painting reached Spanish collections at the time. All the paintings on display in the Prado were purchased later. Many of them belonged to the collection of Philip V and Elizabeth Farnese, who shared the 18th-century fondness for small, decorative pictures by Dutch masters. Later Charles III purchased Rembrandt's splendid *Artemisia* from the Marquis de la Ensenada and Charles IV before he became King acquired works by Ruisdael, Steenwijck and Metsu.

In spite of their relatively small number, however, the works by Dutch masters exhibited in the Prado convey a good idea of the trends and style of this school. Stomer and Salomon de Bray can be considered representative of early 17th-century painting with its Caravaggesque influence in the play of light and shade, which can also be observed in Rembrandt. His above-mentioned *Artemisia* is a masterpiece among his early works and a magnificent example of his artistic genius.

A *Philosopher* attributed to Salomon Koninck is the only work worthy of mention among his followers. The small easel paintings intended to adorn the comfortable interiors of Dutch burghers' homes can be divided into *genre* pictures, still lifes and landscapes, all of them interpreted with exquisite taste, almost like miniatures, and refined colouring with predominance of ochres, greens and greys including touches of reds and yellows, which are a delight to behold. Among the still-life painters, Pieter Claesz, Willem Heda and Jan Davidsz de Heem are admirably represented. Metsu's *Dead rooster* is one of the most outstanding works in the Prado's collection of Dutch masters. The *genre* painters are best represented by four of Ostade's works or by Bramer's biblical and mythological scenes interpreted in a realistic, popular vein. There are also examples of the various trends of landscape painting; sea-pieces are represented by Dubbels' *Seaport in Winter* or by Vlieger's and Willaerts' *Seascapes;* among the winter landscapes, so characteristic of Holland, there is a fine work by Droochsloot; the series by Wouwermans is the best in the field of landscapes with battles or hunting scenes. Finally, the Prado possesses various landscapes by Italianate landscape painters like Poelenburgh, Both and Swanevelt and other typically Dutch ones like Van Goyen and Ruisdael.

> **ANTUM, Aert van** (?) (active in Amsterdam 1604-1618). Amsterdam School. He was a sea painter in the manner of Hendrick Vroom, the creator of this kind of painting, whom he resembled in his realistic and meticulous depictions of warships and sea battles; he did not yet show interest in describing atmospheric effects as other artists later in the 17th century.
>
> 2159 «**Naval battle between a Turkish and a Spanish warship**» (Wood, 37 ×58 cm). This work is considered midway between the styles of Antum and Vroom.
>
> **BACKER, Adriaen** (Amsterdam 1636-1684). Amsterdam School.
>
> 2557 «**A general**» (Canvas, 126 × 106 cm). This is a very decorative Baroque portrait which was originally ascribed to Rigaud due to its realistic treatment of details and psychological study of the sitter.

BLOEMAERT, Adriaen (Utrecht c. 1609-1666).
2046   See Meiren, van der, in Flemish Masters.
BOTH, Jan (Utrecht c. 1618-1652). Utrecht School. Both studied in Utrecht with Bloemaert and soon travelled to Rome as many of his Dutch colleagues interested in landscape painting. There he became acquainted with the work of Claude Lorrain, whose light and atmospheric effects attracted him, although he used them in depicting real nature and not idealized landscapes like Claude; Both filled his scenes with small, popular figures, generally painted by his brother Adriaen. Both's works served as a bridge between Italian-style and the more down-to-earth Dutch landscapes.
2058   **«Landscape with hermit»** (Canvas, 153 × 222 cm).
2059   **«View of Tivoli»** (Canvas, 160 × 155 cm). This is a very beautiful landscape with its striking light contrasts in the foreground and the trees and shrubs subtly silhouetted against the clear background.
2060   **«The baptism of the eunuch of the Queen Candace»** (Canvas, 212 × 155 cm). This work illustrates a passage from the Acts of the Apostles. The figures have been attributed to Both's brother Adriaen or to J. Miel.
2061   **«Shepherds with their flock»** (Canvas, 213 × 153 cm).
2062   **«The Aldobrandini Garden in Frascati»** (Canvas, 210 × 155 cm). This attractive work shows a different aspect of Both's work, as a painter of everyday life. The figures are considered to be by his brother Adriaen.
2064   See Swanevelt.
2066   **«Cascade with anglers»** (Canvas, 210 × 155 cm). This is possibly one of Both's most placid works, with a certain melancholy and lonely mood floating over the landscape, which derives from Italian models.
BRAMER, Leonard (Delft 1596-1674). Delft School. Bramer received a varied and independent training. He travelled to Italy early in life and visited various cities before settling in Rome. He was attracted by real-life painting, by the Bassanos in Venice and the *bamboccianti* in Rome. After being involved in a brawl he had to leave Rome six years later and settled in Delft, where his small mythologies and religious pictures made him famous. His nocturnal lighting effects, brilliant colouring and energetic technique produced a very original style that has been regarded as a forerunner of Rembrandt's.
2069   **«Hecuba's grief»** (Copper, 45 × 59 cm). The subject of this work is actually the discovery of the bodies of Hero and Leander drowned in the Hellespont as a result of their love.
2070   **«Abraham and the three angels»** (Wood, 47 × 74 cm). Signed. Like the preceding work, this is a fine example of Bramer's delicate, energetic style; he interpreted both religious and mythological subjects, as well as scenes from everyday life, which, however, are always pervaded by a certain air of mystery.
BRAY, Salomon de (b. Amsterdam 1597; d. Haarlem 1664). Haarlem School.
2097   **«Offering»** (Wood, 89 × 71 cm). In the past this work was attributed both to Philip Koninck and Greber. Now, after the discovery of a preparatory sketch by de Bray, it is unanimously accepted as an original by the latter. He was a painter and architect; he made the acquaintance of the Italian Tenebrist style thanks to the works of colleagues who had studied in Rome. This *Offering* is a very fine work with striking light contrasts, masterly, highly-detailed rendering of draperies and classically proportioned composition. X-ray studies have revealed that originally a male head was painted under the amphora that the female figure is holding, so that it is believed that the painting was first intended to be a *Salome with the head of John the Baptist.*
BREENBERGH, Bartolomeus (b. Deventer 1599; d. Amsterdam 1657). Amsterdam School.
2293   **«The bishop's blessing»** (Canvas, 96 × 112 cm). Although this work was originally attributed to the Flemish artist Pourbus, it is evident that it is by Breenbergh, especially since a signed preparatory sketch exists for one of the figures. Breenbergh was primarily an Italianate landscape painter, a friend of Poelenburgh with whom he lived in Rome. This work in the Prado, however, shows him as a painter of interiors in the best Dutch tradition with an interest in realistic rendering, generous arrangement of space and light contrasts.
BREKELENKAM, Quiring Gerritsz van (b. Zwammerdam c. 1620; d. Leyden 1668). Leyden School.
2136   **«Old woman»** (Wood, 48 × 36 cm). This work bears an apocryphal signature of Teniers. It is one of Brekelenkam's most interesting works and

reflects an intimate aspect of Dutch painting. Brekelenkam studied under Gerrit Dou and Gabriel Metsu; here he takes pleasure in depicting a homely interior with extremely realistic details in the still life.

CLAESZ or Claeszon, Pieter (b. Burg Steinfort 1598; d. Haarlem 1660). Haarlem School.

2753 **«Still life»** (Wood, 83 × 66 cm). Signed and dated 1637. This is the finest example in the Prado of a Dutch still life with its sobriety, transparent clear shapes and harmonious, sensitive lighting effects. It is a characteristic feature of Claesz' style that apart from these typically Dutch elements he adds a study of the atmosphere that envelops his objects, with refined colouring in a reduced range of colours that brings out the different materials in a masterly fashion. The composition is striking in its simplicity.

2753. Claesz. Still life. 2103. Metsu. Dead rooster.

CUYP, Benjamin Gerritsz (Dordrecht 1612-1652). Dordrecht School.
2077 See Momper, Jan de, in Flemish Masters.
2984 **«The Adoration of the shepherds»** (Wood, 81 × 65 cm). Benjamin Cuyp's style has its origin in that of Rembrandt, although his interpretation is on a more modest scale; he used dark shades with which he sometimes attempted to reproduce the great master's golden touches. His figures appear almost uncouth in their naturalistc portrayal and his religious scenes, like this one, are interpreted with a popular and at times somewhat candid simplicity.

CUYP, Jacob Gerritsz (Dordrecht 1594-1652). Dordrecht School.
2167 **«Portrait of a man»** (Oval panel, 78 × 70 cm). The sitter has been identified as Jan van Oldenbarneveldt, a Dutch politician executed in The Hague in 1619. Jacob Cuyp is best known as a portraitist and reveals here an extremely realistic approach and a fondness for *chiaroscuro*, both typical features of this school of painting, as well as sober colouring and a psychological study of the sitter.

DOU, Gerrit (Leyden 1613-1675), Copy. Leyden School.
2078 **«Old man with a book»** (Wood, 23 × 21 cm). This is a copy or an imitation of an original by Dou kept in the Hermitage in Leningrad.

DROOCHSLOOT, Joost Cornelis (Utrecht 1586-1666). Utrecht School.
2079 **«Winter landscape with skaters»** (Canvas, 71 × 111 cm). Signed and dated 1629. This is an example of a type of landscape painting, that of frozen water-ways with figures skating, that was very much appreciated in Holland and had its origin in Pieter Bruegel and his followers a hundred years earlier. Droochsloot was not an exceptional artist, but with these skaters he achieved a vivacious, colourful scene, rigorously arranged with a bright, distant horizon and typically Dutch atmospheric effects.

DUBBELS, Hendrick (Amsterdam 1620-1676). Amsterdam School.
2080 **«Seaport in winter»** (Canvas, 67 × 61 cm). Dubbels specialized in seapieces and in this work he enlarged on the subject of a port and ships by adding a winter landscape with skaters and other figures. The work is delicate in its details, perfectly and harmoniously arranged and the artist appears to have taken pleasure in the play of different shades of white, with which he filled the scene.

FRITS or **Fris, Pieter** (b. Amsterdam 1627; d. Delft 1708). Delft School.

2081 **«Orpheus in the Underworld»** (Canvas, 61 × 77 cm). Signed and dated 1652. Only three works are known by this artist; for this reason the present work is important. Frits' style is somewhat archaic and clearly reminiscent of Bosch, especially in the fantastic interpretation of the scene and the reddish blaze of the fire. The meticulously executed little figures are pleasing with their brilliant colouring.

GLAUBER. See Boudewyns in Flemish Masters.

GOYEN, Jan van (b. Leyden 1596; d. The Hague 1656). The Hague School.

2978 **«Landscape»** (Canvas, 38 × 58 cm). This is a fine example of the style of one of the most outstanding Dutch landscape painters. Van Goyen never tired of travelling through his native country and left his impressions admirably reflected on his canvases. This work belongs to his mature period, when he simplified his compositions. A few trees, a house and a country path in a wide expanse of countryside with a distant horizon lost in the mist are sufficient subject-matter for his works, in which atmospheric effects prevail and light values are expressed in almost monochromatic shades limited to greens and browns with various tones of grey, applied with rapid brushstrokes which achieve an intensely realistic effect.

GREBER. See de Bray.

HEDA, Willem Klaesz (Haarlem 1594-1680/82). Haarlem School. Together with Pieter Claesz, Heda was one of the most outstanding representatives of the Haarlem school of still-life painters. Like Claesz, he used a simple type of composition consisting of few still-life elements arranged on a table, for example a glass, some oysters, the remains of a meal on metal plates, pieces of bread, all enveloped by a unifying atmosphere with subtle contrasts of light and harmonious colouring. In comparison with Claesz' simple compositions, Heda's are more decorative and varied.

2754 **«Still life»** (Canvas, 54 × 71 cm). Signed and dated 1657.

2755 **«Still life»** (Canvas, 52 × 74 cm). This is the most elaborate and overladen of Heda's compositions.

2756 **«Still life»** (Canvas, 52 × 73 cm). Signed. The clock is possibly meant to symbolize Time, as is frequent in this kind of painting.

HEEM, Jan Davidsz de Heem (b. Utrecht 1606; d. Antwerp 1683). Heem was renowned throughout Europe as a still-life artist. He lived most of his life in Antwerp and combined Dutch refinement with a touch of Flemish opulence in his works, which were copied and imitated over and again by his many followers. His rich, decorative still lifes are composed of flowers and juicy-looking fruit combined with ornately worked metal utensils and delicate pieces of crystal. *Chiaroscuro* is used to set off the refined range of greys and ochres; a symbolic reference to the transience of life and beauty underlies the apparent reality of his works.

2089 **«Still life»** (Wood, 43 × 81 cm). Signed. Next to the rich fruit and utensils there is a clock, symbol of Time.

2090 **«Still life»** (Wood, 49 × 64 cm). Signed. Here also the first signs of decay on the fruit allude to Time and the transience of beauty.

HEEM (?).

1997 **«Valour and Abundance in a garland of flowers and fruits»** (Wood, 84 × 54 cm). Although this work has been ascribed to Heem, its style is closer to that of the exuberant and colourful Flemish Masters.

HEEM, Follower.

2091 See Benedetti in Flemish Masters.

2093 See Benedetti in Flemish Masters.

HOBBEMA. See Ruisdael, Follower.

JOHNSON or JANSSEN, Cornelis Janssen van Ceulen (b. London 1593; d. Utrecht 1664).

2588 **«Portrait of a young man»** (Canvas, 74 × 60 cm). This is a very sober portrait whose elegance is related to works by Van Dyck, whom Johnson imitated in Holland.

KONINCK, Salomon (Amsterdam 1609-1656). Amsterdam School.

2974 **«A philosopher»** (Wood, 71 × 54 cm). Recently this work has been ascribed by art historians to Abraham van der Hecke, one of Koninck's imitators; but independently of whether it was painted by the master or his pupil, it is an interesting and exquisitely beautiful work and in this Museum represents the circle of Rembrandt followers in Amsterdam. Here we find the latter's strong *chiaroscuro,* the brown and golden tones, the ample space around the figure of the meditating philosopher, a subject that also appealed to Rembrandt; but it reveals greater attention to ornamentation, like the sheen on the textiles or still-life details, which suggest a more superficial, decorative artist who lacked Rembrandt's profound psychological approach.

LIN, Herman van (active in Utrecht between 1659-1670).

2120 **«Encounter of Cavalry troops»** (Canvas, 61 × 50 cm). Although it was originally attributed to Eglon van der Neer, this battle piece has recently been considered by art critics to correspond to Lin's style; the composition's geometric pattern is very precise and contributes towards the violent impression of the skirmish, while the dark, looming clouds at the top of the picture also heighten this feeling of tenseness.

METSU, Gabriel (b. Leyden 1629; d. Amsterdam 1667). Leyden School.

2103 **«Dead rooster»** (Canvas, 57 × 40 cm). Signed. This is considered Metsu's most important work as a still-life painter and at the same time one of the most remarkable examples of this branch of Dutch painting. Its admirable finish and enamel-like technique reveal the refined style of the Leyden School. Metsu's strong *chiaroscuro* reflects the influence of Rembrandt, but he used short, meticulous brushstrokes to render the dead rooster's plumage in an incredibly realistic manner; the heavy bird hangs in a perfectly balanced and rigorously geometric composition. Another accomplishment is the range of colours: the bird's whiteness is silhouetted against a dark background and the only tone that enlivens the work is the red of the crest.

MIEREVELT, Michiel Hans van (Delft 1567-1641). Delft School. Mierevelt was one of the most famous portraitists of the Delft School and painted in accordance with the prevailing Dutch taste for sober compositions and a highly-detailed portrayal of the sitter including precise description of face, hands and clothes. He left numerous works in which he portrayed members of the aristocracy and wealthy bourgeois circles.

2106 **«A Dutch lady»** (Wood, 121 × 91 cm). It is a high-quality work, but cannot be ascribed to Mierevelt with absolute certainty.

2976 **«Portrait of a lady»** (Canvas, 63 × 51 cm). Signed. The sitter was Elisabeth von Bronckhorst and the work is a fine example of Mierevelt's meticulous and highly-detailed portraits.

2977 **«Portrait of a gentleman»** (Canvas, 63 × 51 cm). This work is considered to be the companion piece to the preceding portrait; the sitter was probably William of Bavaria, the husband of Elisabeth von Bronckhorst.

NEER, Eglon Hendrick van der. See Herman van Lin.

2121. Ostade. Concert in the country.

OSTADE, Adriaen van (Haarlem 1610-1684). Haarlem School. Ostade was a follower of Frans Hals and developed on a little-known branch of the latter's artistic production: that of his small *genre* pictures, around which Ostade centred all his work. He was also influenced by the Flemish artist Adriaen Brouwer (see Flemish Masters) and found a constant source of inspiration in scenes from everyday life, in taverns and home interiors, festivities, brawls and drunkenness in humble, sometimes even miserable settings, which he interpreted in a very satirical and at times burlesque spirit, while on other occasions his tone is symbolic and moralizing, in fitting with the strict, Puritan outlook of Protestant beliefs. Ostade used Rembrandt's light contrasts; the colouring of his works is refined, with predominance of ochres and greens, interrupted at times by very harmonious touches of reds and whites or pale blues. His interiors are spacious and pervaded by unifying light and his shapes are blurred to the point of abstraction.

2121 **«Concert in the country»** (Wood, 27 × 30 cm). Signed. This and the following Nos. were purchased by Charles IV before he became King.

2122 **«A country kitchen»** (Wood, 23 × 29 cm). Signed.

2123 **«Villagers singing»** (Wood, 24 × 29 cm). Signed and dated 1632. This is a companion piece to the preceding work and an example of his early style.

2126 **«Concert in the country»** (Wood, 29 × 40 cm). Signed and dated 1638.

OSTADE, Follower.

2124 **«The five Senses: Sight»** (Wood, 23 × 32 cm).

2125 **«The five Senses: Hearing»** (Wood, 23 × 32 cm). This is a pendant to the preceding No. and both are possibly copies of untraceable originals by Van Ostade intended to symbolize the five senses in *genre* pictures.

PALAMEDESZ, Anthon. See Van der Lamen in Flemish Masters.

PALTHE, Gerard (b. Degenkamp 1681; d. Deventer c. 1750).

2127 **«Young man drawing»** (Wood, 20 × 24 cm). Signed. This is not a particularly high-quality example of 18th-century Dutch painting; it follows on the artistic trends of the preceding century with its intimate mood and artificial light effects.

PARCELLIS or Porcellis. See Jan Peeters in Flemish Masters.

POELENBURGH, Cornelis van (Utrecht 1586-1667). Utrecht School. Dutch landscape painter; together with Breenbergh, with whom he studied in Rome, Poelenburgh was one of the most outstanding Dutch representatives of Italianate landscape painting. He used cool tones in his colouring and his compositions always contain classical ruins or mythological scenes to evoke Antiquity in the same way as the Italian artists. Many painters imitated his style.

2129 **«Diana's bath»** (Copper, 44 × 56 cm). The figures are very delicate and the trees stand out against the *sfumato* background.

2130 **«Landscape with ruins»** (Wood, 42 × 56 cm). The pastoral scene is combined with a real Roman landscape.

POTTER, Paulus (b. Enkhuijzen 1625; d. Amsterdam 1654). Amsterdam School.

2131 **«Landscape with two cows and a goat»** (Wood, 30 × 35 cm). Signed and dated 1652. This is an example of another of the most frequent branches of Dutch painting: landscapes with animals where these become the central part of the scene. Potter was the best representative of this kind of painting, which was very popular in Holland and reproduced the true Dutch countryside.

REMBRANDT, Harmensz van Rijn (b. Leyden 1606; d. Amsterdam 1669). Rembrandt was born in the heart of a peasant family in Leyden; his father was a miller and wanted his son to receive a humanistic education «to serve his city and his fatherland in the best possible way», according to biographers' accounts. He attended the University of Leyden, but his talent for painting made his father decide to let him follow his artistic inclination. He entered the studio of Jacob van Swanenburg, a little-known painter of architectural settings and scenes of Hell, who does not seem to have made much of an impression on Rembrandt. He moved to Amsterdam, a more important cultural centre than his native town, and studied under Pieter Lastman, who belonged to the group of Dutch Caravaggists, from whom Rembrandt learnt his particular technique in contrasting light and shade effects. However, the young artist soon became independent and by 1632 he had settled definitively in Amsterdam. He developed a style of his own, creative, original and personal, which was already completely formed at an early age. He started to produce paintings with biblical subjects, philosophers lost in meditation and his first self-portraits,

2132. Rembrandt. Artemisia.

2131. Potter. Landscape with two cows and a goat.

which he repeated many times during his lifetime. He lived in the Jewish quarter of Amsterdam most of his life and the constant contact with the Jewish community, its rites and clothing can be discerned in the somewhat exotic, at times Oriental air of many of his works. He was attracted by age-worn faces, meditating poses, spacious rooms with a somewhat gloomy, dusty and silent air pervaded by a mysterious half-light and broken at times by a golden ray that makes the scene appear both real and fantastic, whereas on other occasions the light seems to emanate from the figures themselves. Rembrandt's technique was at first meticulous, but later turned energetic, executed with thick brushstrokes, and finally left the shapes unfinished; his rich colouring, which at the outset consisted of warm, glowing colours, gradually turned darker, like the tragedy of his own life. In 1634, at the age of 28 and in a comfortable economic position, he married Saskia, the daughter of an important antique dealer in Amsterdam; she was the love of his life and a faithful companion, but she died young, leaving him alone with his small son, Tito. On the other hand, Rembrandt was a fervent collector of works of art, jewelry and musical instruments and this collector's passion was the cause of his financial ruin since he spent enormous sums of money on works of art. In 1656 he had to sell his house and collections in order to pay his debts and move into one of the poorest quarters of Amsterdam. Aged, far from his friends and forgotten by his former patrons who no longer understood his very personal kind of painting, he received another blow in 1668 when his son Tito died, which probably accelerated his own death the following year. One of the greatest artists of all times ended his life in poverty and obscurity.

2132 **«Artemisia»** (Canvas, 142 × 153 cm). Signed and dated 1634. This is the only work in the Prado that is without doubt by Rembrandt; it is one of his earlier masterpieces, painted in 1634, the year he married Saskia, a prosperous and happy period of his life. The work has been interpreted in two different manners: some critics consider that it represents Artemisia about to drink the cup containing the ashes of her dead husband Mausolus, whereas others believe that it is Sophonisba preparing to drink the poison sent her by her husband to avoid her falling into the hands of Scipio. It is at all events a tribute to conjugal love and faithfulness, probably dedicated to Rembrandt's wife Saskia, who, according to some critics, sat for the artist for this work. It is a very beautiful painting with its majestically monumental figure, the effects of light and *chiaroscuro* and the mysterious half-light in the background where we catch a glimpse of an old woman who seems to be a passive spectator to the dramatic scene.

2808 «Self-portrait» (Canvas, 81 × 65 cm). This is considered an excellent copy after an original kept in London.
REMBRANDT, Follower.

2133 «Young girl with a barrel» (Canvas, 95 × 71 cm). Some art critics consider that this follower of Rembrandt did not belong to the Dutch School.
RUISDAEL, Jacob van (b. Haarlem 1628/29; d. Amsterdam 1682). Ruisdael was one of the best Dutch landscape painters and represents the most Classicist trend in this branch. He used mellow brushwork to enrich the surface of his paintings, trees and distant villages and with his fast, vibrating touches he made nature come to life in a way unknown before, which anticipated 18th-century English landscape painters. Characteristic features of Ruisdael are vast spaces extending as far as the eye can see and dark green tones that render perfectly his shady woodlands at times pervaded by a deeply melancholy and lonely mood.

1728 «Woodland» (Wood, 55 × 61 cm). This landscape reflects a dramatic view of nature.

1729 «Woodland» (Wood, 61 × 61 cm). Signed. These two works were purchased by Charles IV.
RUISDAEL, Follower.

2860 «Landscape» (Wood, 40 × 65 cm). Signed. This work was originally attributed to Hobbema, but art historians consider the signature to be false and the style related to that of Ruisdael's followers.
SCHALCKEN, Godfried (b. Made 1643; d. The Hague 1706). The Hague School. A portraitist and *genre* painter, Schalken specialized in small, exquisitely finished pictures which were very much appreciated by Dutch collectors, especially in the 18th century. He left in particular nocturnal scenes with artificial lighting which produces attractive light contrasts.

2135 «Effect of artificial light» (Canvas, 58 × 47 cm). Signed. Portrait of a man by candlelight.

2587 «Man in a feathered cap» (Wood, 18 × 15 cm). The perfection and highly-refined details recall miniature work.
SCHOEFF, Johannes Pietersz (b. The Hague 1608; d. Bergen after 1666).

2087 «River scene» (Wood, 49 × 76 cm). Signed. Schoeff was a landscape painter of secondary importance, a pupil of Van Goyen whose bright, atmospheric style he followed very closely, although less vigorously.
SMITS, Theodorus (Dordrecht (?) c. 1635-1707). Dordrecht School.

1847 «Still life» (Wood, 26 × 35 cm). Smits was a still-life artist who painted in the traditional Dutch style without reaching the level of the great masters.
STEENWIJCK «the Younger», Hendrick van (b. Amsterdam c. 1580; d. London 1649). Steenwijck was a Dutch representative of the branch of architectural paintings, church interiors and views of cities, in which he used simple elements and a rather forced perspective. His compositions are generally small and executed with masterly, highly-detailed technique, precise draughtsmanship and mellow colouring.

2138 «Jesus before Pontius Pilate» (Copper, 41 × 50 cm). The artificial light effects break the monotony of the scene.

2139 «St. Peter denying Christ» (Copper, 42 × 50 cm). The companion piece to the preceding No., this work represents a very attractive scene in

2974. Koninck. A philosopher.   2808. Rembrandt. Self-portrait.

which the light effects emphasize the architectonic elements leaving the groups of figures in a mysterious half-light.

STEENWYCK, Pieter van (active in Delft mid-17th century).

2137 **«Emblem of Death»** (Wood, 34 × 46 cm). Signed. This is an example of a *Vanitas* still life in the sober, refined, highly-detailed and masterly style of the Leyden School. The elements of the composition, such as the skull on the book in the centre, allude to the vanity of knowledge and science, and the musical instruments symbolize the transience of worldly pleasures.

STOMER, Matthias (b. Amersfoort c. 1600; d. Sicily after 1650). Little is known of the biography of Stomer, who possibly studied in Utrecht to judge by his style, similar to that of Honthorst. In 1630 he is known to have been in Rome, where the naturalistic style of the Caravaggists appealed to his Northern sensibility, anxious to convey concrete, life-like scenes; Stomer also adopted Caravaggio's striking light contrasts in his works and was one of the first, with Honthorst and Terbruggen, to introduce Tenebrism in Holland.

127 **«Roman charity»** (Canvas, 128 × 144 cm). There are doubts about attributing this work to Stomer; it represents a frequent scene in Italian painting: the aged Cimon being fed by his daughter in prison.

1963 **«The incredulity of St. Thomas»** (Canvas, 125 × 99 cm). In the past this work has been attributed both to Honthorst and Terbruggen, but now it is generally accepted by art critics as a work by Stomer due to the brownish and reddish tones of its colouring, smooth flesh textures and energetic, wide, hard brushstrokes. It is an excellent work and a good example of the Dutch Caravaggists.

SWANEVELT, Herman van (b. Woerden c. 1600; d. Paris 1655). Utrecht School. Together with Breenbergh and Poelenburgh, Swanevelt was one of the artists who in the first half of the 17th century painted idealized and classical landscapes in the Italian manner. He lived in Rome in the same house as Claude Lorrain (see French Masters), which was a decisive factor in forming his style; like his French colleague, Swanevelt showed a preference for central, orderly compositions, golden late-afternoon light effects and small figures that seem lost in his landscapes. On his return from Italy he settled in Paris and visited Holland frequently, thus contributing towards spreading this kind of classical landscape painting in these countries.

2063 **«Landscape with St. Rosalia of Palermo»** (Canvas, 158 × 234 cm). Here the artist shows interest in the dramatic effects of a stormy sky.

2064 **«Landscape with St. Bruno»** (Canvas, 158 × 232 cm). Like the preceding landscape, this work was attributed to Jan Both, but current opinion among art critics considers it to be by Swanevelt. The highly-detailed rendering of the small garden in the centre is characteristic of Northern-born artists.

2065 **«Landscape with St. Benedict»** (Canvas, 158 × 232 cm). This work belongs to the same series as the two preceding ones. They came from the Buen Retiro Palace and were commissioned by Philip IV together with others by Claude Lorrain and Poussin for a series of landscapes with hermits.

2141 **«Landscape with a river and anglers»** (Canvas, 210 × 156 cm). This work was also commissioned by Philip IV.

VLIEGER, Simon de (b. Rotterdam 1601; d. Weeps 1653). Rotterdam School.

1581 **«Seascape»** (Wood, 41 × 60 cm). A Dutch marine painter, Vlieger's works contain wide expanses of open sea near coastlines with fantastic, decorative rocks. He showed an exquisite sense for atmospheric and aerial perspective.

VOLLENHOVEN, Herman van (active in Utrecht in the first half of the 17th century.

2142 **«Dead birds»** (Wood, 26 × 36 cm). Signed and dated. This is a realistic and precisely executed still life.

WIERINGEN, Cornelis Claesz van (Haarlem 1560-1643). Haarlem School.

2143 **«Naval combat»** (Wood, 43 × 90 cm). Signed. Wieringen painted seapieces and naval battles with a profusion of highly-finished detail and excellent draughtsmanship; the atmospheric sense shown by later artists is still missing in his works.

WILLAERTS, Adam (b. Antwerp 1577; d. Utrecht 1639). Utrecht School.

1899 **«Seascape»** (Canvas, 83 × 125 cm). Signed and dated 1621. This work is characteristic of Willaerts' sea-pieces, in which he introduced anecdotic elements to represent seashores or quays enlivened by small figures.

WITENWAEL or Uytewael, Joachim (Utrecht c. 1566-1638). Utrecht School.

2151. Philips Wouwermans. In front of an inn.

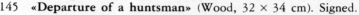

2157   «The Adoration of the Shepherds» (Wood, 62 × 99 cm). Signed and
dated 1625. Witenwael belonged to the generation of Dutch Mannerist
artists. He lived in Italy, particularly in Venice, at the end of the 16th
century. His work reveals the influence of Venetian artists, specially
the Bassanos (see Italian Masters). His figures are elongated and energetic,
in Mannerist-style precarious poses and the brilliant enamel-like technique
emphasizes the vivid yellows, reds and dark greens of his palette.
WOUWERMANS, Philips (Haarlem 1619-1668). Haarlem School.
Wouwermans specialized in *genre* pictures, battles, hunting scenes, stables
with soldiers, etc., his chief characteristic being that very finely and naturalistically depicted horses appear in all his paintings. His attractive works
were very much appreciated in the 18th century and could be found in
every important collection in Europe, as was the case in that of Philip V
and Elizabeth Farnese, whose paintings are now distributed between the
Prado and the royal collection. Wouwermans possibly studied under Frans
Hals in Haarlem, but he soon travelled to Rome, where he stayed for ten
years and was in contact with the *bamboccianti,* who painted realistic
scenes of popular, everyday life. Wouwermans' style is elegant; with fine
brushstrokes and an exquisite range of colours he conveyed an impression
of transparent atmosphere in his landscapes with their hazy backgrounds
and very decoratively arranged trees which recall the brightness of artists
like Dughet and Claude Lorrain, also active in Rome at the time.

2145   «Departure of a huntsman» (Wood, 32 × 34 cm). Signed.

1728. Ruisdael. Woodland.

2146   «Two horses» (Wood, 33 × 32 cm). Signed. This work is characteristic of
Wouwermans in its atmospheric feeling stressed by the wide expanse at the top.
2147   «Departure for a hunt» (Canvas, 76 × 105 cm).
2148   «Hare-hunt» (Canvas, 77 × 105 cm). Signed. It could be a pendant to the
preceding No. to judge by its measurements and subject-matter. The view
of the landscape is also the same, with its high horizon line and the plain
seen from a raised viewpoint making the small, vividly-coloured figures
appear lost in the landscape.
2149   «Hawking scene» (Canvas, 50 × 66 cm). The style of this work is the
same as that of the two preceding pictures.
2150   «Departure for a hunt» (Canvas, 80 × 70 cm). Signed. This work includes
the Fountain of Neptune as a decorative motif and reminder of the artist's
stay in Rome.
2151   «In front of an inn» (Wood, 37 × 47 cm). Signed. This is one of the

2087. Schoeff. River scene.

finest of Wouwermans' works in the Prado, with its highly-detailed depiction of the inside of the inn stables and the bright door-opening which gives the composition an extremely realistic touch.

2152   «Stopover in front of a tavern» (Canvas, 61 × 73 cm). Signed.

2154   «Combat between lancers and foot soldiers» (Canvas, 60 × 71 cm). Signed. This is a sample of Wouwermans' battle pieces, a widespread branch of painting in 17th-century Europe, devastated by constant warfare, and very popular with collectors.

2748   «Landscape with a windmill» (Wood, 19 × 25 cm). This work is not by Wouwermans; it is probably by an early 17th-century Flemish artist.

ANONYMOUS DUTCH MASTERS

1978   «Louise Henriette of Orange-Nassau» (Canvas, 37 × 32 cm). She was the daughter of Frederick Henry of Nassau and married the Elector of Brandenburg, Frederick William.

2160   «Ships braving a storm» (Wood, 37 × 56 cm).

2165-6 See C. van Huynen in Flemish Masters.

2167   «Jan van Oldenbarnevelt» (Wood, 78 × 60 cm). See Cuyp.

2751   «Landscape with a shepherd and sheep» (Wood, 20 × 25 cm).

2752   «Landscape with shepherds» (Wood, 20 × 25 cm). This is the companion piece to the preceding No.

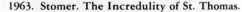

1963. Stomer. The Incredulity of St. Thomas.

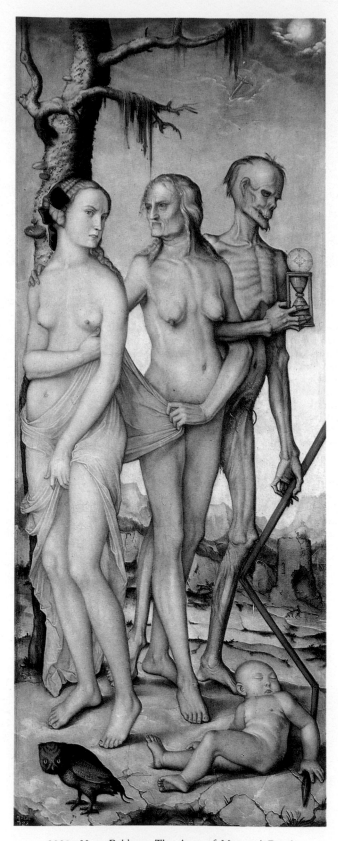

2220. Hans Baldung. The Ages of Man and Death.

2179. Albrecht Dürer. Self-portrait. (detail)

GERMAN MASTERS

The collection of works by German masters in the Prado is surprisingly small considering the close political ties between Spain and the Empire during the 16th century. It is difficult to understand why hardly any German paintings reached the royal collections at the time. Possibly the artistic sensibility of the Emperor Charles V and his son Philip II was too Italianized to appreciate the dramatic, expressionistic style of the German masters, so far removed from the formal beauty and mythological themes of 16th-century Mediterranean Classicism. However, thanks to gifts made to Philip IV and also to purchases in the 17th-century, the Prado now possesses some important 16th-century works, for example four paintings by the great German Renaissance artist Albrecht Dürer which are very fine examples of this brilliant master's art and aesthetic values. Dürer's followers are represented by Baldung Grien and Cranach, whose painting illustrates the trend towards Mannerism in the mid-16th century, with a linear, fantastic vein full of moralizing allegories that denote deeply rooted Gothic origin underlying the outward Renaissance elegance. There is nothing by other great masters like Grünewald or Altdorfer and even the small *Portrait of an old man* attributed to Holbein, although it is an excellent work, has not been definitively accepted by art critics as genuine.

The only example of 17th-century German art is a small copper-plate by Elmsheimer, very representative and characteristic of his style. The vast, flamboyant German Baroque is not represented in Spain and we have to wait until the 18th century to find a really outstanding artist, Anton Raffael Mengs, one of the pioneers of Neo-Classicism, but whose works still have a Rococo flavour. He was Court Painter to King Charles III, who called him to Spain to decorate the cupolas of the Royal Palace in Madrid on its completion. Mengs is well represented in the Prado, both with elegant portraits and religious paintings.

2184. Amberger. The wife of the goldsmith Jörg Zörer.

AMBERGER, Christoph (Augsburg 1500-1561/2).
2183   «The goldsmith Jörg Zörer from Augsburg» (?) (Wood, 78 × 51 cm). Amberger was an excellent portrait-painter and probably studied in Augsburg under Hans Burgkmeir; to judge by his realistic style he must have been acquainted with Holbein's portraits. His late works reveal Venetian influence: it should be borne in mind that Titian lived and worked in Augsburg for over a year. In this portrait and the following one Amberger paints in the pure German tradition. The clear-cut forms and naturalistic portrayal of the sitters are stressed by the imaginary wooden background, which all contributes towards producing an extraordinarily realistic effect.
2184   «The wife of the goldsmith Jörg Zörer» (Wood, 68 × 51 cm).
BALDUNG GRIEN, Hans (b. Schwäbisch-Gmünd 1484/5; d. Strasbourg 1545). Baldung Grien was a painter and engraver who trained in Dürer's workshop in Nuremberg, where he studied the Italian Renaissance discoveries with regard to figure proportions and composition. The evolution of his own personal style began after his return to Strasbourg in

1508; although derived from that of his master, it became more expressive, bolder and strikingly dramatic, whereas the stylized and refined character of his late works brings them close to the Mannerist style that had
begun to pervade art at the time as a result of the political and religious
crisis affecting Europe.

2175. Cranach. Hunt in honour of Charles V near the Castle of Torgau.

2219 «Harmony or the Three Graces» (Wood, 151 × 61 cm). See No. 2220.
2220 «The Ages of Man and Death» (Wood, 151 × 61 cm). This is the companion piece to the preceding work; they exemplify the moralizing allegories
characteristic of the Middle Ages, combined with mythological elements
typical of the Renaissance. Due to their extreme delicacy, elongated figures, refined details and colouring they should probably be dated towards
the end of Baldung Grien's life. The mellow female nudes of the *Harmony*
panel, with their gay expressions and delicate draperies, contrast with the
dramatic, arid landscape, disconcerting expressions of the two women and
appalling figure of Death in the *Ages of Man.*
CRANACH, Lucas Sunder or Munder von Cranach, called «Cranach
the Elder» (b. Kronach 1472; d. Weimar 1553). The evolution of Cranach's painting runs along similar lines to that of Baldung Grien. His early
dramatic and expressionistic style gradually became more elegant, refined
and abstract with a fantastic and sensuous touch that relates him to Manner-

2176. Cranach. Hunt in honour of Charles V near the Castle of Torgau.

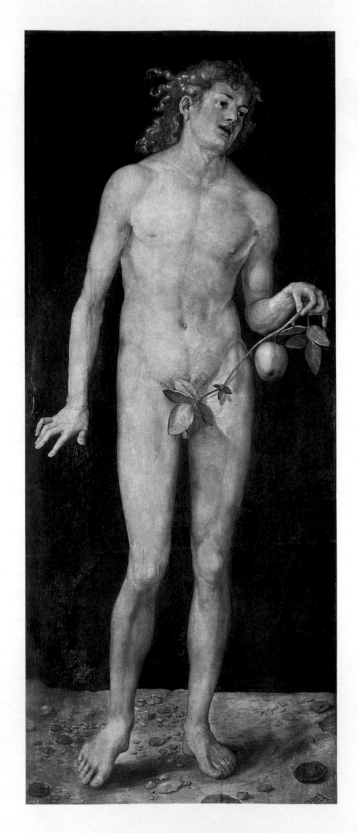

2177. Albrecht Dürer. Adam.

2178. Albrecht Dürer. Eve.

ism. A further important element in his works is the landscape; during a stay in Vienna he became one of the representatives of the Danube School of landscape-painters, for whom nature was an excuse for elaborate and decorative flights of fancy. Cranach was Court Painter to the Saxon Elector Frederick the Wise and a friend of Luther.

2175 **«Hunt in honour of Charles V near the Castle of Torgau»** (Wood, 114 × 175 cm). Signed and dated 1544. See No. 2176.

2176 **«Hunt in honour of Charles V near the Castle of Torgau»** (Wood, 118 × 177 cm). The panels show two aspects of a hunt organized by the Elector in honour of the Emperor, who, incidentally, was to take the former prisoner three years later at the battle of Mühlberg (see Titian). The artist's son, Lucas Cranach «the Younger», probably collaborated on this work. The landscape occupies practically the entire background and acts as a setting for the different scenes of the stag hunt, depicted with great liveliness, colouring and detail. For modern spectators there is possibly a somewhat archaic and ingenuous air about the representation of these two scenes.

2180. Dürer. Portrait of an unknown man.

DÜRER, Albrecht (Nuremberg 1471-1528). Dürer was the first Renaissance painter in Northern Europe. Son of a goldsmith, he received his first training in his father's workshop and was later apprenticed to the artist Michael Wolgemut, who taught him painting and engraving, the latter being particularly important in Dürer's art. He travelled to Italy and in 1494 he was to be found studying the principles of Renaissance art in Venice, especially the central concept of space, mathematical harmony of the composition and the search for ideal beauty. He visited other Italian cities and after a second period in Venice in 1505 returned to Nuremberg, where he wrote a treatise on proportion in the human figure and on perspective, which had a widespread influence among Northern artists in the 16th century. In Dürer's painting we find monumental Italian-style forms, his figures reveal a sense of mass and plasticity, beauty and poise that is all far-removed from the world of Gothic art; however, of Gothic and in particular German origin are Dürer's brilliant colouring, his fondness for meticulous technical execution and accuracy, which contributes towards making his work one of the milestones in the history of universal art.

2177 **«Adam»** (Wood, 209 × 81 cm). Signed with the monogram AD. See No. 2178.

2178 **«Eve»** (Wood, 209 × 80 cm). Signed and dated 1507. These two panels were sent as a gift to Philip IV by Queen Christina of Sweden; they are two of Dürer's most important works and the first life-size nude paintings in Northern European art. Dürer painted them in 1507, after his second visit to Venice; he has used the Biblical theme to make a study of the proportions of the human figure. The long bodies and flowing forms, especially in *Eve,* still have a Gothic flavour, whereas the intensely emotional expressions and grand fullness of the forms bear witness to the influence of the Classical Mediterranean world.

2179 **«Self-portrait»** (Wood, 52 × 41 cm). Signed and dated 1498. This portrait, painted when Dürer was twenty-six years old, is a masterpiece and exemplifies the new standing of the artist at the time of the Renaissance. Far-removed from the world of the Medieval craftsman, with an aloof, elegant and self-assured air Dürer asserts his personality as a man of letters and intellectual who belonged to the most cultured circles of his time, a man whose features should be known by his contemporaries and illustrate the fame, success and wealth that he had attained by means of his art. His technique, highly detailed description and deeply expressive gaze all reveal a true master. This work was purchased by Philip IV from the estate of King Charles I of England.

2180 **«Portrait of an unknown man»** (Wood, 50 × 36 cm). Signed and dated 1524. It has not been possible to identify the sitter, whose energetic personality is indicated by Dürer here in the tension of his hands, tight, thin lips and knitted brows. The expressive power of the portrait is heightened by the intense light on the man's features and the reduced surrounding space.

ELSHEIMER, Adam (b. Frankfurt-on-the-Main 1578; d. Rome 1610). This German-born artist travelled to Venice early in life, attracted by the art of Tintoretto with its brilliant colouring and strongly contrasted light, but later he settled in Rome. There he produced small landscape paintings, which sometimes included Biblical or mythological scenes; the shadiness of nature in these pictures gives them an air of mystery, an impression that is heightened by nocturnal light, moonlight or artificial light that emphasizes the contrasts. His works were very successful and due to their small size and copper plates they were exported throughout Europe.

2181 **«Ceres and Stellio»** (Copper, 30 × 25 cm). Dating from about 1608, this small copper-plate was engraved and also reproduced in painting several times. It represents a scene from Ovid's *Metamorphoses:* in her search for her daughter Proserpine, the goddess Ceres arrives at the cottage of an old woman whom she asks for water; while she is drinking a young boy approaches and taunts her and the offended goddess transforms him into a tiny lizard. With its nocturnal lighting and depiction of the small, shiny leaves, the work is very characteristic of Elmsheimer.

2181. Elsheimer. Ceres and Stellio.

FRANKFURT, Master of (active between 1460 and 1515/20).
1941 **«St. Catherine»** (Wood, 79 × 27 cm). See No. 1942.
1942 **«St. Barbara»** (Wood, 79 × 27 cm). This and the preceding panel were originally two wings of a triptych. The anonymous master worked in

2182. Hans Holbein. Portrait of an old man.

Frankfurt until 1490 and after 1491 he is known to have been in Antwerp. His style was eclectic, inspired in Flemish masters such as van Orley and van Cleve, whose forms and colouring he imitated.

HOLBEIN, Hans Holbein «the Younger» (?) (b. Augsburg 1497/8; d. London 1543).

2182   **«Portrait of an old man»** (Wood, 62 × 47 cm). The attribution of this work to Holbein is questioned by some art critics, who ascribe it to Joos van Cleve's mature period. Its excellent quality is evident: the masterly treatment of the black draperies is matched by the wonderful psychological characterization of the sitter with his weary expression and disdainful turn of the mouth. With its intense expressiveness and meticulous, highly realistic details both in the draperies and in the wrinkled face and crooked nose, this portrait seems to be related to the more penetrating and keener character of German rather than Flemish painting.

KAUFFMANN, Angelica (b. Chur, Switzerland 1741; d. Rome 1807). She was the daughter of a painter, from whom she received her first training as an artist. In 1763 she was in Rome in contact with the cultural circles that created the Neo-Classical movement, whose principal artists as well as the art scholar Winckelmann were among her friends. Her painting follows the Neo-Classical trend in style and composition. She lived in England for a few years, where her works were highly successful, but then returned to Rome, where she spent rest of her life. She received the highest honours as an artist: she was one of the founding members of the Royal Academy in London and also a member of the Academies of Painting of Rome, Bologna, Florence and Venice.

2473   **«Anna von Escher van Muralt»** (Canvas, 110 × 86 cm). This portrait is characteristic of Angelica Kauffmann's work, with its rich colouring and elegant, distinguished manner of presenting the sitter. The landscape background with Classical monuments is very much in keeping with the taste of the time.

MECKENEN, Israhel van (Bocholt c. 1450-1503).

2185   **«St. Jerome»** (Wood, 53 × 70 cm). This artist is best known for his engravings, a large number of which have been handed down to us. The same expressiveness as in his prints can be found in his pictorial work, together with a fondness for broken lines, ample folds, distorted poses and somewhat grotesque, caricature-like faces, all of which is exemplified in this *St. Jerome* ascribed to him in the Prado.

MENGS, Anton Raffael (b. Aussig, Bohemia 1728; d. Rome 1779). Mengs' importance as an artist consists primarily in his role in founding and propagating the Neo-Classical movement. The son of a painter from Dresden, his style is by no means limited to his native country; early in life he accompanied his father to Rome and by the age of eighteen he was engaged in the study of Classical art, Michelangelo and Raphael, which was to prove essential for his later work. On his return to Dresden in 1746 he was appointed Court Painter to Augustus III. However, the cultural environment of Rome attracted him too much; in 1748 he returned to Italy, visiting Venice, Parma and Bologna to study the painting of these famous schools before settling in Rome. In 1752 he was accepted as a member of the Academy of San Luca, made the acquaintance of the German art scholar Winckelmann and joined the circle of artists developing the new style. From then on Mengs' art spread the Neo-Classical style throughout Europe. Charles III of Spain appointed him Court Painter and he spent almost ten years in Madrid, where he exerted an important influence both as a painter (decorations in the Royal Palace, portraits) and as honorary Director of the Academy of San Fernando on the young generation of Spanish artists (Maella, Bayeu, Goya, Vicente López). The Prado possesses a large number of his portraits, the most important side of his work. They are flattering, courtly portraits with elegant, often affected poses, which are however redeemed by the brilliant, enamel-like technique with which Mengs achieves flesh tones resembling fine porcelain and wonderfully realistic effects in silks, laces and other textiles.

2186   **«Maria Josepha of Lorraine, Archduchess of Austria»** (Canvas, 128 × 98 cm). Daughter of Francis I and Maria Theresa of Austria, she died when she was about to marry Ferdinand IV of Naples.

2187   **«Infante Don Antonio Pascual of Bourbon»** (Canvas, 84 × 68 cm). He was a son of the Spanish King Charles III and Maria Amalia of Saxony, born in 1755.

2188 «**Charles IV of Spain as a Prince**» (Canvas, 152 × 110 cm). This sober portrait is reminiscent of Velázquez in the way the prince is presented in hunting dress against a landscape background.

2189 «**Maria Luisa of Parma as Princess of Asturias**» (Canvas, 152 × 110 cm). Daughter of the Duke of Parma, she married the future Charles IV of Spain. This is one of Mengs' most delicate portraits, where he portrayed the grace and vivaciousness of Maria Luisa in her youth; the details of her dress are also depicted in a masterly fashion.

2190 «**Ferdinand IV, King of Naples**» (Canvas, 179 × 130 cm). Signed and dated 1760. Son of the Spanish King Charles III, he was born in Naples in 1751 and later became King of the Two Sicilies.

2191 «**The Archduke Francis of Austria, later Emperor**» (Canvas, 144 × 97 cm). Son of Leopold and Maria Luisa and grandson of the Spanish King Charles III, he became Emperor in 1792 and father-in-law of Napoleon.

2192 «**The Archduke Ferdinand and Archduchess Marianne of Austria**» (Canvas, 147 × 96 cm). These were two of Charles III's grandchildren, son and daughter of Leopold and Maria Luisa.

2193 «**The Archduchess Theresa of Austria**» (Canvas, 144 × 105 cm). Daughter of the Grand Duke of Tuscany, born in 1767, she became Queen of Saxony by her marriage to Anton Clement of Saxony.

2194 «**Maria Caroline of Lorraine, Queen of Naples**» (Canvas, 130 × 153 cm). Daughter of Francis I and Maria Theresa of Austria, she married Ferdinand IV of Naples, son of Charles III.

2195 «**Infante Don Javier of Bourbon**» (Canvas, 82 × 69 cm). He was a son of the Spanish King Charles III.

2196 «**Infante Don Gabriel of Bourbon**» (Canvas, 82 × 69 cm). He was another of Charles III's sons.

2197 «**Self-portrait**» (Wood, 62 × 50 cm). The simplicity and vivaciousness of this self-portrait contrast with Mengs' courtly portraits.

2198 «**Leopold of Lorraine, Grand Duke of Tuscany and later Emperor**» (Canvas, 95 × 72 cm). Son of the Empress Maria Theresa of Austria, he was Grand Duke of Tuscany and Emperor, as Leopold II, from 1790-92.

2199 «**Maria Luisa of Bourbon, Grand Duchess of Tuscany and later Empress**» (Canvas, 116 × 107 cm). She was a daughter of Charles III and married Leopold of Lorraine.

2200 «**Charles III**» (Canvas, 154 × 110 cm). This was the official portrait of the King and for this reason a large number of copies were made. It is a conventional work which still contains some flamboyant Baroque details.

2201 «**Queen Maria Amalia**» (Canvas, 154 × 110 cm). The wife of Charles III, Maria Amalia of Saxony, had died before Mengs came to Spain, so that this portrait must have been painted after another portrait or miniature. The colouring and the description of the draperies are highly attractive.

2202 «**An Apostle**» (Canvas, 63 × 50 cm). See No. 2203.

2203 «**An Apostle**» (Canvas, 63 × 50 cm). These two works were preparatory studies for the *Ascension* in Dresden, which Mengs completed in Madrid in 1769. The technique is soft and very light.

2204 «**The Adoration of the Shepherds**» (Wood, 258 × 191 cm). This work was painted in Rome in 1770 and it is important in Mengs' religious painting; it follows the Italian tradition originated by Correggio of *Adorations* with strongly contrasted nocturnal light effects. The Gloria of the angels also reflects the influence of Correggio.

2205 «**Repentant Mary Magdalene**» (Canvas, 110 × 89 cm). This work with its serene, ordered composition reveals devotional feeling.

2206 «**St. Peter preaching**» (Canvas, 134 × 98 cm). The splendidly realistic figure of the saint stands out in this sober, serene composition.

2568 «**Maria Luisa of Parma**» (Canvas, 48 × 38 cm). This was a preliminary study for a portrait now kept in the Metropolitan Museum in New York. Its unfinished state heightens the impression of spontaneity and vividness.
ROOS, Philipp Peter Roos, called «**Rose of Tivoli**» (b. Frankfurt 1657; d. Rome 1705). He was a German artist who settled in Rome and painted *genre* scenes with very realistic landscapes as a setting for popular scenes, with shepherds and their flocks, in which animals occupy a large proportion of the composition.

2208 «**Shepherd with his flock**» (Canvas, 94 × 130 cm).

2211 «**Shepherdess with goats and sheep**» (Canvas, 196 × 290 cm). The technique is vigorous and very decorative; the artist takes pleasure in light and atmospheric effects.

2568. Anton Raffael Mengs. Maria Luisa of Parma.

2473. Kauffmann. Anna von Escher van Muralt.

VOLLARDT, Jan Christian Vollaert or Vollardt (b. Leipzig 1709; d. Dresden 1769). He was a German landscape painter, well acquainted with Italian art, and his works are inspired in paintings by 17th-century artists such as Dughet. His landscapes are delicate and decorative, with a fine sense of space and light, and ample, bright horizons.

2820 **«Landscape»** (Canvas, 38 × 51 cm). Signed and dated 1758.

2821 **«Landscape»** (Canvas, 38 × 51 cm). Signed and dated 1758. This is a companion piece to the preceding work.

WERTINGEN, Hans Schwabmaler von Wertingen (?) (b. ?; d. Landshut 1533).

2216 **«Frederick III, German Emperor»** (Wood, 47 × 32 cm). Frederick III was Duke of Austria, born in 1415, and became Emperor in 1440; he was the father of Maximilian I. Wertingen was a lesser artist who painted glass decorations and miniatures; this meticulous and highly detailed portrait reveals the latter technique.

ANONYMOUS GERMAN MASTERS.

2037 **«Portrait of an unknown man»** (Canvas, 51 × 42 cm). The attribution of this 18th-century portrait is doubtful; some art critics consider it to be the work of a German contemporary of Mengs.

2276 **«Empress Elisabeth Christina of Brunswick»** (Canvas, 96 × 76 cm). Daughter of Ludwig Rudolf of Blackenburg, she married the Archduke Charles who became Holy Roman Emperor.

2705 **«Charles V»** (Wood, 97 cm in diameter). This portrait shows the Emperor at the age of about thirty.

2790 **«Self-portrait»** (Canvas, 80 × 64 cm). This is an 18th-century work.

2200. Mengs. Charles III. 2201. Mengs. Queen Maria Amalia.

2204. Mengs. The Adoration of the Shepherds.

ENGLISH MASTERS

It has already been mentioned that the reason why the Prado has so few works by Dutch and French masters was primarily political; the same applies to English painting. As a result of the Reformation, Spain and England were enemies from the 16th century on, a state of affairs that lasted until the end of the 18th century. This no doubt accounts for the fact that there were no English works to be found in the Spanish royal collections. However, the Prado now possesses a small selection of 18th-century and early 19th-century English painting. Works by the important landscape painters are missing, as well as Hogarth's satirical paintings, but there is a good display of portraits from this brilliant period of English history, which are the fruit of recent purchases. Gainsborough, Reynolds, Romney and Lawrence are now represented in the Prado and even if these works are not their most famous masterpieces, they do at least illustrate the elegant, noble style and rapid, brilliant technique of the English masters.

GAINSBOROUGH, Thomas (b. Sudbury, Suffolk, 1727; d. London 1788). Gainsborough was one of the most noteworthy representatives of 18th-century English painting. Primarily a landscape painter and portraitist, he trained in London, where he studied the European schools of painting, Dutch and Flemish landscape painting and Van Dyck's portraits. The latter's style had a decisive influence on his work as a portraitist; the numerous portraits he painted are elegant and refined and his wealthy, fashionable sitters, although apparently devoid of feeling and maybe somewhat aloof and self-assured, do not lose their vivaciousness and true-to-life air. The artist's technique is light and transparent and brings out the sheen of textures in a delicate, subtle manner.

2979 **«Dr. Isaac Henrique Sequeira»** (Canvas, 127 × 102 cm). Sequeira was a Portuguese Jew and Gainsborough's doctor.

2990 **«Mr Robert Butcher of Walttamstan»** (Canvas, 75 × 62 cm). Great simplicity is the key-note of this work.

HOPPNER, John (b. Whitechapel 1758; d. London 1810). An English landscape and portrait painter, Hoppner's style derives from that of Reynolds, although evidently he does not reach the latter's standard. His technique is light and sometimes almost sketch-like, which gives his works vivaciousness and movement.

2474 **«Portrait of an unknown lady»** (Wood, 64 × 55 cm). It has been repainted.

3040 **«Mrs. Thornton»** (Canvas, 61 × 74 cm). The sitter's melancholy air is characteristic of Hoppner, as well as the sketch-like technique with long brushstrokes that make the forms appear unfinished.

LAWRENCE, Sir Thomas (b. Bristol 1769; d. London 1830). Lawrence succeeded Reynolds in the post of Court Painter to George III and painted in the same grandiose manner; he was an important figure in English portraiture in the late 18th and early 19th centuries. The style of courtly portraits is necessarily more lavish and decorative than that of portraits painted for wealthy, non-aristocratic circles, but in spite of his extremely rhetoric approach and elegant, prepared poses, Lawrence never lost sight of his sitters' inmost character, which is captured in his best works with absolute mastery.

3001 **«John Vane, 10th Earl of Westmoreland»** (Canvas, 247 × 147 cm). Here Lawrence was evidently inspired by Van Dyck's style to judge by the sitter's elegant, haughty air; Lawrence conjured up all his technical skill to render the rich draperies using light, brilliant brushwork and extremely modern touches in the loose brushstrokes of the landscape background or the Earl's magnificently portrayed head.

2979. Thomas Gainsborough. Dr. Isaac Henrique Sequeira.

2990. Gainsborough. Robert Butcher.   **3012. Lawrence. Miss Marthe Carr.**

3011 **«Lady from the Storer family»** (Canvas, 240 × 148 cm). This work shows a more sober approach than in the preceding courtly portrait and the sitter is portrayed in a calm setting with a landscape background; Lawrence again demonstrates his exquisite technique in the draperies and colour.

3012 **«Miss Marthe Carr»** (Canvas, 76 × 64 cm). This is a wonderful portrait, spontaneous and intimate, and Lawrence has captured the sitter's gesture with great sensibility; the landscape and the transparent silk texture of the white dress are depicted with a definitely modern technique.

OPIE, John (b. St. Agnes 1761; d. London 1807).

3084 **«Portrait of a gentleman»** (Canvas, 100 × 90 cm). The sitter is admirably characterized.

RAEBURN, Sir Henry (b. Stockbridge 1756; d. Edinburgh 1823).

3116 **«Portrait of Mrs. MacLean of Kinlochlaine»** (Canvas, 75 × 63 cm). Raeburn has been called the «Scottish Reynolds» and this portrait bears witness to his debt to the great English master. It is an admirable work in which the artist used long, energetic brush-strokes, allowing the canvas to show through, to capture the sitter's haughty, resolute character.

REYNOLDS, Sir Joshua (b. Plympton 1723; d. London 1792). Together with Gainsborough, Reynolds was one of the greatest 18th-century English portraitists. He received a varied training; after studying art in London he visited Italy (1750-52) and familiarized himself with Italian art; he was particularly attracted by Venetian colouring and the Roman Classicist movement. His career as an artist really began after his return to London when he set up as a portraitist and painted aristocratic and other distinguished sitters. He created a grandiloquent kind of portrait in which he sometimes portrayed his sitters with mythological or religious symbols. He evidently found inspiration for his most intimate portraits in

2986. Reynolds. Portrait of Mr. James Bourdieu.

Van Dyck's work, which influenced all English portraiture, but also in the more sober Dutch masters such as Rembrandt and Frans Hals.

2858 «**Portrait of a clergyman**» (Canvas, 77 × 64 cm). This is typical of Reynolds' most simple portraits where he concentrated on portraying his sitter's face, in this case reflecting all his keenness and intelligence, leaving the rest in the shade.

2986 «**Portrait of Mr. James Bourdieu**» (Canvas, 121 × 61 cm). Dated 1765. This work is also characteristic of Reynolds in his most moderate and sober aspect. It is evidently reminiscent of Van Dyck and possibly also, to a lesser degree, of Venetian colouring and technique.

RIGAUD, John Francis (b. Turin 1742; d. Packington Hall 1807).

2598 «**Three favourite air travellers**» (Oval copper, 36 × 31 cm). This work is almost a *genre* painting and represents a candid and highly-detailed description of an ascent in balloon performed in 1785 by the Italian Vicenzo Lunardi, the Englishman George Biffin and Mrs. Letitia Ann Suge, the first Englishwoman to ascend in a balloon.

2853. Roberts. The Torre del Oro in Seville.

2852. Roberts. The Castle of Alcalá de Guadaira.

ROBERTS, David (b. Edinburgh 1796; d. London 1864).

2852 «**The Castle of Alcalá de Guadaira**» (Canvas, 40 × 48 cm). See No. 2853.
2853 «**The Torre del Oro in Seville**» (Canvas, 39 × 48 cm). Signed and dated 1833. Although these are minor works by Roberts, they are representative of the style of this artist, who travelled throughout Spain between 1833 and 1836 and recorded on his canvases and in water colours different aspects of the Spanish towns and countryside in an exotic, romantic mood that contributed towards spreading this notion of Spain throughout Europe.

ROMNEY, George (b. Dalton-in-Furness 1734; d. Kendal 1802). He was a portraitist trained in the English tradition of elegant and aristocratic portraits, which he enriched with his knowledge of the new Neo-Classical style that he had studied in Paris in 1764 and in Rome from 1773 to 1775.

2584 «**An English gentleman**» (Canvas, 76 × 64 cm). This is a sober and elegant portrait of not very high quality.

3013 **«Portrait of Master Ward»** (Canvas, 126 × 102 cm). This is a very attractive portrait in which Romney follows Gainsborough's moderate, simple style in painting the child in a landscape setting. The sitter is portrayed in an admirably naturalistic manner, in an indolent pose and with a dog sitting at his feet, during a break in his games.

SHEE, Sir Martin Archer (b. Dublin 1769; d. Brighton 1850).

3000 **«Mr. Storer»** (Canvas, 239 × 148 cm). See No. 3014.

3014 **«Anthony Gilbert Storer Esq.»** (Canvas, 240 × 148 cm). Signed and dated 1815. This is the companion piece to the preceding portrait; both are examples of early 19th-century English portraiture, sober and elegant, representing the sitters in their own surroundings. The more interesting work is probably the second one of a gentleman looking through a collection of prints.

ANONYMOUS ENGLISH MASTERS

2407 **«Charles II of England»** (Canvas, 105 × 86 cm). Charles II was born in 1630 and reigned from 1660 to 1685.

2410 **«James II of England»** (Canvas, 105 × 86 cm). James II was the son of Charles I; he was born in 1633 and became King of England in 1685, being obliged to go into exile in 1688.

2550 **«Ferdinand VII»** (Canvas, 80 × 74 cm). This portrait was originally ascribed to a Spanish painter from Cadiz, but is now considered to be the work of an anonymous English artist.

2879 **«The 1st Count of Vilches»** (Canvas, 75 × 64 cm). This is the work of one of Lawrence's followers.

2858. Sir Joshua Reynolds. Portrait of a clergyman.

SCULPTURE

The collection of sculptures in the Prado consists of over 500 pieces, many of them of excellent quality and great historical and artistic value; the majority were purchased by Spanish kings from the 16th century on, others were gifts to the royal family or donations to the Prado Museum and some are the result of comparatively recent purchases. The oldest sculptures in the Prado date from before the Classical Period; the most interesting is possibly a head of the Sumerian *King Gudea* from about 2300 B. C. (No. 435), or an Egyptian *Falcon* in basalt with inlaid agates as eyes dating from about 350 B. C., in the Saite period.

Some of the Classical sculptures belonged to the collection that Philip II kept in the Alcázar in Madrid, which consisted chiefly of busts of Roman emperors or unknown personalities which were used to decorate Renaissance palaces, many of them being 16th-century copies of antique originals. It is certain that the so-called *Venus of Madrid* (No. 44) and the *Venus with a shell* (No. 86), both found in the town of Sagunto, belonged to Philip II. The former is of finer quality and under the delicate folds we can observe the prototype of the Venus of Capua, the Roman work inspired in an original by the Greek sculptor Lysippus, who also made the more famous Venus de Milo.

Only one antique sculpture reached Spain during the reign of Philip IV: the *Apotheosis of Claudius* (No. 225), which Cardinal Ascanio Colonna sent the King as a gift soon after it had been discovered during excavations on the Via Appia in Rome. It consists of an eagle with outspread wings holding in its claws Jupiter's thunderbolt and on its back a bust of the Emperor Claudius (copy of an untraceable original). The technique is interesting since the trepan has been used, which enabled the artist to make deep incisions in the marble, thus achieving an expressive play of light and shadow.

Antinous.

The largest group of Classical sculptures consists of works purchased by Philip V and Queen Elizabeth Farnese in 1724 from the heirs of Prince Livio Odescalchi; this was one of the most famous collections in Rome and had been assembled by Christina of Sweden during the time she lived there. These works then decorated the Palace at La Granja until they were moved to the Prado Museum in 1839. There they were exhibited together with others that the Spanish ambassador in Rome, Nicolás de Azara, who had carried out excavations in Tivoli in 1779, gave to Charles IV. Among other interesting sculptures a beautiful *Bronze head* (No. 99) deserves special mention; it is a fragment of a colossal statue believed to represent Alexander the Great, a Hellenistic original from the 3rd century B. C., with forcefully modelled facial features and hair. A delicate, vivacious bronze *Boy running* (No. 165) is also Hellenistic, a 3rd-century imitation of Praxiteles' prototype of *Hypnos;* there is a copy after the latter in the Prado (No. 89), but resting on one foot only to achieve greater elegance. The so-called *San Ildefonso group* (No. 28) is also Hellenistic, dating from the 1st century B. C.; its interpretation is controversial, some critics considering the two young male figures to represent the twins Castor and Pollux, while others regard them as the Greek heroes Orestes and Pylades. This very Classicist work is eclectic in concept and combines a model related to those of Polyclitus (the youth on the right) with another more stylized and flowing figure reminiscent of Praxiteles, to which a head of the Emperor Hadrian's favourite Antinous has been added at some later date; the features can be compared with those of the colossal *Bust of Antinous* (No. 60) here in the Museum. The *Faun with a kid* (No. 29) is an excellent Roman copy after a bronze sculpture from the 3rd century B. C.; art scholars have always drawn attention to the pathetic expression on its face and the impression of movement conveyed by its body. The small *Atenea Parthenos* (No. 47) is a copy after Phidias' statue in ivory and gold for the Parthenon in Athens; it offers us an opportunity to study the monumentality and beauty of one of the most famous, now untraceable, works by the greatest of all Greek sculptors. The statue of *Diadumenes* (No. 88) is an example of the characteristic serene and harmonious style of another of the Greek sculptors of the Golden Age, Polyclitus, and is

99. Bronze head.

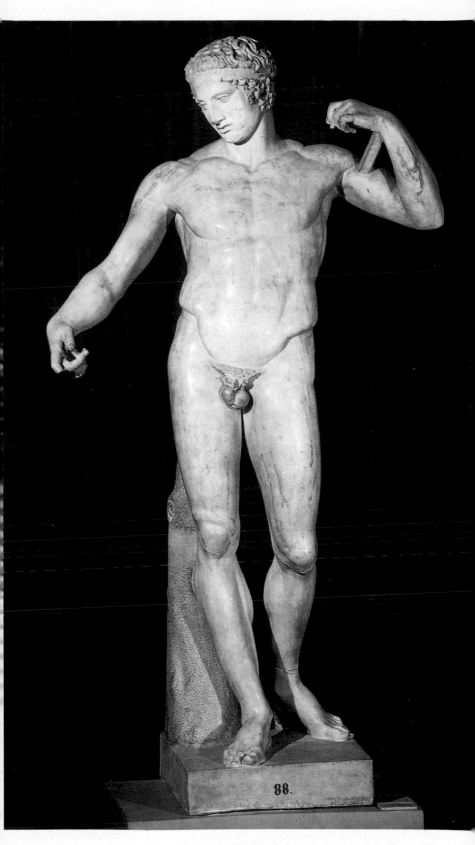

88. Style of Polyclitus. Diadumenes.

Youth.   Apollo.

considered the finest of all the copies of the original bronze. The *Venus with a dolphin* (No. 31) is another of the masterpieces of this collection; it belongs to the type of «modest Venus» who covers her nakedness with her arms and is another version of the ones kept in Rome and Florence. A series of sculptures of *Muses* and *Bacchantes* should also be mentioned as they were the prototypes that inspired Renaissance and Baroque artists. One of the most beautiful sculptures in this Museum is a *Sleeping Ariadne* (No. 167) with her slender, naturalistically sculptured figure covered by simple draperies. Several marbles deserve attention, such as the *Satyr at rest* (No. 30), restored by the sculptor Bernini in the 17th century, an elegant *Roman lady* (No. 67), larger than life-size, an *Augustus as a priest* (No. 170), with his toga covering his head while he offers a sacrifice to the gods, a colossal statue of *Jupiter* (No. 5) and a *Kneeling Venus* (No. 33) which has been repeated many times. The Roman busts include an *Augustus* (No. 119), a *Sabine* (No. 210), *Marcus Aurelius* (No. 213), *Juba of Mauritania* (No. 358), a *Roman lady* (No. 117) and *Aristogiton* (No. 78).

There is also a collection of bronzes that were brought from Italy by Velázquez or purchased by Philip IV. They are Renaissance works inspired in or copied after famous sculptures of Classical Antiquity. The finest examples are the *Espinarius* (No. 163), the *Venus* (No. 171) attributed to the Florentine sculptor Bartolomeo Ammannati and a *Hermaphrodite* (No. 223) which is said to have been the model for Velázquez's *Rokeby Venus* (now kept in the National Gallery, London).

Another homogeneous series of Renaissance bronze and marble sculptures consists of busts of the Emperor Charles V and his family done by the Italian sculptors Leone Leoni (1509-1590) and his son Pompeo Leoni (1533-1608), who were Court artists in the service of Charles V. In style these works are derived from Michelangelo, but their finish and precise detail remind us that these two artists trained as goldsmiths. They include a bust of the *Emperor Charles V* (No. 271), a life-size statue of the *Empress Isabella* (No. 260) with richly decorative draperies, another of the Queen of Hungary *Maria of Austria* (No. 263) with severely sculptured draperies and the most interesting of the series, an *Emperor Charles V and Fury,* representing the Emperor dominating in a majestic and serene pose a nude male figure writhing at his feet which represents the Fury of Heresy. His Roman armour can be removed, revealing him in the heroic nude pose of the Roman emperors.

Finally, the Prado possesses several Romanesque painted wooden sculptures including two figures of the *Virgin and Child* from the fresco-decorated chapel of Santa Cruz in Maderuelo, another Flemish late-Gothic *Virgin and Child* and a Castilian *Christ crucified.* But the most interesting works in this section are without doubt two figures of *Epimetheus* and *Pandora* attributed to El Greco; they have the characteristic elongated forms and are the only extant examples of the artist's work as a sculptor. Various bronze equestrian statues of different monarchs, including one of *Charles II* by the Italian sculptor Giovanni Battista Foggini (1652-1725) and another of *Louis XIV* by the French artist François Girardon (1628-1715), are examples of late 17th-century and early 18th-century sculpture.

321. San Ildefonso Group.

THE DAUPHIN'S TREASURE. COINS AND MEDALS. DECORATIVE ARTS

In the various exhibition rooms of the Prado a number of attractive and original works of the so-called «lesser» or decorative arts will catch the visitor's eye. These include jewels, crystal and silverware, coins, medals, pieces of furniture, tapestries, armour and porcelain.

The interesting group of works of art known as the «Dauphin's Treasure» is one of the finest collections of its kind and consists of cut crystal glassware, jewels and different vessels made of precious stones and metals, all of exceptional quality and immense artistic value since they illustrate the «industrial» angle of Renaissance and Baroque art. The «Dauphin's Treasure», as it is called in the royal inventories, was kept at the La Granja Palace; it belonged to Philip V of Bourbon, son of the Grand Dauphin, who inherited part of his father's collection on the latter's death in 1712 (the other part of the collection went to the Dauphin's French heirs and is now kept in the Louvre). The enlightened king Charles III deposited these pieces in his Natural History collection in 1776. During the Napoleonic invasion they were sent to Paris, in 1813, along with many other works of art requisitioned by the French troops, but fortunately they were returned to Spain two years later, although 12 pieces disappeared and others were damaged in transportation. But this was not the end of the Treasure's misfortunes: in 1918, 11 pieces were stolen from the Prado showcases and another 35 were damaged. However, in spite of thefts and other accidents, the «Dauphin's Treasure» is still a magnificent collection. It includes a number of goblets made of precious stones or rock crystal, set in richly worked gold and adorned with enamel, precious stones, cameos and leaf motifs. The agates, jaspers, lapis lazuli and turquoises used for these vessels were all specially selected for their colouring and vein. The beautifully cut rock crystal glasses with their leaf-like decorations were probably the work of 16th-century Milanese artists. The cameos that adorn these pieces are Renaissance in style and possibly also Milanese. They depict mythological scenes and portraits; among the latter the likenesses of the French kings Francis I and Henry IV as well as Cardinal Richelieu and others can be distinguished, a reminder that these objects belonged to the French royal family. The most outstanding pieces of this Treasure include the cameo caskets (Nos. 31-32), an onyx salt-cellar with a gold mermaid (No. 1), little agate boats with dragons (Nos. 3, 6 and 19), an agate perfume container with cameos (No. 34), a rock crystal peacock (No. 110), a boat with a tortoise (No. 78) and a goblet with hunting scenes (No. 79).

The collection of coins and medals was bequeathed to the Prado in 1915 by Don Pablo Bosch and consists of 146 Spanish coins and 852 medals from Italy and other countries. The latter include 15th-century medals by Matteo di Pasti with

Onyx salt-cellar with a gold mermaid.

the heads of Sigismondo Malatesta and Alfonso V of Aragón and those made by the sculptor Leone Leoni in the 16th century for Charles V and Philip II. There are several 16th-century French medals by Matteo di Nassaro with the heads of Francis I and Henry II and other 17th-century examples by famous medallists like Guillaume Dupré and Jan Roettiers. The most interesting medals from Germany are those of Hernán Cortés, Anne of Hungary and Charles V attributed to Hagenauer, and from England a series of naval battles by John Croker from the reign of Queen Anne. There are also examples of 18th-century Spanish medals by Tomás Prieto and Jerónimo Antonio Gil, who worked for Charles III and Charles IV.

The collection of decorative arts includes pieces of furniture the finest of which are possibly the marble tables inlaid with stones which are distributed throughout the Museum. Some are Italian, the 16th and 17th-century tables are Neapolitan and those of the 18th century come from the Spanish Buen Retiro Factory. In the room where paintings by Italian *Quattrocento* artists are exhibited there are also some Italian *cassone*, examples of typical Renaissance wedding chests. The so-called *papeleras* from the Fernández Durán Legacy are writing desks with drawers, decorated with ivory, ebony or silver. The pieces of antique Talavera ceramics, Sèvres porcelain and La Granja glassware also belonged to the same legacy, as well as 16th and 17th-century Spanish armour, some arms and finally the tapestries, including two Flemish tapestries from about 1630 by Geraert Peemans on the *Victory and Triumph of Titus* and others by Willen Pannemaker of Brussels which belonged to a series on *Tales about Mercury*.

Italian console table.

DRAWINGS

The Prado possesses a large collection of almost 4,000 drawings which are displayed occasionally in special exhibitions. The basis of this collection consisted of drawings which originally belonged to the royal family; in 1930 it was enlarged by the Fernández Durán Legacy which included some 3,000 drawings. A large number of artists are represented here. Those of the Spanish school are particularly interesting as their work offers a fine survey of the historical and stylistic development of drawing in Spain since the 15th century. One of the earliest displays is a highly attractive 15th-century architectonic project by Juan Guas for the church of San Juan de los Reyes in Toledo; the 16th century is represented by Becerra, Navarrete, Carducho and Caxés; from the 17th century there are examples of drawings by important painters such as Alonso Cano, Ribera, Claudio Coello, Carreño and Ribalta. But the most numerous section is that of 18th-century drawings: the Prado has about 400 studies by Francisco and Ramón Bayeu for works they carried out as Court painters. There is also a large collection of drawings by Maella, as well as studies by other artists such as José del Castillo, Luis Paret, Mariano Salvador Carmona, etc.

The second largest section is that of Italian drawings, which also includes some very fine works. Among 16th-century works, a series by Luca Cambiaso deserves special mention and from the 17th century those of the Bolognese Classicists Annibale Carracci, Domenichino, Guido Reni, Lanfranco and Guercino, although there are also admirable drawings by Roman and Florentine painters. Tiepolo, Donato Creti, Corrado Giaquinto and Gaetano Gandolfi are the most outstanding names among the 18th-century Venetian, Bolognese and Neapolitan artists. The French, German and Dutch schools are not very adequately represented; the finest examples are probably the drawings attributed to Rubens.

However, the Prado has a special attraction which makes it a cause of admiration and envy: its important collection of over 450 drawings by Goya. The majority of

Goya. Because she knew how to make mice.　　　　Goya. La toilette.

Goya. The sickness of Reason.

Goya. The literary ass.

them were acquired in 1866 and 1888, although some were bequeathed to or purchased by the Prado in the present century. They include the famous albums known as the Sanlúcar and Madrid albums. The former dates from 1797 and comprises rapid sketches made by Goya from scenes of everyday life at the Duchess of Alba's country house in Andalusia. The latter is later in date and contains scenes of life at Court, as well as a series of imaginative sketches, many of them based on studies from the Sanlúcar album, which reveal Goya's critical spirit and satirical approach to the society of his time. He used many of these drawings for his series of etchings *Los Caprichos* (1799). The most interesting are probably: *Ni así la distingue, Que se la llevaron, A caza de dientes, Bien tirada está, el Sueño de la razón produce monstruos,* etc. Another series of drawings are the *Disasters of War* which Goya used for his etchings with the same title. They are probably the most direct and realistic of Goya's graphic works: almost all of them are done in red pencil, many date from the time of the Peninsular War and convey Goya's reflections on the cruelty, horrors and misery of war. The Prado also possesses the preparatory sketches for the *Tauromaquia* etchings. Goya was an enthusiastic bullfight-lover and in these works he represents the most important stages of a bullfight in a particularly lively and striking manner. In the *Proverbs,* which are difficult to interpret, Goya offers us another example of his satirical approach to society, in particular to the political régime of King Ferdinand VII. He uses various different techniques: red chalk, black pencil, pen and water-colours. Goya's drawings, etchings and engravings are exhibited periodically and are without doubt one of the Prado's chief attractions. They afford an opportunity to understand the artist's genius and the creative process of his work, as well as his skill in conveying a vibrating, naturalistic vision of life and death.

Goya. The dream of Reason.

Goya. I am still learning.

BIBLIOGRAPHY

ANGULO IÑIGUEZ, Diego: Catálogo de las Alhajas del Delfín. Museo del Prado, Madrid, 1955.
— Pintura del siglo XVI. Ars Hispaniae XII, Madrid, 1954.
— Pintura del siglo XVII, Ars Hispaniae XV, Madrid, 1958.
ANGULO IÑIGUEZ, D. & PÉREZ SÁNCHEZ, A. E.:
— Pintura madrileña. Primera mitad del siglo XVII. Madrid, 1969.
— Pintura toledana. Primera mitad del siglo XVII. Madrid, 1972.
ARNÁEZ, Rocío: Museo del Prado. Dibujos españoles del siglo XVIII, A-B. Madrid, 1975.
BERNT, Walther: The Netherlandish Painters of the Seventeenth Century, 3 vols. London, 1970.
BLANCO, Antonio: Museo del Prado. Catálogo de la Escultura. Madrid, 1957.
BUENDÍA, J. Rogelio: El Prado Básico. Madrid, 1973.
CEBALLOS, Isabel de & BRAÑA, María: Museo del Prado. Catálogo del Legado Fernández Durán (Artes Decorativas). Madrid, 1974.
CHUECA GOITIA, Fernando: El Museo del Prado. «Misiones de Arte», Madrid, 1952.
DÍAZ PADRÓN, Matías: Museo del Prado. Catálogo de Pinturas. Escuela Flamenca del siglo XVII. Madrid, 1975.
FERNÁNDEZ BAYTON, Gloria: Museo del Prado. Principales adquisiciones de los últimos diez años. Madrid, 1969.
FREEDBERG, Sidney: Painting in Italy 1500-1800. Harmondsworth, 1971.
FRIEDLANDER, Max: Early Netherlandish Painters, 14 vols. Leyden, 1967.
GERSON, H. & KUILE, E. H.: Art and Architecture in Belgium 1600-1800. Harmondsworth, 1960.
GUDIOL RICART, José: Pintura Gótica. Ars Hispaniae. Madrid, 1955.
LAFUENTE FERRARI, E.: Breve Historia de la Pintura Española. Madrid, 1953.
— El Prado. Del Románico al Greco. Madrid, 1976.
— El Prado. Pintura Española, siglos XVII-XVIII, 2 vols. Madrid, 1978.
— El Prado. Pintura nórdica. Madrid, 1977.
— El Prado. Escuela italiana y francesa. Madrid, 1977.
PANOFSKY, Erwin: Early Netherlandish Painting. Its Origin and Character. New York, 1971.
PÉREZ SÁNCHEZ, A. E.: Museo del Prado. Dibujos Españoles de los siglos XV al XVII. Madrid, 1972.
— Museo del Prado. Madrid, 1974.
— Pasado, presente y futuro del Museo del Prado. Madrid, 1976.
— Pintura italiana del siglo XVII en España. Madrid, 1967.
— Pintura italiana del siglo XVII. Exposición conmemorativa del 150 aniversario de la fundación del Museo del Prado. Madrid, 1970.
SALAS, Javier de: Museo del Prado. Adquisiciones de 1969 a 1977. Madrid, 1978.
SÁNCHEZ CANTÓN, F. J.: Museo del Prado. Catálogo. Madrid, 1972.
— Escultura y Pintura del siglo XVIII. Francisco de Goya. Ars Hispaniae XVII. Madrid, 1958.
URREA FERNÁNDEZ, Jesús: Pintura Italiana del siglo XVIII en España. Valladolid, 1977.
VALDIVIESO, Enrique: Pintura holandesa del siglo XVII en España. Valladolid, 1973.

INDEX OF ARTISTS

INDEX OF PAINTINGS

According to catalogue number

Catalogue No.	Page	Catalogue No.	Page	Catalogue No.	Page	Catalogue No.	Page
1	191	74	206	148	209	243	221
2	191	75	203	149	214	244	222
3	242	76	203	150	239	245	222
4	199	77	203	151	216	246	244
5	200	78	206	152	216	247	222
6	191	80	219	153	216	248	223
7	261	81	219	157	216	252	226
8	191	83	242	159	216	256	245
9	182	84	207	160	216	257	245
10	182	85	261	161	216	258	245
11	261	86	220	162	216	259	245
12	191	87	212	163	216	262	224
13	268	88	207	165	216	263	224
14	244	89	207	166	216	264	224
15	192	91	212	167	217	265	224
16	192	92	212	168	217	266	226
17	194	93	213	171	217	269	226
18	194	94	213	172	217	270	261
18a	194	95	209	178	217	271	226
20	207	96	209	179	217	272	226
21	195	97	209	181	217	273	227
22	195	98	256	182	217	275	227
23	195	99	209	183	217	276	227
25	195	100	261	184	217	277	227
26	195	101	210	185	217	278	227
27	195	102	210	186	217	279	227
28	195	103	215	187	217	280	227
29	195	104	215	188	217	281	227
30	195	105	215	189	217	282	227
31	195	106	215	190	217	283	230
32	195	107	215	191	218	284	230
33	194	108	215	193	218	287	231
34	194	109	215	194	218	288	218
36	194	110	215	195	218	289	220
39	195	111	210	196	218	290	234
40	195	112	210	197	218	291	245
41	195	115	210	198	218	292	235
42	254	117	210	200	219	293	235
43	195	118	210	201	219	294	235
44	195	119	210	202	219	295	116
45	195	120	210	203	219	296	238
47	198	121	211	208	239	297	238
48	198	122	200	209	239	298	238
49	198	123	26	210	241	299	238
50	198	124	26	211	241	300	238
51	226	125	26	212	241	301	238
53	223	126	26	213	241	302	238
53a	199	127	292	214	241	303	239
54	199	128	211	215	241	304	239
55	261	129	211	216	241	305	239
56	188	130	223	218	241	313	239
57	224	131	211	219	241	315	239
58	230	132	206	220	241	319	239
59	200	134	212	226	241	322	241
59a	202	135	212	229	241	323	241
60	200	136	212	232	219	324	242
61	200	137	212	233	219	326	242
62	200	138	212	234	220	327	223
63	202	139	213	235	220	328	242
65	202	141	199	236	220	329	210
66	202	142	213	237	214	330	243
67	63	143	213	238	214	331	243
68	203	144	213	239	220	332	243
69	203	145	213	240	221	334	243
70	206	146	207	241	222	335	243
72	203	147	214	242	221	336	243

Catalogue No.	Page	Catalogue No.	Page	Catalogue No.	Page	Catalogue No.	Page
337	243	415	251	501	257	619	27
338	243	416	224	502	257	620	34
341	243	417	251	504	220	621	27
342	243	418	251	510	209	622	27
344	244	419	251	511	260	623	27
345	231	420	252	512	260	625	30
346	231	421	252	513	260	626	30
348	231	422	252	519	261	627	30
349	220	423	254	522	260	629	30
351	244	424	254	523	230	632	30
352	244	425	252	524	230	633	30
353	218	426	252	525	230	635	31
354	245	427	252	528	116	636	31
355	247	428	252	533	254	637	31
356	247	429	253	535	261	638	31
357	247	430	253	537	224	639	31
358	247	431	253	539	280	639a	31
359	247	432	253	540	211	640	32
360	247	433	253	542	212	641	32
361	247	434	253	543	223	642	32
362	247	436	253	547	211	643	31
363	246	437	253	549	198	644	32
364	246	438	253	550	198	645	32
364a	246	439	253	552	212	646	32
365	246	440	253	555	192	647	32
365a	246	441	254	556	192	648	32
366	248	442	254	563	244	649	32
367	249	443	254	566	223	650	32
368	261	444	254	569	234	651	32
369	248	445	254	571	35	652	116
370	248	446	254	573	218	653	34
371	248	447	254	576	198	654	34
372	199	448	221	577	192	656	113
373	248	452	254	577a	192	657	34
374	248	457	254	579	243	658	35
377	248	458	255	580	261	659	35
378	248	459	255	581	245	660	35
379	248	461	255	582	215	661	35
380	226	462	255	583	246	662	35
381	247	463	255	584	116	663	35
382	248	464	255	585	22	664	35
383	247	465	255	587	22	665	35
384	248	466	255	588	22	666	35
385	248	468	255	590	22	671	35
386	248	469	255	591	22	672	38
387	247	470	255	592	23	673	38
388	248	471	226	593	23	680	38
389	248	472	223	594	23	687	38
390	248	473	256	595	23	689	38
391	248	474	256	596	23	690	38
392	248	475	256	597	23	694	62
393	248	476	234	598	23	696	38
394	249	477	242	599	23	697	38
395	249	478	256	600	24	698	38
396	249	479	230	601	24	699	38
397	249	480	260	603	24	700	38
398	249	482	256	604	24	701	38
399	249	483	256	605	24	702	38
400	247	484	249	606	24	703	38
401	249	485	194	607	24	704	39
402	226	486	256	609	26	705	116
404	203	487	257	610	26	706	116
406	261	489	260	611	26	707	116
407	250	490	260	—	—	708	116
408	250	491	257	612	26	709	116
409	250	492	257	613	26	710	116
410	250	494	257	614	27	714	42
411	250	497	257	615	27	715	42
412	251	498	257	616	27	716	42
413	251	499	257	617	27	719	46
414	251	500	257	618	27	720	46

Catalogue No.	Page	Catalogue No.	Page	Catalogue No.	Page	Catalogue No.	Page
721	46	786	53	873	64	972	74
722	46	787	54	874	64	973	75
723	46	788	54	875	64	974	75
724	46	789	54	877	200	975	75
725	47	790	54	878	66	976	75
726	47	791	54	879	66	977	75
727	47	792	54	880	66	978	75
728	47	793	54	883	66	979	75
729	47	794	54	885	64	980	75
730	47	795	54	886	64	981	75
731	47	796	54	887	91	982	78
732	49	797	54	888	67	983	81
733	49	798	54	889	107	984	78
734	49	799	54	890	22	985	81
735	49	800	54	893	22	986	81
736	49	800a	54	894	22	987	78
737	49	801	54	895	22	989	78
738	49	802	54	896	22	990	81
739	49	803	54	897	22	991	81
740	49	804	54	898	22	992	35
740a	49	805	54	899	22	994	78
740b	49	806	58	899a	67	995	78
740c	49	807	58	901	70	996	78
740i	49	808	58	902	67	996a	78
740j	49	809	58	903	70	997	78
740h	24	810	58	906	70	998	78
741	49	811	58	907	70	999	79
742	49	812	58	909	70	1000	79
743	50	813	58	910	70	1001	79
744	50	814	58	911	70	1002	79
745	50	815	58	912	70	1005	79
746	50	817	58	915	70	1006	79
747	50	819	58	919	70	1012	81
748	50	820	61	924	70	1015	81
749	51	821	59	927	70	1016	81
750	51	822	59	929	70	1017	81
751	51	823	59	930	70	1018	81
752	51	824	59	931	70	1020	81
753	51	825	59	932	70	1022	82
754	52	826	60	933	70	1023	82
755	52	827	60	934	70	1024	82
756	52	828	60	935	70	1025	82
757	52	829	60	936	70	1026	82
758	52	830	61	937	70	1030	92
759	52	831	61	938	70	1031	92
760	52	832	61	943	70	1032	82
761	52	832a	61	944	70	1034	82
762	52	833	61	946	70	1035	82
763	52	836	62	947	70	1036	92
764	52	837	62	948a	70	1037	116
765	52	838	62	951	34	1038	82
766	52	839	62	952	34	1040a	82
767	52	840	62	953	34	1040b	82
768	52	841	62	954	34	1041	83
769	52	842	62	955	34	1042	83
770	53	843	66	956	34	1043	83
771	53	844	62	957	71	1044	83
772	53	846	62	958	70	1045	83
773	53	848	62	959	70	1046	83
774	53	849	66	960	74	1047	83
775	53	850	66	961	74	1048	84
776	53	851	66	962	74	1049	84
777	53	852	66	963	74	1050	84
778	53	853	62	964	74	1051	84
779	53	854	62	965	74	1052	84
780	53	855	62	966	74	1053	84
781	53	858	63	967	74	1054	84
782	53	859	63	968	74	1055	84
783	53	860	63	969	74	1056	84
784	53	861	92	970	74	1057	84
785	53	871	63	971	81	1059	84

Catalogue No.	Page	Catalogue No.	Page	Catalogue No.	Page	Catalogue No.	Page
1730	177	1805	183	1889	187	2039	177
1731	174	1806	183	1890	187	2040	175
1732	131	1807	183	1891	187	2041	175
1733	179	1808	183	1892	187	2042	175
1734	179	1809	183	1894	188	2043	175
1735	179	1810	183	1899	292	2044	175
1736	179	1811	183	1900	188	2045	135
1737	179	1812	183	1901	188	2046	154
1738	179	1813	183	1904	188	2048	122
1739	180	1814	183	1905	178	2049	123
1740	180	1815	183	1906	178	2050	126
1741	180	1816	183	1907	178	2051	126
1742	180	1817	183	1908	179	2052	123
1743	180	1818	183	1909	179	2054	126
1744	180	1819	183	1910	179	2055	126
1744-P	177	1820	184	1911	179	2056	124
1745	180	1821	184	1912	179	2058	284
1746	180	1822	184	1914	179	2059	284
1747	180	1823	184	1915	148	2060	284
1748	180	1825	184	1916	189	2061	284
1749	180	1826	184	1917	189	2062	284
1750	180	1827	184	1918	189	2063	292
1751	180	1828	184	1919	154	2064	292
1752	180	1829	184	1920	158	2065	292
1753	180	1830	184	1921	135	2066	284
1754	180	1831	184	1924	189	2069	284
1755	180	1832	184	1925	39	2070	284
1756	180	1833	184	1927	120	2072	138
1757	180	1834	184	1928	120	2073	139
1758	180	1835	184	1929	120	2074	139
1759	180	1836	184	1930	154	2075	139
1760	186	1839	184	1932	158	2076	139
1761	180	1843	184	1933	120	2077	156
1762	180	1844	184	1934	159	2078	285
1763	180	1845	184	1935	120	2079	285
1764	180	1846	184	1937	156	2080	285
1765	181	1847	291	1938	156	2081	286
1766	186	1848	184	1940	281	2082	126
1767	180	1849	127	1941	303	2083	126
1768	180	1851	180	1942	303	2084	126
1770	180	1852	184	1943	151	2085	126
1771	180	1853	184	1949	150	2087	291
1772	180	1854	185	1950	110	2088	138
1774	181	1855	185	1953	189	2089	286
1775	181	1856	139	1954	181	2090	286
1776	181	1857	189	1955	117	2091	120
1779	181	1858	185	1957	158	2093	120
1780	181	1859	185	1958	150	2095	150
1781	181	1860	185	1959	189	2096	130
1782	181	1861	186	1961	182	2097	284
1783	184	1862	186	1962	182	2099	163
1784	184	1865	186	1963	292	2100	163
1785	182	1866	186	1965	211	2101	163
1786	182	1867	186	1969	211	2103	287
1787	182	1868	186	1971	182	2104	156
1788	182	1869	186	1977	162	2105	156
1789	182	1870	186	1978	295	2106	287
1790	182	1871	186	1985	261	2107	157
1791	182	1872	186	1986	150	2108	157
1793	182	1873	186	1990	242	2109	157
1794	182	1875	186	1991	179	2110	157
1795	183	1876	186	1994	179	2111	157
1796	183	1877	186	1995	189	2112	157
1797	183	1879	121	1997	286	2113	157
1798	183	1880	186	1999	189	2114	157
1799	183	1882	186	2002	177	2115	157
1800	183	1884	187	2022	189	2116	157
1801	183	1885	130	2024	181	2117	157
1802	183	1886	188	2035	189	2117bis	157
1803	183	1887	148	2037	308	2118	157
1804	183	1888	187	2038	177	2119	157

Catalogue No.	Page	Catalogue No.	Page	Catalogue No.	Page	Catalogue No.	Page
2120	287	2204	306	2292	263	2410	314
2121	288	2205	306	2293	284	2414	279
2122	288	2206	306	2294	279	2416	255
2123	288	2207	153	2295	282	2417	282
2124	288	2208	306	2296	268	2420	282
2125	288	2211	306	2297	268	2421	81
2126	288	2211a	218	2298	274	2422	83
2127	288	2213	135	2299	274	2424	215
2128	160	2216	308	2302	275	2425	63
2129	288	2217	189	2303	275	2435	282
2130	288	2219	299	2304	276	2437	282
2131	288	2220	299	2305	212	2440	64
2132	290	2223	138	2306	277	2441	153
2133	291	2227	31	2307	276	2441a	61
2135	291	2229	63	2308	276	2442	114
2136	284	2231	263	2309	276	2443	22
2137	292	2232	263	2310	276	2444	60
2138	291	2233	162	2311	276	2445	60
2139	291	2234	263	2312	277	2446	54
2141	292	2235	230	2313	277	2447	54
2142	292	2236	263	2314	213	2448	55
2143	292	2237	264	2315	200	2449	55
2145	294	2238	264	2316	277	2450	55
2146	294	2239	268	2317	277	2451	26
2147	294	2240	264	2318	277	2452	26
2148	294	2241	265	2320	277	2453	26
2149	294	2242	265	2322	277	2454	175
2150	294	2243	265	2323	277	2455	175
2151	294	2244	34	2325	278	2456	175
2152	295	2247	265	2326	278	2457	175
2154	295	2249	265	2329	278	2458	175
2155	121	2250	212	2330	278	2459	175
2157	294	2251	269	2332	278	2460	177
2159	283	2252	272	2333	278	2461	175
2160	295	2253	272	2334	278	2462	256
2163	146	2254	273	2335	279	2463	256
2165	150	2255	273	2336	279	2464	246
2166	150	2256	273	2337	279	2465	202
2167	285	2257	273	2343	279	2466	202
2171	84	2258	273	2345	282	2467	268
2172	84	2259	273	2346	263	2468	268
2173	84	2260	273	2347	280	2469	282
2175	302	2261	273	2348	280	2470	134
2176	302	2262	268	2349	280	2472	114
2177	302	2263	268	2350	280	2473	305
2178	302	2264	269	2352	282	2474	310
2179	303	2265	278	2353	281	2476	198
2180	303	2266	278	2354	281	2477	191
2181	303	2267	269	2355	265	2478	202
2182	305	2268	269	2358	279	2480	24
2183	298	2269	269	2359	282	2481	24
2184	298	2270	269	2364	120	2482	24
2185	305	2271	269	2365	264	2483	24
2186	305	2272	269	2367	280	2484	64
2187	305	2273	270	2369	274	2485	24
2188	306	2274	268	2371	282	2486	24
2189	306	2276	308	2372	282	2487	24
2190	306	2277	270	2375	282	2488	24
2191	306	2278	270	2376	279	2489	24
2192	306	2279	282	2380	274	2491	24
2193	306	2280	270	2381	279	2493	24
2194	306	2281	270	—	—	2494	178
2195	306	2282	272	2387	269	2495	42
2196	306	2283	272	2390	279	2496	209
2197	306	2284	272	2391	279	2497	64
2198	306	2285	272	2392	191	2498	64
2199	306	2286	273	2394	279	2499	64
2200	306	2287	273	2396	282	2500	64
2201	306	2288	274	2400	274	2501	31
2202	306	2289	274	2407	314	2502	31
2203	306	2291	274	2409	263	2503	34

Catalogue No.	Page	Catalogue No.	Page	Catalogue No.	Page	Catalogue No.	Page
2504	35	2581	39	2692	159	2769	223
2505	117	2582	94	2693a	118	2770	70
2506	90	2583	35	2693b	118	2771	81
2507	23	2584	313	2694	178	2772	81
2508	23	2585	261	2695	124	2773	61
2509	92	2586	153	2696	147	2774	61
2510	91	2587	291	2697	158	2775	93
2511	92	2588	286	2698	127	2776	93
2512	70	2589	261	2699	189	2777	81
2514	61	2590a	268	2700	135	2778	118
2516	117	2591	274	2701	189	2779	118
2517	117	2592	282	2702	189	2780	39
2518	90	2593	94	2703	138	2781	55
2519	111	2594	114 ·	2704	189	2782	55
2520	24	2595	64	2705	308	2783	55
2521	26	2596	91	2706	153	2784	55
2522	26	2597	279	2707	118	2785	55
2523	26	2598	313	2708	261	2786	27
2524	55	2599	26	2709	27	2787	27
2525	152	2600	91	2711	260	2788	280
2526	146	2631	206	2715	202	2789	282
2527	155	2634	24	2716	147	2790	308
2528	155	2635	189	2718	189	2791	282
2529	30	2636	189	2719	138	2792	192
2530	117	2637	30	2720	118	2793	274
2531	24	2638	209	2721	118	2794	275
2532	117	2640	215	2722	187	2795	275
2533	32	2641	139	2723	138	2796	275
2534	117	2643	142	2724	153	2797	27
2535	39	2644	60	2725	159	2799	273
2536	39	2645	60	2726	158	2800	32
2537	117	2646	268	2727	158	2801	154
2538	117	2647	39	2728	181	2802	84
2539	185	2648	189	2729	179	2803	115
2540	187	2649	32	2730	179	2804	85
2541	39	2650	55	2731	127	2805	111
2542	142	2651	282	2732	184	2806	30
2543	155	2652	63	2734	148	2807	91
2544	151	2653	163	2735	148	2808	291
2545	81	2654	135	2736	148	2809	79
2546	55	2656	70	2737	148	2810	261
2547	55	2657	79	2738	148	2811	177
2548	55	2658	279	2739	149	2816	135
2549	90	2659	261	2740	149	2817	156
2550	314	2660	244	2741	149	2818	151
2551	261	2662	110	2742	149	2819	60
2552	154	2663	153	2743	149	2820	308
2553	110	2664	151	2744	149	2821	308
2554	110	2665	117	2745	149	2822	124
2555	83	2666	61	2746	120	2823	124
2556	146	2668	117	2747	120	2824	249
2557	283	2669	117	2748	295	2825	188
2562	82	2670	117	2749	153	2828	38
2563	82	2671	117	2750	153	2829	118
2564	202	2672	127	2751	295	2830	118
2565	146	2673	117	2752	295	2832	38
2566	175	2674	117	2753	285	2833	118
2567	163	2675	27	2754	286	2834	118
2568	306	2676	117	2755	286	2835	118
2569	146	2677	27	2756	286	2836	93
2570	120	2678	83	2757	188	2837	93
2571	67	2680	61	2758	261	2838	200
2572	115	2681	117	2759	202	2839	200
2573	63	2682	26	2760	261	2840	200
2574	27	2683	61	2761	218	2841	213
2575	93	2684	91	2762	218	2842	213
2576	93	2686	117	2763	218	2843	223
2577	93	2687	117	2764	261	2844	231
2578	93	2688	222	2765	261	2845	79
2579	63	2689	222	2766	261	2849	35
2580	178	2691	246	2767	261	2852	313

Catalogue No.	Page	Catalogue No.	Page	Catalogue No.	Page	Catalogue No.	Page
2853	313	2962	91	3055	118	3153	224
2854	263	2965	85	3057	185	3159	35
2855	263	2966	27	3058	61	3161	82
2856	55	2968	241	3060	79	3178	218
2857	55	2970	62	3061	31	3179	218
2858	313	2971	81	3062	31	3180	34
2860	291	2972	81	3064	34	3181	84
2861	92	2974	286	3074	154	3185	30
2862	56	2975	93	3075	147	3186	82
2870	90	2976	287	3077	91	3187	82
2872	71	2977	287	3078	93	3188	215
2873	107	2978	286	3079	23	3189	242
2874	60	2979	310	3080	23	3192	215
2875	83	2984	285	3081	111	3193	216
2876	39	2986	313	3084	312	3194	209
2877	61	2987	281	3085	126	3195	218
2879	314	2988	61	3086	35	3196	118
2880	157	2989	261	3087	38	3197	118
2881	157	2990	310	3088	32	3201	27
2882	234	2991	83	3090	241	3202	279
2883	279	2992	115	3091	220	3203	111
2884	189	2993	218	3092	224	3204	216
2885	282	2994	71	3102	38	3209	157
2886	282	2995	56	3103	38	3210	138
2888	115	2996	110	3105	84	3212	66
2889	60	2997	39	3106	92	3214	91
2890	60	2998	39	3107	92	3217	275
2891	60	3000	314	3108	91	3218	275
2892	60	3001	310	3110	27	3220	38
2893	22	3002	61	3111	118	3222	92
2894	34	3004	84	3112	118	3224	57
2895	56	3006	115	3113	57	3225	66
2896	56	3007	246	3114	38	3226	66
2897	42	3008	79	3116	312	3227	66
2898	56	3009	115	3120	34	3228	34
2899	56	3010	115	3122	215	3229	81
2900	246	3011	312	3124	222	3232	138
2902	111	3012	312	3125	38	3233	91
2903	107	3013	314	3126	27	3236	57
2907	224	3014	314	3128	64	3239	226
2908	206	3015	118	3129	66	3242	81
2909	206	3016	118	3130	66	3243	246
2910	206	3017	64	3131	215	3254	57
2911a	70	3018	64	3132	215	3255	57
2912	81	3027	35	3134	30	3256	35
2913	126	3028	118	3135	38	3259	261
2918	42	3029	91	3136	91	3262	61
2919	91	3030	23	3137	175	3265	32
2922	91	3039	39	3138	23	3265	107
2926	212	3040	310	3139	23	3524	282
2935	39	3041	30	3140	64	3974	235
2936	39	3043	220	3141	64	4180	198
2937	39	3044	85	3142	282	4181	198
2938	39	3045	56	3144	148	4195	269
2939	192	3046	38	3146	234	4196	269
2940	34	3047	57	3147	71	s. n.	115
2943	220	3048	177	3148	115	s. n.	116
2944	254	3049	270	3149	94	s. n.	195
2956	31	3051	34	3150	118	s. n.	206
2957	38	3052	81	3151	207	s. n.	210
2961	110	3053	90	3152	207	s. n.	216

INDEX OF BLACK AND WHITE
ILLUSTRATIONS(*)

(*) Many of these illustrations, which include the most representative works in the Prado, are reproduced in detail in order to make the best use of the given space.

INDEX OF COLOUR PLATES

TITLES PUBLISHED
ON THE PRADO
MUSEUM

A BASIC GUIDE TO THE PRADO
José Rogelio Buendía
THE KEY TO THE PRADO
Consuelo Luca de Tena and
Manuela Mena
GOYA, drawings
Enrique Lafuente Ferrari
BOSCH, reality, symbol and
fantasy
Isidro Bango Torviso and
Fernando Marias
GOYA, obra, vida, sueños
José Manuel Pita Andrade
MURILLO, sombras de la tierra,
Luces del cielo
Enrique Valdivieso
GUIDE TO THE PRADO
Consuelo Luca de Tena and
Manuela Mena
LOS CAPRICHOS DE
FRANCISCO DE GOYA Y
LUCIENTES
Camilo José Cela

SILEX EDICIONES. Madrid.